American Urbanism

Recent Titles in
Contributions in American History
Series Editor: Jon L. Wakelyn

American Urbanism

A HISTORIOGRAPHICAL REVIEW

Edited by Howard Gillette, Jr.,
and Zane L. Miller

Contributions in American History, Number 125

GREENWOOD PRESS
New York • Westport, Connecticut • London

Library of Congress Cataloging-in-Publication Data

American urbanism.

(Contributions in American history, ISSN 0084-9219 ;
no. 125)
    Bibliography: p.
    Includes index.
    1. Cities and towns—United States—History.
2. Cities and towns—United States—Historiography.
I. Gillette, Howard. II. Miller, Zane L. III. Series.
HT123.A6665 1987   307.7′6′0973   86-29614
ISBN 0-313-24967-9 (lib. bdg. : alk. paper)

Library of Congress Catalog Card Number: 86-29614
ISBN: 0-313-24967-9
ISSN: 0084-9219

First published in 1987

Greenwood Press, Inc.
88 Post Road West
Westport, Connecticut 06881

Printed in the United States of America

∞™

The paper used in this book complies with the
Permanent Paper Standard issued by the National
Information Standards Organization (Z39.48-1984).

10 9 8 7 6 5 4 3 2 1

Contents

American Urbanism

Introduction

HOWARD GILLETTE, JR.

This book has grown out of the conviction that the proliferation of work in U.S. urban history has created the need for a ready resource book for students of cities, not just those in academic settings but also in associated fields of urban planning, historic preservation, museums, and historical societies. Although specialized journals, such as the *Journal of Urban History* and, before its recent termination as a separate entity, *Urbanism Past and Present*,[1] and annotated bibliographies published by Gale and Clio presses[2] have provided useful reference materials, we have felt that because the field was in transition, a review of existing literature required critical treatment. The chapters that follow, then, fill two functions: they point readers to the cumulated body of historical literature on U.S. cities and suggest the possibilities, as well as some of the limitations, of urban history.

Central to the timing of this book is the transitional nature of urban history as a distinctive field of study. The surge in interest in the subject in the 1960s brought differences in method, as Michael Ebner has described them, most notably between an ecological approach advanced by Eric Lampard and an environmental, or city-building approach called for by Roy Lubove.[3] Scholars differed on priorities for research, and even such a leading contributor to the field as Stephan Thernstrom questioned urbanism as a valid topic in itself.[4]

Despite such differences, urban historians shared the belief that they had an unusual opportunity to contribute to the solution of contemporary problems and that to do so they had to overcome the restraints of a professional culture that separated them from colleagues in associated disciplines in the social sciences and from the city itself.[5] On the first count, the early work of Sam Bass Warner, Jr., revealed a reformist strain common to the field.[6] On the second count, interdisciplinary collaboration formed a central premise for conferences that provided both the initial definition and the first work associated with what came to be called the new urban history.[7] Theodore Hershberg made such an approach the cornerstone of the Philadelphia Social History Project, the most advanced research unit of its kind to stem from the period.[8]

Success could be measured in the usual academic terms: in the outpouring of research, the introduction of urban history series by major scholarly presses, the formation of the *Journal of Urban History* in 1974, and the growth of course offerings on the subject around the country.[9] To some degree urban practitioners took note; professional planners included more history in their journals, and some public agencies hired urban historians as consultants for environmental and transportation studies. University programs in public history and historic preservation helped bridge the gap between theory and practice in urban studies.

Even with all these achievements recorded, one cannot help but be struck in the 1980s by a shift in mood as well as purpose among urban historians. The Philadelphia Social History Project has ended now, with Hershberg reaching the bleak conclusion that "neither the dialogue nor the task" of the integration of knowledge has really begun.[10] A new collection of urban essays stands out for the lack of quantitative research of the kind that generated the first distinctive urban studies of the early 1970s.[11] While the reformist approach to cities is not yet dead,[12] Sam Bass Warner, Jr., is among those who have publicly renounced such an approach. Some other scholars contend that new directions in the field represent the abandonment of both the pioneering methods and the social concerns of the 1960s.[13] Thernstrom's once lonely challenge to the appropriateness of spatially bound urban studies is increasingly shared by those struck by the diffusion of urban functions over space and of urban values throughout the culture. Peter Saunders, for instance, in taking up the major theorists of the city, concludes that "the city in contemporary capitalism is no longer the basis for human association (Weber), the locus of the division of labour (Durkheim), or the expression of a specific mode of production (Marx), in which case it is neither fruitful nor appropriate to study it in its own right."[14]

To a degree urban historians have been victims of their own success. The creation of a journal devoted solely to urban history offered an outlet for research but diminished interest among other interdisciplinary journals—notably *Social Science History* and the *Journal of Interdisciplinary History*—in carrying their work. The creation of separate journals of social history, urban affairs, and historical geography further splintered the field. Still, as the chapters in this book suggest, prospects for achieving a more holistic view of cities have advanced in the last generation. Students of architecture and urban planning, as Richard Longstreth and Eugenie Birch demonstrate, have widened their historical perspective beyond the physical environment to incorporate social and cultural elements as well. Historians have also incorporated spatial concepts advanced by geographers, as Edward Muller and Carl Abbott show, bringing about a fuller sense of the processes of urban development. If a passion for social change no longer dominates the literature, there is no lack of deep criticism today of the tenets behind urban development, as many of the chapters in this book demonstrate. If specifically interdisciplinary research has lagged, the prospects for a greater integration of knowledge through an understanding of cities are not nearly so bleak as Hershberg would suggest.

Coming into the 1980s, as Alan Marcus' lead chapter in this collection suggests, a shared commitment to reform made it difficult for historians to examine the past on its own terms. Looking for an idyllic period of social harmony in contrast to the turbulent 1960s, they focused on the problems brought on by urban-industrial change—to the point of missing some of the larger context in which urbanization proceeded. As the passion for change has receded in the past decade, it has been possible to take a more dispassionate look at cities. Now a research agenda that has included many disparate case studies in the past can be extended, as Kathleen Conzen suggests, to explain the many differences among cities, as well as their changing role in larger social, economic, and cultural systems.[15]

Such an approach necessarily encompasses some redefinition. Just as Ebner concluded his 1981 review of the field with a call for pluralistic approaches to the city, William Sharpe and Leonard Wallock, in recognizing that *city* and *locale* are no longer synonymous, suggest broadening the definition of urbanism. "As used now," they write in their thoughtful introduction to *Visions of the Modern City*, "the word 'city' no longer refers simply to a changing morphology with certain easily identifiable characteristics like population concentration and high-density building but rather to a new pattern of life and thought, a physical, social, and psychological construct for which the earlier city is only a point of departure."[16]

Such a definition does not necessitate abandonment of the focus on concentrated settlement patterns, for the processes of urbanization are too important to be ignored by any student of American civilization. As Charles Tilly writes, "The conjunction of capitalism and state making created the contemporary Western city, with its extraordinary concentration of large workplaces, residential segregation by class, high-priced central locations, massive governmental intervention to assure the profitable use of those central locations, huge but shaky systems of transportation, and political struggle over the collection and allocation of municipal revenues."[17] Each aspect of urbanism Tilly describes might appropriately be studied independently, but taken as a whole they point directly to the central research question Thernstrom posed in 1971: how urbanization reshaped society.

Tilly's comments reflect the commitment made by Lewis Mumford almost fifty years ago to make the city the central focus for the study of modern life. Mumford's base outside an academic setting relieved him from the start from the disciplinary boundaries that scholars have worried so much about in the past generation. Nor was he confined in considering the city to sources that could be quantified, a criticism of some of the "new urban history." For him the fates of cities and civilization were inextricably linked, and thus the effort to separate them was unthinkable. "The city, as one finds it in history," he wrote in 1938, "is the point of maximum concentration for the power and culture of a community. . . . Here is where the issues of civilization are focused."[18] More systematic studies were necessary before Mumford's generalizations about cities as agents of capitalism could be tested, and surely recent research on mobility, labor, race and ethnicity, and urban infrastructure has offered the kind of evidence for such testing. As some of the missing ingredients of the urban histories of the past two decades are now being supplied through the examination of the means by which politics, capitalism, and modes of thought affected experience, the possibilities of a larger picture emerge.

The chapters in this book are presented with an appreciation for the pluralism that has characterized the field and with the hope that greater knowledge of the range of work completed will be helpful in the ongoing reassessment of recent scholarship. Not every aspect of American urbanism is thoroughly covered here, though we have attempted to identify the major strands—physical as well as social, imaginative as well as analytical—that contribute to making urban history a distinctive field. In the spirit of the revival of the field in the 1960s, we have encouraged our authors to cross disciplinary lines, choosing not to confine our treatment of the contributions of single disciplines but to look more at different aspects of the urban phenomenon, whatever the scholarly source. We thus provide chapters on work, not on economics, and on race and ethnicity, not sociology or anthropology. In the light of the shifting definition of cities, we have purposely cast a wide net to include chapters on neighborhoods, towns, suburbs, and regions, all as they relate to central questions of urbanism.

Portions of the chapters by Alan Marcus, Jon Teaford, Patricia Mooney Melvin, Michael Ebner, Carol O'Connor, Carl Abbott, and Robert Dykstra and William Silag appeared earlier in the 1985 bibliography edition of the *American Quarterly*. Some of those essays have been expanded for this book, and we are grateful to both the authors for their extra work and the American Studies Association for permission to adapt the essays for this book. We hope that if our assessment is correct—that the field of urban history is in transition—then this book will serve both as a guide to where we have been and where we might go in the years ahead.

Notes

1. For a history of how *Urbanism Past and Present* evolved out of the *Urban Historians' Newsletter*, see the commentary by Blake McKelvey and A. Theodore Brown

in the inaugural issue (Winter 1975–1976). The magazine has since merged with *Urban History Review* published by the University of Winnipeg, Canada.

2. John D. Buenker, Gerald Michael Greenfield, and William J. Murin, *Urban History: A Guide to Information Sources* (Detroit: Gale Research Company, 1981), and Neil Shumsky and Timothy Crimmins, eds., *Urban America: A Historical Bibliography* (Santa Barbara: Clio Press, 1983).

3. Michael H. Ebner, "Urban History: Retrospect and Prospect," *Journal of American History* 68 (June 1981): 69–84, cites especially Eric E. Lampard, "American Historians and the Study of Urbanization," *American Historical Review* 67 (October 1961): 49–61, and Roy Lubove, "The Urbanization Process: An Approach to Historical Research," *Journal of the American Institute of Planners* 33 (January 1967): 33–39.

4. Stephan Thernstrom, "Reflections on the New Urban History," *Daedalus* 100 (Spring 1971): 360–62.

5. Michael Frisch, "American Urban History as an Example of Recent Historiography," *History and Theory* 18 (October 1979): 350–77, and Thomas Bender, "The Erosion of Public Culture: Cities, Discourses, and Professional Disciplines," in Thomas L. Haskell, ed., *The Authority of Experts: Studies in History and Theory* (Bloomington: Indiana University Press, 1984), pp. 83–106.

6. In both tone and content, Warner caught the spirit of a reformist age, as when he wrote that his goal was "to attempt to use history to replace the diffuse fears and sporadic panics which now characterize the popular perceptions of our cities . . . by presenting people with their history" to help them to "choose for themselves intelligently what needs to be done and what can be done to build humane cities in America." Sam Bass Warner, Jr., *The Urban Wilderness: A History of the American City* (New York: Harper & Row, 1972), p. 4. See also Richard C. Wade, "An Agenda for Urban History," in George Athan Billias and Gerald N. Grob, eds., *American History: Retrospect and Prospect* (New York: Free Press, 1971), pp. 367, 398.

7. Stephan Thernstrom and Richard Sennett, eds., *Nineteenth-Century Cities: Essays in the New Urban History* (New Haven: Yale University Press, 1969), and Leo F. Schnore, ed., *The New Urban History: Quantitative Explorations by American Historians* (Princeton: Princeton University Press, 1975).

8. See the prologue to Theodore Hershberg, ed., *Philadelphia: Work, Space, Family, and Group Experience in the 19th Century* (New York: Oxford University Press, 1981), and Hershberg, "The New Urban History: Toward an Interdisciplinary History of the City," *Journal of Urban History* 5 (November 1978): 3–40, reprinted in *Philadelphia*.

9. See Diana Klebanow and Bayrd Still, "The Teaching of American Urban History," *Journal of American History* 55 (March 1969): 843–47.

10. Theodore Hershberg, "Toward an Interdisciplinary History of the American City," *Journal of Urban History* 8 (August 1982): 484.

11. Derek Fraser and Anthony Sutcliffe, eds., *The Pursuit of Urban History* (London: Edward Arnold, 1983).

12. See, for instance, Kenneth Fox, *Metropolitan America: Urban Life and Urban Policy in the United States, 1940–1980* (Jackson: University of Mississippi Press, 1986).

13. Bruce M. Stave, "A Conversation with Sam Bass Warner, Jr.: Ten Years Later," *Journal of Urban History* 11 (November 1984): 83–113; Terrance J. McDonald, "The Pursuit of Urban History: To the Rear March," *Historical Methods* 18 (Summer 1985): 113–16, and his response to Hershberg in *Journal of Urban History* 8 (August 1982): 455.

14. Peter Saunders, *Social Theory and the Urban Question* (New York: Holmes & Meier, 1981), p. 13.

15. Kathleen Neils Conzen, "The New Urban History: Defining the Field," in James B. Gardner and George Rollie Adams, eds., *Ordinary People and Everyday Life: Perspectives on the New Social History* (Nashville: American Association for State and Local History, 1983), pp. 270–91.

16. William Sharpe and Leonard Wallock, eds., *Visions of the Modern City*, Proceedings of the Heymen Center for the Humanities (New York: Columbia University, 1983), p. 22.

17. Charles Tilly, "History: Notes on Urban Images of Historians," in Lloyd Rodwin and Robert M. Hollister, eds., *Cities of the Mind: Images and Themes of the City in the Social Sciences* (New York: Plenum Press, 1984), pp. 131–32.

18. Lewis Mumford, *The Culture of Cities* (New York: Harcourt and Brace, 1938), p. 3.

1 ———— Back to the Present: Historians' Treatment of the City as a Social System During the Reign of the Idea of Community

ALAN I MARCUS

Recently historians have approached the issue of the American city as a social system in several ways. Social historians, including those adept in the techniques and jargon of the social sciences, conclude that cities are and always have been social systems. Surely whenever more than one person resides in a place, a social relationship among inhabitants is established. And whenever someone or something intervenes—whether institution, religion, government, or the like— that relationship becomes systematized; a social system is formed, complete with inequities and power relationships. Those conditions seem implicit in definitions of the terms *social* and *system*. But once historians accept this social history formulation and set the nature of social systems in that fashion, their subsequent efforts become rigidly circumscribed. Their assumptions restrict analysis to iden- tifying and measuring the impact of those socioeconomic forces that presumably fortified or dissipated societal bonds; consideration is thus limited to the process of city building and decay.[1]

Modern intellectual and cultural historians of the city advocate a similar agenda but from a different angle. They affirm that urbanites "thought and acted in a world conditioned by their experiences" and seek to develop an "ecology of knowledge." Asking "how did ideas about the city . . . change as Americans confronted the industrial city" and "how did Americans develop new cultural ideals that would give meaning and coherence to their lives in an increasingly urban environment," these scholars maintain that "maps of social reality lose their usefulness in the face of rapid and extensive social change." In this case, assumptions about the nature of experience and social change and their relationship to ideas bound the issue. These assumptions restrict historians to identifying and measuring the impact of those socioeconomic experiences—social forces—that fortified or dissipated ideas of coherence; consideration is limited to the process of idea building and decay.[2]

Since this intellectual-cultural history program is less well known than that of the social historians, a brief description will prove helpful. One wing adopts a modest focus. It identifies groups of people who purportedly underwent or shared remarkably similar experiences; they were subjected to the same socioeconomic forces. This common experience resulted in shared ideas. Indeed, ideas become group specific, the property of groups; these historians often write of ideas of elites, doctors, lower classes, Jews, and blacks. In short, what one has experienced in some real, objective sense dictates not only what one thinks but also who one truly is. The historian's task, then, becomes to determine which experiences were most significant, to select experiences and rank them.[3] The other portion of the modern intellectual-cultural history fraternity differs from the former only in its practitioners' choice of the locus of experience; it portrays the relevant experience as pervasive, not restricted to a particular site or group. It too finds idea-building engines in social forces. Industrialism, urbanization, and immigration come immediately to mind, but Marxism, capitalism, and others have been relegated by these scholars to the social forces category as experience; once their powers were unleashed, everything else was ordained (unless another force intervened).[4]

The intellectual-cultural history and social history approaches greatly reduce scholars' vision and utility. Exclusive emphasis on the impact of social forces casts historians as environmental determinists who engage in the crudest form of mass psychohistory. Their stimulus-response model of human behavior seems as simplistic in its adherence to experience as that of the sociobiologists and their reliance on heredity. More to the point, neither approach is so rigorous as to rule out other modes of analysis. Inquiries into the degree of systematization or the character of experience quickly degenerate into considerations of abstract, speculative, and peculiaristic quantities. Identifying these nebulous quantities and assigning them relative strengths ultimately devolves into a series of qualitative judgements; it results in equally abstract, speculative, and peculiaristic considerations of whether particular forces were positive or negative and to what degree. As with beauty, those assessments are in the eyes of the beholder.

A handful of historians have adopted yet another approach. They have concluded, in effect, that the quest for understanding processes of city and idea building is best left to philosophers, clerics, and divines. They take ideas seriously but in a way different from earlier intellectual historians. Instead of tracing unit ideas or recounting the utterances of intellectuals, these scholars consciously examine the past for ideas of the city's nature in the past. Roy Lubove and M.

Christine Boyer are among those approaching the urban past in this manner. Perhaps the attractiveness of this approach to these investigators stemmed from their books' topics; both have considered designers—urban planners—people who chose to articulate a vision of the city's nature. What these historians have uncovered about these visionaries is exciting. They have found that ideas of what cities were or ought to have been are locked in time but not in place. They have discovered in each instance that contemporaries offered a remarkably similar view, regardless of geographical location. Boyer is especially forceful on that theme.[5]

To be sure, the similarities to which Boyer and Lubove point may be attributed to the subject of their investigations and reflect nothing more than a professional subculture or disciplinary methodology; they could be products of a particular ecology of knowledge. That sort of analysis loses credence, however, when compared with some of the recent work on the history of urban politics. Those who accentuate ideas in their examinations have determined that there was marked agreement at particular times about the nature of the municipality although not about strategy, politics, or other specifics. And this agreement seemed to depend only on time, not location or discipline. For example, Kenneth Fox has identified notions held jointly by the federal Census Bureau's urban statisticians and the National Municipal League's members. Michael Frisch has found similar views among the emerging urban political scientists, while Gerald Frug has pointed to common definitions among legal experts. Jon Teaford's latest book is more provocative. Trying to understand why subsequent generations of scholars have persisted in labeling late nineteenth-century city government a conspicuous failure, Teaford finds that bosses and reformers across the United States shared a common set of perceptions about city government's structure and function, disagreeing only over who should hold power. This conflict produced a series of political compromises among factions discontented with compromise, a situation that engendered heated statements and vituperative public displays as both sides sought to beat back the other. To Teaford, then, city government during this period has an image problem as partisans deprecated their foes in the struggle for power; that wrangling, not the operations of government, is what has captivated later observers. In effect, he exposes the reformer-boss dichotomy as a matter not of vision of the city but of politics.[6]

Teaford's insights into the relationship between the ideas of bosses and reformers are revealing. They suggest that competitors often agreed on the framework in which political maneuver occurs. And when examined in conjunction with the research of Fox, Frug, Frisch, Lubove, and Boyer on the same period, a further implication is clear. There seemed to have existed at least during the late nineteenth and early twentieth centuries a broad-based, overarching common notion about what cities were or ought to have been, and it appeared to know no geographical, disciplinary, or even class or ethnic bounds.

That a sole notion of the city dominated a particular epoch of American history poses a challenge to the scholarship of most historians and other social scientists. Urban geography, demography, racial composition, occupational characteristics,

and the like differed markedly during the period from place to place; the diverse
social realities of cities, coupled with their inhabitants' single vision of the city's
nature, cast doubt on the validity of the social forces explanation of the late
nineteenth- and twentieth-centuries' urban past. While these two simultaneous
occurrences indicate instead that the idea of the city had little in common with
social realities, the work of Teaford and others also implies something more.
The idea of the city's nature apparently bounded possibilities. It governed what
contemporaries perceived when they examined the cityscape, and what they
perceived provided the basis for what they did or sought to do. More simply,
what people have recognized has been their reality.

Such a claim is not nearly as bold as it first appears. A broad-based agreement
about basics during a certain period is necessary for discussion and debate; a
shared vision of the nature of reality allows contemporaries to engage in con-
versations and arguments. But the existence of a common perception of the
nature of reality does not mean that political differences among antagonists are
insignificant or that motivation among individuals does not differ. The diversity
of enterprises conducted and groups active during any single time indicates that
motivation and politics are important. Yet those differences manifest themselves
within the context of the broad consensus about reality. In essence, ideas cir-
cumscribe the debates over, as well as the nature of, public action.

The attempt to delineate ideas of the nature of cities in the past need not be
limited to the late nineteenth and early twentieth centuries. Urban dwellers have
always tried to explain—explicitly or implicitly—their fascination and frustration
with cities, as well as their relationships to those places. These explanations
have been in effect definitions of what cities at particular times seem to be or
ought to be. And as in the case of the late nineteenth and early twentieth centuries,
these definitions frame public problems and suggest potential remedies.

History pursued in this manner is akin to cladistics.[7] French scholars, such as
Alexandre Koyre, Claude Levi-Strauss, and Michel Foucault, have taken the
lead among social scientists in working through this approach. In the United
States, Henry D. Shapiro and Zane L. Miller, both of the University of Cincinnati's ironically titled Center for Neighborhood and Community Studies, have
extended the examination's terms during the last decade, and not just with respect
to cities.[8] Its partisans agree that before historians can ask why, they need to
answer what; before city- or idea-building engines can be selected—before a
discussion of those processes can be meaningful—the dimensions of past realities
have to be uncovered. That sets the agenda at attempting to reconstruct the nature
of past realities, at investigating the taxonomy of past realities. These scholars
seek to identify those broad, arching visions of the past, each of which generated
attempts at explanation, spawned patterns of action, and yielded literatures of
advocacy. These explanations, actions, and advocacies constitute the fossil record
of historians as they try to build again, to understand, the nature of the realities
of the past; these fossilized artifacts and articulations, found in the public and
private record, are the result of definitions of what cities seemed to have been

or ought to have been. An essay on the sequence of visions of the city's nature since the mid-nineteenth century therefore must incorporate some fossils. Indeed, only by comparing the fossil record can it be determined when—and if—contemporaries viewed cities as social systems.

The quest for past realities alters the traditional understanding of the importance of the past's prominent men and women. Rather than portray them as great thinkers, as individuals who invented, discovered or caused the emergence of a new city vision, these historians reevaluate the relationship of these distinguished figures to their contemporaries and turn the time-honored interpretation on its head. Fame and influence in this view is not the product of unusualness or insightfulness but typicality. Eminence is the public recognition of the ability to express in words and deeds those often unspoken, widely held visions of reality's nature; it is the capacity to tell contemporaries in a clear fashion what everybody already knew. In that sense, prominent individuals are commoners, popular spokespersons, who provide broad glimpses into the realities of the past.

The role of social forces in historical analysis also undergoes drastic reinterpretation. These historians maintain that -izations and -isms are names, not explanations, and that that confusion functions to disguise what is not known. These scholars then look beyond the almost occult connotations of the verbiage to unmask what did in fact occur. To these men and women, social forces are not agents of change but decisions and results, another form of public activity; rather than producers of mind (engines) these forces become manifestations of mind (events). And these events provide additional evidence through which to approach an understanding of the past. Two questions can be asked. What assumptions about the nature of reality made these events appropriate, usable, even desirable, and how did they seem appropriate, usable, even desirable? The latter issue is as crucial as the former.

Mid-nineteenth-century cities have not received as much attention as one would expect from recent scholars. Despite the relative neglect, the few who have studied the period in the last decade and a half have provided some valuable insights. Perhaps the most significant for this essay is that mid-century urban society seemed to operate according to principles different from the societies that followed it. For example, Paul Boyer has pointed to the virtual absence of successful single-issue reform organizations prior to the mid-1850s. Kathleen Conzen has accentuated accommodation rather than autonomy in her study of Milwaukee's mid-century Germans. Thomas Bender has suggested that the period's municipal colleges and universities specialized in the teaching of manners and morals—behavior. And Michael Frisch has found that the citizens of Springfield, Massachusetts, made no attempt to organize the city and its population either functionally or in some other hierarchical manner prior to the 1870s.[9]

These instances point to the strangeness of mid-nineteenth-century cities, implying that their inhabitants placed an unprecedented emphasis on uniformity. That emphasis provides the key to understanding this period's vision of cities.

The idea of the mid-century city was predicated on the notion that its residents could constitute a homogeneous group. The reason that homogeneity seemed conceivable stemmed from the focus on behavior—manners, discipline, and morals—as habits learned and as habits that could be changed. Indeed, a plastic or malleable population held out hope of homogeneity because it seemed only to depend on the conversion of the ill-formed or malformed.

A few important exceptions to that formulation existed. Neither blacks nor some religious groups, such as the Mormons, seemed capable of learning the habits necessary to live in cities; they apparently were unable to undergo the conversion experience. As a consequence of these limitations, they had to be tightly regulated, as with black codes in the North or slavery in the South, or excluded, as from Nauvoo. Those labeled intractable were placed outside the city even as they lived within it. They remained apart from mid-nineteenth-century urban life.[10]

But blacks and practitioners of unacceptable religions made up only a small fraction of the mid-century population. The rest seemed able to live happily, healthfully, and successfully in American cities. That crime, vice, filth, street begging, and disease were detected in cities indicated to contemporaries only that homogeneity had not yet been achieved; the reality of cities was different than it could and should be. Urbanites explained the persistence of these social evils by blaming foreigners, the dangerous classes, children who had grown up without moral training, or the like. In virtually every instance, those culpable were identified as strangers to the city, as newcomers unfamiliar with the proper mode of behavior for American urban life. Such was the explanation for even those perpetrators who had lived in the city all their lives.[11]

The method to rid cities of this plague of newcomers was straightforward. Individuals engaging in the social evils had to be retaught—retooled or retrained—to exist as part of a social unit. Reformation was of great moment. Failure to develop and acquire proper behavior held dire consequences for both individuals and the city. These men and women would not only destroy themselves but also affect the lives of others. In addition, their displays could prove infectious and undermine proper behavior generally. Improper activity was a disease likely to spread.

Division of urban residential space also reflected the idea of a city population bifurcated by behavior. Mid-century urbanites recognized concentrations of newcomers in their midst; New York's Five Points and Cincinnati's Over-the-Rhine stood as examples. Surveys of these areas fortified the linkage between geography and behavior. Observers called these places pockets of iniquity, hotbeds of crime and vice, fever nests, or some such thing. In all cases, those who commented said that inhabitants of these areas lived in miserable and degraded circumstances and stressed the need to reform these residents' behavior. Defining places as plagued by newcomers heightened anxiety and accelerated the concentration process. Few men and women of means chose to expose themselves and their families to continued risk. Rather than remain in or near an area identified as overwhelmed by newcomers, they fled to more respectable parts of the city or to settlements beyond the city limits. Often their previous dwellings were sub-divided and rented to several families.[12]

In effect, mid-century cities were composed of but two groups: those who exhibited proper behavior and those who did not but could be taught. Membership in the latter seemed ephemeral, moreover, though it appeared likely that the ranks would be replenished by more recent arrivals. That broad assumption guided public action. Citizens formed institutions to teach proper behavior, to cleanse the city of environmental nuisances caused by the as yet uninitiated, and to protect themselves generally from the habits of newcomers. Historians have studied these attempts at reformation in some depth, demonstrating that the years after about 1840 marked the zenith of American benevolence; city residents created an impressive variety of organizations, asylums, and agencies—both church related and otherwise—to educate and, as a consequence of this education, transform newcomers. In many cases, city missionaries served as the medium through which these reform efforts were transacted. Although each reformist enterprise generally employed its own missionaries, these men and women pur-sued their mandate in similar ways. They scoured the city to search out unfor-tunates and identified the causes of their plight. After classifying these people according to the training they lacked, missionaries attempted to furnish the missing, appropriate education to remedy deficiencies.[13]

Scholars have been even more careful to recount the emergence of municipal government. During this period, cities received from state legislatures the right and power to erect on a full-time basis police, fire, health, and social service departments. They gained permission to institute regular garbage collection and to lay house to main sewer lines. In effect, cities were awarded the authority to protect and restore the urban environment year round; they could remove at regular intervals the debris of society, whether household refuse or the broken bodies and spirits of those destroyed by their lack of preparation for mid-nine-teenth-century American urban life.[14] Despite the multiplicity of social inven-tions, and although city dwellers clearly realized that the action of the maltutored or untutored affected others, mid-nineteenth-century urbanities did not syste-matize the population or urban space. Indeed, they could not. There existed no real, fundamental differences among citizens; city residents seemed to differ only by behavior—appropriate or inappropriate—and proper behavior could be learned. Cities constituted units, not systems.

The mid-century notion of cities stood in stark contrast to its late nineteenth-and early twentieth-centuries' counterpart. Contemporaries identified these places during the later period as cauldrons of diversity; they were far more discriminating than their predecessors. Most fundamental was the persistent attempt to identify the population by type. Late nineteenth-century Americans erected numerous rigid characterization schemes, dividing the populous by class, national racial group, religion, profession, intelligence, and even body type.

These social taxonomies had important consequences because those articulating them (and others) acted as if the divisions they had crafted were critical and real; these distinctions formed the basis for social action. Concerned citizens studied the groups that they had already defined, reaffirmed that each held limited capacities or capabilities, and then worked to see that their reaffirmations served as the foundation of social policy. An often important corollary and result of these studies was the identification of type with geography. As Sam Bass Warner, Jr., has recently noted, the slum in the United States was a late nineteenth-century conception, a union of geography and class. Jacob Riis had gone further. Some ninety years earlier, he treated the slum as a composite entity, as a series of discrete neighborhoods. Although he joined class and geography, Riis also included religion and nationality. The result was to make each slum neighborhood racially or religiously distinct, typified by its inhabitants' national racial or religious characteristics.[15]

The description of urban residential neighborhoods in terms of geography, class, religion, and nationality was not restricted to slum districts. Robert A. Woods and Albert J. Kennedy extended the model shortly after the turn of the century to identify lower, middle, and upper working-class neighborhoods, arguing that together these places constituted a zone of emergence. Zane L. Miller has built on this work and maintained that late nineteenth-century urbanities detected a slum, a zone of emergence, and a periphery. Like the slum and the zone, the periphery was socioeconomically homogeneous—upper class—and composed of several neighborhoods, each of which was characterized by a religious or national group. But Miller also mentions another factor. Some late nineteenth-century neighborhoods were further defined by occupation or profession, yet other manifestations of type.[16]

Type, then, seemed to stand as the organizing principle for residential neighborhoods, with type identified as class, nationality, religion, or occupation. The remaining area of the city was also differentiated by type but in the sense of activity or function. Residential areas were seen as geographically distinct from commercial ones. Heavy industry appeared to be relegated to yet another city section. Like residential neighborhoods, both commercial and industrial districts seemed composed of a number of subdistricts, each of which exhibited a more precise specialization. For example, late nineteenth-century Americans usually situated financial institutions in close proximity to one another and recognized a tendency for hospitals and doctors' offices to agglomerate. This functional arrangement of urban space was not limited to economic activities. Service, pleasure, and entertainment districts also abounded. Indeed, few cities lacked thriving tenderloin and tavern areas. Even fewer were without park districts and parkways. Other sorts of pleasures could be found just outside city limits where restrictions placed on municipal corporations were not in force. For instance, racetracks generally served cities from beyond their borders.[17]

By dividing urban space according to function and by residence, people in the late nineteenth and early twentieth centuries defined cities as complex and diverse. But they also identified them as entities, a notion that placed a premium on uncovering the principles that systematized relations by ordering the many different parts. Economics played that role for Adna Weber, with intra-urban and interurban transportation networks making industrial organization possible. Richard Hurd stressed a more complicated arrangement. Seeking to reduce urban development to a series of universals, he espoused as his social adhesive the concept of total social relations, which he defined as the sum of the economic, political, and social interactions of city residents. To Hurd, the city was like a living organism. Its business center was the heart, its streets the arteries, its parks the lungs, its railroad depots and wharves the mouths, its telephone and telegraph lines the nerves, and its inhabitants the protoplasm.[18] Although few contemporaries agreed precisely with his formulation, a much larger number supported the sentiments and offered their own analogies. Most compared cities to hierarchically arranged organisms but objected to Hurd's designation of the vital organs. Each had individual choices; churches, businesses, and professional organizations were among the most frequently cited as indispensable. To these men and women, the question was not whether the city was a social organism but which parts served as the organism's brain and heart.

Members of these groups did more than talk. They also moved to assume the exalted positions that they had set out for their groups. For example, consortiums of ministers not only pleaded with city residents to conduct their affairs according to Christ's teachings but also worked to enact legislation to prevent backsliding. Individual congregations hammered on the same theme and established organizations to further the goal. Church-affiliated social settlements, aid societies, and the like bore witness to that drive. So too did the sponsorship of nondenominational Christian preachers. Touring the nation's cities, these pastors delivered the message in spellbinding fashion. The business crusade was more one-dimensional. Its proponents tended to concentrate on civic administration, asserting that government regularly made business-like decisions and ought to operate by business principles. As a consequence, businessmen's clubs pressed for laws rationalizing city accounting practices and for experts—businessmen—to hold municipal offices, especially the position of comptroller. Professionals cast a far broader shadow. Their claims seemed boundless. Maintaining that they were entitled to decide virtually every question for the city, these self-proclaimed professionals based that assertion on the profession of scientific or technical expertise; they claimed competence held by no others and demanded authority as the only means to further the public interest. Put another way, these people argued that they possessed the ability to reduce the city and its facets to a formulaic prescription, arrived at impartially because it was done scientifically. As a result of their employment of the scientific method, their conclusions were not subject to debate. All that was required to get urban society to function at peak efficiency was for professionals to gain the power necessary to implement their recommendations and plans.[19]

This professional revolution found expression in numerous ways: drives for staffing municipal service departments with full-time, paid professionals; formation of municipal research institutes to study the city; creation of a profession of city managers; systematization and professionalization of private philanthropic work; and establishment of a city planning profession. It also produced considerable tensions. Battles among professionals over standing frequently erupted as several different professions staked out the same niche and moved to fill it. Contests between professionals and others resulted because both insisted on their right to rule. Sometimes these disputes spawned a vicious competition for the votes of the lower and middle classes and immigrants because these groups' numerical superiority gave them the balance of political power. Often, however, compromise resulted as rivals agreed to form an uneasy alliance to beat back a common foe; they chose to share authority as the lesser evil.[20]

To sum up the case, urbanites in the late nineteenth and early twentieth centuries presumed that cities were composed of diverse groups, each of which had particular merits and liabilities. But while each group was discrete—its characteristics could be isolated and studied—what made cities cites were the relationships of the groups to each other. Because these groups varied according to capacity and capability, each had to be assigned to its proper task; relationships had to be systematized in hierarchical fashion. Only in that way could cities operate smoothly and at peak efficiency. In this view, cities were social systems of discrete, fixed, and diverse hierarchically arranged parts.

This notion of the city did not persist much beyond the second decade of the twentieth century. Historians of urban planning and politics prove helpful in elucidating the decline of the vision of cities as social systems and the rise of a new idea. Their analyses indicate that cities ceased some time after about 1920 to be considered as meaningful units. Communities replaced them, and community seemed to imply an area far larger, such as a region or metropolis, or far smaller, such as a suburb or neighborhood. For example, Fox argues that the functionalist model of city administration gave way in the 1930s to the notion of multinucleated, metropolitan community. Lubove catalogs the rise of the extralocal Regional Planning Association of America, and M. Christine Boyer sketches its ambitions. Lubove also maintains that diversification was an important characteristic of the metropolis and that goals of metropolitan planners included the creation of physically integrated, aesthetically satisfying residential environments. Teaford goes further. He recognizes that by the 1920s zoning had become a major issue in suburban life and that each suburb sought to develop a full range of municipal amenities—social, economic, and cultural. He also notes that suburbanites adopted a notion of dual sovereignty in which they became citizens of both the suburb and the metropolitan community.[21]

Although concerns differ, each historian points to the post-1920 idea of metropolis, suburb, or region as more complex than anything articulated by earlier city residents. That suggests that relationships between inhabitants, between urban spaces, and between inhabitants and urban spaces may have been qualitatively different. Those who studied urban places in the 1920s and 1930s certainly argued that case. Robert E. Park claimed that a city was a "centralized decentralized system of local communities,'' by which he meant both that each neighborhood constituted a community and differed from all others—there was at least as much diversity as there had been in the late nineteenth and early twentieth centuries—and that the city was greater than the sum of its parts. These places were total human environments, characterized by constant adjustment—dynamic equilibrium—as they engaged in the seemingly endless process of growth and decline. Geography, ecology, economics, communications, transportation, human nature, and a host of other forces merged as if one continually operating force, forming a kind of ''social metabolism . . . analogous to the anabolic and katabolic [sic] process of [biological] metabolism.'' To Park, cities were tightly integrated units in which the parts constantly changed in relation to each other.[22]

R. D. McKenzie described relationships similarly but in more detail. He did away with cities per se to focus on a larger picture. Arguing that a city was merely the ''center of a constellation of smaller centers,'' he saw the metropolitan community as a subdivided, multinucleated ''complex of centers that are economically and socially integrated in a larger regional unity.'' While each unit of the metropolitan community was marked by ''an ever-increasing refinement of division of labor,'' the community itself was based on ''interdependence of relationship.'' Community interdependence was paramount and a manifestation of ''modern social life.'' It was ''so closely integrated as a whole that no change can occur in any of its phases without affecting other phases in some measure.''

McKenzie did more than define relationships. He also offered a cause for the emergence of metropolitan communities and a means to deal with their problems. Maintaining that the metropolitan community comprised a ''coherent economic and cultural state,'' McKenzie asserted that it stood as the product of a new social force, the ''modern means of communication.'' This force fostered ''bonds of common interest . . . much stronger than any [other] ties.'' Consequences of this union required a dual form of governance. The United States needed ''units of metropolitan scope'' to deal ''with those matters which affect the metropolis as a whole'' but should rely on local governments for all other purposes.[23]

This vision of an urban place as a dynamic, integrated unit greater than the sum of its constituents was not limited to the Chicago sociologists. It framed the efforts of the post-1920 generation of urbanologists generally. Homer Hoyt, Lewis Mumford, Robert and Helen Lynd, Caroline Ware, and W. Lloyd Warner incorporated this view in their work. So too did the New Deal's Resettlement Administration. Conclusions were not always the same, although the approach and assumptions were. For instance, Hoyt attacked Ernest W. Burgess' theory of urban succession for residential areas, favoring sector analysis over concentric rings. Nonetheless, Hoyt attributed neighborhood growth to a confluence of forces—economic, geographic, and social—and claimed that the dynamic relationship among these forces kept residential neighborhoods in constant motion; they were continually changing. Mumford made a distinguished career out of urging Americans to abandon central cities to establish livable, total communities—regional communities—but he identified technology as the critical force. The "old" technology of steel, coal, and steam caused an irreparable ecological imbalance in central cities, which had become megalopolises, soon to become necropolises. The "new" technology of electricity and the automobile seemed to permit the formation of new, different communities, which would ensure a better, more humane future. Ware's study of Greenwich Village was more clinical. Setting out to delineate forces enhancing community cohesion, she found only forces creating cultural confusion and social disorganization.[24]

Urban space, population groups, and problems gained new meaning within the post-1920 framework. Although contemporaries continued to define urban places as composed of diverse peoples and enterprises, they did not do so in terms of the late nineteenth- and early twentieth-centuries' relationship between geography and population. The static system of the earlier period had been replaced by a new post-1920 dynamism. The new dynamism of urban places made permanent ties to particular spots, and permanence generally, appear antithetical; peoples and businesses were merely passing through on their way to someplace else. It was the forces that seemed to hold population groups together—not the land—that were deemed central. Similarly, these groups themselves seemed temporary and somewhat artificial. They simply were manifestations of social forces—usually culture and economics—and remained viable only so long as those forces persisted. Post-1920 Americans also conceived of urban problems as the result of social forces, but the idea of interdependence complicated matters because it did not allow for the isolation and rectification of individual questions. As early as 1933, McKenzie explained the difficulty. When we arrive at an apparently "satisfactory solution of a single problem," we often, he contended, "produce new problems by putting that solution into practice." As a consequence of interdependence, urbanites and analysts measured each problem's severity relativistically; they determined its impact on community cohesion and acted according to that assessment. In essence, urban problems seemed problems necessitating public action only if they damaged markedly the community's cohesiveness.[25]

Agencies created to attack those crucial problems stemmed from similar assumptions. No matter the title—commission or something else—these groups were multidisciplinary; they were interdisciplinary research groups. Their mandate was temporary and problem specific. Organization was cross-disciplinary and functional. Each type of expert examined only certain facets of the larger question, with duties identified and limited by an individual's special expertise. Indeed, no single discipline predominated within these arrangements because each brought a particular, focused skill seemingly necessary for the problem at hand; these groups were not hierarchical but functional. The complexity and interdependence of metropolitan problems precluded any one sector from tackling them independently. The group's activities promised to yield a result, a solution, greater than or different from that of its ununited parts.[26]

The notion of an urban place as a dynamic, highly integrated community of communities formed by a conjunction of social forces cannot be construed as a social system in any meaningful sense. The parts of the system were not permanent or fixed; they simply were manifestations of current social forces and as a consequence likely to undergo frequent redefinition or revision. The likelihood of frequent change, coupled with the idea of interdependence, did not allow systemization to seem anything more than temporary. Cities were networks of social forces, not systems of peoples and places.

The essence of this vision remains popular among urbanologists today. Scholars such as Wilbur R. Thompson and Amos Hawley continue to enjoy among academics a substantial following. As had their predecessors in the 1920s and 1930s, both stress interdependences and erect a supraorganic model of community, though Hawley accentuated transportation and communications as his predominant cohesive forces, while Thompson singled out economics.[27]

This notion of the city also infects contemporary urban history scholarship. Although most modern purveyors of the discipline explicitly discount the value of such an analysis, their work hinges on an idea of the city's nature, a vision; social historians employ ideas much more centrally than they admit and intellectual-cultural historians more centrally than they know. Within the field, two distinct, major interpretative threads have emerged. Neither thread can be reduced to a social history or an intellectual-cultural history approach. Despite differences in each interpretation's thrust and although practitioners have accorded ideas little importance, both ultimately depend on the same vision of the city.

The first begins with a presumption that the municipal or metropolitan essence is or should be culturally holistic; cities and metropolises always have been or should have been cultural totalities. Although often tacit, that assumption is extremely powerful to these scholars. Their task becomes to identify the socioeconomic forces that have increased or loosened community cohesion. Indeed urban biographers often have incorporated this notion in their examinations, and it frequently has served as the centerpiece of local history or community studies. The large-scale introduction of quantitative techniques has merely formalized the evaluation process; urban historians generally use statistics to delineate factors strengthening or inhibiting cultural cohesion—whether each was functional or dysfunctional—and especially to measure the intensity of cultural union. Like many of their narrative history counterparts, quantifiers present their findings in terms of interdependence and community, concepts predicated on their notion of cultural holism.[28]

The second tradition of urban history scholarship seems to reverse the equation. Its practitioners stress separation, distance, and isolation, emphasizing and measuring the strength of what they often label cleavages. These historians usually pinpoint industrialization—sometimes objectified as modernization or villified as corporate capitalism—as the primary dysfunctional force in the urban crucible. Industrialization transformed cities, either from geographic areas in which each nationality had carved out its cultural network into metropolises characterized by spatial segregation according to income, occupation, and nationality or from collections of whole, fulfilled craftsmen into metropolises marked by rigid class antagonisms and individual alienation as workers lost control of the means of production. Despite different verbiage, however, advocates of the industrialization thesis hold much in common with the cultural cohesion group; differences in approach, though not politics, are more apparent than real. At the heart of both types of the industrialization analysis is the romantic idea of an idyllic urban past, one bordering on cultural cohesion, shattered and replaced by a loss of personal identity and underlying dissatisfaction.[29]

That most present-day urban historians depend on a single notion of the city's nature is intriguing. They have achieved a concensus, which remains in effect even as they criticize and dispute one another. Their differences lie not in the realm of ideas of the city but politics; they argue over which -isms or -izations were the key environmental determinants, the most essential and most influential social forces, as well as those forces' efficacy. This consensus provides additional confirmation for the assumption that reality is something defined and that action proceeds from that definition.

That these men and women pursue this path even as they deny the utility or relevance of ideas is ironic. It makes understanding the pre-1920 past difficult. Reliance on the post-1920 notion of what cities are or ought to be obscures what cities before 1920 were. It superimposes the concerns and categories of the mid-twentieth century on the past; it is going back to the present. Those of the past held their own concerns and categories. The study of the past—history—must be done on the past's own terms. It requires good-faith attempts to uncover those past concerns and categories. To do otherwise is to pretend that the past was virtually indistinguishable from the present. The past simply becomes the place to wage present battles. That is ignoring the forest for the trees.

Notes

1. Several historians have produced during the past few years synoptic essays on the state of urban history scholarship. The role of social forces looms prominently in each. See Kathleen Neils Conzen, "Community Studies, Urban History, and American Local History," in Michael Kammen, ed., *The Past Before Us: Contemporary Historical Writing in the United States* (Ithaca: Cornell University Press, 1980), pp. 270–91; Michael H. Ebner, "Urban History: Retrospect and Prospect," *Journal of American History* 68 (June 1981): 69–84; and Jon C. Teaford, "Finis for Tweed and Steffens: Rewriting the History of Urban Rule," *Reviews in American History* 10 (December 1982): 133–49.

2. The quotations are from Steven J. Diner, *A City and Its Universities: Public Policy in Chicago, 1892–1919* (Chapel Hill: University of North Carolina Press, 1980), p. 10; Charles Rosenberg, "Towards an Ecology of Knowledge: On Discipline, Context, and History," in Alexandra Oleson and John Voss, eds., *The Organization of Knowledge in Modern America, 1860–1920* (Baltimore: Johns Hopkins University Press, 1979), pp. 440–55; and Thomas Bender, *Toward an Urban Vision: Ideas and Institutions in Nineteenth-Century America* (Lexington: University Press of Kentucky, 1975), p. ix.

3. See, for example, Charles E. Rosenberg, "Social Chaos and Medical Care in

Nineteenth-Century America: The Rise and Fall of the Dispensary," *Journal of the History of Medicine and Allied Sciences* 29 (January 1974): 32–54, and "Inward Vision and Outward Glance: The Shaping of the American Hospital, 1818–1914," *Bulletin of the History of Medicine* 53 (Fall 1979): 346–91; Sylvia Doughty Fries, *The Urban Idea in Colonial America* (Philadelphia: Temple University Press, 1977); Sam Bass Warner, Jr., "The Management of Multiple Urban Images," in Derek Fraser and Anthony Sutcliffe, eds., *The Pursuit of Urban History* (London: Edward Arnold, 1983), pp. 383–94; and Blaine A. Brownell, "The Idea of the City in the American South," in Fraser and Sutcliffe, *Pursuit,* pp. 138–50.

4. See, for instance, Richard Sennett, *The Fall of Public Man: On the Social Psychology of Capitalism* (New York: Knopf, 1977); Christopher Lasch, *Haven in a Heartless World: The Family Besieged* (New York: Basic Books, 1977); and David F. Noble, *America by Design: Science, Technology, and the Rise of Corporate Capitalism* (New York: Knopf, 1977). For a discussion of Marxist analysis, see Paolo Ceccarelli, "*Ex Uno Plures:* A Walk through Marxist Urban Studies," in Lloyd Rodwin and Robert M. Holliser, eds., *Cities of the Mind: Images and Themes of the City in the Social Sciences* (New York: Plenum Press, 1984), pp. 313–35.

5. Roy Lubove, *The Progressives and the Slums: Tenement House Reform in New York City, 1890–1917* (Pittsburgh: University of Pittsburgh Press, 1962); and M. Christine Boyer, *Dreaming the Rational City: The Myth of American City Planning* (Cambridge, Mass.: MIT Press, 1983), esp. the Introduction.

6. Kenneth Fox, *Better City Government: Innovation in American Urban Politics, 1850–1937* (Philadelphia: Temple University Press, 1977), pp. 63–89; Michael H. Frisch, "Urban Political Images in Search of a Historical Context," in Rodwin and Hollister, *Cities of the Mind,* pp. 197–232; Gerald E. Frug, "The City as Legal Concept," in Rodwin and Hollister, *Cities of the Mind,* pp. 233–90; and Jon C. Teaford, *The Unheralded Triumph: City Government in America, 1870–1900* (Baltimore: Johns Hopkins University Press, 1984), esp. p. 9.

7. For the scope and concerns of cladistics, see, for example, Walter Henning, *Phylogenetic Systematics,* trans. D. D. Davis and R. Zangcrly (Urbana: University of Illinois Press, 1979); and Thomas Duncan and Tod F. Stuessy, eds., *Cladistics: Perspectives on the Reconstruction of Evolutionary History,* Columbia Perspectives on the Reconstruction of Evolutionary History (New York: Columbia University Press, 1984).

8. See, for instance, Alexandre Koyre, *From the Closed World to the Infinite Universe* (Baltimore: Johns Hopkins University Press, 1957); Claude Levi-Strauss, *The Savage Mind* (Chicago: University of Chicago Press, 1966); and Michel Foucault, *The Order of Things: An Archaeology of the Human Sciences* (New York: Vintage, 1970) and *The Birth of the Clinic: An Archaeology of Medical Perception* (New York: Vintage, 1975). An essay that considers a possible political implication of some aspects of Foucault's work is François Bedarida, "The French Approach to Urban History: An Assessment of Recent Methodological Trends," in Fraser and Sutcliffe, *Pursuit,* pp. 403–4. Also see "The Neo-Structuralism of Michel Foucault," in Robert Wuthnow, James Davison Hunter, Albert Bergesen, and Edith Kurzwell, eds., *Cultural Analysis* (Boston: Routledge and Kegan Paul, 1984), pp. 133–78. For Miller, see, for example, *Suburb: Neighborhood and Community in Forest Park, Ohio, 1935–1976* (Knoxville: University of Tennessee Press, 1981), and "The Rise of the City," *Hayes Historical Journal* 3 (Spring and Fall 1980): 73–84. For Shapiro, see *Appalachia on Our Mind: The Southern Mountains and Mountaineers in the American Consciousness, 1870–1920* (Chapel Hill: University of

North Carolina Press, 1978), and "Neighborhood and the Family—The Larger Setting: The Emergence of Ideas and Their Implication," in Thomas L. Jenkins, ed., *Home and Family in the 1980s* (Cincinnati: Better Housing League of Greater Cincinnati, 1984), pp. 44–67.

9. Paul Boyer, *Urban Masses and Moral Order in America, 1820–1920* (Cambridge, Mass.: Harvard University Press, 1978), p. 84; Kathleen Neils Conzen, *Immigrant Milwaukee, 1836–1860: Accommodation and Community in a Frontier City* (Cambridge, Mass.: Harvard University Press, 1976); Thomas Bender, "The Erosion of Public Culture: Cities, Discourses, and Professional Disciplines," in Thomas Haskell, ed., *The Authority of Experts: Studies in History and Theory* (Bloomington: Indiana University Press, 1984), pp. 84–106; and Michael H. Frisch, *Town into City: Springfield, Massachusetts, and the Meaning of Community, 1840–1880* (Cambridge, Mass.: Harvard University Press, 1972).

10. For evidence of attempts at regulation or exclusion, see Phillip J. Staudenhaus, *The African Colonization Movement, 1815–1865* (New York: Columbia University Press, 1961); Letitia Woods Brown, *Free Negroes in the District of Columbia, 1790–1846* (New York: Oxford University Press, 1972); Richard C. Wade, *Slavery in the Cities: The South, 1820–1860* (New York: Oxford University Press, 1964); Robert F. Flanders, *Nauvoo: Kingdom on the Mississippi* (Urbana: University of Illinois Press, 1965); and Ray Allen Billington, *The Protestant Crusade, 1800–1860: A Study of the Origins of American Nativism* (New York: Macmillan, 1938).

11. Boyer, *Urban Masses*, pp. 65–120; Alan I Marcus, "National History through Local: Social Evils and the Origins of Municipal Services in Cincinnati," *American Studies* 23 (Fall 1981): 23–29. Also see T. S. Arthur, *Ten Nights in a Bar-Room, and What I Saw There* (New York: Hurst and Co., 1852).

12. See, for example, John Griscom, *The Sanitary Condition of the Laboring Population of New York, with Suggestions for its Improvement* (1845; New York: Arno Press, 1971); Samuel C. Busey, *Immigration: Its Evils and Consequences* (1856; New York: Arno Press, 1969); Charles Loring Brace, *The Dangerous Classes and Twenty Years Work Among Them* (New York: Tiffin, 1872); William Channing, ed., *The Memoir and Writings of James Handasyd Perkins*, 2 vols. (Cincinnati: Trueman and Spofford, 1851); and *Cincinnati Daily Commercial*, March 2, 1855.

13. For benevolence, see, for instance, Ian R. Tyrrell, *Sobering Up: From Temperance to Prohibition in Antebellum America, 1800–1860* (Westport, Conn.: Greenwood Press, 1979); Roy Lubove, "The New York Association for the Improving of the Condition of the Poor: The Formative Years," *New York Historical Society Quarterly* 43 (July 1959): 307–28; Elizabeth M. Geffen, "Philadelphia Protestantism Reacts to Social Reform Movements Before the Civil War," *Pennsylvania History* 30 (April 1963): 192–211; and Jay P. Dolan, *The Immigrant Church: New York's Irish and German Catholics, 1815–1865* (Baltimore: Johns Hopkins University Press, 1975), esp. pp. 121–40.

14. For the institution of municipal services, see, for example, Marcus, "National History through Local"; Ernest S. Griffith and Charles R. Adrian, *A History of American City Government: The Formation of Traditions, 1775–1870* (Washington, D.C.: University Press of America, 1983); James F. Richardson, *Urban Police in the United States* (Port Washington, N.Y.: Kennikat Press, 1974); John C. Schneider, *Detroit and the Problem of Order: A Geography of Crime, Riot, and Policing* (Lincoln: University of Nebraska Press, 1980); Arlen Dykstra, "Rowdyism and Rivalism in the St. Louis Fire Department, 1850–1857," *Missouri Historical Review* 69 (October 1974): 48–64; Stephen F. Ginsberg, "Above the Law: Volunteer Fireman in New York City," *New York History*

50 (April 1969): 165–86; and Louis P. Cain, "Raising and Watering a City: Ellis Sylvester Chesbrough and Chicago's First Sanitation System," *Technology and Culture* 13 (July 1972): 356ff.

15. Sam Bass Warner, Jr., "Slums and Skyscrapers: Urban Images, Symbols, and Ideology," in Rodwin and Hollister, *Cities of the Mind,* pp. 181–95; and Jacob Riis, *How the Other Half Lives: Studies among the Tenements of New York* (1890; New York: Hill and Wang, 1957).

16. Robert A. Woods and Albert J. Kennedy, *The Zone of Emergence: Observations of the Lower Middle and Upper Working Class Communities of Boston, 1905–1914,* ed. Sam Bass Warner, Jr., 2d ed. (Cambridge, Mass.: MIT Press, 1969); and Zane L. Miller, *Boss Cox's Cincinnati: Urban Politics in the Progressive Era* (New York: Oxford University Press, 1968).

17. Jon Teaford, *City and Suburb: The Political Fragmentation of Metropolitan America, 1850–1970* (Baltimore: Johns Hopkins University Press, 1979), pp. 5–31; Harold L. Platt, *City Building in the New South: The Growth of Public Service in Houston, Texas, 1830–1910* (Philadelphia: Temple University Press, 1983), pp. 78–84, 184–85; and David R. Goldfield and Blaine A. Brownell, *Urban America: From Downtown to No Town* (Boston: Houghton Mifflin, 1979), pp. 202–40.

18. Adna Ferrin Weber, *The Growth of Cities in the Nineteenth Century: A Study in Statistics* (New York: Macmillan, 1899), esp. p. 183; and Richard M. Hurd, *Principles of City Land Values* (New York: n.p., 1903), esp. pp. 17–18.

19. See, for example, Walter Rauschenbusch, *Christianity and the Social Crisis* (New York: Macmillan, 1907); Robert D. Cross, ed., *The Church in the City* (Indianapolis: Bobbs-Merrill, 1967); Aaron Ignatius Abell, *The Urban Impact on American Protestantism 1865–1900* (Cambridge, Mass.: Harvard University Press, 1943); Kenneth Sturges, *American Chambers of Commerce* (New York: Moffat, Pard and Co., 1915); Melvin G. Holli, *Reform in Detroit: Hazan S. Pingree and Urban Politics* (New York: Oxford University Press, 1969); Martin J. Schiesl, *The Politics of Efficiency: Municipal Administration and Reform in America, 1880–1920* (Berkeley: University of California Press, 1977); Samuel P. Hays, "The Politics of Reform in Municipal Government in the Progressive Era," *Pacific Northwest Quarterly* 55 (October 1964): 157–69; Alan I Marcus, "Professional Revolution and Reform in the Progressive Era: Cincinnati Physicians and the City Elections of 1897 and 1900," *Journal of Urban History* 5 (February 1979): 183–207; and Simon N. Patten, *The New Basis of Civilization* (New York: Macmillan, 1907).

20. Teaford, *Unheralded Triumph,* pp. 132–216; Miller, *Boss Cox's Cincinnati,* pp. 124–60; Marcus, "Professional Revolution"; Roy Lubove, *The Professional Altruist: The Emergence of Social Work as a Profession* (Cambridge, Mass.: Harvard University Press, 1965); and Janet R. Daly, "Early City Planning Efforts in Omaha, 1914–1920," *Nebraska History* 66 (Spring 1985): 48–73. Ernest S. Griffith has amassed a great deal of material on city government during this period. See his *A History of American City Government: The Conspicuous Failure, 1870–1900* (New York: Praeger, 1974), and *A History of American City Government: The Progressive Years and Their Aftermath, 1900–1920* (New York: Praeger, 1974).

21. Fox, *Better City Government,* 138–81; Roy Lubove, *Community Planning in the 1920s: The Contributions of the Regional Planning Association of America* (Pittsburgh: University of Pittsburgh Press, 1964); Boyer, *Dreaming the Rational City,* pp. 175–261; Roy Lubove, *Twentieth Century Pittsburgh: Government, Business and Environmental Change* (New York: John Wiley and Sons, 1969), pp. 87–105; and Teaford, *City and Suburb,* pp. 105–70.

22. Robert E. Park, Ernest W. Burgess, and Roderick D. McKenzie, *The City* (1925; Chicago: University of Chicago Press, 1967), esp. pp. 52–54.

23. R. D. McKenzie, *The Metropolitan Community* (1933; New York: Russell and Russell, 1967), particularly pp. v, 49, 116, 308, 312. Also see Louis Wirth, "Urbanism as a Way of Life," *American Journal of Sociology* 44 (July 1938): 1–24.

24. Homer Hoyt, *The Structure and Growth of Residential Neighborhoods in American Cities* (Washington, D.C.: Government Printing Office, 1939); Robert S. Lynd and Helen Merrell Lynd, *Middletown: A Study in American Culture* (New York: Harcourt, Brace and World, 1929), pp. 496–502, and *Middletown in Transition: A Study in Cultural Conflicts* (New York: Harcourt, Brace and World, 1937), esp. pp. 487–510; Caroline F. Ware, *Greenwich Village, 1920–1930: A Comment on American Civilization in the Post-War Years* (Boston: Houghton Mifflin, 1935), particularly pp. 422–24; and W. Lloyd Warner, ed., *Yankee City* (New Haven, Conn.: Yale University Press, 1963), esp. pp. 1–34. Warner's 1963 book is an abridgement of the Yankee City Series, published between 1941 and 1947. For Mumford's work, see, for instance, *The Culture of Cities* (New York: Harcourt, Brace and World, 1938), *The City in History: Its Transformations, and Its Prospects* (New York: Harcourt, Brace and World, 1961), and *The Urban Prospect* (New York: Harcourt, Brace and World, 1968). Also see Harlan Paul Douglass, *The Suburban Trend* (New York: Century, 1925), pp. 271–303.

25. McKenzie, *Metropolitan Community*, p. vii.

26. See, for instance, Robert B. Fairbanks, "Housing the City: The Better Housing League and Cincinnati, 1916–1939," *Ohio History* 89 (Spring 1980): 158–80, and "From Better Dwellings to Better Community: Changing Approaches to the Low-Cost Housing Problem, 1890–1925," *Journal of Urban History* 11 (May 1985): 314–34; *Regional Survey of New York and Its Environs* (New York: Committee on Regional Plan of New York and its Environs, 1928) and *Sioux City (Iowa) Journal*, January 4, 1955, February 14, 1956, May 15, 1962. For interdisciplinary research groups in a different vein, see Alan I Marcus and Erik Lokensgard, "Greater Than the Sum of Its Parts: Chemical Engineering, Agricultural Wastes, and the Transformation of Iowa State College, 1920–40," *Annals of Iowa* 49 (Summer 1985): 37–62.

27. Wilbur R. Thompson, *A Preface to Urban Economics* (Baltimore: Johns Hopkins University Press, 1965); and Amos H. Hawley, *Urban Society: An Ecological Approach* (New York: Ronald Press, 1971). Also see, for example, Robert Dahl, *Who Governs?* (New Haven: Yale University Press, 1961); Wallace S. Sayre and Herbert Kaufman, *Governing New York City: Politics in the Metropolis* (New York: Russell Sage Foundation, 1960); and Robert C. Wood, *1400 Governments: The Political Economy of the New York Metropolitan Region* (Cambridge, Mass.: Harvard University Press, 1961).

28. See, for instance, Thomas Bender, *Community and Social Change in America* (Baltimore: Johns Hopkins University Press, 1982); Carol Hoffecker, *Wilmington, Delaware: Portrait of an Industrial City, 1830–1910* (Charlottesville: University of Virginia Press, 1974); Roger W. Lotchin, *San Francisco, 1846–1856: From Hamlet to City* (New York: Oxford University Press, 1974); Richard C. Wade, *The Urban Frontier: The Rise of Western Cities, 1790–1830* (Cambridge, Mass.: Harvard University Press, 1959); and Humbert S. Nelli, *The Italians of Chicago, 1880–1930* (New York: Oxford University Press, 1970). For quantification, see Stephan Thernstrom, *Poverty and Progress: Social Mobility in a Nineteenth Century City* (Cambridge, Mass.: Harvard University Press, 1964) and *The Other Bostonians: Poverty and Progress in a Nineteenth Century American Community* (Chicago: University of Chicago Press, 1972); and Leo F. Schnore, ed., *The*

New Urban History: Quantitative Explorations by American Historians (Princeton: Princeton University Press, 1975).

29. See, for example, Christine Meisner Rosen, "Infrastructural Improvement in Nineteenth-Century Cities," *Journal of Urban History* 12 (May 1986): 211–56; Francis G. Couvares, *The Remaking of Pittsburgh: Class and Culture in an Industrializing City, 1877–1919* (Albany: State University of New York Press, 1984); Oliver Zunz, *The Changing Face of Inequality: Urbanization, Industrial Development, and Immigrants in Detroit, 1880–1920* (Chicago: University of Chicago Press, 1982); Susan E. Hirsch, *Roots of the American Working Class: The Industrialization of Crafts in Newark, 1800–1860* (Philadelphia: Temple University Press, 1978); Alan Dawley, *Class and Community: The Industrial Revolution in Lynn* (Cambridge, Mass.: Harvard University Press, 1976); and Richard Sennett, *Families Against the City: Middle Class Homes of Industrial Chicago, 1872–1890* (Cambridge, Mass.: Harvard University Press, 1970). Also see Charles Tilly, "History: Notes on Urban Images of Historians," in Rodwin and Hollister, *Cities of the Mind*, pp. 119–32.

2 ———— The City in American Culture

HOWARD GILLETTE, JR.

The city, as one finds it in history, is the point of maximum concentration for the power and culture of a community . . . here is where human experience is transformed into viable signs, symbols, patterns of conduct, systems of order. Here is where the issues of civilization are focused.

Lewis Mumford, *The Culture of Cities* (1938)

Perhaps it is only appropriate that the most eloquent argument for examining the city as the central agent of civilization would have been offered by one of America's first great urbanists but also one whose sweeping approach to the subject would have been largely rejected by the most recent generation of urban historians. Suggestive as Lewis Mumford's approach to urbanization was, it ran counter to the tides of specialization, and as the task of interpreting America's urban heritage passed to practitioners of a "new" urban history, who emphasized tangible and quantifiable aspects of urbanism, the more qualitative aspects of urban culture, especially the analysis of imaginative and perceptual views of cities, were relegated to a relative backwater in the field. To the cultural historian was assigned everything that did not otherwise fit established specializations, a situation much like that for social history a generation ago.

A few nonurban specialists, especially in American Studies, tackled competing intellectual concepts of city and country, and ultimately the middle landscape, as Leo Marx was to call the type of community forms that attempted to combine the best of both worlds. Provocative as such studies were when they first appeared, they seemed crude according to the subsequent standards of modern historiography, and as a consequence they remained largely apart from the field that was being defined as urban history. Only in recent years has there been a shift whereby symbolic manifestations of the city and countryside have been perceived in ways that can be considered central to contemporary trends of urban analysis. With new visions for reading the city that draw on a range of sources, in literature, popular culture, and the arts, new possibilities for synthesis have emerged.

Peter Brooks suggested the need for such perceptual awareness of cities in 1977. Looking particularly at Balzac's treatment of Paris, Brooks depicted an effort to uncover the basis of an urban semiotic through discovering the codes that would allow the "undifferentiated surfaces of modern urban existence to reveal their systematic meaning." One way to read those patterns lay in language, but even more generally, Balzac contended, the city itself acted as theater where obscure activity revealed a latent behavioral text. Balzac, Brooks contends, virtually invented the nineteenth century "by bringing to consciousness the very shape of modernity as a set of texts subject to our reading and interpretation."[1]

While European historians have taken the lead in interpreting those texts, as exemplified by Steven Marcus' treatment of Manchester in the 1840s as a paradigm for changes in Western culture, such efforts have been employed as well in American urban history.[2] Marcus himself has applied the concept to a reading of Saul Bellow and Thomas Pynchon as his contribution to an important book dedicated to various means of reading the city, in both the United States and abroad.[3] Stuart Blumin, an early contributor to the new social and urban history, has examined popular writing to uncover urban codes of behavior, as suggested by Brooks.[4] Other scholars in several disciplines have interpreted a variety of cultural clues offered by urban phenomena. In visual as well as written materials, critics are examining manifestations of culture for insight into the nature of urbanism.

Such approaches would seem long overdue. Although John Agnew and his colleagues are quite correct in asserting that social scientists have paid inadequate attention to such intangible aspects of culture as attitudes, values, and beliefs, it appears that humanists have been asking questions comparable to those asked by social scientists for some time.[5] Early studies of the urban novel by George Arthur Dunlap and Blanche Gelfant pointed to the value of such works for social historians, and studies of urban poetry by Robert Walker showed how this work anticipated concepts of social segmentation and separation in cities that would be systematized only later by America's first sociologists.[6] More recently, Adrienne Siegel's examination of nineteenth-century popular literature has tackled the central question asked by Stephan Thernstrom in *Poverty and Progress* and countless successors: what lay behind the myth of social mobility in the nineteenth-century city?[7] Bernard Rosenthal, in illustrating through travel accounts and other popular literature the underlying urban assumptions behind the development of the West, has enlivened an earlier interpretation of the role of cities on the frontier by Richard Wade.[8]

The cultural roots of American urbanism originated abroad in the transmission of distinct values and beliefs to the first settlers. The best known of these lay in what Perry Miller called an Augustian strain of piety, in which Americans adopted the goal of attempting to establish a godly city on a hill, which would stand apart from the corrupted cities they had left behind.[9] Bernard Rosenthal suggests that such a vision placed a particularly heavy burden on Americans. Augustine had intended merely to prepare mortals for the certain vicissitudes of the world; John Winthrop charged his followers with actually carrying out that mission by choosing between dichotomized cultures on earth, one promising "curses upon us til we be consumed out of the good land" and the other offering such "a praise and glory, that men shall say of succeeding plantations the Lord make it like that of New England."[10]

As New Englanders set about fulfilling their mission, they conceived their towns in physical plan as well as in social arrangement as bulwarks against the disorders of the cities left behind. Boston and Philadelphia, Sylvia Fries suggests, were rural in inspiration, based on principles of individual property holding and a shared belief in social hierarchy and religious conviction. Although Savannah was platted in a more secular age when classicism, especially the example of Republican Rome, more than the Bible provided inspiration, it too sought to promote moral improvement through city building, this time relying on the integration of the countryside with the city as the necessary means for securing social stability. Although towns were recognized as agents of trade and commerce, they were conceived primarily, Fries argues, as the means of instilling virtue.

At the heart of America's early ambivalence toward the city lay the success of those towns in commercial terms. William Bradford's well-known lament about the disintegration of Plymouth Colony as the forces of individualism were released with advanced prosperity was magnified in Boston, which by the 1640s was being accused of the same sins as the London of the 1620s. Ultimately, Fries suggests, Boston had to be abandoned as the embodiment of a city on the hill, even as other experiments, at New Haven, Providence, and elsewhere, attempted to recover a purer model. Penn's hopes for Philadelphia as a "green country town" free of corruption were compromised before he could even survey the city, as impracticalities of site and demand for land crushed his hope to concentrate property in the hands of a select leadership group of country proprietors.[11]

By the advent of the new republic, a religious interpretation of advancing civilization had given way to a secular one, typified by Benjamin Franklin's *Autobiography*, which Charles Sanford has described as a secularized *Pilgrim's*

Progress with Philadelphia as a neoclassical city on a hill.[12] With the decline of the utility of religious metaphors, Americans found recourse in another European tradition, that of pastoral literature. But, as Leo Marx suggests, it was modified in America in a sentimentalized belief that people could live in a middle landscape between nature's primitivism and civilization's authority. Americans remained hostile to European cities, especially as they industrialized, but they attempted to retain the benefits of their own commercial seaports. This was true, according to Marx, not only of Jefferson, as he grudgingly accepted the necessity of cities in the contest with England leading up to the War of 1812. It was also true of leading writers such as Ralph Waldo Emerson, who had been previously identified by Lois White and Morton White as a leading antagonist to the city, at least until the 1840s, when he noted several times that machinery and transcendentalism were compatible.[13]

Marx's book, written during the nascent stage of the American Studies movement, extended to the subject of urbanism the broad terms of cultural history introduced most notably by Henry Nash Smith and R. W. B. Lewis.[14] America, according to their interpretation, had been conceived in secular terms as a garden, where a new American Adam, redeemed by contact with nature and natural values, would thrive free from the Old World corruption associated with over-civilized cities. As civilization advanced in the eastern United States, the West was perceived as the virgin territory where the myth of American innocence could still be pursued. To these general propositions Michael Cowan added in *City of the West* a detailed examination of Ralph Waldo Emerson's effort to reconcile the facts he observed of urban-industrial advancement with the continuing myth of an uncorrupted West. Although Cowan admits that Emerson scarcely paid attention to the streets and buildings of real cities, he nonetheless contends that Emerson recognized his as the "Age of Cities" and thus looked to his role as a writer as the agent "to convert the vivid energies acting at this hour in New York and Chicago and San Francisco into universal symbols." While Cowan does not deny the importance of Emerson's retreat from Boston to Concord in 1834 or of his famous distinction five years later between cities as places of artificial learning and the country as the true school of reason, he nonetheless sees Emerson as committed to reconciling the different poles of experience.[15] Like other romantics, Emerson felt that cities were hostile to natural experience, but along with other American writers, in contrast to Europeans, Emerson tried to blur the distinction between the urban and the natural. Although Americans admitted an urban-rural dichotomy, they denied its universality or necessity. Most important, by transmitting the Christian metaphor of his forbearers to modern terms, Emerson managed, according to Cowan, to revive the role of the writer as reformer committed, as he said, to the belief that "the test of a civilization is the power of drawing the most benefits out of cities."[16]

The myth-and-symbol approach exemplified by Marx and Cowan found other practitioners, most notably Alan Trachtenberg in *Brooklyn Bridge: Fact and Symbol*.[17] While distinctions made in this approach between broad ideas and tangible facts drew some criticism,[18] the approach continued to be used in treating such widely divergent subjects as the founding of Washington as the national capital, the work of Henry James, and the imaginative treatment of the Vietnam war.[19] Recently the importance of efforts to fuse urban and rural perceptions has been reconfirmed in the work of James Machor, who identifies the tradition as "urban pastoralism," in which writers sought an environment blending "the pastoral attributes of freedom, simplicity and probity with the urban qualities of community, sophistication and progressive development."[20]

Indeed, the other major classical writers have been described as sharing Emerson's effort to incorporate a vision of both city and countryside. While Poe, Hawthorne, Melville, and Cooper all made the effort, like Emerson, to engage the urbanization process, each of them ultimately was so repelled by the expansion of commercialism associated with urbanism, Cynthia Stout suggests, that they retreated from an observed physical and temporal reality into the realm of private imagination. Unlike Balzac in Paris or Dickens in London, they chose not to detail the impact of industrialization on particular places.[21] Even Walt Whitman, who has been considered the most public and urban of these critics, followed the same path in the aftermath of the Civil War, when he no longer utilized the vital images of his beloved New York as the core of his work.[22]

In *Toward an Urban Vision*, Thomas Bender presents the most sympathetic and sophisticated treatment of the urban pastoral synthesis, which he describes as a contrapuntal relationship between city and country derived from the interplay of the New England version of early American agrarian ideals and the modernizing forces associated with the industrial city. Arguing that "cultural ideals provide a vocabulary of symbols or metaphors for interpreting, predicting, and relating to social experience," he describes the rise of new ideologies intended to resolve the dissonance between inherited ideals and everyday experience by supplying the meaning that older symbols no longer provided. From Jefferson, through the promoters of the Lowell industrial experiment, to the efforts to mediate urbanism through the park plans of Frederick Law Olmsted and the social reforms of Charles Loring Brace, Bender sees recurring efforts to reconcile the city with prevailing ideals through the preservation of "nature and spontaneity in an increasingly artificial and rationally organized environment." Such efforts to achieve balance, however, were soon overwhelmed by the advance of urban development and its popular acceptance. Although a critic like Henry David Thoreau might complain that the principle of textile production was "not that mankind may be well and honestly clad, but . . . that the corporations may be enriched," his warning was lost on the general public.[23]

It is the isolation of such critics from popular thought and their ultimate tendency to write in abstractions rather than to deal directly with the particulars of urban development that has discouraged social scientists from taking this body of cultural criticism into fuller account. Yet while Bernard Rosenthal agrees that America's major writers failed in their effort to achieve an imaginative synthesis, by broadening his own study to include popular literature at mid-century, he succeeds both in identifying the salience of the issues raised by those writers and in describing how images of the city and the West were assimilated into daily life.

For most people, Rosenthal contends, the city was the logical extension of the wilderness, which in an age of commercialism was assumed to give way under man's cultivating hand to civilization as represented by cities. Thus the train (as before it the canal) was not perceived as an intrusion violating nature, as Leo Marx has argued, but as the purveyor of the fruits of civilization. In contrast to Europeans who constantly commented on the apparent denigration of nature by Americans, Rosenthal suggests that fallen trees, roads, and, ultimately, cities were broadly considered as signs of advancement. "Railroads and canals will make one broad garden of Michigan," ran one typical comment, to which Rosenthal responds, although "there were those who worried about the 'garden' of pastoral imagination becoming mechanized, as Leo Marx has shown, they were few. For most, the machine *was* the garden." In the nineteenth century, he argues, the word *garden* had moved from older religious and aesthetic referents toward a commercial metaphor, as "in a land whose very birth implied the idea of a journey toward something better, it was entirely logical that in the passage to the West, the ultimate goal—however remote from nature—could be the garden. This garden, which in imagination—if not always in practice—might be the wonderful cities rising in the West, became in America the verbal configuration for the journey's end, just as the 'garden' or the 'city' had traditionally been the goal in the Christian model from which America in large measure drew its paradigm."[24]

The underlying optimism with which the mass of Americans appeared to embrace the advance of urbanism as described by Rosenthal is reaffirmed by Carl Abbott's study of western boosterism and by Lester H. Cohen, who writes that "promoters underscored the point that building towns and cities, developing trade and manufacturing—extending civilization further westward—were the aims of settlement; and these aims cast doubt on the notion that the frontier was depicted as a natural paradise. The 'garden' was not depicted as what already existed; rather it was what *might* exist, given industry and the arts of civilized society."[25]

Other studies indicate, however, that the resolution of the facts of urbanism with the consequent revolution in social relations was more difficult for that same mass of middle-class Americans. At one level, as Stuart Blumin and Hans Bergmann have argued, it was crucial for Americans to feel that the new urban system was intelligible. Taking a clue from Peter Brooks, Blumin suggests that even the formulaic tales of a gifted writer like George Foster helped his many followers to read the complex city around them. Calling Foster the "neglected grandfather of urban realism," Blumin suggests that by identifying distinct zones within the city, Foster managed to create what Anselm Straus has called the "shared symbolization" of the metropolitan "social world." Thus, behind the dark shadows of the evils he described lay an assuring message to readers that the complex city they were exposed to was intelligible.[26] Bergmann's treatment of the role of panoramic vistas at mid-century, whether in visual or printed form, parallels Blumin's study in suggesting that such visions "functioned to acknowledge a new immensity of urban scale at the same time as it created an image of the city as a single comprehensible whole." The heroes of what Bergmann calls the panoramic gothic narrative, among whom he includes George Foster, are those who in exploring the underside of the city demonstrate by their careful investigation that disorder can be removed. As such, these forms served, Bergmann asserts, "the ideological work of its culture in suggesting that the city, despite its growth and extent, can be pictured: it is explicable."[27]

Popular literature did not, however, always serve a positive role, even as it might have functioned to assure readers that urban change was both intelligible and manageable. While Raymond Wohl's treatment of the country boy myth is sympathetic to the ways Horatio Alger in particular helped provide direction for the mass of new migrants to the city, Adrienne Siegel is more critical.[28] By failing to deal with the underlying contradictions of the new urban environment, popular narrative, she contends, offered a "hollow myth of the city as a place where the stalwart could hold fast to agrarian righteousness while at the same time pursuing material abundance. . . . By denying the reality of diminishing opportunities for social mobility in the city, this fiction whetted the appetite for urban life of those who no longer wished to till the soil." Although popular literature denounced the evil aspects of cities, in the process it managed to broadcast the lure of city. Most particularly it veiled the clash of values between moralism and materialism and thus helped quiet social tensions. "Saturating the reader with a flood of happy endings," Siegel writes, "it carried the encouraging news that the city was part of God's kingdom and that those imbued with the discipline of Calvinistic morality could reach a state of grace in a terrain that contained both good and evil."[29]

If popular literature instilled newcomers to the city with illusions, those already established there made their own efforts to deal with the social complexity of burgeoning cities. Noting the magnitude of the country-to-city migration, Karen Halttunen broadens the examination of the country boy myth by showing how members of the middle class tried to protect themselves. Faced with the breakdown of a deferential social system and consequent fluidity in a world of strangers, they sought in rules of dress, etiquette, and ritual the means to define and assert standards of right behavior. By criticizing those who would manipulate the rules for their own personal ends—the confidence man and the painted lady— they focused their own anxieties about the underlying nature of social change.[30] In his study of etiquette books, John Kasson argues that such writing served not just to assure readers but also to instill in them shame as the consequence of failing to conform to dominant standards of accepted behavior. In this fashion, the purveyors of etiquette accommodated themselves to a capitalistic society that affected urban behavior by extending "the values of the increasingly urban, industrial, bureaucratic society deep into the texture of everyday life, even into the individual personality."[31] A specialized result of that response, Barbara Berg suggests, was the creation of the woman-belle ideal as a vision of domestic order designed to compensate men for the vicissitudes felt in the workplace and the retreat of agrarian pastoralism before advancing industrialism. "The woman," Berg writes, "quietly tucked away at home, creating a haven of peace and order, provided a salubrious contrast to the shrill urban milieu. As the repository of all virtue and morality, women became the substitute for a bountiful nature who nourished and nurtured, purified, and sustained. Blissfully noncompetitive, she remained unsullied by a corrupt world. She emulated the serene garden, free from the rampant vying for money, power, and position so characteristic of industrial cities."[32]

It is these bourgeois attempts to assert order that attracted the early attention of Richard Sennett. Attacking first the tendency of middle-class families to retreat from the responsibilities of public life into the privacy of the home and then to abandon the city altogether in the obsessive search for order in the suburbs, Sennett ultimately concluded that the signs once used to communicate among strangers had given way to symbols ripe for manipulation. Through the advances of capitalism and secularism, people and their appearances had become commodified, to the detriment of the possibilities of communities of strangers, which Sennett identifies as working well in eighteenth-century London and Paris. While Sennett's work has drawn its share of criticism (for, among other things, oversimplifying the role and function of the Victorian home), he succeeded nonetheless in encouraging further studies of the ways the bourgeois middle class attempted to project their values and outlook on other city dwellers.[33]

Victorian culture rested on a concept of the maintenance of strict rules of decorum, which were challenged by the dramatic growth and increased heterogeneity of the city. Paul Boyer documents the moral response of the middle class to urban change, detailing how, with the decline in the salience of religion, other means of projecting order were employed.[34] His broad synthesis adds to previous work that detailed some of these changes. The establishment in the mid-nineteenth century of parks as pleasure grounds for the masses was a relatively permissive means of asserting social control. The advent of progressivism brought with it a more assertive approach in the form of organized recreational activity.[35] To this were added cultural institutions, including museums, libraries, symphony orchestras, and universities, which, according to Helen Horowitz, were intended to "purify the city and to generate a civic renaissance."[36] Even department stores could aspire to uplift the urban masses as they adopted modes similar to the museum of architecture and decoration as well as methods of exhibiting.[37]

The area of entertainment became a particularly vital arena for Victorian reformers, who hoped to direct the leisure time of workers into socially acceptable channels. The advent of nickelodeons posed a serious threat, breaking down as it did rules established in the elite theaters of the nineteenth century separating sexes and classes from one another. Social reformers, calling for a "redemption of play," managed to redirect both the content of film and the physical environment of the performance through the buildup of elaborate movie palaces to embody the ideal of polite order. "While theater managers sought to achieve an air of pleasurable entertainment rather than of moral uplift," John Kasson writes, "they adopted both the trappings and the etiquette of artistic performance that had been established by the elite institutions in the late 19th century, and generalized it for mass audiences in the 20th."[38] Even an area that successfully thwarted reform efforts, such as the amusement park, proved less an alternative to established norms than genteel critics feared. According to Kasson, Coney Island promised city dwellers freedom from the constraints of daily life but in fact offered only a "fantastic replication of that life." Marking the shift in a culture based on production to one of consumption, such amusement parks thus represented a "cultural accommodation to the developing urban-industrial society in a tighter integration of work and leisure than ever before."[39] Although we have only a few examples of how the intended beneficiaries of such efforts reacted by creating spaces and activities of their own, the centrality of such efforts to the reforming ethos has become well recognized.[40]

Both Blumin and Siegel suggest that the popular efforts to reconcile urban contradictions could not survive the effects of the Civil War and subsequent intensification of urban anomalies. In failing to come to terms with the city, the popular literature of the prewar years, Siegel argues, paved the way for the despondent, disillusioned urban literature of a later era.[41] Also in the postwar era, Blumin reports, those who picked up the same symbolic zones described by George Foster abandoned his confident expectation that reintegration of different symbolic spaces was still possible, accepting instead polarization as an apparently permanent feature of metropolitan life, still to be marveled at, perhaps, but no longer to be lamented. As he quotes one writer, "If New York is a city of contrasts, it is because it is a little world of itself, and must necessarily be made up of all the elements of good and evil."[42]

With the advent of progressivism, both writers and painters felt a social obligation to encourage the improvement of cities.[43] Yet a review of a range of studies of urbanism at the turn of the century reveals continuing efforts to reconcile increasingly apparent contradictions within the modern metropolis. Popular accounts, like those detailed in an earlier period by Siegel and Rosenthal, managed still to romanticize the industrial aesthetic. Drawing on photographs, guidebooks, and other popular views of cities, John Stilgoe describes how even smoke and tenements could be glorified. Seen from the Pullman car, the internal workings of factories could be forgotten as the city offered a coherent, inspiring panorama. Photographers captivated by the pervasive industrial landscape could find beauty in worker housing nestled at the base of gigantic steel mill smokestacks. Given new legitimacy through their inclusion in art galleries, these photographs helped convince remaining doubters that the industrial zone was beautiful.[44]

While early critics of the divided city—Henry George, Henry Demarest Lloyd, and Edward Bellamy—are frequently cited as precursors to the social criticism of the progressive era, they could not, according to John L. Thomas, escape in their utopian writings the pull of an earlier, simpler time. Each in his own way, according to Thomas, built his vision for the future by calling forth the "picture of recovered innocence in a natural order where self-sufficient yeomen live out virtuous lives untouched by commercialism and free from the envy bred by wealth.[45] Even the early sociologists and social workers who wanted to reform the city at the turn of the century sought in the dynamic and fluid city to reassert the physical and social benchmarks they associated with the small towns from which they came.[46]

If this was another kind of escapism, it was enhanced, according to Peter Hales, by the way photographers encouraged viewers to see the city. Like Bergmann, Hales argues that the photographs of urban buildings in the late nineteenth century provided a means of making the city intelligible. Like Kasson, he suggests that such images were far from neutral but served as active agents to instill a proper sense of place. High-angled views of monumental buildings that left out or diminished people around them served, he says, to make the pictorial city more awesome, more orderly, and more civilized than the reality. "In this," he writes, "the grand-style taxonomy reveals its grounding in widely held ideas about the American city: the hope that order could be wrested out of chaos, the belief that nature and nurture could then coexist in the urban world, and the dream that what resulted would be a civilization as great, as monumental, as magnificent as any that Greece, Rome or Napoleonic France had ever known. By plucking buildings out of their immediate surroundings and revealing them, within the picture's frame, in their grandest and most awesome perspective, these photographs served to celebrate the city's monumental symbols and to promulgate the composite mythos of prosperity and permanence."[47]

Rather than accepting the 1893 Columbian Exposition in Chicago as the origin of the city beautiful movement, Hales suggests that grand-style photography served to pave the way for the themes of monumentality and order that the fair consciously attempted to project, not the least by granting a monopoly to photograph the grounds to one of the exponents of the grand style. While Hales suggests that the use of photography by social reformers upset this carefully crafted vision of the city by consciously projecting the disorder in people's lives, he nonetheless concludes that even these reform efforts were grounded in a nostalgic vision of community.[48]

Neither writers nor artists, it seems, reacted to the changes advanced in the city by corporate capitalism simply by detailing what they saw. Rather, in complex ways, they revealed the wrench of social change. In the strategies they employed to deal with that change, they suggest much about the nature of cultural adaptation to urbanism. While some of the literature on the critical reaction to cities at the turn of the century has retained the earlier attempt to derive an anti-urban tradition, a handful of scholars have revealed more complex patterns of observation.

In Amy Kaplan's examination of *A Hazard of New Fortunes*, William Dean Howells' reaction to his move from small town to city is seen as more than the simple anti-urbanism that has sometimes been ascribed to him. Citing Paul Boyer, Kaplan places Howells in the tradition of those who would make the city intelligible and reassuring for his middle-class readers. By keeping what Raymond Williams calls a "knowable community" in the foreground, Howells helps distance his middle-class characters from the threatening world of workers, immigrants, and slums. Like Stilgoe, Kaplan shows how Howells suggests that by observing such aspects of the city at a comfortable distance from the speeding trains of the "L," passengers could repress that "useless" information about the city that failed to conform to a coherent vision. By drawing the line between classes, the city was divided into two separate and unequal camps, veiling the antagonism between them. "What comes into view as background, as cityscape," Kaplan writes, "becomes visible as an arena for social agency. Against this setting, the colony of characters in the foreground stands out as a synecdoche for the whole city—the knowable urban community."[49]

As the book evolves, however, Howells allows, through the vehicle of a strike, the boundary line to be penetrated as the ugly aspects of public life invade even the sanctity of the private home. In destabilizing the family unit, Kaplan asserts, the strike renders it as alien and threatening as the surrounding city. The strike scene "exposes the violent course that the narrative itself must take to articulate and control the conflicts that inform the representation of the city," she writes. And yet, in the end, Howells reasserts the boundary line separating background from foreground. Although characters cannot retreat to their rural homes, as they do in Howells' earlier Boston novels, he allows the threatening city to recede into the background, not to be picked up again in his future writing. Angered by the Haymarket incident and the failure of his colleagues to react against the violence of the state, Howells briefly attempted to challenge through his narrative strategy the separation of the middle class from the broader context of the city. In the end, however, he adopted conventions that were every bit as reassuring and unrealistic as the grand style photographers.[50]

Other studies of fiction at the turn of the century explore further urban contradictions, exemplified most dramatically in the placement of a monumental fair amid Chicago's slums in 1893 and the growing prominence of the skyscraper towering over low-cost housing. Guy Szuberla, for instance, describes how Henry Blake Fuller and Theodore Dreiser provide evidence of what he calls the "urban sublime," a complex response to the material evidence of the city combining both exhilaration and terror. Seen as a parallel to a rural sublime in which skyscrapers were replacing mountains and the infinite stretch of the city the rolling fields of the plains, Szuberla suggests that each writer attempted to convey and grapple with these contradictory feelings.[51] Both Alan Trachtenberg and Michael Cowan uncover a similar reaction by Henry James in *The American Scene*. While James cannot help but be impressed by the aesthetics of the new buildings, he quickly identifies them as symbols of aggressive corporate capitalism and as threats to the historic identity of cities through the obliteration of the scale of a remembered past.[52]

Students of painting and photography have also identified the importance of the reaction to the skyscraper. Also employing the term *urban sublime*, Dominic Ricciotti notes how the underlying terror suggested by such a powerful aesthetic presence was mediated by techniques borrowed from the French to soften the image by placing the context at dusk or at night or in snow or mist.[53] Trachtenberg affirms this picture in looking at the photographer Alfred Steiglitz. By attempting to render the city more beautiful than could be commonly seen, Trachtenberg argues, Steiglitz participated in the larger progressive movement in the attempt to "remake the city in the imagination as a place of order, of form, of distanced experience, even in the face of perceptions of disorder, formlessness, and threat."[54] In adopting a theme from the anthropologist Clifford Geertz, Sam Bass Warner, Jr., adds that such images served an ideological function of re- solving deeper conflicts within the culture. "The skyline photographers—by their special point of view, by stepping away, and by turning skyscrapers into abstract compositions—solved this political and economic conflict between the democratic and capitalistic elements of contemporary ideology," he writes. "In their hands, the skyscrapers were not corporate towers at all, they were art objects in a landscape, and therefore, these photographers moved the skyscraper image from a position of conflict in the ideology to the older position of the tradition of civic pride."[55]

In a similar vein, Christine Boyer's treatment of the ideas of planners not in programmatic so much as in ideological terms leads her to conclude that they attempted literally to bring true the images that photographers had abstracted from the seemingly unmanageable nineteenth-century city. Their goal was to erect a facade behind which the disorders of daily living of those not fortunate enough to participate in the abundance generated by advancing industrialism would be hidden.[56] In presenting this viewpoint, Boyer sounds much like Steven Mar- cus in his description of the Manchester Friedrich Engels encountered in the 1840s, where the well-to-do were shielded from exposure to the poor by the wall of shops that lined the broad avenues connecting their homes and places of work.[57]

The literature on women in cities offers yet another strand in the history of efforts to mediate the effects of advancing urbanism. Marlene Stein Wortman, for instance, argues that an important exception to the social scientific thrust was offered by women reformers of the progressive era, as they argued that the solution to urban problems lay in the extension of those values nourished in the home into the public arena. In what would be called "municipal housekeeping," women worked to cleanse the environment, regulate leisure time, and recommit schools to community service as part of the effort to "domesticate the city."[58] In the area of literature, Sidney Bremer suggests that Chicago's women writers offered a more positive communal and organic view of their city than the better- known male authors, who stressed the disruptive effects of industrialism.[59]

Behind the ambivalent responses of writers and artists to the new city lay an even deeper shift in Western culture manifest especially in cities and analyzed by Jean-Christophe Agnew. With the expansion of a market economy and the subsequent undermining of established social moorings, individuals looked for ways to make sense of their changing world. For some, there was the familiar refuge of the pastoral myth with its image of a harmonious, nonpecuniary past. A more complex effort to deal with the effects of a nascent market economy could be found in the theater, where in a self-conscious effort to reflect on the play itself, the actors, by confronting the contradictions of their own performance, could invoke the larger problems of exchange: questions of authenticity, accountability, and intentionality.

Although Agnew confines his treatment of America to a discussion of Melville's *The Confidence Man*, he nonetheless attributes to that work a critique every bit as penetrating as the Elizabethan theater had been. Melville appeared to adopt, as Agnew writes, "the principles by which Adam Smith and his American disciples had wanted the bourgeois world to be knowable, reliable, and workable, namely, the transactional or 'performance' principles of commercial capitalism." In fact, Agnew suggests, Melville attempted to attack in his prose the pervasiveness of monetary exchange and its effect on what Karl Marx called the "language of commodities," in which money's arithmetical precision provided a sense of order to shifting social mores even as it preserved "the element of arbitrariness common to the commercial and natural worlds." Melville's critique had no more effect on the American public than Thoreau's did; his book languished, and even his publisher failed.[60] But Agnew's critique has found resonance among other scholars who, in assessing the power of market values, stress the way urbanism and modernism have become practically indistinguishable in the twentieth century.

William Sharpe and Leonard Wallock make this point in noting that as civilization and cities have become increasingly associated with one another, "the age-old boundaries of city and countryside still obtain, but already there is an erosion of the distinction between the two in the nonmaterial and mental realms." The emphasis thus shifts, they suggest, to the "psychological, internalized landscape of the city and its effects on human consciousness." Quoting Raymond Williams, they note the profound alteration of thought involved: "The forces of action have become internalized, and in a way there is no longer a city, there is only man walking through it."[61] Such is an apt description of Steven Marcus' contribution to their book. For Saul Bellow, Marcus asserts, the urban experience has been the modern experience. Within the historical conception of the corrupting market, the city "with its 'treelessness,' and its 'unnatural, too-human deadness' . . . has become man's new nature, and the conscious substance of Bellow's novelistic discourse." In Bellow's early work, the city thus signifies culture in a manner much like that employed by Balzac or Dickens. With time, however, Marcus argues, the city has appeared to Bellow more problematic as older structures of signification appear to be in a state of decomposition. Like Mumford's concept of megalopolis, the city in the process of deterioration,

Bellow's vision evolves to suggest that the great bourgeois achievement, the modern metropolis, has collapsed.[62]

While Marcus contends that it is still up to critics to read the city, Jackson Lears takes a somewhat different approach even as he accepts the presumption that modernism and urbanism have become inseparable. While Lears' work can hardly be described as urban, its adoption of the cultural framework for analysis from the Italian Marxist Antonio Gramsci offers a new means for bridging the gap between social scientists and humanists. Describing Gramsci's concept of hegemony as a dynamic process in which one group dominates others in the cultural as well as economic and political spheres, Lears argues that the concept offers the opportunity for intellectual and cultural historians to place ideas within a social matrix. Gramsci's work, Lears asserts, "offers a point of departure for trying to understand how ideas actually function in society. His concept of hegemonic consensus acknowledges differences in wealth and power even in 'democracies' and seeks to show how these inequalities have been maintained or challenged in the sphere of culture."[63] While Lears approaches a specifically urban experience only once in illustrating Gramsci's thesis, other scholars, notably John Kasson, Paul Boyer, Sidney Bremer, and Jean-Christophe Agnew have applied the hegemonic concept to overtly urban themes.

In the kind of ambiguity about the city other scholars have identified in American artists, Lears perceives, like Agnew, an uneasiness rooted in the decline of autonomous selfhood under the impact of a market economy. For him, modernism is inescapably tied up with the maturation of a consumer culture. Thus while Gunter Barth can describe the emerging urban institutions of the department store and popular entertainment as means by which city dwellers fashioned order for themselves, other scholars in the mode of Lears' cultural criticism suggest that city dwellers were more acted upon than acting in their own right.[64] Elizabeth Ewen, for instance, suggests that with the shift of film-making to Hollywood came a message designed not to liberate the mass of immigrant women who had flocked to the early silent features but to tie them to increased consumption through the beguiling presentation of dress, manners, fashion, and sexual imagery.[65] William Leach sees a more positive effect in the ways urban department stores helped break down established female inhibitions. Nonetheless he locates women's new freedom within the constraints of consumer culture, not on the more liberating possibilities of production of goods or on ownership of property.[66] From advertising and popular amusements concentrated in cities, Lears and Richard Wrightman Fox argue, emerged new forms of cultural hegemony.[67] Again, Jean-Christophe Agnew takes this view to the most critical limit, arguing that the extension of goods through a "radically defamiliarized material and symbolic landscape" ultimately transformed society itself into a market place. "The 'fluid medium' of the mass market," he writes, "dissolves the social and cultural sediment in which symbolic forms are embedded; it continually and systematically dislodges the meaning that humans have always expressed through and attached to their own artifacts."[68] In parallel fashion,

Michael Gilmore traces the alienation of America's classic writers from their audience as even their writing becomes commodified in a modern age. A text like Melville's *The Confidence Man*, Gilmore asserts, "from which the author has banished all reminder of his presence, mirrors the world of the modern economy, where objects are produced in factories and exchanges mediated by money."[69]

The gap between the symbolist and the hegemonic schools of analysis that open and close this review of urban commentary appears today to be so wide as to be practically unbridgeable. Both groups have attempted to make connections between social facts and the values, symbols, and myths that inform and guide Americans in their everyday lives, and yet both their sources and their assumptions about American culture have been very different. The symbolists have drawn largely on the skills of literary critics, while a new school of American studies scholars has been more influenced by cultural anthropology. Both groups, however, have stressed a commitment to depicting and analyzing those important disjunctions between the facts of cities and how they have been conceived. In their studies they have been drawn inevitably to sources usually neglected in the social sciences. In the process, both schools have returned to the presumption that informed Lewis Mumford's work: that cities have been the chief agent of civilization. Deepening the analytic approach offered by Mumford, a new generation of scholars has reminded us that the full story of cities remains not just what actually happened there but how cities were perceived and related to. Unlike social historians who frequently cite one another and build on each other's work, those adopting a cultural vision appear more isolated from one another, their work less representative of a particular strain within urban history. Nonetheless, they offer in their assessments of the private as well as the public manifestations of urban life, the imaginative as well as the actual, some compelling notions of the links between urbanization and American civilization.

Notes

1. Peter Brooks, "The Text of the City," *Oppositions* 8 (Spring 1977): 7–11. See also Peter Brooks, "Romantic Antipastoral and Urban Allegories," *Yale Review* 64 (Autumn 1974): 11–26. More recently Patricia Tobin has reiterated the belief that "for poetic script, as well as for the camera eye, the city functions within a sign-system—one that is available for our reading and writing, coding and decoding, exhaustion and replenishment." "The City in Post-Romantic Figuration," *Comparative Literature Studies* 18 (March 1981): 49.

2. Steven Marcus, *Engels, Manchester, and the Working Class* (New York: Random House, 1974).

3. Steven Marcus, "Reading the Illegible: Some Modern Representations of Urban Experience," in William Sharpe and Leonard Wallock, eds., *Visions of the Modern City*, Proceedings of the Heyman Center for the Humanities (New York: Columbia University, 1983), pp. 228–43.

4. Stuart M. Blumin, "Explaining the New Metropolis: Perception, Depiction, and Analysis in Mid-Nineteenth Century New York City," *Journal of Urban History* 11 (November 1984): 9–38. For examples of his contributions to the "new" urban history, see "Mobility and Change in Ante-Bellum Philadelphia," in Stephan Thernstrom and Richard Sennett, eds., *Nineteenth-Century Cities: Essays in the New Urban History* (New Haven: Yale University Press, 1969), pp. 165–208, and *The Urban Threshold: Growth and Change in a Nineteenth Century American Community* (Chicago: University of Chicago Press, 1976).

5. John A. Agnew, John Mercer, and David E. Sopher, *The City in Cultural Context* (Boston: Allen and Unwin, 1984), p. vii.

6. George Arthur Dunlap, *The City in the American Novel* (1934; New York: Russell & Russell, 1962); Blanche Housman Gelfant, *The American City Novel* (Norman: University of Oklahoma Press, 1954); Robert H. Walker, *The Poet and the Gilded Age* (Philadelphia: University of Pennsylvania Press, 1963), pp. 53–54, and "The Poet and the Rise of the City," *Mississippi Valley Historical Review* 49 (June 1962): 85–99.

7. Adrienne Siegel, *The Image of the American City in Popular Literature, 1820–1870* (Port Washington, N.Y.: Kennikat Press, 1981), and Stephan A. Thernstrom, *Poverty and Progress: Social Mobility in a Nineteenth Century City* (Cambridge, Mass.: Harvard University Press, 1964).

8. Bernard Rosenthal, *City of Nature: Journeys to Nature in the Age of American Romanticism* (Newark: University of Delaware Press, 1980), and Richard C. Wade, *The Urban Frontier: The Rise of Western Cities, 1790–1830* (Cambridge, Mass.: Harvard University Press, 1959).

9. Perry Miller, *The New England Mind: The Seventeenth Century* (New York: Macmillan, 1939), chap. 1.

10. Rosenthal, *City of Nature*, pp. 192–93.

11. Sylvia Doughty Fries, *The Urban Idea in Colonial America* (Philadelphia: Temple University Press, 1977).

12. Charles L. Sanford, *The Quest for Paradise: Europe and the American Moral Imagination* (Urbana: University of Illinois Press, 1961), pp. 123–25.

13. Leo Marx, *The Machine in the Garden* (New York: Oxford University Press, 1964). See also Marx's essay, "The Puzzle of Anti-urbanism in Classic American Literature," in Michael C. Jaye and Ann Chalmers Watts, eds., *Literature and the Urban Experience* (New Brunswick, N.J.: Rutgers University Press, 1981), and Jack Lark Bryant, "A Usable Pastoralism: Leo Marx's Method in *The Machine in the Garden*," *American Studies* 16 (Spring 1975): 63–72. Morton White and Lucia White, *The Intellectual Versus the City: From Thomas Jefferson to Frank Lloyd Wright* (Cambridge, Mass.: Harvard University Press 1962), and Morton White, "The Philosophers and the Metropolis in America," in Werner Z. Hirch, ed., *Urban Life and Form* (New York: Holt, Rinehart, and Winston, 1963), pp. 81–89 set the framework for the debate that ensued over the anti-urban tradition in America. Blaine A. Brownell, "The Agrarian and Urban Ideals: Environmental Images in Modern America," *Journal of Popular Culture* 5 (Winter 1971): 576–87, makes a more positive case for the ways different images can help make the environment more susceptible for human understanding. Don S. Kirschner provides a more specialized treatment of the subject in *City and Country: Rural Responses to Urbanization in the 1920s* (Westport, Conn.: Greenwood Publishing Corporation, 1970), while Andrew Lees, *Cities Perceived: Urban Society in European and American*

Thought, 1820–1940 (New York: Columbia University Press, 1985), provides a broader and updated review of the subject.

14. Henry Nash Smith, *The Virgin Land: The American West as Symbol and Myth* (Cambridge, Mass.: Harvard University Press, 1950), and R. W. B. Lewis, *The American Adam: Innocence, Tragedy and Tradition in the Nineteenth Century* (Chicago: University of Chicago Press, 1955).

15. This distinction, which is taken up by many critics, including the Whites and Lees, is also addressed by Robert A. Gross, "Transcendentalism and Urbanism: Concord, Boston, and the Wider World," *Journal of American Studies* 18 (December 1984): 361–81.

16. Michael H. Cowan, *City of the West: Emerson, America, and Urban Metaphor* (New Haven: Yale University Press, 1967), pp. 3–4, 182, 20.

17. Alan Trachtenberg, *Brooklyn Bridge: Fact and Symbol* (New York: Oxford University Press, 1965), p. 137, argues that the Brooklyn Bridge "embodied physically the forces, emotional as well as mechanical, which were shaping a new civilization."

18. Bruce Kuklick, "Myth and Symbol in American Studies," *American Quarterly* 24 (October 1972): 435–50.

19. J. P. Dougherty, "Baroque and Picturesque Motifs in L'Enfant's Design for the Federal Capital," *American Quarterly* 26 (March 1974): 23–36; Paul Rosenzweig, "James's Special Green Vision: *The Ambassadors* as Pastoral," *Studies in the Novel* 13 (Winter 1981): 367–87; John Hellmann, *American Myth and the Legacy of Vietnam* (New York: Columbia University Press, 1986), pp. 171–204.

20. James L. Machor, "The Garden City in America: Crevecoeur's Letter and the Urban-pastoral Complex," *American Studies* 23 (Spring 1982): 71, and "Urbanization and the Western Garden: Synthesizing City and Country in Ante-Bellum America," *South Atlantic Quarterly* 81 (Autumn 1982): 413–28. See also Patricia Hunt, "North American Pastoral: Contrasting Images of the Garden in Canadian and American Literature," *American Studies* 23 (Spring 1982): 39–68.

21. Janis P. Stout, *Sodoms in Eden: The City in American Fiction Before 1860* (Westport, Conn.: Greenwood Press, 1976). See also Robert H. Byer, "Mysteries of the City: A Reading of Poe's 'The Man of the Crowd,' " in Sacvan Bercovitch and Myra Jehler, eds., *Ideology and Classic American Literature* (Cambridge: Cambridge University Press, 1986), pp. 221–46; Sidney H. Bremer, "Exploring the Myth of Rural America and Urban Europe: 'My Kinsman, Major Molineux' and 'The Paradise of Bachelors and the Tartarus of Maids,' " *Studies in Short Fiction* 18 (Winter 1981): 49–57; Thomas Bender, "James Fenimore Cooper and the City," *New York History* 51 (April 1970): 287–305; John Henry Raleigh, "The Novel and the City: England and America in the Nineteenth Century," *Victorian Studies* 11 (March 1968): 291–328; Paul McCarthy, "City and Town in Melville's Fiction," *Washington State University (Pullman) Research Studies* 38 (September 1970): 214–29; and Alfred Kazin, "Fear of the City, 1783–1983," *American Heritage* 34 (February-March 1983): 14–23.

22. M. Wynn Thomas, "Walt Whitman and Mannahatta-New York," *American Quarterly* 34 (Fall 1982): 362–78. Echoing Stout, James L. Machor says of Whitman, "Like other Americans, Whitman searched for an urban home in virgin territory, but he did so by directing his quest to a landscape of thought, to planes yet unmapped in imagination." "Pastoralism and the American Urban Ideal: Hawthorne, Whitman, and the Literary Pattern," *American Literature* (October 1982): 335. As part of his assessment that most major writers failed to grapple with American urbanism, David Weimar writes

of Whitman, "Having introduced the city to American poetry, he displayed considerable uncertainty as to what to do with it." *The City as Metaphor* (New York: Random House, 1966), p. 33.

23. Thomas Bender, *Toward an Urban Vision: Ideas and Institutions in Nineteenth Century America* (Lexington: University Press of Kentucky, 1975), pp. viii, 194, 49.

24. Rosenthal, *City of Nature*, p. 62. See also Rosenthal, "The Urban Garden: Nineteenth Century Views of the City," *Texas Studies in Literature and Language* 20 (Spring 1978): 119–38.

25. Carl Abbott, *Boosters and Businessmen: Popular Economic Thought and Urban Growth in the Antebellum Middle West* (Westport, Conn.: Greenwood Press, 1981), and Lester H. Cohen, "Eden's Constitution: The Paradisiacal Dream and Enlightenment Values in Late Eighteenth-Century Literature of the American Frontier," *Prospects* 3 (1977): 91.

26. Blumin, "Explaining the New Metropolis," p. 23, cites Anselm Strauss, *Images of the American City* (Glencoe, Ill.: Free Press, 1961), p. 67.

27. Hans Bergmann, "Panoramas of New York, 1845–1860," *Prospects* 10 (1985): 119, 128.

28. Raymond Wohl, "The 'Country Boy' Myth and Its Place in American Urban Culture: The Nineteenth-Century Contribution," *Perspectives in American History* 3 (1969): 77–156. See also Eric Monkkonen, "Socializing the New Urbanites: Horatio Alger, Jr.'s Guidebooks," *Journal of Popular Culture* 11 (Summer 1977): 77–87.

29. Siegel, *Sodoms in Eden*, pp. 175–76. See also Siegel, "When Cities Were Fun: The Image of the American City in Popular Books, 1840–1870," *Journal of Popular Culture* 9 (Winter 1975): 573–82.

30. Karen Halttunen, *Confidence Men and Painted Women: A Study of Middle-class Culture in America, 1830–1870* (New Haven: Yale University Press, 1982).

31. John F. Kasson, "Civility and Rudeness: Urban Etiquette and the Bourgeois Social Order in Nineteenth Century America," *Prospects* 9 (1984): 162–63.

32. Barbara J. Berg, *The Remembered Gate: Origins of American Feminism: The Woman and the City, 1800–1860* (New York: Oxford University Press, 1978), p. 264.

33. Richard Sennett, *Families Against the City: Middle-Class Homes of Industrial Chicago, 1872–1890* (Cambridge, Mass.: Harvard University Press, 1970), *The Uses of Disorder: Personal Identity and City Life* (New York: Knopf, 1970), *The Fall of Public Man* (New York: Knopf, 1976), and T. J. Jackson Lears, "The Two Richard Sennetts," *Journal of American Studies* 19 (April 1985): 81–94.

34. Paul Boyer, *Urban Masses and Moral Order in America, 1820–1920* (Cambridge, Mass.: Harvard University Press, 1978).

35. Galen Cranz, *The Politics of Park Design: A History of Urban Parks in America* (Cambridge, Mass.: MIT Press, 1982), makes the distinction between parks as pleasure grounds and as objects for progressive reform. For Frederick Law Olmsted's role in parks, see the interpretive essays by Albert Fein, "The American City: The Ideal and the Real," in Edgar Kaufmann, Jr., *The Rise of the American City* (New York: Praeger, 1970), and Geoffrey Blodgett, "Frederick Law Olmsted: Landscape Architecture as Conservative Reform," *Journal of American History* 62 (March 1973): 869–89. On the organization of play, see Dominick Cavallo, *Muscles and Morals: Organized Playgrounds and Urban Reform, 1880–1920* (Philadelphia: University of Pennsylvania Press, 1981), and Bernard Mergen, *Play and Playthings: A Reference Guide* (Westport, Conn.: Greenwood Press, 1982), pp. 87–98. On the regulation of dance halls, see Elisabeth I. Perry, " 'The General

Motherhood of the Commonwealth': Dance Hall Reform in the Progressive Era,'' *American Quarterly* 37 (Winter 1985): 719–33. On public baths, see David Glassberg, ''The Design of Reform: The Public Bath Movement in America,'' *American Studies* 20 (January 1979): 5–21.

36. Helen Lefowitz Horowitz, *Culture and the City: Cultural Philanthropy in Chicago from the 1880s to 1917* (Lexington: University Press of Kentucky, 1976). Kathleen D. McCarthy, *Noblesse Oblige: Charity and Cultural Philanthropy in Chicago, 1849–1929* (Chicago: University of Chicago Press, 1982), adds a complementary theme that cultural institutions provided elaborate stage settings for the controlled interaction of rich and poor. For a broad review of cultural institutions in an urban setting, see McCarthy's essay, ''Creating the American Athens: Cities, Cultural Institutions, and the Arts, 1840–1930,'' *American Quarterly* 37 (Bibliography Issues 1985): 426–39.

37. Remy G. Saisselin, *The Bourgeois and the Bebelot* (New Brunswick, N.J.: Rutgers University Press, 1984), pp. 41–49.

38. John F. Kasson, ''Urban Audiences and the Organization of Entertainment in the Late 19th and Early 20th Centuries,'' *Henry Ford Museum and Garfield Village Herald* 14 (1985): 11–12. See also Larry May, *Screening Out the Past: The Birth of Mass Culture and the Motion Picture Industry* (New York: Oxford University Press, 1980), esp. chaps. 1–4.

39. John F. Kasson, *Amusing the Million: Coney Island at the Turn of the Century* (New York: Hill & Wang, 1978), pp. 108, 106.

40. Francis G. Couvares, in tracing the substitution of a mass for a parochial working-class culture, reports how workers appropriated space for their own park, even though it had not been so designed. *The Remaking of Pittsburgh: Class and Culture in an Industrializing City, 1877–1919* (Albany: State University Press of New York, 1984), p. 119. See also Betsy Blackmar, ''Re-walking the 'Walking City': Housing and Property Relations in New York City, 1780–1840,'' *Radical History Review* 21 (Fall 1979): 131–50; Roy Rosenzweig, ''Middle-Class Parks and Working-Class Play: The Struggle over Recreational Space in Worcester, Massachusetts, 1870–1910,'' *Radical History Review* 21 (Fall 1979): 31–46; and Roy Rosenzweig, *Eight Hours for What We Will: Workers and Leisure in an Industrial City, 1870–1920* (Cambridge: Cambridge University Press, 1983).

41. Siegel, *Image of the American City*, pp. 176–77.

42. Blumin, ''Explaining the New Metropolis,'' p. 30.

43. Joseph J. Kwiat, ''The Social Responsibilities of the American Painter and Writer: Robert Henri and John Sloan; Frank Norris and Theodore Dreiser,'' *Centennial Review* 21 (Winter 1977): 19–35, and Joel C. Mickelson, ''Correlations Between Art and Literature in Interpreting the American City: Theodore Dreiser and John Sloan,'' in Joel C. Mickelson, ed., *Images of the American City in the Arts* (Dubuque, Iowa: Kendall/Hunt, 1978), pp. 20–25.

44. John Stilgoe, *Metropolitan Corridor: Railroads and the American Scene* (New Haven: Yale University Press, 1983), pp. 96–97.

45. John L. Thomas, ''Utopia for an Urban Age: Henry George, Henry Demarest Lloyd, Edward Bellamy,'' *Perspectives in American History* 6 (1972): 135–63. See also the concluding chapter of Thomas' *Alternative America: Henry George, Edward Bellamy, Henry Demarest Lloyd and the Adversary Tradition* (Cambridge, Mass.: Belknap Press of Harvard University Press, 1983), pp. 354–66.

46. Jean B. Quandt, *From Small Town to the Great Community: The Social Thought*

of Progressive Intellectuals (New Brunswick, N.J.: Rutgers University Press, 1970), and Boyer, *Urban Masses and Moral Order,* pp. viii, 280.

47. Peter B. Hales, *Silver Cities: The Photography of American Urbanization, 1893– 1915* (Philadelphia: Temple University Press, 1984), p. 72.

48. Ibid., pp. 215–17.

49. Amy Kaplan, " 'The Knowledge of the Line': Realism and the City in Howells's *A Hazard of New Fortunes,"* *PMLA* 101 (January 1986): 71, 74. Kaplan cites Raymond Williams' important book, *The Country and the City* (New York: Oxford University Press, 1973), p. 202.

50. Ibid., p. 78. See also Gregory L. Crider, "William Dean Howells and the Antiurban Tradition: A Reconsideration," *American Studies* 19 (Spring 1978): 55–64, and Jacqueline Tavernier-Courbin, "Towards the City: Howells' Urbanization in *A Modern Instance," Modern Fiction Studies* 24 (Spring 1978): 111–28.

51. Guy Azuberla, "Making the Sublime Mechanical," *American Studies* 14 (Spring 1973): 83–93, and "Theodore Dreiser at the World's Fair: The City without Limits," *Modern Fiction Studies* 23 (Autumn 1977): 369–79.

52. Alan Trachtenberg, "The American Scene: Versions of the City," *Massachusetts Review* 8 (Spring 1967): 281–95, and Michael Cowan, "Walkers in the Streets: American Writers and the Modern City," *Prospects* 6 (1981): 292. See also Peter Buitenhuis, "Aesthetics of the Skyscraper: The Views of Sullivan, James and Wright," *American Quarterly* 9 (Fall 1957): 316–24.

53. Dominic Ricciotti, "Symbols and Monuments: Images of the Skyscraper in American Art," *Landscape* 25, no. 2 (1981): 22–29. See also Nicholas Taylor, "The Awful Sublimity of the Victorian City," in A. J. Dyos and Michael Wolff, eds., *The Victorian City: Images and Realities* (London: Routledge and Kegan Paul, 1973), 2:431–48.

54. Alan Trachtenberg, "Image and Ideology: New York in the Photographer's Eye," *Journal of Urban History* 10 (August 1984): 264–65.

55. Sam Bass Warner, Jr., "Slums and Skyscrapers: Urban Images, Symbols, and Ideology," in Lloyd Rodwin and Robert M. Hollister, eds., *Cities of the Mind: Images and Themes of the City in the Social Sciences* (New York: Plenum Press, 1984), p. 194. Warner cites Clifford Geertz's article, "Ideology as a Cultural System," in D. W. Apter, ed., *Ideology and Discontent* (New York: Free Press, 1964), pp. 47–76.

56. M. Christine Boyer, *Dreaming the Rational City: The Myth of American City Planning* (Cambridge, Mass.: MIT Press, 1983), pp. 3–6.

57. Steven Marcus, "Reading the Illegible," in Dyos and Wolff, *Victorian City,* 1:257–76.

58. Marlene Stein Wortman, "Domesticating the Nineteenth Century City, " *Prospects* 3 (1977): 531–72. See also Suellen M. Hoy, " 'Municipal Housekeeping': The Role of Women in Improving Urban Sanitation Practices, 1880–1917," in Martin V. Melosi, ed., *Pollution and Reform in American Cities, 1870–1930* (Austin: University of Texas Press, 1980), pp. 173–98.

59. Sidney H. Bremer, "Lost Continuities: Alternative Urban Visions in Chicago Novels, 1890–1915," *Soundings* 64 (Spring 1981): 29–51. See also Blanche H. Gelfant, "Sister to Faust: The City's 'Hungry' Woman as Heroine," in Susan Merrill Squier, ed., *Women Writers and the City: Essays in Feminist Literary Criticism* (Knoxville: University of Tennessee Press, 1984), pp. 265–87.

60. Jean-Christophe Agnew, *Worlds Apart: The Market and the Theater in Anglo-*

American Thought, 1550–1750 (Cambridge, England: Cambridge University Press, 1986), pp. 11–12, 195–203.

61. Sharpe and Wallock, "From 'Great Town' to 'Nonplace Urban Realm': Reading the Modern City," in Sharpe and Wallock, *Visions of the Modern City*, p. 235.

62. Marcus, "Reading the Illegible," in Sharpe and Wallock, pp. 229–30, 239; Lewis Mumford, *The Culture of Cities*, pp. 223–99. On Bellow, see also Steven M. Gerson, "The New American Adam in the Adventures of Augie March," *Modern Fiction Studies* 25 (Spring 1979): 117–28; Sarah Blocher Cohen, "Saul Bellow's Chicago," *Modern Fiction Studies* 24 (Spring 1978): 139–46; and Daniel Walden, "Urbanism, Technology and the Ghetto in the Novels of Abraham Cahan, Henry Roth and Saul Bellow," *American Jewish History* 73 (March 1984): 296–306.

63. T. J. Jackson Lears, "The Concept of Cultural Hegemony: Problems and Possibilities," *American Historical Review* 90 (June 1985): 572. See also Raymond Williams' discussion of hegemony in *Marxism and Literature* (New York: Oxford University Press, 1977), pp. 108–14.

64. Gunther Barth, *City People: The Rise of Modern City Culture in Nineteenth-Century America* (New York: Oxford University Press, 1980).

65. Elizabeth Ewen, "City Lights: Immigrant Women and the Rise of the Movies," *Signs* 5 (Spring 1980): S63–S65.

66. William R. Leach, "Transformations in a Culture of Consumption: Women and Department Stores, 1890–1925," *Journal of American History* 71 (September 1984): 319–42. See also Susan Porter Benson, "Palace of Consumption and Machine for Selling: The American Department Store, 1880–1940," *Radical History Review* 21 (Fall 1979): 199–221.

67. Richard Wightman Fox and T. J. Jackson Lears, *The Culture of Consumption: Critical Essays in American History, 1880–1980* (New York: Pantheon Books, 1983), p. 29.

68. Jean-Christophe Agnew, "The Consuming Vision of Henry James," in ibid., pp. 71–72.

69. Michael T. Gilmore, *American Romanticism and the Marketplace* (Chicago: University of Chicago Press, 1985). In his treatment of Poe, Robert Byer picks up a similar theme, noting that "the crowd's unhealthy vitality mirrors, and is imparted by, the circulation of commodities: It is the vitality of a grotesquely partial humanity in which things have come to represent people." "Mysteries of the City," p. 231.

3 ———— From Culture to Cuisine: Twentieth-Century Views of Race and Ethnicity in the City

ANDREA TUTTLE KORNBLUH

Many books have been written about race and ethnicity in the city. Some assess the urban experience of a particular ethnic or racial group, while others compare the experience of some combination of different groups.[1] This chapter will concentrate on works that explicitly compare the urban experience of immigrants with that of Afro-Americans, for that is the fundamental issue that has preoccupied students of these subjects since 1950. Taking note of a criticism raised by Philip Gleason in 1980 that scholars have not done enough to recognize the nature of past debates about race and ethnicity, this review will examine three distinct periods of American thought about the relationship of race, ethnicity, and urban culture.[2] The first period began in the late nineteenth century, when critics depicted urban society as consisting of a racial hierarchy that ought to be headed by a superior, white Anglo-Saxon majority, a conception that left racial inferiors only the option of conforming, if they could. Next comes a period, beginning around 1915, when the idea of cultural pluralism (the substitution of cultural for racial determinism) caught on. Most recently, starting in the 1950s, students dropped the idea of cultural determinism in favor of the view of the city as an essentially neutral environment in which individuals could voluntarily choose their racial or ethnic cultural identities but where structural barriers impeded the full social acceptance and economic success of some groups.

In the period since the 1950s, three variations on the basic argument can be identified. In the 1960s, the emphasis tended to fall on discrimination—especially against people of color by ethnics as well as white Anglo-Saxon Protestants— as the reason that individuals had not had sufficient opportunity of choice to develop satisfactory racial or ethnic identities and affiliations. During the white ethnic revival of the 1970s, a backlash set in that sought to demonstrate that white ethnics, especially the working class, had also been discriminated against yet nonetheless had managed to forge satisfying and durable ethnic identities and affiliations. While scholarly work rooted in this contemporary view of ethnic and racial conflict continues to appear, the most recent development is an attempt by Olivier Zunz, William J. Wilson, and others to establish economic class as a more important restraint on opportunity than race or ethnicity.[3]

Richmond Mayo-Smith, a professor of political economy and social science at Columbia College, suggested in 1890 that Americans could be divided into three categories: descendants of white people who had been in America by 1790, American Negroes, and descendants of post-1790 immigrants. The colonial descendants, he argued, carried a common English heritage, which included a common language, institutions, and political system. Negroes, he declared, were incapable of fully participating in American social and political life because of their racial characteristics and previous condition of servitude. He predicted they would never "fully amalgamate" with the white population and would remain a problem, although Negro "docility and good nature" guaranteed that they would remain a "comparatively harmless" element in national life. The immigrants posed a graver threat, for they carried "no distinguishing mark, such as color," to distinguish them from the descendants of the colonialists. Noting that foreigners sought out large cities, Mayo-Smith warned that they were becoming powerful enough to begin "overshadowing the native." He was skeptical, moreover, about the possibility that intermarriage would create a new and vigorous American people, for surely good stock would not result from crossbreeding with "the dregs of Europe."[4] Like Mayo-Smith, John R. Commons, another early student of immigration, began his career by proclaiming, in 1903, that the real Americans, Anglo-Saxons who had developed democracy "unhampered by inroads of alien stock," were experiencing the erosion of democracy as immigrants took political power in the northern cities and racial conflict plagued the South.[5]

After 1915, such ideas increasingly came under attack by social critics like Randolph Bourne, who suggested that America's national character lay not in the legacy of Anglo-Saxon institutions but in the future creation of a multicultural society.[6] In 1924, Konrad Bercovici, a Rumanian student of American culture, developed this approach further in a popular travel book, *Around the World in New York*. "New York," Bercovici wrote, "like no other city, offers the best study of the nations of the world, samples of each being centered in different sections within easy reach of one another." He reported on the neighborhoods and cultures of more than twenty nationalities in Manhattan (including Syrians,

Greeks, Jews, Chinese, Italians, Gypsies, Africans, Balkans, Spaniards, French, Germans, Hungarians, Czechoslovakians, and Americans), cataloging each nationality's languages, foods, smells, theaters, libraries, clothing, housing, music, newspapers, coffeehouses, and political participation. From all these groups, he claimed, by "a slow filtering, drop by drop," a new "civilization" was taking shape, "an aggregate" that had "no counterpart."[7]

Bercovici thought that the route to equality for all these diverse ethnic groups was the full development in America of an awareness by each group of its own culture. He predicted that the settlement workers who came to the Greek community "bearing precious gifts in charity," the pre-election "Americanizers" who spoke on street corners, and the public schools that ground out Americans "in the same fashion as sausages" would be unable to bring relief or understanding to the variety of Greeks undergoing the "assimilation process." Instead, salvation would come from their own poets and philosophers, speaking their own language, "appealing to them to be better Greeks first, that they may become better Americans." Like the Greeks, *Around the World in New York* presented Jews as a mixture of peoples, but on the Lower East Side these diverse Jews had created a thriving culture based on Yiddish, a language that, Bercovici noted, many Russian Jews learned only after arriving in New York. Thus for Bercovici, cultural traditions and institutions held national groups together, made them socially and economically viable, and ensured their continued existence. Groups that lacked such institutions and a permanent locale, like the Gypsies, stood in danger of disappearing, for their only strategy for survival consisted of intermarriage into other, stronger cultures.[8]

Harlem's Afro-Americans, said Bercovici, had an "outward tendency" to acquire the characteristics of the people they lived among, but they also had an "undercurrent of self-affirmation, of a desire for a culture all their own." Bercovici argued that all native American art was of Negro origin—"folk-lore, the spirituals, jazz, the dance, and some of the best poetry"—and had been brought by Negroes from Africa to the New World. Therefore he complained about those inhabitants of Harlem who wanted to "cross the line" and try to live among whites as whites, and he applauded "another much better element who refuse to live with whites under false pretenses, who want to live as negroes, race-conscious, who hope by their achievements to compel the white people surrounding them to recognize them as their equals." This latter group sought to educate Negroes to the value of their own literature, poetry, theater, sculpture, painting, and higher education.[9]

The year after the publication of Bercovici's book, Robert E. Park, Ernest W. Burgess, and Roderick D. McKenzie published *The City*, an examination by sociologists of many of the same themes Bercovici raised, including the survival of ethnic group cohesion within urban culture. Burgess argued that the American metropolis consisted of a set of concentric circles, or zones, radiating out from a central business district (CBD). In the zone closest to the CBD, the "so-called 'slums,' " he located "immigrant colonies" ("combining old world heritages and American adaptations'') and an adjacent black belt. McKenzie suggested that the city's natural segregation of different cultural groups both limited and enhanced group development.[10] Park claimed that those immigrant groups that had been able to maintain their "simple village religions and mutual aid organizations" adjusted most successfully to life in America. In addition to maintenance of old ways, however, he thought that a "new sense of racial identity" was developed by those groups under the most attack by the racial and national majorities. Thus, he thought the Negro, the Jew, and the Japanese had developed a "sense of cause" and "group efficiency," which fueled their struggle to maintain their racial status and social and economic viability as urbanites.[11]

While many of the findings of the Chicago sociologists were similar to those of Bercovici, they added a new dimension, the problem of second-generation immigrants who appeared to be in danger of becoming cultureless and thus not subject to social restraints. Culture seemed to be related to geographical location, and Louis Wirth, for example, argued in *The Ghetto* that to leave one's habitat meant leaving its social values and way of life as well. As Wirth wrote, "Once the individual is removed from the soil to which he and his institutions have been attached, he is exposed to the possibility of losing his character and disappearing as a distinct type."[12] This problem came up particularly in the study of juvenile delinquency and gangs. Park suggested that the children of Negro migrants from the South might be prone to demoralization leading to delinquency.[13] Harvey W. Zorbaugh in *The Gold Coast and the Slum* feared that second-generation immigrants in Chicago's ethnic ghettos suffered conflict because they found themselves living in "two social worlds, worlds which define the same situation in very different ways." This gap, Zorbaugh thought, led second-generation immigrant boys to form gangs as a way to "create a social world in which he can live and find satisfaction for his wishes."[14] This analysis suggested that ethnicity might be one kind of group identification, but that other peer groups, whether gangs or professional associations, could create alternative ways for individuals to belong to a community.

In another Chicago study of the 1920s, Charles Edward Merriam reported that Chicago's "racial heterogeneity" presented a major problem in the "development of that common understanding which is the basis of all government." Yet he refused to blame the "ignorant foreigner" for the city's municipal ills, for he depicted immigrant allegiance to neighborhood bosses in ethnic communities as a logical and sensible response, since the "newcomer's political allegiance goes first to those human beings who satisfy his immediate and urgent needs." Like Zorbaugh, moreover, Merriam found that after the first-generation, ethnic solidarity began to erode and the power of "nationalistic leaders declined" because a territorial basis for ethnic communities disappeared as second-generation immigrants scattered around the city in new housing, business, and marriage patterns. "Class interests, religious interests, regional differences," all soon became as important as the "bonds of nationalistic solidarity."[15]

Merriam found a lessening of the role of ethnicity in the political participation of the city's Irish, Poles, Scandinavians, Bohemians, Czechs, Italians, Lithuanians, Greeks, and Slavs, but the situation differed somewhat for Negroes, whose political importance had grown with their increasing numbers and the exodus of white voters to the suburbs. Unlike the ethnics, the Negro population had no tendency to scatter. Concentrated in the black belt on the South Side, Merriam feared that unlike other second-generation immigrants, Negroes were less able to shake off the rule of predatory politicians. This desire for Negro politicians, Merriam feared, led the South Side to choose representatives who were not of a high caliber, but he found the trend hopeful, part of a "rising sense of dignity and responsibility."[16]

The concern in the 1920s among students of the city for ethnic culture and urban culture persisted into the 1930s and 1940s. In 1932, Clyde Vernon Kiser suggested in *Sea Island to City* that urban culture itself functioned as a dynamic factor in creating the culturally pluralistic city. Kiser took issue with the idea that Negro migration could be attributed simply to racial friction or landlessness, for neither of these existed in the Sea Islands. Nor was he convinced that the boll weevil infestation or the curtailment of the supply of European labor was sufficient explanation for the Negro migration. Using the testimony of migrants themselves, he concluded that they came to urban areas not simply for economic improvement but to participate in city life or urban culture. This movement from the unhurried agricultural community to the modern urban life of Harlem Kiser characterized as a "manifestation of revolt against the mode of life afforded in St. Helena." Thus Sea Island migrants shared the "fundamental desires" of all other individuals "involved in the general drift from rural areas to urban centers," and racial, religious, and political problems played little part in the decision to migrate. Instead, Sea Island migrants went to the cities seeking good jobs and the stimulation of urban culture.[17]

Like Kiser, Caroline Ware was interested in New York City's urban culture, but she feared that it was not sufficiently strong to hold together the city's diverse ethnic groups. In her study of Greenwich Village, she found ethnic divisions were more important than those based on geography or economic class. She discovered that "for practically every aspect of local life the several ethnic groups had separate institutions and distinctive ways and were more or less firmly separated from each other by social barriers." Although by 1930 most of the city's Negro population was centered in Harlem, Ware's discussion of the social relations of Greenwich Villages's Negroes is similar to her description of the Jews, Italians, Irish, Germans, and Spaniards. Politics and public schools pulled these diverse populations together, but the social distances between groups caused Ware to worry that the neighborhood no longer had any "assimilative powers." Greenwich Village was a geographic area, but, Ware declared, there was no close relationship between the groups, and thus it was "no longer a community." The neighborhood was heading toward "social disorganization and cultural confusion," for there was no "social cement" to make a whole out of the separate fragments of old cultures. Ware thought this was not a problem unique to Greenwich Village but one common to other urban communities.[18]

Ware expanded her discussion of ethnic communities in an article in the 1938 edition of the *Encyclopedia of the Social Sciences* suggesting that "ethnic denotes race." But she chose to have her definition mean the "more general concept of culture." While race certainly was important "as a differentiating factor," she suggested that it was "more potent when reinforced by differences of culture or status." Ware conceded that American communities were always on the move and that ethnic groups had no permanent neighborhoods, but she thought this did not affect cultural continuity, for that persisted "without reference to geographical location." World War I, she contended, had revealed the continued existence of these ethnic communities across America and led to two opposing responses. On one hand, Americanization programs asserted Nordic superiority, and the Americanization movement resulted in the passage of the quota immigration law. On the other hand, leaders within immigrant communities demanded recognition for their groups as a whole—not just for "exceptional individuals"— and insisted that the incorporation of these groups into the American community must be done on the basis of "respect for differences of inherited tradition and culture." Ware expected this condition to last into the foreseeable future, and she believed ultimately that the ethnic community would become "a relic of a separatist age" as it fell victim to the "unconscious pressure of an integrated economic society and a leveling material civilization."[19]

Some students of ethnicity in the city during the 1920s, 1930s, and 1940s also sought to contrast the rural ethnic experience with the urban. Stow Persons and Marcus Lee Hansen, for example, contended in the 1940s that the urbanization and industrialization of the post–Civil War period altered the experience of immigrants in America.[20] Persons argued that before the Civil War, the immigrant had to Americanize in a rural society, a task simplified by the agricultural background of most immigrants. But by the twentieth century, immigration had "become largely an urban and a class problem." The immigrant became closely associated with the working class, and economic conflicts between groups of workers (native and immigrant) became transformed into race problems and cultural conflict. As a result, unlike their agrarian predecessors, urban immigrants of the early twentieth century developed persisting ethnic ghettos in urban slums.[21]

The rural-urban dichotomy also attracted the attention of the National Resources Committee in its contribution to *When Peoples Meet: A Study in Race and Culture Contacts*. Its essay, "Cultural Diversity in American Life," suggested that the cultural heritage of most rural groups in the United States involved "few sharp breaks with tradition" and less strain on the part of immigrant groups who shared in the pioneering experience of claiming the frontier West. City life differed, however, for urban civilization had to cope with successive waves of immigrants from different sources, immigrants who had to adjust to a new national culture and a new urban way of life. The more recent migration of the Negro "peasant" and of white "native colonial stock" of the cotton areas and "southern highlands" indicated that the problem of "cultural assimilation" in American cities was neither primarily an ethnic nor a racial problem but rather an issue of accommodating "rural patterns of living and contemporary urban ways."[22]

Robert E. Park had suggested a similar division in his introduction to Charles S. Johnson's *Shadow of the Plantation*, where he discussed the distinction between "folk culture" and the majority American culture. Negro peasants of the black belt, the Acadians of southwestern Louisiana, the Mennonites, the Pennsylvania Dutch, the mountain whites of Appalachia, and the Mexicans of New Mexico, though distinct groups, shared common cultural characteristics: a history in the form of unrecorded ballads and legends and isolation from other groups in a particular rural geographical area. Once removed from their places of origin, said Park, these folk cultures were in transition from a simple primitive culture to modern industrial and urban civilization. Once individuals left this marginal rural culture and came to the city, they were no longer folk. They became instead the proletariat.[23]

Like Robert Park, to whom they dedicated *Black Metropolis,* St. Clair Drake and Horace R. Cayton depicted city life as a culture distinct from the rural South. Negroes were becoming "city people," and in cities, they claimed, "the problem of the Negro in American life appears in its sharpest and most dramatic form." And it was in cities, they hoped, that the "Negro problem" would finally be settled. Chicago had offered its previous migrants anonymity, impersonal relationships, and a complex division of labor, all of which fostered free competition and socioeconomic mobility. But the white residents of Chicago had attempted to confine southern Negroes to a fixed status through discrimination in employment and housing opportunities, creating for blacks the social and psychological problems of segregation. But the very nature of city life—anonymity, impersonal relations, and a complex division of labor—the study implied, would urbanize Chicago's rural blacks and provide them the potential to overcome their social and psychological problems and segregation itself as urbanism undermined the hostility of white ethnic groups by making them more tolerant.[24]

Through the work of Bourne and Bercovici, Ware, Park, and Drake and Cayton runs the thread of culture, especially urban culture, as a tangible part of the migrant-immigrant experience. For those who studied race and ethnicity in the city in the years from 1920 to 1945, the city was much more than the geographical space and physical setting where immigrant life took place. The city itself influenced the ways in which people lived and worked. The newcomers to the city could not avoid becoming participants in urban culture, nor could they choose the way they interacted with that culture.

By the 1950s, however, the discourse about urban life, race, and ethnicity began to alter. In that decade, as Zane L. Miller recently suggested, began a "revolt against culture as a given way of life"—a rejection of cultural determinism—in which a new importance was attached to individuals rather than groups as the basic social units.[25] In this new world, urban culture no longer played a role in shaping the behavior of groups. Instead, the experiences of the immigrants in determining their own identity and commitments became paramount.

Oscar Handlin and Will Herberg authored two influential books symptomatic of the new tendency to emphasize individual choices over the role of urban culture. In this new literature of the 1950s, individuals were assumed to be free to choose their own social identities, which could be ethnic or religious or a combination of the two. It is this concern with individual choice, and the factors that encouraged or discouraged its exercise, that has characterized the recent literature on race, ethnicity, and the city. Thus the scholars of mobility, whether they sought to discover how social and geographical mobility produced "American exceptionalism" rather than socialism or to argue that any ethnic group could "pull itself up by the bootstraps," agreed that the unit to examine was the individual.

Handlin's *The Uprooted* reversed the traditional exploration of what the immigrant had done to or for urban America by looking at how the immigrant experienced becoming American. Handlin suggested that the experience of the individual immigrants who made the choice to come to America was more important to study than the cultural group to which they belonged. In his view, the rural culture the immigrants left behind was collective, traditional, and based on a passive acceptance of life. The choice to leave was an individual choice, the antithesis of peasant values, and in the act of making that choice the peasant became an American, for America was a nation of individuals unrestrained by the prison of culture. And while the immigrants tried to recreate familiar institutions from the old country, these new institutions were consciously created and thus very different from those of the Old World.[26]

The immigrant that Handlin described in 1951 was an alienated and isolated individual. Arguing that the history of immigration "is a history of alienation and its consequences," Handlin described this alienation as a product of the broken homes, interruptions in familiar life, and separation from familiar surroundings caused by emigration. But this alienation, although difficult, was not pathological, for it was a necessary condition for the existence of individuals. The newcomers to America became foreigners and ceased "to belong." Without habitual patterns to conform to, the uprooted individuals were faced with continual choices. "No man," Handlin wrote, "could escape choices that involved, day after day, and evaluation of his goals, of the meaning of his existence, and of the purpose of the social forms and institutions that surrounded him."[27]

America was distinguished not by its culture but by being the place where immigrants "discovered what it was to be an individual, a man apart from place and station." In their flight, immigrants discovered the "unexpected, invigorating effects of recurrent demands upon the imagination, upon all our human capacities." Although the descendants of the immigrants of the nineteenth century had become rooted in American soil, Handlin cautioned his fellow Americans that they should remember having been "strangers in the land" and refuse to let "our nest become again a moldy prison holding us in its tangled web of comfortable habits." Cutting the bonds of habit and tradition had proved difficult for the immigrants, but out of that experience came the liberation of the individual, and even though they were no longer immigrants, Americans should remain individuals.[28]

In his equation of American character with individualism, Handlin differed sharply from his predecessors who had suggested that assimilation of ethnics and Afro-Americans could come through either the development by each group of its own cultural strength or through abandoning cultural groups to join "American culture." Unlike his predecessors (the scholars of the 1920s, 1930s, and 1940s), Handlin was not concerned with the problem of cultural diversity at all, for he saw the country not in terms of competing ethnic and racial groups but as a collection of individuals. What most distinguished his Americans was the fact that they were free of culture. Their actions were a result not of determinism but of choice.

A few years later, Will Herberg made a similar argument in another influential book highlighting the enduring significance of religion in the analysis of American social life and history. In *Protestant-Catholic-Jew*, Herberg suggested that the descendants of American immigrants shed their immigrant culture and language but not their religion. For third-generation ethnics in a nation of individuals, the religion of their grandparents became a route to social identity, and Americans became increasingly identified as Catholic, Protestant, or Jew. Like Handlin, Herberg viewed these third-generation Americans as consciously choosing to identify themselves by their religion rather than their ethnic culture. Within each of these religions an ethnic merging took place, making America not a single melting pot but a triple one and a place of religious pluralism. The underside of this pluralism, however, was the assumption that all Americans had to have some religious identification, and failure to do so was viewed as "un-American." In Herberg's America, one could not choose not to choose a religious identification.[29]

Handlin, however, continued to pursue the notion of a generic immigrant experience of alienation (or liberation) from cultural imperatives that he had suggested in *The Uprooted*. He made this explicit in his 1959 study, *The Newcomers*, an analysis of the apparent immobility of Negroes and Puerto Ricans in New York City. Here he argued that in choosing to move to the city, these two groups were simply following the pattern of older immigrant groups and would go through similar stages of adjustment. Thus they could be expected to develop communal institutions, responsible leadership, and individual "will and energy" and rise in urban America just like everyone else.[30] Others, however, were less sanguine about the availability of choices of black Americans. Gilbert Osofsky accepted the assumption that individuals should be free to make choices, but he concluded that since the end of slavery in the North, the Negro ghetto had remained remarkably enduring. For him, the ghetto formed and persisted because of "enforced Negro economic and social immobility" resulting from "an enervating and destructive racism." In the preface to the second edition of his book, Osofsky responded even more explicitly to Handlin's argument in *The Newcomers*. "To insist that blacks are simply the most recent ethnics in the city," he wrote, "is deficient history and deficient social commentary." Handlin, Osofsky complained, had ignored the fact that black migration to the North had begun a hundred years before, in the first half of the nineteenth century. Handlin also failed to note the diverging patterns of political participation for native-born urban blacks and immigrants. Suffrage was denied to blacks in the 1840s and 1850s "at the very moment the great masses of Irish and German immigrants were using political power as a principal weapon of advancement and acculturation." Osofsky argued that an outlook that claimed merely that Americans were a "nation of immigrants" did not take into consideration the vast implications of racism in American history. Thus it could not help explain "why our cities are burning."[31]

Scholars of immigration history like Rudolph J. Vecoli who found fault with Handlin's picture of the immigrant experience also agreed, without saying so, with much of Handlin's orientation. In "Contadini in Chicago: A Critique of *The Uprooted*," Vecoli argued that the typical south Italian peasant came not from the countryside but from a rural city. In those cities, Vecoli contended, solidarity was based not on the community but on the family, and peasant economic interests were individual or familial, not communal. Thus the traits of individualism that Handlin had identified as distinctly American Vecoli characterized as indigenous to peasant life, as part of the cultural baggage of immigrants. Rather than emphasizing alienation in America, however, Vecoli argued that the immigrant lived a life "sheltered within his ethnic colony from the confusing complexity of American society." Like Handlin, though, Vecoli was concerned with barriers to the exercise of free choice by immigrants, and he reported that the employment options available to Italians in Chicago had been limited by both the persistence of Old World customs and discrimination by American employers.[32]

Most students of race and ethnicity in the 1960s agreed, however, that blacks had fared even worse than Italians or other white immigrants, and Nathan Glazer and Daniel P. Moynihan in *Beyond the Melting Pot* sought the source of this extraordinary black immobility. Glazer, who wrote the chapters on Negroes, Puerto Ricans, Jews, and Italians, described Negroes as immigrants who came to the city without skills or strong institutions and who found no well-organized ethnic community within which to start their new life. Unlike other immigrants, Negroes did not bring with them a foreign culture that provided peculiar needs that could be met by black entrepreneurs within the migrating group, and they also lacked, according to Glazer, the immigrants' clannishness, close family ties, and the tradition of saving that could have served as foundations for the development of a black business class. Thus Negroes were less successful at self-help because they could not view themselves as other ethnic groups did—"the Negro is only an American, and nothing else," with no peculiar "values and culture to protect" and an exceptionally "weak" family structure in addition. Since Glazer and Moynihan viewed New York City as a collection of competing ethnic groups, they found the Negro, because of his very Americanness, to be an unsuccessful competitor in the battle for urban spoils, a classic victim of discrimination for whom the ethnic neighborhood had not been a staging ground for mobility.[33]

From a different perspective but in a similar way, Allan H. Spear examined Chicago's black ghetto and discovered that its existence was due to discrimination, not the choice of its inhabitants. Negroes had a longer Chicago history than any other ethnic group, but the ghetto was not created primarily by black community ties. Instead, he found the ghetto was "primarily the product of white hostility." Other ethnic minorities shared wider occupational opportunities as well as a broader range of choices about residential areas. By 1915, Spear argued, Chicago blacks could not be described as simply another of Chicago's many ethnic groups. Instead they suffered from systematic discrimination in housing, employment, public accommodation, and municipal services, as well as frequently violent attacks. Spear's Chicago of 1915 was not a world of cultural pluralism but a biracial society.[34]

While Spear could document the rhetoric of cultural pluralism that accompanied the rise of the black ghetto in the early twentieth century, he argued that ethnic autonomy was not a real option for the black community. First, the black community was not sufficiently developed economically to be "truly independent." Second, black community institutions and facilities were inferior. Thus Spear concluded that Negro leaders had "neither the experience nor the resources to create an adequate community life of their own." The separatism of these Negro leaders was not a "free choice" but a condition mandated by the hostility and oppression of the white community. At base, the Negro community, unlike the Irish, Poles, Jews, and Italians, was not tied together by a common linguistic, cultural, or religious tradition. Blacks were united by a common oppression.[35]

The 1960s saw the development of an important new way to measure the comparative success of individuals in the competition of urban life: the systematic study of individual social mobility with quantitative analytic techniques. Inaugurated in 1964 by Stephan Thernstrom's *Poverty and Progress*, these books provided a new method for examining the relationship of race, ethnicity, social class, and mobility. Among Thernstrom's discoveries was the fact that the nineteenth-century urban working class included many transients "drifting from city to city according to the dictates of the labor market." Thernstrom distinguished between this rootless proletariat and the settled property-owning laboring class. Among the latter, occupational mobility provided one way to measure social mobility, but Thernstrom argued that property accumulation was also a valid measure of social advance. For immigrants, he said, home ownership was a particularly important measure of progress, and parents frequently sent children to work rather than to school in order to marshal the wage-earning capacity of the entire family in this pursuit. Thus for working-class families of nineteenth-century Newburyport, social mobility was not cumulative, and upward mobility was not inherited. Instead, the choice made by a father to purchase a house might in fact limit the mobility options of the children.[36]

Building on Thernstrom's work, the Philadelphia Social History project began research in April 1969. This project was originally undertaken as a comparative study of blacks and Irish and German immigrants "to determine whether the burdens and disabilities faced by black Americans were peculiar to their historical experience or simply obstacles which every immigrant group entering society had to overcome." In "A Tale of Three Cities," the concluding essay in *Philadelphia: Work, Space, Family, and Group Experience in the Nineteenth Century*, the first major publication of the Philadelphia Social History Project, Theodore Hershberg, Alan N. Burstein, Eugene P. Ericksen, Stephanie W. Greenberg, and William L. Yancey argued that immense differences separated the experiences of Philadelphia's urban immigrants and its black migrants. These groups came to the city in different historical periods and encountered vastly different economic and social systems. White racism limited Afro-American opportunity in a unique way by creating intensely discriminatory employment and housing practices not faced by other groups. Thus in modern Philadelphia Afro-Americans continue to live in areas left behind by the "processes of modern urban-industrial development." To enable black Americans to "enter the American mainstream," Philadelphia would have to make "major structural changes and perhaps some form of preferential treatment . . . at all levels of public and urban policy."[37]

While most who compared the relative success of immigrants and blacks in the city found that immigrants fared better, by the early 1970s proponents of the white ethnic revival began to argue that immigrants, especially Catholics, also had been adversely affected by the dominant culture. In *The Rise of the Unmeltable Ethnics*, Michael Novak claimed that like the blacks, Chicanos, Native Americans (Indians), Jews, and America's PIGS (Novak's acronym for Poles, Italians, Greeks, and Slavs) suffered at the hands of entrenched WASP (white Anglo-Saxon Protestant) power. Novak began his work by complaining that the "phrase 'white racist' has become for the Left what 'communism' was for Joe McCarthy: an indiscriminate scare word designed to prevent clear thought and apt strategy." Novak described his PIGS as primarily working class, with attachments to community, Catholicism, family, stability, and roots that stood in sharp contrast to the professional, intellectual, rootless traits of the WASP ruling class. Novak took the idea of cultural pluralism, originally developed as a model of each group striving for cultural excellence, and transformed it into an argument defending a kind of residual peasant culture striving for self-defense. Novak argued that the WASP professional's alienation from community and a group value system allowed the development of programs for the racial integration of public schools, which he saw as an attack on ethnic communities.[38]

Novak's argument was challenged by Melvin Steinfield's *Cracks in the Melting Pot*. The essays in this anthology covered the repression and discrimination experienced by Native Americans, Afro-Americans, Chicanos, Filipinos, Asian-Americans, and American Jews. Steinfield also included a chapter entitled "Other Ethnic Minorities: Immigration and Discrimination" and noted that "it is not always the nativist majority which has erected barriers to those who wanted to assimilate, or which has become irritated when assimilation was shunned by the minority itself." Steinfield suggested that other minorities (many of Novak's PIGS) "have been absorbed quite well into the American mainstream" after having undergone "considerable difficulty" earlier. These difficulties had limited the kinds of choices the older minorities had been able to make in the past, but the discrimination faced by these ethnics was a historical issue, not a contemporary dilemma.[39]

Like Steinfield, Kenneth L. Kusmer documented the differing opportunities available to immigrants and Afro-Americans in his comparison of the experiences of Cleveland's black community with those of the city's white ethnic groups. He studied the differing opportunities blacks and ethnic groups encountered in employment, home ownership, and housing segregation in the years from 1870 to 1930. During the period before World War I, he said, Italians and Rumanians had been even more segregated from the native white population than Afro-Americans, and other white ethnic groups also tended to cluster within "fairly well restricted sections of the city." By 1920, however, the pattern changed, and the segregation of foreign born from native whites began to decline at the same time that the black community was becoming even more concentrated.[40]

Thomas Lee Philpott in a study of Chicago also compared the residential patterns of immigrants with those of blacks in the late nineteenth and early twentieth centuries but argued that Chicago's immigrants never experienced the separate community life that Afro-Americans endured in the ghetto. While the black neighborhoods grew increasingly homogeneous, the immigrant sections remained random mixtures of European populations striving to remain all white. Unlike the ethnic clusters, in black ghettos segregation was "practically total, essentially involuntary, and also perpetual." Philpott argued that unlike blacks, white ethnics were assimilated "on their own terms as much as the reformers" and without forfeiting their identity and that they joined with their native neighbors to draw the color line. To the question frequently asked by ethnic Americans, "If we did it, why couldn't they?" Philpott answered that "contrary to popular and academic tradition," immigrants never experienced the ghetto and therefore never had to escape it, for urban American blacks faced a unique kind of "residential confinement."[41]

David R. Goldfield and Blaine A. Brownell's *Urban America: From Downtown to No Town* supported Philpott's argument and challenged the traditional interpretation that immigrants had been rural peasants in Europe who became overwhelmed by American cities. Few immigrant districts in American cities were homogeneous, they wrote, and those clusters that developed resulted as much from lack of housing, stages in life cycle of immigrant families, or employment opportunities as from ethnicity. Immigrants were quick to adopt the prevailing white view about black inferiority and fought to protect their neighborhoods from black "invasions." In reaction, urban blacks "sought to establish a separate society, a much more self-contained and isolated one than the immigrants had formed to preserve their foreign heritages." In contrast to immigrant institutions with overseas roots, which had voluntarily formed "to ease the transition to urban America and to retain the traditions of the past," black institutions, with the important exception of the black church, "came into existence as a result of blacks' exclusion from the white urban world."[42]

Arnold R. Hirsch's *Making the Second Ghetto: Race and Housing in Chicago, 1940–1960* described the dynamic process of ghetto maintenance and assessed the roles played by different elements of the white community in that process. Hirsch argued that the concern with neighborhood solidarity and communal stability of unassimilated inner-city ethnics led them to play an important role in supporting the creation of the second ghetto (the post–World War II expansion of Chicago's black belt) and in shaping the direction of the city's public housing program. In an argument similar to that of Michael Novak, Hirsch differentiated between the attitudes and actions of the "ethnic" Catholic working class and the middle-class professionals of Hyde Park. The working-class Catholics "played a central role" in resisting neighborhood integration and led "communal riots" against unwanted black neighbors. The Hyde Park residents were both more open to racial integration and less a real community, for their unity was based on middle-class aspirations, not ethnic heritage. The ethnic Catholics were further distinguished by their zeal for home ownership and, unlike the residents of Hyde Park, their roots in their community. Hirsch also offered readers an updated version of the myth of the "wandering Jew," claiming that Jews were traditionally more geographically mobile than other ethnic groups and hence less likely to own their own homes. Jews thus did not feel the territorial imperative to defend their community that so strongly motivated the Catholic ethnics and were thus less resistant to racial integration since they could easily move on.[43]

Like Hirsch, Julia Blackwelder studied the relationship of class, ethnicity, and mobility, but she added the category of gender. She examined the impact of the depression on Anglo, black, and Mexican-American women and found that women in these groups faced different conditions and developed different strategies depending on their family status and "caste," a position in society ascribed by outsiders. Each caste had its own culture, which also influenced women's behavior. By separating caste from culture, Blackwelder was able to develop a much more sophisticated picture of the interrelationship between discrimination imposed from the outside and the cultural restraints or choices that come from within the group.[44]

By the late 1970s scholars of immigration history began publishing books that characteristically opened with a criticism of Oscar Handlin's picture of immigrants as alienated individuals in the process of breaking from the bondage of culture. While Handlin had argued that the choice to leave the old country set immigrants on their flight to freedom, more recent scholars claimed that immigrants had not made clear-cut choices between Old World culture and New World alienation. Instead they ascribed to their ethnics a flexible, malleable culture, one that could survive the sea of change and provide the new Americans with a variety of options to help them adjust to urban life. Virginia Yans-McLaughlin, for example, centered her work on the adaptation of the Italian family to life in Buffalo. In evaluating the Italian family she suggested that one could interpret with equal validity its stability as "either the successful transmission of a strong heritage" or as a "successful adaptation of Old World patterns to new situations." Thus Yans-McLaughlin and others argue that Handlin errs in describing immigrants as choosing to leave Old World culture behind. But like Handlin, she emphasizes the role of individual choice as her immigrants select the aspects of Italian culture that seem most useful in the New World. Their lives are not determined by their culture.[45]

This point is made even more explicitly in Donna R. Gabaccia's *From Sicily to Elizabeth Street*, which establishes the framework within which Sicilian immigrants made choices by describing the cultural ideals, environmental possibilities, and social behavior of the immigrants. Gabaccia disputes Yans-McLaughlin's claim that Italian newcomers remained culturally a folk for the first generation. Instead, Gabaccia suggests that immigrants were easily able to "strip down" their culture without undergoing either a "painful" or a "disorienting cultural process." Gabaccia's immigrants are able to make choices to conduct their lives in different ways and at the same time can continue to justify these changes as being faithful to traditional Sicilian ideals.[46]

Like Gabaccia, who focused her attention on how the change in housing stock from Sicily to New York City's tenements affected immigrant lives, James Borchert in 1980 examined alley life in Washington, D.C., and discovered residents sustained by a resilient culture. Afro-American alley residents, he discovered, despite harsh conditions were "able to shape and control their own lives within the economic, social and political limits imposed by the dominant white society." Rural behavior first learned in the South was not abandoned once ex-slaves reached the city. Rather it continued to provide guidance for urban living. "Because their cultural heritage was rich and complex," Borchert claimed, "migrants could choose from among several appropriate or acceptable courses of action." Borchert suggested that "urban experience does not impose itself on the migrant" but "provides a set of choices, the perception of which is determined by the extent to which one can recognize them, and influenced by the weighting given by culture and an individual's own experience."[47]

While Borchert depicted black urban migrants creating "meaningful worlds that permitted both survival and a sense of identity and belonging," other recent assessments of urban life have been considerably less enthusiastic about the degree of choice and creativity made available to black residents of the urban ghetto. Elizabeth Hafkin Pleck, who examined black poverty in nineteenth-century Boston, found persistent racial barriers in employment that meant that Boston's black population displayed American aspirations for mobility but could not find avenues to economic progress. Contemporary black poverty is thus not the result of limited black aspirations and low economic status but of "high aspirations and low status," the latter of which can be attributed to employment discrimination in Boston, not to slavery or the rural culture of blacks.[48]

Economic mobility also attracted the attention of Olivier Zunz in his study of Detroit, *The Changing Face of Inequality*, which traces the city's development from a collection of semi-autonomous ethnic communities in the nineteenth century to a society structured by class in the twentieth century. Accompanying the changes in industrial production between 1880 and 1920 came a geographical reorganization of residential neighborhoods that destroyed an older plural model of opportunity, which had allowed members of an ethnic group to achieve mobility within their ethnic communities. By 1920, with the development of large-scale industrialization, all ethnic groups had to compete for employment in one economic arena, thus making class a more salient influence on experience than ethnicity.[49]

William J. Wilson also recognized the growing importance of class in limiting the possibilities for social mobility among black city dwellers. Like Zunz, Wilson found that the twentieth-century development of corporate capitalism led to a change in the relative importance of race and class in determining opportunity for mobility. Since mid-century, the development of a new economic structure aided the growth of the black middle class even as it created a semi-permanent underclass in the ghettoes. Before the middle of the twentieth century, however, race discrimination was more important than class.[50]

Wilson also took pains to explain that blacks failed to develop the political influence characteristic of ethnic groups. First, substantial black migration to urban areas did not occur before World War I so that "by 1920 blacks were already several decades behind European immigrant ethnics in developing institutional capabilities for urban life." Second, and to Wilson far more important, blacks alone faced "systematic exclusion" from the urban political system. Wilson argued that European immigrants and their descendants used urban political machines to gerrymander ghetto neighborhoods so as to undermine the "political participation, strength, and potential of the burgeoning black urban population." Excluded from real participation in white-controlled city machines, blacks were deprived of the kind of political development experienced by white immigrant ethnics. As a result, they could not use "ethnic patterns and prejudices as the primary basis for interest-group and political formations" and could not "build upon these to integrate a given ethnic community into the wider politics of the city and the nation." Thus to exert political influence, the black middle class was forced to resort to the "extrainstitutional civil rights movement." The growth of black political power that occurred after mid-century was due, Williams claimed, to the demise of political machines, which was part of the shift of the concentration of power away from political parties to complex corporate bureaucracies.[51]

Like Zunz and Wilson, John Bodnar placed his description of the urban experience of immigrants in *The Transplanted* in a historical framework of developing capitalism and class analysis. For Bodnar, the experience of all immigrant groups can be divided into two "separate but related worlds which might be termed broadly working class and middle class." "The fragile link between the generations of the last century and the current one," he contended, "is not necessarily cultural or emotional as much as it is the shared need to respond to an evolving capitalism." And just as Handlin, Borchert, and other scholars since the 1950s have declared, Bodnar suggests that today's Americans, like their ancestors, "need to choose from available but limited life paths." Suggesting that previous attempts to generalize about the experience of immigrants have assumed a common experience shared by all, Bodnar argues that different life choices influenced by different cultures, different ideologies, and different opportunities have created a diverse pattern of immigrant experience. A more useful approach, he suggests, is to think of the process of immigration as a relationship between the "changing imperatives of the marketplace and the diverse responses of human beings." The individuals who undergo this are not, in his scheme, helpless victims "simply manipulated by leaders, their class standing, or their culture." Instead, they are "active participants in a historical drama whose outcome is anything but predictable." The culture and the mentality of these immigrants, Bodnar wrote, "was a blend of past and present and centered on the immediate and the attainable."[52]

The theme of choice in ethnic cultural options is highlighted in Zelda Stern's *The Complete Guide to Ethnic New York*. When she published this book in 1980, Stern claimed it was the first of its kind, but it was similar in many, though superficial, ways to Bercovici's book of more than fifty years earlier. Like Bercovici, she identified ethnic neighborhoods and gave a thumbnail history of each group's history in New York. Many of the seventeen ethnic groups she discussed had been described by Bercovici, but she added both the East and West Indian communities, as well as the Japanese, Puerto Ricans, South Americans, and Scandinavians. Many of her communities had relocated since Bercovici had studied them, but more important, few of the ethnic communities she identified continued to be the population centers of the group because middle-class ethnics had scattered around the city. The ethnic neighborhoods that continued to be vibrant were those that continued to receive new immigrants, like Chinatown and Greek Astoria. Outside these functioning ethnic neighborhoods, she offered tours of historic and "symbolic" centers that still contained ethnic shrines, like Harlem's Apollo Theater (Stern pointed out that New York's largest contemporary black ghetto was located in Brooklyn's Bedford-Stuyvesant, but she offered no tour tips for that area).[53]

Unlike Bercovici, Stern does not discuss the religious beliefs, the economic activities, or the political inclinations of different ethnic groups. She saves her descriptive powers for food, offering the culinary history and a menu glossary for each ethnic group, as well as a quality rating and price range for various ethnic restaurants. For Stern, New York City is a consumer's delight of edible cultural diversity. In "what other city," she asks, "can you have breakfast at an Italian cafe, lunch at a Japanese sushi bar, tea at a German konditorei, and dine at a Hungarian restaurant—all in the same day?"[54]

This smorgasborg of cultures serves a very different function than Bercovici's brand of cultural pluralism. For him, each group needed to develop its own culture to become American. In his world—the world of 1920 to 1950—everyone belonged to a particular culture, and that culture—whether rural, urban, Afro-American, or ethnic—was commonly regarded as determining the fate of the individual. An individual might, though with considerable stress and strain, change cultures through geographic relocation, but one could not be a peasant and thrive in an urban environment. After 1950 and the demise of interest in cultural determinism, individuals came to be regarded as exercising, within limits, critical choices about which elements of their culture to keep or discard. Historians now argue about which elements particular groups sought to preserve or abandon, but most agree that culture is not a fixed deterministic agent but rather a set of options. For Zelda Stern, as for most other contemporary commentators, ethnic culture is seen as an optional item of consumption. But if ethnic culture is now depicted as malleable, the economic system that limits the mobility aspirations of Americans appears more problematic. Today, as Wilson suggests, the primary line of distinction is drawn not between ethnic groups but between those who can afford to eat out and the inner-city poor of all groups who line up at the doors of soup kitchens and relief agencies.[55]

Notes

1. For an introduction to this literature, see Stephan Thernstrom, ed., *Harvard Encyclopedia of American Ethnic Groups* (Cambridge, Mass.: Belknap Press of Harvard University Press, 1980); *Journal of American Ethnic History; International Migration Review;* and Donald H. Parkerson's review article, "Race and Ethnicity in the Industrializing City," *Journal of Family History* 10 (Winter 1985): 402–9.

2. Philip Gleason, "American Identity and Americanization," in *Harvard Encyclopedia*, p. 58.

3. Olivier Zunz, *The Changing Face of Inequality: Urbanization, Industrial Development, and Immigrants in Detroit, 1880–1920* (Chicago: University of Chicago Press, 1982); William J. Wilson, *The Declining Significance of Race: Blacks and Changing American Institutions*, 2nd ed. (Chicago: University of Chicago Press, 1980).

4. Richmond Mayo-Smith, *Emigration and Immigration: A Study in Social Science* (1890; New York: Charles Scribner's Sons, 1895), pp. 62–65.

5. John R. Commons, "Race and Democracy," in Moses Rischin, ed., *Immigration and the American Tradition* (Indianapolis: Bobbs-Merrill, 1976), p. 282. Some representatives of minorities also spoke in these racial terms at the turn of the century. See,

for example, Zane L. Miller, "Cincinnati Germans and the Invention of an Ethnic Group," *Queen City Heritage: The Journal of the Cincinnati Historical Society* 42 (Fall 1984): 13–22; W. E. B. Du Bois, *The Philadelphia Negro* (1899; New York: Schocken Books, 1967).

6. Randolph Bourne made a similar argument eight years earlier in "Trans-national America," *Atlantic Monthly* 118 (July 1916): 86–97. Bourne suggested that the recognition of the "Failure of the Melting Pot" and the discovery of the existence of diverse nationalistic feelings came as a shock to Americans during World War I. Rather than assimilating, immigrant cultures seemed to be growing in strength. A redefinition of Americanism was called for, a vision of America as a federation of nations. Although Bourne pointed out that the first colonialists had not adopted the culture of the American Indian but had slavishly followed British styles, he did not include the American Negro in his description of cultures that made up America. Nor did he include Arab or Chinese immigrants but limited his discussion to European immigrants.

7. Konrad Bercovici, *Around the World in New York* (New York: Century Company, 1924), pp. 14–15, 23.

8. Ibid., pp. 60–61, 74, 205.

9. Ibid., pp. 20, 213, 243.

10. Ernest W. Burgess, "The Growth of the City: An Introduction to a Research Project," and Roderick D. McKenzie, "The Ecological Approach to the Study of the Human Community," both in Robert E. Park, Ernest W. Burgess, Roderick D. McKenzie, eds., *The City* (1925; Chicago: University of Chicago Press, 1967), pp. 54–55, 78.

11. Robert E. Park, "Community Organization and the Romantic Temper," in Park et al., *The City*, pp. 127, 122.

12. Louis Wirth, *The Ghetto* (Chicago: University of Chicago Press, 1928), p. 286. Interestingly, Wirth cites Bercovici's argument that immigrant colonies in New York appear to locate in the same geographical pattern that the mother countries assume on the map of Europe. He finds the pattern is a little different in Chicago, but there is "an unmistakable regularity in the association between local immigrant groups, and particularly between the Jews and their neighbors" (p. 227). Bercovici appears to have been regarded as an expert on New York City's Jewish community, for Wirth also quotes from a Bercovici article titled "The Greatest Jewish City in the World," *Nation,* September 12, 1923, p. 261. For a recent discussion of the changing relationship between geographic place and culture, see Henry D. Shapiro, "The Place of Culture and the Problem of Identity," in Allen Batteau, ed., *Appalachia and America: Autonomy and Regional Dependence* (Lexington: University Press of Kentucky, 1983), pp. 111–41.

13. Robert E. Park, "Community Organization and Juvenile Delinquency," in Park et al., *The City*, p. 108.

14. Harvey W. Zorbaugh, *The Gold Coast and the Slum: A Sociological Study of Chicago's Near North Side* (Chicago: University of Chicago Press, 1929), pp. 154, 155.

15. Charles Edward Merriam, *Chicago: A More Intimate View of Urban Politics* (New York: Macmillan, 1929), pp. 134, 136–38.

16. Ibid., p. 146.

17. Clyde Vernon Kiser, *Sea Island to City: A Study of St. Helena Islanders in Harlem and Other Urban Centers* (New York: Columbia University Press, 1932), pp. 142, 144.

18. Caroline F. Ware, *Greenwich Village, 1920–1930: A Comment on American Civilization in the Post-War Years* (Boston: Houghton Mifflin, 1935), pp. 127, 422.

19. Caroline F. Ware, "Ethnic Communities," *Encyclopedia of the Social Sciences* (1931; New York: Macmillan, 1948), 5:607–13.

20. Marcus Lee Hansen, *The Immigrant in American History* (1940; New York: Harper Torchbook, 1964), pp. 167–68.

21. Stow Persons, "The Americanization of the Immigrant," in David F. Bowers, ed., *Foreign Influences in American Life* (Princeton: Princeton University Press, 1944), p. 50.

22. National Resources Committee, "Cultural Diversity in American Life," in Alain Locke and Bernhard J. Stern, eds., *When Peoples Meet: A Study in Race and Culture Contacts* (New York: Progressive Education Association, 1942), pp. 706–19.

23. Robert E. Park, Introduction to Charles S. Johnson, *Shadow of the Plantation* (1934; Chicago: Midway Reprint, 1979), pp. x–xi. Park also suggests that Robert Redfield, another University of Chicago social scientist, offered a useful definition of "folk" in *Tepoztlan, A Mexican Village: A Study of Folklife* (Chicago: University of Chicago Press, 1930). Folk were people with a common stock of tradition, with continuity from generation to generation without needing to rely on the printed page. Folk people always had a local habitat, which was always located in the country. Any folklore found in the city was diminishing; as Redfield described it, urban folklore was "always a vestige."

24. St. Clair Drake and Horace R. Cayton, *Black Metropolis: A Study of Negro Life in a Northern City* (New York: Harcourt, Brace and Company, 1945), p. 755.

25. Miller, "Cincinnati Germans," pp. 19, 22 n.24.

26. Oscar Handlin, *The Uprooted* (New York: Grosset & Dunlap, 1951). See also Oscar Handlin, *Boston's Immigrants: A Study in Acculturation* (Cambridge, Mass.: Harvard University Press, 1941).

27. Ibid., pp. 4, 6.

28. Ibid., pp. 305, 306–7.

29. Will Herbert, *Protestant-Catholic-Jew: An Essay in American Religious Sociology* (1955; University of Chicago Press, 1983), pp. 27, 36–40.

30. Oscar Handlin, *The Newcomers: Negroes and Puerto Ricans in a Changing Metropolis* (Cambridge, Mass.: Harvard University Press, 1959), pp. 118–19.

31. Gilbert Osofsky, *Harlem: The Making of a Ghetto,* 2nd ed. (1963; New York: Harper Torchbook, 1971), p. xvi. Other studies of Harlem include James Weldon Johnson, *Black Manhattan* (1930; New York: Atheneum, 1968); Nathan Irvin Huggins, *Harlem Renaissance* (New York: Oxford University Press, 1971); and Mark Naison, *Communists in Harlem during the Depression* (Urbana: University of Illinois Press, 1983).

32. Rudolph J. Vecoli, "Contadini in Chicago: A Critique of *The Uprooted,*" *Journal of American History* 51 (December 1964): 407–17.

33. Nathan Glazer and Daniel Patrick Moynihan, *Beyond the Melting Pot: The Negroes, Puerto Ricans, and Irish of New York City* (Cambridge, Mass.: MIT Press, 1963), p. 53. The suggestion that Afro-Americans had no culture was challenged by a whole series of books documenting black culture, among them Charles Keil, *Urban Blues* (Chicago: University of Chicago Press, 1966), and Herbert Gutman, *The Black Family in Slavery and Freedom, 1750–1925* (New York: Pantheon Books, 1976).

34. Allan H. Spear, *Black Chicago: The Making of a Negro Ghetto, 1890–1920* (Chicago: University of Chicago Press, 1967), esp. pp. 5–8, 227–29.

35. Ibid., p. 227.

36. Stephan Thernstrom, *Poverty and Progress: Social Mobility in a Nineteenth Century City* (Cambridge, Mass.: Harvard University Press, 1964), pp. 199, 136–37, 152–56.

37. Hershberg, *Philadelphia*, pp. vi, 485. Among the mobility studies are Stephan Thernstrom, *The Other Bostonians: Poverty and Progress in the American Metropolis, 1880–1970* (Cambridge, Mass.: Harvard University Press, 1973); Howard Chudacoff, *Mobile Americans: Residential and Social Mobility in Omaha, 1880–1920* (New York: Oxford University Press, 1972); Dean R. Essinglinger, *Immigrants and the City; Ethnicity and Mobility in a Nineteenth-Century Midwestern Community* (Port Washington, N.Y.: Kennikat Press, 1975); Thomas Kessner, *The Golden Door: Italian and Jewish Immigrant Mobility in New York City, 1880–1915* (New York: Oxford University Press, 1977); and Humbert S. Nelli, *Italians in Chicago 1880–1930: A Study in Ethnic Mobility* (New York: Oxford University Press, 1970).

38. Michael Novak, *The Rise of the Unmeltable Ethnics: Politics and Culture in the Seventies* (New York: Macmillan, 1972), pp. 7, 35–38. See also Andrew M. Greely, "In Defense of Ethnics," in his *Building Coalitions* (New York: New Viewpoints, 1974), pp. 353–79. Greely attacks the "liberal elite" for their view of ethnics as "conservative defectors" in the 1972 presidential election. For a more recent assessment of the experiences of East Central Europeans, see Ewa Morawska, *For Bread with Butter: Life-Worlds of East Central Europeans in Johnstown, Pennsylvania, 1890–1940* (New York: Cambridge University Press, 1985). Melvin G. Holli and Peter d'A. Jones criticized Novak's image of the WASP in *Ethnic Chicago, Revised and Expanded* (Grand Rapids, Mich.: William B. Erdmans Publishing Company, 1984), p. 2. They claimed the "mythical WASP" had never existed, for long before the arrival of the new immigrants of the late nineteenth century, mainstream American culture had been forged out of English, Scotch-Irish, Welsh, Dutch, Swedish, American Indian, black, German, and other subcultures. The new immigrants had thus encountered not an Anglo-Saxon Puritan culture but one that was "already melted." Lewis M. Killian's *White Southerners* (1970; Amherst: University of Massachusetts Press, 1985) argued that white southerners were a distinct ethnic group and acted as if they were members of a minority. For a discussion of the ethnic revival that treats ethnic groups as interest rather than racial or cultural groups, see Kenneth Fox, *Metropolitan American: Urban Life and Urban Policy in the United States, 1940–1980* (Jackson: University Press of Mississippi, 1986), pp. 107–36.

39. Melvin Steinfield, *Cracks in the Melting Pot: Racism and Discrimination in American History* (New York: Glencoe Press, 1973), pp. 175–76.

40. Kenneth L. Kusmer, *A Ghetto Takes Shape: Black Cleveland, 1870–1930* (Chicago: University of Chicago Press, 1976), pp. 42–43. Other studies of ghetto development include Paul A. Groves and Edward K. Muller, "The Evolution of Black Residential Concentrations in Late 19th Century Cities," *Journal of Historical Geography* 1 (April 1975): 169–91; and Reynolds Farley, "The Urbanization of Negroes in the United States," *Journal of Social History* 1 (Spring 1968): 241–58.

41. Thomas Lee Philpott, *The Slum and the Ghetto: Neighborhood Deterioration and Middle-Class Reform, Chicago, 1880–1930* (New York: Oxford University Press, 1978), pp. xv–xvii. It should be noted that Philpott was a student of Richard C. Wade, who argued in *Slavery in the Cities: The South, 1820–1860* (1964; New York: Oxford University Press, 1975), that mid-nineteenth-century urban conditions had undermined slavery and brought forth segregation as a means of governing race relations.

42. David R. Goldfield and Blaine A. Brownell, *Urban America: From Downtown to No Town* (Boston: Houghton Mifflin, 1979), pp. 250, 270.

43. Arnold R. Hirsch, *Making the Second Ghetto: Race and Housing in Chicago, 1940–1960* (New York: Cambridge University Press, 1983), pp. 78, 189–90, 194, 203–

4. Other assessments of post-1940 urban race relations include Dominic J. Capeci, Jr., *Race Relations in Wartime Detroit: The Sojourner Truth Housing Controversy of 1942* (Philadelphia: Temple University Press, 1984); and David R. Colburn, *Racial Change and Community Crisis: St. Augustine, Florida, 1877–1980* (New York: Columbia University Press, 1985). Like Hirsch, Christopher Silver in *Twentieth-Century Richmond: Planning, Politics and Race* (Knoxville: University of Tennessee Press, 1984) is concerned with the relationship between public policy and changing urban racial divisions.

44. Julia Blackwelder, *Women of the Depression: Caste and Culture in San Antonio, 1929–1939* (College Station: Texas A&M University Press, 1984), pp. 7–10. See also Dolores Janiewski, *Sisterhood Denied: Race, Gender, and Class in a New South Community* (Philadelphia: Temple University Press, 1985), for a discussion of Durham, North Carolina, women workers.

45. Virginia Yans-McLaughlin, *Family and Community: Italian Immigrants in Buffalo, 1880–1930* (Ithaca: Cornell University Press, 1977), p. 261.

46. Donna R. Gabaccia, *From Sicily to Elizabeth Street: Housing and Social Change among Italian Immigrants, 1880–1930* (Albany: State University of New York Press, 1984), p. 115. See also David Kertzer and Dennis Hogan, "On the Move: Migration in an Italian Community, 1865–1921," *Social Science History* 9 (Winter 1985): 1–23.

47. James Borchert, *Alley Life in Washington: Family, Community, Religion, and Folklife in the City, 1850–1970* (Urbana: University of Illinois Press, 1980), pp. 223, 240. Borchert's work followed in the tradition established during the 1970s by John Blassingame, *The Slave Community: Plantation Life in the Antebellum South* (New York: Oxford University Press, 1972); Gutman, *The Black Family;* and Lawrence W. Levine, *Black Culture and Black Consciousness: Afro-American Folk Thought from Slavery to Freedom* (New York: Oxford University Press, 1977).

48. Elizabeth Hafkin Pleck, *Black Migration and Poverty: Boston, 1865–1900* (New York: Academic Press, 1979), pp. 207–8. See also James Oliver Horton and Lois E. Horton, *Black Bostonians: Family Life and Community Struggle in the Antebellum North* (New York: Holmes and Meier, 1979).

49. Zunz, *Changing Face of Inequality,* see esp. pp. 400–403.

50. Wilson, *Declining Significance of Race,* pp. 120–21. James O. Horton and Lois E. Horton take issue with Wilson's analysis of the relative importance of class and race in "Race and Class," *American Quarterly* 35 (Spring-Summer 1983): 155–68.

51. Wilson, *Declining Significance of Race,* pp. 78–79, 81–82, 86–87.

52. John Bodnar, *The Transplanted: A History of Immigrants in Urban America* (Bloomington: Indiana University Press, 1985), pp. 208, xv, xx, 211. See also John Bodnar, Roger Simon, and Michael P. Weber, *Lives of Their Own: Blacks, Italians, and Poles in Pittsburgh, 1900–1960* (Urbana: University of Illinois Press, 1981).

53. Zelda Stern, *The Complete Guide to Ethnic New York* (New York: St. Martin's Press, 1980).

54. Ibid., p. 1.

55. Stephen Steinberg claims in *The Ethnic Myth: Race, Ethnicity, and Class in America* (New York: Atheneum, 1981), that ethnic pluralism was built on systematic inequality and that as long as ethnicity is associated with class disadvantage, there is powerful reason to opt for assimilation. Andrew Stein, "Children of Poverty," *New York Times Magazine,* June 8, 1986, suggests that youth and gender ("the feminization of poverty") are more important than race in determining who will be poor. This point is also made in Daniel Patrick Moynihan's new book, *Family and Nation* (New York:

Harcourt Brace Jovanovich, Publishers, 1986). My analysis of the state of ethnic-black urban history differs from that of Jo Ann Eady Argersinger in her review essay, " 'Second-Generation' Ethnic Studies," *American Quarterly* 34 (Fall 1982), which argues that ethnic history to that date had failed to address the "relationship between class and ethnicity." It should be noted, however, that Argersinger concentrated her attention on books written in the 1970s. For the argument that race is still the primary factor, see Alphonso Pinkney, *The Myth of Black Progress* (New York: Cambridge University Press, 1984).

4 ———— Work and the Workplace in the City: Toward a Synthesis of the "New" Labor and Urban History

LEONARD WALLOCK

"Just as the plantation was the typical product of the antebellum Southern system and the small farm of the Northern agricultural order, so the city was the supreme achievement of the new industrialism." Thus concluded Arthur M. Schlesinger, Sr., in his landmark study, *The Rise of the City, 1878–1898*, published over a half-century ago. The fundamental role played by industrial development in urban growth was a theme Schlesinger reiterated in 1940 when he urged further study of "The City in American History." Not until the 1960s, however, did historians of the working class and the city begin focusing in detail on the relationship between industrialization and urbanization. Their belated response to Schlesinger's call may be explained in large part by the way in which American labor and urban history had evolved. In each of these fields, historians faced conceptual barriers that had to be overcome before the industrialization process could be placed in an ecological framework. Only in the last two decades have researchers broken out of the confines imposed by the "old" labor and urban history. In doing so, they have not only provided a rich body of literature on work and the workplace in the American city but they have reconceived the meaning of the terms *labor* and *urban*.[1]

The conceptual foundations of American labor history were laid in the first quarter of the twentieth century by John R. Commons and his associates. Known for their institutional approach, members of the Wisconsin school focused on three principal themes: trade unionism, collective bargaining, and political organization. Regarding capitalism from the perspective of classical economics, they explained its evolution by detailing the historical extension of markets. Thus the " 'conflict of labor and capital' " became instead a "conflict of market and labor, of merchant and wage-earner, of prices and wages." This schema informed not only Commons' study "American Shoemakers, 1648–1895," which appeared in 1909, but also the monumental *History of Labour in the United States* that he coauthored in 1918. The assumptions these labor economists made about working-class behavior were most clearly articulated by Selig Perlman, who took job-conscious unionism to be its motivational key. The political efforts of Commons and his associates—to legitimate trade unionism within the context of a capitalist economy—set narrow limits on their vision of working-class experience. As a result, explains David Brody, "for all that they contributed to our knowledge of the labor movement, [they] left us otherwise nearly ignorant of the history of the American worker."[2]

Those who wrote *History of Labour in the United States* devoted surprisingly little attention to the subject of work and its urban context. Although they analyzed the development of industry in general and the evolution of certain trades in particular, such as shoemaking, printing, and moulding, Commons and his associates focused primarily on wages, hours, and working conditions. Changes in the forces and relations of production were deemed significant only to the degree that they affected the bargaining power of trade unions. This limited perspective on work had profound consequences for the writing of American labor history. It left what David Montgomery calls "three issues of critical importance" largely unexplained:

1) the social relations peculiar to industrial production, 2) the changing and conflicting forms of social consciousness created by people in their efforts to cope with those relationships, and 3) the impact of workers' consciousness and activities on the rest of society.

Not only the social but the ecological dimension of work was largely absent from the studies done by Commons and his associates. Occasionally their *History of Labour in the United States* acknowledges the importance of the urban environment. For example, we learn that in the early nineteenth century labor's awakening "to a feeling of class solidarity was made possible by the growth of cities" and that at mid-century, the "great demand for buildings . . . in New York" aided the journeymen carpenters in winning their strike. However, emphasizing as they did the extension of markets, members of the Wisconsin school failed to investigate systematically the urban dimension of work and working-class experience.[3]

While the field of labor history emerged from a dominant school of thought, urban history developed without an overarching scheme of conceptualization.

For this reason, early writings on the American city reflected a diversity of approaches. The oldest genre was composed of what Roy Lubove termed urban biographies. Begun in the 1880s and 1890s as an effort to record local history, these biographies "lack[ed] any significant conceptual framework; or fail[ed] to distinguish between urban and national history." Closely related to biographies were topical studies, which sought to explain a particular facet of urban development. First appearing in the 1930s but dating mainly from the 1960s, these works dealt with "cities or life in cities, but rarely with urban history as distinguished from social, economic, or political history in the context of cities." Another genre, which began to proliferate in the mid-1960s, included studies of the urban environment: architecture, design, housing, planning, economic development, transportation, and land use. According to Lubove, these environmental studies pointed toward a more satisfying definition of urban history because they focused on the "process of city building over time." While Lubove called for the further study of the city as an artifact, other urbanists, such as Eric Lampard, proposed to investigate the city as an ecological complex. Regardless of their differences, these critics agreed on the need to conceptualize urban history as a dynamic, interrelated process. To use a pertinent example, the biographical, topical, and environmental studies of the city all dealt with industrialization, but none of them adequately explained the logic of its development or the full range of its consequences.[4]

Despite such conceptual limitations, the "old" labor and urban history produced some studies concerned with work and the workplace in the city. The best-known examples of this literature are the monographs of New England's factory towns written in the 1930s and 1940s. Not only did they depict the labor process of textile workers, but they revealed how the "ambitions and exploitation of capitalist enterprise" were, according to Sean Wilentz, "congealed in the very architecture of the mills, the mansions, and the rows of workers' housing." Early accounts of individual trade unions, written during the opening decades of this century, also addressed the topic of work and its setting. Especially noteworthy is Don Lescohier's "The Knights of St. Crispin, 1867–1874," which analyzed the kinds of work and range of workplaces in which nineteenth-century shoemakers found employment. The most ambitious of these early attempts to weave work into the urban fabric were made by historians of immigration and ethnicity. In his portrait *Boston's Immigrants,* Oscar Handlin sketched the relationship between the "economic" and "physical adjustment" of the city's Irish immigrants, using a model of population secession similar to the one adopted by the Chicago school of urban sociologists.[5]

During the last two decades, the subject of work and the workplace in the city has become one of paramount importance to authors of the "new" labor and urban history. A focal point of their research has been the contrasting experiences of workers in three types of nineteenth-century cities: single-industry towns, seaboard cities, and industrial centers. The first type included early nineteenth-century textile towns located mostly in New England, whose European counterparts were found in Lancashire and Lyons. While the basic outlines of the textile paradigm have been long established, recent scholarship has added to our appreciation of its complexities and variations.[6] In his study of Rockdale, a Pennsylvania mill village, Anthony Wallace analyzed in great detail the process and organization of textile production, as well as the cultural and political battles that took place between manufacturers and workers. Thomas Dublin's *Women at Work* delineated the efforts of mill owners in Lowell, Massachusetts, to impose work discipline and moral supervision on female factory hands and revealed how patterns of work and housing promoted solidarity among these young women. Single-industry towns devoted to shoemaking have also inspired new interest among historians. In *Class and Community*, Alan Dawley depicted the erosion of skills experienced by shoemakers in Lynn, Massachusetts, due to the introduction of the putting-out system, the central shop, and the factory. Despite resistance by male and female shoemakers, the growth of industrial capitalism transformed the work, family, politics, and built environment of antebellum Lynn.[7]

Until just a few years ago, the textile paradigm continued to serve as a model for the rise of nineteenth-century capitalist manufacture and thereby to obscure understanding of the economic transformation experienced by the great seaboard cities. In the 1970s, a number of European historians, especially Raphael Samuel, began to question the "orthodox account of the industrial revolution [which] concentrates on the rise of steam power and machinery, and the spread of the factory system." Samuel argued that a "vast amount of capitalist enterprise was organized on the basis of hand rather than steam-powered technologies" and that industry grew not by means of a linear take-off but through a process of combined and uneven development. Bringing these insights to bear on U.S. Census data, Bruce Laurie and Mark Schmitz identified five distinct work settings (factories, manufactories, sweatshops, households, and artisan shops) combining several methods of production in mid-nineteenth-century Philadelphia. In *Proprietary Capitalism*, Philip Scranton also made use of census data to demonstrate that the "small, separate, specialized firms" within Philadelphia's industry had themselves departed from the industrial model introduced at Lowell. The most far-reaching critique of the textile paradigm to date appeared in Sean Wilentz's *Chants Democratic*. Wilentz coined the term *metropolitan industrialization* to describe New York's "labyrinth of factories and tiny artisan establishments, central workrooms and outworkers' cellars, luxury firms and sweatwork strapping shops."[8]

The same uneven pattern of development that was the hallmark of capitalist manufacture in seaport cities also emerged in the industrial centers of the Northeast and Midwest. In *Roots of the American Working Class*, Susan Hirsch devised a three-stage model to represent Newark's industrialization between 1830 and 1860. Using the division of labor and mechanization as her criteria, Hirsch outlined the stages in which traditional crafts declined and modern industry arose. Tracing the history of eight crafts, she discovered that by 1860 "they differed significantly in extent of mechanization, wage level, percentage of women employed, and the average size of the shop.'' This heterogeneous labor process tended to place boundaries on the class consciousness felt by Newark's journeymen and to promote exclusive, craft unionism among them. These findings dovetail with those of Steven Ross, whose *Workers on the Edge* assessed the development and consequences of industrial capitalism in Cincinnati. Ross divided the city's history into three eras: the Age of the Artisan (1788–1843), the Age of Manufacturing (1843–73), and the Age of Modern Industry (1873–1890). Taking his readers "Inside the Workplace," Ross indicated how industrialization fragmented Cincinnati's manufacturing work force into four groups: small-shop artisans, factory artisans, factory laborers, and outworkers. As in Newark, through the 1860s, this diversity of work experience inhibited the formation of a unified working-class consciousness. Beginning in the 1870s, however, the birth of modern industry created a greater uniformity in the process and conditions of work that helped inspire broader class consciousness and labor solidarity in Cincinnati.[9]

The development of capitalist manufacture, whether in single-industry towns, seaport cities, or industrial centers, had far-reaching consequences for urban workers. In the case of artisans, it meant the debasement of their crafts and the creation of new occupational hierarchies, even if the process was far more uneven, complex, and prolonged than previously recognized. Just as outwork, sweating, and factory labor transformed the crafts, so too did they alter the character of the artisan household. In late eighteenth- and early nineteenth-century Lynn, the shoemaker's entire family was often employed under the putting-out system. With the rise of the central shop, shoe production began relocating outside the home. After the introduction of sewing machines in 1852, the number of women employed in the industry declined markedly, and most of those who remained were put to work in factories. Beginning in the 1880s, large numbers of "machine girls" joined the shoe factory labor force. In Newark, where most artisans proved capable of supporting their families, industrialization had a different impact: in the mid-nineteenth century, the craftsmen's household contracted to a nuclear family, and the craftsman's wife devoted herself to domestic labor. The new economic order recast not only the work and family but the community life of artisans as well. In Troy, New York, moulders and puddlers usually settled near the mills in which they found employment. Within these worker communities, there existed ethnic neighborhoods whose strong family ties and kinship networks laid the foundations for an impressive range of religious, social, and political institutions that developed alongside trade unions. As a result, such worker neighborhoods as Harmony Hill or the "iron wards" of South Troy assumed the character of a cohesive working-class community. Although it varied significantly from one locale to another, during the nineteenth century this process of community building occurred in such disparate environments as Philadelphia's textile district of Kensington and Lynn's shoe-making neighborhoods of Brickyard and Highland.[10]

Investigating how the experience of work varied according to skill, gender, ethnicity, race, class, and life cycle has been one of the seminal contributions of the "new" labor and urban history. Despite the fact that several monographs on women in industry appeared during the opening decades of this century and that female employment assumed an important role in Schlesinger's *The Rise of the City*, not until the 1970s did an extensive literature on urban working women appear.[11] U.S. Census data indicate that during the late nineteenth century, females found employment in such low-paying occupations as domestic service, sewing, clerical work, teaching, nursing, sales, and textile manufacture. Early in the twentieth century, the proportion of women in domestic service declined as more industrial and white-collar jobs became available. In both Europe and the United States, the critical factor determining whether a woman worked outside the home was the city's industrial structure. According to Susan Kleinberg, U.S. cities with narrow industrial bases and heavy industry, such as Pittsburgh, had a low proportion of women in the labor force, but urban areas with narrow industrial bases and light industry, such as Lowell and other textile centers, had a high proportion of women and children in the work force. Just as in Europe, in the United States the patterns of family economy that migrants and immigrants brought with them to the city also affected women's labor force participation. That newcomers chose different means of reconciling cultural traditions with economic needs and urban employment opportunities is evident from case studies of Italians in Buffalo (Virginia Yans-McLaughlin), French-Canadians in Manchester, New Hampshire (Tamara Hareven), Eastern European Jews in New York City (Alice Kessler-Harris), and blacks in several locales (Elizabeth Pleck).[12] While working-class women found employment in households, shops, and factories, middle-class women entered such "genteel" professions as nursing, teaching, and clerical work.[13] In general, unmarried women worked outside the home, while married women labored within the home except in times of financial need.

Having redefined work to include unpaid as well as paid tasks, historians are finally coming to recognize the importance of women's contributions to what Louise Tilly and Jon Scott have termed the "family wage economy." Throughout the nineteenth and early twentieth centuries, a minority of married women earned wages doing home work. The most widely known examples of such women include the seamstresses of New York and Philadelphia and the shoebinders of eastern Massachusetts. However, the great majority of married women engaged in household labor that went unpaid. Wives and children often assisted male artisans in trades that required sewing: hatmaking, shoemaking, tailoring, and harness and saddlemaking. Married women shored up the family budget by renting out rooms, offering meals, and providing housekeeping services to boarders and lodgers. In "'Urbanization and the Malleable Household,'" John Modell and Tamara Hareven concluded that well into the twentieth century boarding and lodging was common, taking place in 15 to 20 percent of urban households at any one time. Long regarded as being unproductive, housework was the most common and least recognized labor performed by women. Since the mid-1970s, a number of scholars, including Ann Oakley, Heidi Hartmann, Rae André, and Susan Strasser, have illustrated the ways in which housework constitutes productive labor in its own right. Far from being immune to the pressures of industrialization, housework, like other occupations, was rationalized in the late nineteenth and early twentieth centuries. The introduction of labor-saving technologies into the home did not reduce the time women devoted to housework, since it was accompanied by an increase in their standards of housekeeping and an expansion of their role as consumers.[14]

Though previously neglected, the history of urban free blacks became a vital topic of research during the last two decades. Recent findings demonstrate that the work experience of black men and women differed in fundamental respects from that of their white counterparts. In the antebellum period, urban free blacks were employed as laborers, servants, or in other menial tasks. Based on a statistical analysis of city directories and manuscript census returns from the first half of the nineteenth century, Leonard Curry concluded that free blacks suffered from "widespread discrimination" in urban labor markets, making their chances of economic advancement "highly unlikely." Between 1800 and 1850 such discrimination not only persisted but, in most cities grew worse. Occupational opportunities for free black males were greatest in the Lower South and deteriorated progressively from the Upper South to New England. After the Civil War, most urban blacks continued to work in unskilled and service jobs, and those with skills were often displaced by immigrants and excluded by trade unions. According to the census, in 1870 the rate of labor force participation among black women was three times greater than among white women. In the years before and during World War I, large numbers of southern blacks migrated to northern cities. By the 1920s, many black men had entered the industrial labor force, especially in northern centers of manufacture, such as Detroit and Pittsburgh. Even so, "their work patterns continued to diverge from those of white men" and were marked by "chronic underemployment and sporadic unemployment." As in the past, black women supplemented family earnings usually by toiling as maids, cooks, and washerwomen. According to Jacqueline Jones in *Labor of Love, Labor of Sorrow*, an exceptionally high percentage of black wives found work outside the home, "in 1920, five times higher than the women in any other racial or ethnic group." These employment patterns were reinforced by the segregation of blacks in Northern ghettos.[15]

During the 1970s and 1980s, as women's and Afro-American history burgeoned, immigration history experienced a renaissance. Profiting from the increased study of immigrant groups, historians renewed long-standing debates over the significance of ethnicity and class for urban workers. In his influential essay, "Work, Culture, and Society in Industrializing America," Herbert Gutman emphasized the recurrent tension that existed between the "preindustrial" habits and values of nineteenth-century migrant and immigrant workers and the discipline imposed on them by modern industry. According to Gutman, the repetition of this first-generation experience—among rural migrants in the early nineteenth century, artisans in the middle decades, and peasant immigrants in the closing years of the century—accounted for the resistance to industrialization that each generation of workers displayed. Other scholars have disputed Gutman's thesis because of its questionable juxtaposition of preindustrial and industrial society and its abandonment of class for cultural analysis.[16] The relationship of ethnic to class consciousness has been another much-debated topic. Some historians have argued that immigrant culture enhanced class solidarity; others have suggested that ethnic ties just as easily fragmented class identity.[17] The significance of ethnicity and class for urbanization is a subject that has also provoked lively discussion among historians. Using a labor-shed analysis of census data, Theodore Hershberg and his associates concluded that industrial location rather than ethnicity determined patterns of residence in nineteenth-century Philadelphia. By contrast, employing a block-frontage analysis of census data, Olivier Zunz found that during the 1880s, ethnicity was the principal factor influencing settlement patterns in Detroit, but that by the 1920s, class had become the primary determinant of residential location in the city. Regardless of their outcome, these debates illustrate a growing concern on the part of historians with what David Montgomery has called the "delicate interaction of class and ethnicity."[18]

However much the work experience may have varied for different groups in nineteenth- and twentieth-century America, the labor process under capitalism embodies certain unifying elements. Since the early 1970s, historians have come to view the workplace as a contested terrain. This perception, founded in Marxist theory, was strengthened by the appearance of Harry Braverman's *Labor and Monopoly Capital* and David Noble's *America by Design*. They argued two related propositions in regard to capitalism: first, that the labor process must be continually transformed in accordance with profit maximization and shop floor control; and second, that a fundamental interdependence exists between technology and the social relations of production. Their discovery that "modern technology reflects in its very design the need to assert managerial control over the labor force" was, according to Christopher Lasch, "one of the most important advances in recent social theory."[19] Instead of passively assenting to the "logic of capital," workers resisted by mounting a struggle for control over the labor process. David Montgomery traced the successive stages these struggles assumed among skilled industrial workers in the nineteenth and early twentieth centuries while at the same time delineating the moral code on which they rested. Resistance to capitalist relations of production was by no means confined to skilled, industrial workingmen. Whether employed in domestic service, the needle trades, textile mills, shoemaking factories, or department stores, women also devised shop floor and sometimes unionizing strategies to exercise control over work.[20]

Inspired by the writings of E. P. Thompson, Eric Hobsbawm, George Rudé, and other European scholars, in the last fifteen years American labor historians have begun piecing together the social identities of working people: their ethnic backgrounds, religious beliefs, craft traditions, family lives, associational networks, and leisure-pursuits.[21] A pioneering effort at reconstructing the cultural differences that existed among nineteenth-century artisans was made in 1976 by Alan Dawley and Paul Faler in "Working-Class Culture and Politics in the Industrial Revolution." Focusing on the shoemakers of Lynn, Massachusetts, they argued for the existence of three cultural types among these artisans: traditionalists, rebels, and loyalists. Building on the insights of Dawley and Faler, in 1980 Bruce Laurie completed his history, *Working People of Philadelphia, 1800–1850*, which divided its subjects into four broad categories: rationalist radicals, radical revivalists, traditionalists, and revivalists. Laurie advanced beyond the work of his predecessors in two respects. First, he examined the evolution and transformation of these groups in the light of ethnic, religious, economic, and political influences. Second, he maintained that in addition to possessing distinct beliefs, customs, and institutions, the members of each subculture gravitated toward one or another of the five work settings whose existence in antebellum Philadelphia he had previously documented. The importance of linking work experience and social identity has been demonstrated by other scholars in studies of Pawtucket, Rhode Island, during the early nineteenth century, Cincinnati during the mid-nineteenth century, and Detroit during the 1930s. Such research has served to remind us that battles within the workplace must be seen as part of a larger struggle for class and cultural hegemony that occurred in nineteenth- and twentieth-century American cities.[22]

The recent analyses of workers' control and working-class subcultures were developed partly in response to an earlier generation's scholarship: institutional studies done by the Wisconsin school of labor economists. Ironically, the greatest efforts to synthesize this new literature have been made not by historians but by a new generation of labor economists. In *Contested Terrain*, Richard Edwards maintained that during the nineteenth and twentieth centuries, "continuing conflict in the workplace and employers' attempts to contain it . . . brought the American working class under the sway of three quite different systems for organizing and controlling their work": simple control based on the personal authority of the entrepreneur, structural control embedded within the labor process, and bureaucratic control growing out of the social structure of the firm. During the twentieth century, uneven development among these forms of managerial control segmented labor markets and created three enduring "fractions" within the working class: the working poor found mostly in rural areas or central cities; the traditional proletariat living in urban working-class communities; and the middle layers occupying the suburban rings around major cities or urban neighborhoods isolated from the poor. Each fraction was also characterized by "its distinct job experiences, distinct community cultures, and distinct consciousness." For Edwards such fragmentation provided the key to explaining why a class-conscious workers' movement failed to emerge in the United States. This model was expanded and refined when, in 1982, David Gordon, Richard Edwards, and Michael Reich co-authored *Segmented Work, Divided Workers*.

Examining the long swings of capitalist accumulation, they identified three periods of change in the organization of work and structure of labor markets in
the United States: initial proletarianization (1820s–1890s); the homogenization
of labor (1870s–World War II); and the segmentation of labor (1920s–present).
They also concluded that labor market segmentation was the central factor in
the "unmaking" of the American working class.[23]

Since the 1960s, a new history of work and the workplace in the city has been
written. Moving beyond the conceptual boundaries of their predecessors, its
authors have articulated several common themes. In the nineteenth century,
capitalist manufacture followed alternative paths of development in single-
industry towns, seaboard cities, and industrial centers. As a result, work assumed
different forms within a variety of urban settings, which included households,
sweatshops, artisan shops, manufactories, and factories. The emergence of industrial capitalism not only transformed the labor process but recast the household
and community life of working people as well. This is not to imply, however,
that members of the working class experienced the transition to capitalism in
precisely the same ways. In fact, work varied significantly depending on skill,
gender, ethnicity, race, and life cycle. Even so, the labor process under capitalism
was distinguished by certain unifying elements. Throughout the nineteenth and
twentieth centuries, the point of production was a contested terrain where workers
of all types carried on shop floor and sometimes unionizing strategies to resist
exploitation. Although often a powerful resource for making common cause,
cultural traditions among workers frequently limited their sense of class solidarity. The segmentation of workers into several labor markets and their separation into different urban neighborhoods also placed boundaries on their
identification as members of a class. What a synthesis of these recent findings
will look like is as yet unclear. However, any new interpretive framework in
the field of labor history will have to begin with a dynamic conception of
industrialization and urbanization that treats work and the workplace as variable,
working-class experience as multidimensional, and the city as determinative. It
is in this sense that the terms *labor* and *urban* when applied to social history
have now assumed a new meaning.

Notes

The sources in this chapter are intended to be representative rather than comprehensive.
Neither doctoral dissertations nor unpublished papers have been included. A more com-
plete listing of the relevant literature may be found in Maurice F. Neufeld, Daniel J.
Leab, and Dorothy Swanson, eds., *American Working Class History: A Representative
Bibliography* (New York: R. R. Bowker Company, 1983) and *Labor in America: A
Historical Bibliography* (Santa Barbara: Clio Press, 1985).

1. Arthur Meier Schlesinger, *The Rise of the City, 1878–1898* (New York: Macmillan,
1933), p. 79 and "The City in American History," *Mississippi Valley Historical Review*
27 (June 1940): 43–66. Since the mid-1960s, economic historians and geographers have
produced an impressive body of research on industrialization and urbanization: Jeffrey

G. Williamson and Joseph A. Swanson, "The Growth of Cities in the American Northeast, 1820–1870," *Explorations in Entrepreneurial History*, 2nd ser. 4 (Fall 1966): supplement, 3–101; Allan Pred, *The Spatial Dynamics of U.S. Urban-Industrial Growth, 1800–1914: Interpretive and Theoretical Essays* (Cambridge, Mass.: MIT Press, 1966); David T. Gilchrist, ed., *The Growth of the Seaport Cities, 1790–1825* (Charlottesville: University of Virginia Press, 1967); Simeon J. Crowther, "Urban Growth in the Mid-Atlantic States, 1785–1850," *Journal of Economic History* 3 (September 1976): 624–44; John Burk Sharpless, *City Growth in the United States, England and Wales, 1820–1861: The Effects of Location, Size and Economic Structure on Inter-Urban Variations in Demographic Growth* (New York: Arno Press, 1977); Diane Lindstrom, *Economic Development in the Philadelphia Region, 1810–1850* (New York: Columbia University Press, 1978); Diane Lindstrom and John Sharpless, "Urban Growth and Economic Structure in Antebellum America," in Paul Uselding, ed., *Research in Economic History: An Annual Compilation of Research* (Greenwich, Conn.: JAI Press, 1978), pp. 161–216; Allan Pred, *Urban Growth and City-Systems in the United States, 1840–1860* (Cambridge, Mass.: Harvard University Press, 1980).

2. John R. Commons, "American Shoemakers, 1648–1895: A Sketch of Industrial Evolution," *Quarterly Journal of Economics* 24 (November 1909): 78, 81; idem, *Labor and Administration* (New York: Macmillan, 1913); idem, et al., *History of Labour in the United States*, 4 vols. (New York: Macmillan, 1918–1935), 2:6–7; Selig Perlman, *A History of Trade Unionism in the United States* (New York: Macmillan, 1922); idem, *A Theory of the Labor Movement* (New York: Macmillan, 1928); David Brody, "The Old Labor History and the New: In Search of an American Working Class," *Labor History* 20 (Winter 1979): 112.

3. David Montgomery, "To Study the People: The American Working Class," *Labor History* 21 (Fall 1980): 485; Commons et al., *History of Labour*, 1:176–77, 582. For other assessments of the contribution made by Commons and his associates, see Thomas A. Krueger, "American Labor Historiography, Old and New: A Review Essay," *Journal of Social History* 4 (Spring 1971): 277–85; Robert H. Zieger, "Workers and Scholars: Recent Trends in American Labor Historiography," *Labor History* 13 (Spring 1972): 245–66; Herbert G. Gutman, "Work, Culture, and Society in Industrializing America, 1815–1919," *American Historical Review* 78 (June 1973): 531–88; Alan Dawley, *Class and Community: The Industrial Revolution in Lynn* (Cambridge, Mass.: Harvard University Press, 1976), pp. 31–32, 180–83; Robert Ozanne, "Trends in American Labor History," *Labor History* 21 (Fall 1980): 513–21; Melvyn Dubofsky, "Give Us That Old Time Labor History: Philip S. Foner and the American Worker," *Labor History* 26 (Winter 1985): 118–37.

4. Eric Lampard, "American Historians and the Study of Urbanization," *American Historical Review* 67 (October 1961): 49, 54, 60–61; Roy Lubove, "The Urbanization Process: An Approach to Historical Research," *Journal of the American Institute of Planners* 33 (January 1967): 33, 35, 37; Theodore Hershberg, "The New Urban History: Toward an Interdisciplinary History of the City," *Journal of Urban History* 5 (November 1978): 5–8; Eric E. Lampard, "Urbanization and Social Change: On Broadening the Scope and Relevance of Urban History," in Oscar Handlin and John Burchard, eds., *The Historian and the City* (Cambridge, Mass.: MIT Press, 1963), pp. 233–34, 237; Michael H. Ebner, "Urban History: Retrospect and Prospect," *Journal of American History* 68 (June 1981): 71–74. For two other recent reflections on urban history, see Michael Frisch, "American Urban History as an Example of Recent Historiography,"

History and Theory 18 (October 1979): 350–77; Kathleen Neils Conzen, "Community Studies, Urban History, and American Local History," in Michael Kammen, ed., *The Past Before Us: Contemporary Historical Writing in the United States* (Ithaca: Cornell University Press, 1980), pp. 270–91.

5. Sean Wilentz, *Chants Democratic: New York City and the Rise of the American Working Class, 1788–1850* (New York: Oxford University Press, 1984), p. 6; Caroline Ware, *The Early New England Cotton Manufacture: A Study in Industrial Beginnings* (Boston: Houghton Mifflin, 1931); Vera Shlakman, "Economic History of a Factory Town: A Study of Chicopee, Massachusetts," *Smith College Studies in History* 20, nos. 1–4 (October 1934-July 1935); Hannah Josephson, *The Golden Threads: New England's Mill Girls and Magnates* (New York: Duell, Sloan and Pearce, 1949); Jacob H. Hollander and George E. Barnett, eds., *Studies in American Trade Unionism* (New York: Henry Holt and Co., 1906); George E. Barnett, "The Printers: A Study in American Trade Unionism," *American Economic Association Quarterly*, 3rd ser. 10 (October 1909); Don D. Lescohier, "The Knights of St. Crispin, 1867–1874: A Study in the Industrial Causes of Trade Unionism," *Bulletin of the University of Wisconsin*, no. 355 (Madison, 1910); Oscar Handlin, *Boston's Immigrants: A Study in Acculturation*, rev. ed. (Cambridge, Mass.: Harvard University Press, 1959); Robert Ernst, *Immigrant Life in New York City, 1825–1863* (New York: Columbia University Press, 1949).

6. Walter Licht, "Labor and Capital and the American Community," *Journal of Urban History* 7 (February 1981): 219–38; Sean Wilentz, "Artisan Origins of the American Working Class," *International Labor and Working Class History* 19 (Spring 1981): 1–22; Lynn H. Lees, "Metropolitan Types," in H. J. Dyos and Michael Wolff, eds., *The Victorian Cities: Images and Realities*, 2 vols. (London: Routledge and Kegan Paul, 1973), 1:413–28; Wilentz, *Chants Democratic*, p. 6; Olivier Zunz, *The Changing Face of Inequality: Urbanization, Industrial Development, and Immigrants in Detroit, 1880–1920* (Chicago: University of Chicago Press, 1982), pp. 16, 20, 92.

7. Anthony F. C. Wallace, *Rockdale: The Growth of an American Village in the Early Industrial Revolution* (New York: Alfred A. Knopf, 1978); Thomas Dublin, *Women at Work: The Transformation of Work and Community in Lowell, Massachusetts, 1826–1860* (New York: Columbia University Press, 1979); Dawley, *Class and Community*, p. 97. On single-industry towns in the early and mid-nineteenth century, see also Thomas Dublin, "Women, Work, and Protest in the Early Lowell Mills: 'The Oppressing Hand of Avarice Would Enslave Us,' " *Labor History* 16 (Winter 1975): 99–116; Lisa Vogel, "Hearts to Feel and Tongues to Speak: New England Mill Women in the Early Nineteenth Century," in Milton Cantor and Bruce Laurie, eds., *Class, Sex, and the Woman Worker* (Westport, Conn.: Greenwood Press, 1977), pp. 64–82; Philip S. Foner, *The Factory Girls* (Urbana: University of Illinois Press, 1977); Gary Kulik, "Pawtucket Village and the Strike of 1824: The Origins of Class Conflict in Rhode Island," *Radical History Review* 17 (Spring 1978): 5–37; Daniel J. Walkowitz, *Worker City, Company Town: Iron and Cotton-Worker Protest in Troy and Cohoes, New York, 1855–84* (Urbana: University of Illinois Press, 1978); Paul G. Faler, *Mechanics and Manufacturers in the Early Industrial Revolution: Lynn, Massachusetts, 1780–1860* (Albany: State University of New York Press, 1981); Jonathan Prude, *The Coming of Industrial Order: Town and Factory Life in Rural Massachusetts, 1810–1860* (New York: Cambridge University Press, 1983); John S. Garner, *The Model Company Town: Urban Design Through Private Enterprise in Nineteenth-Century New England* (Amherst: University of Massachusetts Press, 1984); Barbara M. Tucker, *Samuel Slater and the Origins of the American Textile Industry,*

1790–1860 (Ithaca: Cornell University Press, 1984). On single-industry towns in the late nineteenth and early twentieth centuries, see Stanley Buder, *Pullman: An Experiment in Industrial Order and Community Planning, 1880–1930* (New York: Oxford University Press, 1967); Tamara K. Hareven and Randolph Langenbach, *Amoskeag: Life and Work in an American Factory-City* (New York: Pantheon, 1978); Philip T. Silvia, Jr., "The Position of Workers in a Textile Community: Fall River in the Early 1880s," in Milton Cantor, ed., *American Working-Class Culture: Explorations in American Labor and Social History* (Westport, Conn.: Greenwood Press, 1979), pp. 189–207; John T. Cumbler, *Working-Class Community in Industrial America: Work, Leisure, and Struggle in Two Industrial Cities, 1880–1930* (Westport, Conn.; Greenwood Press, 1979); Tamara K. Hareven, *Family Time and Industrial Time* (New York: Cambridge University Press, 1982). The typology of cities adopted here is intended to be suggestive rather than definitive. It makes no mention of commercial cities, frontier communities, and other nineteenth-century urban formations. It identifies a wide range of settlements as single-industry towns, though significant differences existed among them. Finally, it does not take account of the stages in which cities developed.

8. Raphael Samuel, "The Workshop of the World: Steam Power and Hand Technology in Mid-Victorian Britain," *History Workshop*, no. 3 (1977): 45, 58; Michael P. Hanagan, "The Logic of Solidarity: Social Structure in Le Chambon-Feugerolles," *Journal of Urban History* 3 (August 1977): 409–26; Brighton Labor Process Group, "The Capitalist Labour Process," *Capital and Class* 1 (Spring 1977): 3–26; Bruce Laurie and Mark Schmitz, "Manufacture and Productivity: The Making of an Industrial Base, Philadelphia, 1850–1880," in Theodore Hershberg, ed., *Philadelphia: Work, Space, Family, and Group Experience in the 19th Century* (New York: Oxford University Press, 1981), pp. 53–65; Bruce Laurie, *Working People of Philadelphia, 1800–1850* (Philadelphia: Temple University Press, 1980), pp. 3–30; Philip Scranton, *Proprietary Capitalism: The Textile Manufacture at Philadelphia, 1800–1885* (New York: Cambridge University Press, 1983), p. 3; Wilentz, *Chants Democratic*, pp. 12–13, 107–42. See also David Montgomery, "The Working Classes of the Pre-industrial American City, 1780–1830," *Labor History* 9 (Winter 1968): 3–22; Gary B. Nash, *The Urban Crucible: Social Change, Political Consciousness, and the Origins of the American Republic* (Cambridge, Mass.: Harvard University Press, 1979); Howard B. Rock, *Artisans of the New Republic: The Tradesmen of New York City in the Age of Jefferson* (New York: New York University Press, 1979); Charles G. Steffen, "Changes in the Organization of Artisan Production in Baltimore, 1790 to 1820," *William and Mary Quarterly*, 3rd ser. 36 (January 1979): 101–17; Edward K. Spann, *The New York Metropolis: New York City, 1840–1857* (New York: Columbia University Press, 1981); Sharon V. Salinger, "Artisans, Journeymen, and the Transformation of Labor in Late Eighteenth-Century Philadelphia," *William and Mary Quarterly*, 3rd ser. 40 (January 1983): 62–84; Charles G. Steffen, *The Mechanics of Baltimore: Workers and Politics in the Age of Revolution, 1763–1812* (Urbana: University of Illinois Press, 1984); David Bensman, *The Practice of Solidarity: American Hat Finishers in the Nineteenth Century* (Urbana: University of Illinois Press, 1985).

9. Susan E. Hirsch, *Roots of the American Working Class: The Industrialization of Crafts in Newark, 1800–1860* (Philadelphia: University of Pennsylvania Press, 1978), pp. xix, 21–22, 24, 130; Steven J. Ross, *Workers on the Edge: Work, Leisure, and Politics in Industrializing Cincinnati, 1788–1890* (New York: Columbia University Press, 1985). See also Zunz, *Changing Face of Inequality*; Roy Rosenzweig, *Eight Hours for What We Will: Workers and Leisure in an Industrial City, 1870–1920* (New York:

Cambridge University Press, 1984); Frank G. Couvares, *The Remaking of Pittsburgh: Class and Culture in an Industrializing City, 1877–1919* (Albany: State University of New York, 1984); Richard J. Oestricher, *Solidarity and Fragmentation: Working People and Class Consciousness in Detroit, 1875–1900* (Urbana: University of Illinois Press, 1986).

10. Licht, "Labor and Capital," pp. 219–20, 229–32; Wilentz, "Artisan Origins," p. 18; Dawley, *Class and Community*, pp. 46, 57, 77; Hirsch, *Roots*, pp. 53–76; Walkowitz, *Worker City, Company Town*, pp. 156–57; Laurie, *Working People*, pp. 11, 16, 33–34, 53–66; Scranton, *Proprietary Capitalism*, pp. 138, 177–223 and "Milling About: Family Firms and Urban Manufacturing in Textile Philadelphia, 1840–1865," *Journal of Urban History* 10 (May 1984): 259–84. Both Walkowitz and Scranton emphasized that while ethnic and religious ties could promote working-class solidarity, they could also discourage the formation of class-based alliances. During the last twenty years, comparatively little has been written about the impact of industrialism on unskilled workers. Much of what we know must be gleaned from the studies of artisans already cited or from the works on ethnicity and immigration listed in notes 17 and 18.

11. Susan J. Kleinberg, "The Systematic Study of Urban Women," in Cantor and Laurie, eds., *Sex, Class*, pp. 20–42; Maurine Weiner Greenwald, "Historians and the Working-Class Woman in America," *International Labor and Working Class History* 14/15 (Spring 1979): 23–32; Elaine Tyler May, "Expanding the Past: Recent Scholarship on Women in Politics and Work," *Reviews in American History* 10 (December 1982): 216–33. The early studies of women workers include Elizabeth Beardsley Butler, *Women and the Trades: Pittsburgh, 1907–08* (New York: Charities Publication Committee, 1909); Edith Abbott, *Women in Industry* (New York: D. Appleton and Company, 1910); Anne Marion MacLean, *Wage-Earning Women* (New York: Macmillan, 1910); Margaret F. Byington, *Homestead: The Households of a Mill Town* (New York: Charities Publication Committee, 1910). For recent surveys of women and work, see Barbara Mayer Wertheimer, *We Were There: The Story of Working Women in America* (New York: Pantheon, 1977); Leslie Woodcock Tentler, *Wage-Earning Women: Industrial Work and Family Life in the United States, 1900–1930* (New York: Oxford University Press, 1979); Susan Estabrook Kennedy, *If All We Did was to Weep at Home: A History of White Working-Class Women in America* (Bloomington: Indiana University Press, 1979); Alice Kessler-Harris, *Out to Work: A History of Wage-Earning Women in the United States* (New York: Oxford University Press, 1982); Julie A. Matthei, *An Economic History of Women in America: Women's Work, the Sexual Division of Labor, and the Development of Capitalism* (New York: Schocken, 1982); Lynn Y. Weiner, *From Working Girl to Working Mother: The Female Labor Force in the United States, 1820–1980* (Chapel Hill: University of North Carolina Press, 1985).

12. On wage-earning women and the family, see Joan Scott and Louise Tilly, "Women's Work and the Family in Nineteenth Century Europe," *Comparative Studies in Society and History* 17 (January 1975): 36–64; Louise A. Tilly and Joan W. Scott, *Women, Work, and Family* (New York: Holt, Rinehart and Winston, 1978); Virginia Yans-McLaughlin, "Patterns of Work and Family Organization: Buffalo's Italians," *Journal of Interdisciplinary History* 2 (Autumn 1971-1972): 299–314; Daniel J. Walkowitz, "Working Class Women in the Gilded Age: Factory, Community, and Family Life among Cohoes, New York Cotton Workers," *Journal of Social History* 5 (Summer 1972): 464–90; Tamara K. Hareven, "Family Time and Industrial Time: Family and Work in a Planned Corporation Town, 1900–1924," *Journal of Urban History* 1 (May 1975): 365–

89; Carol Groneman, " 'She Earns as a Child; She Pays as a Man': Women Workers in a Mid-Nineteenth-Century New York City Community,'' in Cantor and Laurie, eds., *Sex, Class*, pp. 83–100; Laurence A. Glasco, "The Life Cycles and Household Structure of American Ethnic Groups: Irish, Germans, and Native-born White in Buffalo, New York, 1885," in Tamara K. Hareven, ed., *Family and Kin in American Urban Communities, 1700–1930* (New York: New Viewpoints, 1977), pp. 122–43; Virginia Yans-McLaughlin, *Family and Community: Italian Immigrants in Buffalo, 1880–1930* (Ithaca: Cornell University Press, 1977); Elizabeth H. Pleck, "A Mother's Wages: Income Earning Among Married Black and Italian Women, 1896–1912," in Michael Gordon, ed., *The American Family in Social Historical Perspective*, 2nd ed. (New York: St. Martin's Press, 1978), pp. 490–510; Thomas Kessner and Betty Boyd Caroli, "New Immigrant Women at Work: Italians and Jews in New York City, 1880–1905," *Journal of Ethnic Studies* 5 (Winter 1978): 19–31; special issue, "Immigrant Women and the City," *Journal of Urban History* 4 (May 1978): 251–359.

13. On the particular occupations in which women worked, see David M. Katzman, *Seven Days a Week: Women and Domestic Service in Industrializing America* (New York: Oxford University Press, 1978); Daniel E. Sutherland, *Americans and Their Servants: Domestic Service in the United States from 1800 to 1920* (Baton Rouge: Louisiana State University Press, 1981); Faye E. Dudden, *Serving Women: Household Service in Nineteenth-Century America* (Middletown, Conn.: Wesleyan University Press, 1983); Mary H. Blewett, "Work, Gender, and the Artisan Tradition in New England Shoemaking, 1780–1860," *Journal of Social History* 17 (Winter 1983): 221–48; Christine Stansell, "The Origins of the Sweatshop: Women and Early Industrialization in New York City," in Michael H. Frisch and Daniel J. Walkowitz, eds., *Working-Class America: Essays on Labor, Community, and American Society* (Urbana: University of Illinois Press, 1983), pp. 78–103; Joan M. Jensen and Sue Davidson, eds., *A Needle, a Bobbin, a Strike: Women Needleworkers in America* (Philadelphia: Temple University Press, 1984); Ava Baron, "Women and the Making of the American Working Class: A Study of the Proletarianization of Printers," *Review of Radical Political Economics* 14 (Fall 1982): 23–42; Susan Levine, *Labor's True Woman: Carpet Weavers, Industrialization, and Labor Reform in the Gilded Age* (Philadelphia: Temple University Press, 1984); Cindy S. Aron, " 'To Barter Their Souls for Gold': Female Clerks in Federal Government Offices, 1862–1890," *Journal of American History* 67 (March 1981): 835–53; Margery W. Davies, *Woman's Place Is at the Typewriter: Office Work and Office Workers, 1870–1930* (Philadelphia: Temple University Press, 1982); Barbara Melosh, *"The Physician's Hand": Work, Culture and Conflict in American Nursing* (Philadelphia: Temple University Press, 1982).

14. Scott and Tilly, "Women's Work," pp. 36–64; Stansell, "Origins of the Sweatshop," p. 92; Hirsch, *Roots*, p. 38; Kessler-Harris, *Out of Work*, pp. 124–25; Matthei, *Economic History of Women*, pp. 125–26; John Modell and Tamara K. Hareven, "Urbanization and the Malleable Household: An Examination of Boarding and Lodging in American Families," in Hareven, ed., *Family and Kin*, p. 167; May, "Expanding the Past," p. 223; Susan J. Kleinberg, "Technology and Women's Work: The Lives of Working Class Women in Pittsburgh, 1870–1900," *Labor History* 17 (Winter 1976): 58–72; Ann Oakley, *Woman's Work: The Housewife, Past and Present* (New York: Pantheon, 1975); Heidi I. Hartmann, "The Family as the Locus of Gender, Class, and Political Struggle: The Example of Housework," *Signs* 6 (Spring 1981): 366–94; Rae André, *Homemakers: The Forgotten Workers* (Chicago: University of Chicago Press,

88   LEONARD WALLOCK

1981); Susan Strasser, *Never Done: A History of American Housework* (New York: Pantheon, 1982); Jeanne Boydston, "To Earn Her Daily Bread: Housework and Antebellum Working-Class Subsistence," *Radical History Review* 35 (1986): 7–25.

15. Leonard P. Curry, *The Free Black in Urban America, 1800–1850* (Chicago: University of Chicago Press, 1981), pp. 21, 31–32; William H. Harris, *The Harder We Run: Black Workers since the Civil War* (New York: Oxford University Press, 1982), pp. 7–50, 59; Jacqueline Jones, *Labor of Love, Labor of Sorrow: Black Women, Work, and the Family from Slavery to the Present* (New York: Basic Books, 1985), pp. 111, 160–64, 167. See also John W. Blassingame, *Black New Orleans, 1860–1880* (Chicago: University of Chicago Press, 1973); David M. Katzman, *Before the Ghetto: Black Detroit in the Nineteenth Century* (Urbana: University of Illinois Press, 1973); Ira Berlin, *Slaves Without Masters: The Free Negro in the Antebellum South* (New York: Random House, 1974); Philip S. Foner, *Organized Labor and the Black Worker, 1619–1973* (New York: Praeger, 1974); Kenneth L. Kusmer, *A Ghetto Takes Shape: Black Cleveland, 1870–1930* (Urbana: University of Illinois Press, 1976); Herbert G. Gutman, *The Black Family in Slavery and Freedom, 1750–1925* (New York: Pantheon, 1976); Katzman, *Seven Days a Week*, pp. 184–222; James Borchert, *Alley Life in Washington: Family, Community, Religion, and Folklore in the City, 1850–1970* (Urbana: University of Illinois Press, 1980); Gerald David Jaynes, *Branches Without Roots: The Genesis of the Black Working Class, 1862–1882* (New York: Oxford University Press, 1986).

16. Herbert G. Gutman, *Work, Culture, and Society in Industrializing America: Essays in American Working-Class and Social History* (New York: Vintage Books, 1977), pp. 3–78; David Montgomery, "Gutman's Nineteenth-Century America," *Labor History* 19 (Summer 1978): 416–29; idem, "To Study the People," p. 501.

17. On the relationship between ethnic and class identification, see Harmut Keil, "The German Immigrant Working Class of Chicago, 1875–1890: Workers, Labor Leaders, and the Labor Movement," in Dirk Hoerder, ed., *American Labor and Immigration History, 1877–1920s: Recent European Research* (Urbana: University of Illinois Press, 1983), pp. 156–76; Richard J. Oestreicher, "Industrialization, Class, and Competing Cultural Systems: Detroit Workers, 1875–1900," in Harmut Keil and John B. Jentz, eds., *German Workers in Industrial Chicago, 1850–1910: A Comparative Perspective* (De Kalb: Northern Illinois University Press, 1983), pp. 54–69; John Bodnar, *The Transplanted: A History of Immigrants in America* (Bloomington: Indiana University Press, 1985), pp. 85–116; Ewa Morawska, *For Bread with Butter: Life-Worlds of Eastern Central Europeans in Johnstown, Pennsylvania, 1890–1940* (New York: Cambridge University Press, 1985); Dirk Hoerder, ed., *"Struggle A Hard Battle": Essays on Working-Class Immigrants* (De Kalb: Northern Illinois University Press, 1986); David Montgomery, "The Shuttle and the Cross: Weavers and Artisans in the Kensington Riots of 1844," *Journal of Social History* 5 (Summer 1972): 411–46; Edwin Fenton, *Immigrants and Unions, A Case Study: Italians and American Labor, 1870–1920* (New York: Arno Press, 1975); Laurie, *Working People of Philadelphia*, pp. 137–59.

18. On ethnicity, class, and urban residential patterns, see Eugene P. Ericksen and William L. Yancey, "Work and Residence in Industrial Philadelphia," *Journal of Urban History* 19 (Summer 1978): 416–29; Hershberg, ed., *Philadelphia*, pp. 128–203; Zunz, *Changing Face of Inequality*, pp. 40–59, 326–71; Kathleen Neils Conzen, "Patterns of Residence in Early Milwaukee," in Leo F. Schnore, ed., *The New Urban History: Quantitative Explorations by American Historians* (Princeton: Princeton University Press,

1975), pp. 145–83; idem, *Immigrant Milwaukee, 1836–1860: Accommodation and Community in a Frontier City* (Cambridge, Mass.: Harvard University Press, 1976).

19. Harry Braverman, *Labor and Monopoly Capital: The Degradation of Work in the Twentieth Century* (New York: Monthly Review Press, 1974); David F. Noble, *America by Design: Science, Technology, and the Rise of Corporate Capitalism* (New York: Alfred A. Knopf, 1977); Christopher Lasch, "Mass Culture Reconsidered," *Democracy* 1 (October 1981): 18.

20. Stanley Aronowitz, "Marx, Braverman, and the Logic of Capital," *Insurgent Sociologist* 8 (Fall 1978): 126–46; David Montgomery, *Workers' Control in America: Studies in the History of Work, Technology, and Labor Struggles* (New York: Cambridge University Press, 1979), pp. 9–31; Helen C. Callahan, "Upstairs-Downstairs in Chicago, 1870–1907: The Glessner Household," *Chicago History* 6 (Winter 1977–78): 195–209; Alice Kessler-Harris, "Organizing the Unorganizable: Three Jewish Women and Their Union," *Labor History* 17 (Winter 1976): 5–23; Mary H. Blewett, "The Union of Sex and Craft in the Haverhill Shoe Strike of 1895," *Labor History* 20 (Summer 1979): 352–75; Susan Porter Benson, *Counter Cultures: Saleswomen, Managers, and Customers in American Department Stores, 1890–1940* (Urbana: University of Illinois Press, 1986). On workers' control, see also Stephen A. Marglin, "What Do Bosses Do? The Origins and Functions of Hierarchy in Capitalist Production," *Review of Radical Political Economics* 6 (Summer 1974): 113–74; Michael Burawoy, *Manufacturing Consent: Changes in the Labor Process under Capitalism* (Chicago: University of Chicago Press, 1979); Dan Clawson, *Bureaucracy and the Labor Process: The Transformation of U.S. Industry, 1860–1920* (New York: Monthly Review Press, 1980); Walter Licht, *Working for the Railroad: The Organization of Work in the Nineteenth Century* (Princeton: Princeton University Press, 1983); Herbert G. Gutman and Donald H. Bell, eds., *The New England Working Class and the New Labor History* (Urbana: University of Illinois Press, 1986).

21. For a discussion of European scholarship that has influenced American labor historians, see Gutman, *Work, Culture, and Society*, p. 11.

22. Alan Dawley and Paul Faler, "Working Class Culture and Politics in the Industrial Revolution: Sources of Loyalism and Rebellion," *Journal of Social History* 9 (June 1976): 466–80; Laurie, *Working People of Philadelphia*, pp. 33–83, 161–87; Kulik, "Pawtucket Village," pp. 6, 14–19; Ross, *Workers on the Edge*, pp. 141–92; Peter Friedlander, *The Emergence of a UAW Local, 1936–1939: A Study in Class and Culture* (Pittsburgh: University of Pittsburgh Press, 1975). See also Wallace, *Rockdale*, pp. 243–95; Friedrich Lenger, "Class, Culture, and Class Consciousness in Ante-bellum Lynn: A Critique of Alan Dawley and Paul Faler," *Social History* 6 (October 1981): 317–32; Bryan D. Palmer, "Classifying Culture," *Labour/Le Travailleur* 8/9 (Autumn-Spring 1981–1982): 153–83.

23. Richard Edwards, *Contested Terrain: The Transformation of the Workplace in the Twentieth Century* (New York: Basic Books, 1979), pp. 21, 184, 186, 189, 192; David M. Gordon, Richard Edwards, and Michael Reich, *Segmented Work, Divided Workers: The Historical Transformation of Labor in the United States* (New York: Cambridge University Press, 1982). See also Peter B. Doeringer and Michael J. Piore, *Internal Labor Markets and Manpower Analysis* (Lexington, Mass.: Lexington Books, 1971); Richard C. Edwards, Michael Reich, and David M. Gordon, eds., *Labor Market Segmentation* (Lexington, Mass.: Lexington Books, 1975).

5 ———— New Life for an Old Subject: Investigating the Structure of Urban Rule

JON C. TEAFORD

In 1883, the first volume of the Johns Hopkins University Studies in Historical and Political Science appeared, a scholarly monument to the birth of the history profession in the United States. Focusing on local institutions, this seminal work testified to the profession's early fascination with local government structure, a fascination that during the next few years produced Johns Hopkins monographs on the municipal history of Philadelphia, Boston, Saint Louis, New Haven, New Orleans, and San Francisco.[1] Anyone scanning the table of contents of these early volumes would think that historical and political science was chiefly the study of the development of local government structure. This was the subject on which the nascent profession cut its first teeth and tested its infant skills.

During the following decades, other books and articles tackled the troublesome question of how city government developed. Some journalist-historians like Lloyd Wendt and Herman Kogan focused on the fascinating scoundrels in the municipal past who betrayed the public trust but also left a rich legacy of rumors and tales worth repeating in popular histories.[2] Others like Ernest Griffith remained true to the Johns Hopkins tradition of "historical science" and offered dry but reliable accounts of structural evolution.[3] After the turn of the century, however, the history of city government was never again so near the center of professional concern as it was during the 1880s. Some continued to study the development of urban rule, but the major scholarly skirmishes within the historical profession were not being fought over the origins of mayoral prerogatives or the evolution of municipal powers.

In the 1960s, the much-publicized urban crisis focused unwonted attention on city government and injected some new life into the study of the municipal past. The result was a number of excellent works examining the boss-reform struggle that dominated urban politics between the Civil War and World War II. In his article "The Politics of Reform in Municipal Government in the Progressive Era," Samuel Hays introduced the major theme of these studies when he posited that the conflict between the political machine and civic reformer was a symptom of the social tensions and ethnic divisions fragmenting the American city. Thus the battle between bossism and reform was actually a struggle between the neighborhood, working-class immigrant interests and the native-born business elite who favored centralized rule by strong mayors and expert bureaucrats.[4] Alexander Callow's study of the Tweed Ring, Zane Miller's account of politics in Cincinnati, and Melvin Holli's volume on Detroit accepted this general approach, relating the history of urban rule to changes in the social structure.[5] Holli added a new corollary to the argument, distinguishing between the socioeconomic foundations of social reform and structural reform. Structural reform campaigns to revise the municipal framework and achieve honest, efficient, and inexpensive rule won the greatest following among upper-middle-class business and professional leaders. In contrast, the efforts of social reformers to secure municipal ownership of public utilities and better living conditions for the poor reaped stronger support from the working-class masses. Throughout the pages of Holli's study, as in the works of Callow, Miller, and Hays, demands for reform and expressions of loyalty to the political machine are not ideological positions arising in a socioeconomic vacuum. Instead, in these works urban government rests on an unstable social structure riddled by ethnic animosities, cultural conflicts, and economic rifts.

In the 1970s and the 1980s, other historians have continued to focus on the social, ethnic, and cultural foundations of urban government, applying new techniques to the search for underlying political motives. John Allswang and Martin Shefter have painstakingly computed correlation and regression coefficients for social class, ethnicity, and voter preference in the boss-reform contests of the late nineteenth and early twentieth centuries.[6] Eugene J. Watts has applied political prosopography, collecting and analyzing the social, economic, and occupational characteristics of municipal officeholders in Atlanta between 1865 and 1903.[7] Most recently, a number of essays in a book edited by Ronald P. Formisano and Constance K. Burns on the evolution of Boston politics have emphasized the complex ethnocultural attitudes influencing relations between Yankee reformers and Irish machine politicians.[8] In each of these studies, the authors have accepted the notion that American municipal government is more than the formal flowchart of authority found in traditional civics texts. The history of urban government is as much the story of the changing social structure as it is a chronicle of charters, ordinances, and bureaus.

In the late 1970s and the 1980s, the range of research on the history of urban rule has broadened still further, opening new prospects for future investigation and raising new questions about the municipal past. Increasingly historians are examining not only the social tensions that motivated structural change but studying other significant factors as well. During the past ten years, a number of scholars have realized that a knowledge of social, economic, and cultural origins of boss-reform conflict is necessary but not sufficient for an understanding of the evolution of urban government.

Building on the research of such public works historians as Joel Tarr, some recent studies have attempted to relate the evolution of public services to changes in the governmental framework.[9] In *The Unheralded Triumph: City Government in America, 1870–1900*, I deal, in part, with the development of municipal functions and the consequent impact on the distribution of authority within the formal and informal structure of urban rule. For example, I find that demands for improved fire protection resulted in professional fire department bureaucracies that nurtured an independent power base. Also fire insurance interests formed an extralegal body of decision makers that pressured the cities to maintain first-rate service and allied themselves with the nonpartisan bureaucrats. In virtually every field of municipal endeavor, there was this symbiotic relationship between improved services and a burgeoning professionalism bolstered by private interests eager for the advantage of nonpartisan administration. Thus the development of municipal services in the late nineteenth century was intimately tied to the emergence of career bureaucrats as a new power bloc in the governing structure and was also linked to the mobilization of new pressure groups outside the formal framework of urban rule. Social and ethnic tensions were certainly the catalyst of much structural change and political conflict. But the development of new services created bureaucratic and special-interest factions that transcended ethnic loyalties and forced the redrawing of lines of municipal authority. Irish fire chiefs and Yankee insurance underwriters formed an alliance that centered on their common dedication to a certain public service rather than their ethnic or social standing.[10]

Others have also related the development of the urban infrastructure and public services to the evolving system of city government. In *Stamford in the Gilded Age: The Political Life of a Connecticut Town, 1868–1893*, Estelle F. Feinstein argues that heightened demands for municipal services as well as the emerging political activism of the community's Irish minority forced Stamford to abandon its borough-town form of government and to reorganize as a city. Tracing the history of Stamford's government during a period when its population rose from 10,000 to 16,000, Feinstein describes the conflicts over public works, health policy, schools, and welfare programs, consistently weaving demand for improved services with strands of ethnic and social group antipathy. She does not view Stamford's changing structure of government as solely a product of social tension or as solely a knee-jerk response to the need for sewers or schools. Instead, in Feinstein's study, the structure of government and politics is a rich fabric with social demands and service expectations combined in a complex pattern. A publication of the Stamford Historical Society, Feinstein's work offers much more than the standard local history. It presents a thorough and intelligent analysis of the forces producing governmental change.[11]

More recently Harold L. Platt in *City Building in the New South: The Growth of Public Services in Houston, Texas, 1830–1910* has attempted to interrelate class biases, the development of public services, and the changing structure of municipal rule. After a short survey of the evolution of municipal functions in antebellum Houston, Platt examines the commercial-civic elite that dominated city government during the Reconstruction era and pursued a policy of municipal borrowing in order to finance transportation lines and public construction projects. When depression struck in the mid-1870s, the burden of interest payments brought Houston to its knees, and cries of retrenchment halted ambitious improvement schemes. Throughout the 1880s, an emerging group of ward-centered politicians remained cautious about public expenditures. By the 1890s, however, Houston residents were calling for better services, and voters grew increasingly antagonistic to the city's privately owned public utilities and to the ward-based politicians in city hall. As a result, in 1904 the commercial-civic elite was able to win approval for a commission form of government, thereby sharply curbing the influence of the neighborhood politicians and shifting political power up the social ladder.[12]

Thus both Platt and Feinstein place public services and the creation of the urban infrastructure back into the story of city government. Many early twentieth-century commentators viewed the history of urban rule as a moral struggle between the forces of good represented by reformers and the forces of evil personified by the boss. The development of public services was tangential to their tale, appearing only in the scandal-stained pages when a vivid example of boss venality was needed. In the work of Samuel Hays and other historians of the 1960s, a sharp focus on the social pattern of urban politics similarly precluded much attention on waterworks, sewers, and street lighting. In my work, however, and in the local studies of Stamford and Houston, public services are essential elements in the story of municipal government, not just dependent variables reflecting the social attitudes or the personal immorality of urban decision makers. Fire and police protection, water supply, and garbage collection are the business of city government, and they deserve a central place in the history of urban rule.

Whereas the work of Feinstein and Platt exemplifies a new interest in municipal services, another body of literature is developing that emphasizes the dollars-and-cents factors influencing the governmental structure. In the past, historians of urban government and politics often have written as if their cast of characters operated in a world lacking any fiscal constraints. Morality or social-class biases determined the actions of bosses and reformers; money was no object. Yet in fact money was the root of many problems in city government, and the municipal ledgers tell as much about urban rule as the sensational campaign rhetoric appearing in front-page newspaper columns. What was the effect of the community's economic base on its political structure? And how did the budgetary process direct the course of urban government? In the 1970s and 1980s, these questions finally have attracted the attention of scholars.

Among the works adopting this economic approach to city government is Alan D. Anderson's *The Origin and Resolution of an Urban Crisis: Baltimore, 1890–1930*. Anderson forthrightly asserts that in progressive-era Baltimore, the institutional structure was of secondary importance when compared to technological and economic factors, for politicians "must always operate within the narrow constraints of technological and economic imperatives."[13] Having discarded political institutions as minor elements in municipal decision making, Anderson then proceeds to explain the "urban crisis" of the turn of the century with a dizzying display of economic theory. Anderson believes that American cities suffered a governmental crisis because increased urban population densities resulted in heightened demands for improved municipal services that would make life in the congested city bearable. Moreover, density drove land prices up, increasing costs for the private and public sectors and straining the municipal pocketbook. The electrification of the streetcar and advent of the automobile finally relieved the city treasury by encouraging needed decentralization.

Anderson's analysis is a fascinating exercise in theory, but it does not necessarily rest on a firm factual foundation. First, one may question whether there was a crisis in city government at the turn of the century. Anderson exaggerates the woeful shortcomings of municipal rule, though admittedly Baltimore did not rank among the best-governed American cities. Second, it is difficult to accept Anderson's preoccupation with population densities and land values. Advances in bacteriology rather than population densities were instrumental in the expansion of public health services. The growing influence of the city's engineering bureaucracy may have had a greater impact on expenditures for sewers or reservoirs than did any change in land prices. Economic theories that neglect the myriad of vectors in the decision-making formula can hardly arrive at the correct answer. Third, by focusing on land values, Anderson understates the importance of labor costs for municipal government. With its vast army of firefighters, police officers, teachers, street sweepers, and garbage collectors, city government was a labor-intensive enterprise. Since municipalities garnered the bulk of their revenues from real property taxes, the rise in land values in the urban core might actually benefit the city treasury by reaping increased revenues. In fact, Anderson's theory might work better if turned on its head. High property valuations in the urban core were responsible for a golden age in municipal finances at the turn of the century, an era of fiscal well-being that came to an end when automobile-induced decentralization undermined the central city economy.

Whereas Anderson's work is a great deal of theory based on limited fact, J. Rogers Hollingsworth and Ellen Hollingsworth's *Dimensions in Urban His-*

tory: Historical and Social Science Perspectives on Middle-Size American Cities is all methodology and little results. Dedicated to a "more theoretical level of analysis" than that applied in earlier historical studies of urban government, Hollingsworth and Hollingsworth investigate the statistical relationships of political, socioeconomic, and expenditure variables in late nineteenth-century cities of 10,000 to 25,000 population.[14] First, they present a scheme for categorizing cities in terms of socioeconomic-political structure, labeling some as autocratic communities and others as oligarchic or polyarchic. Next they proceed to empirical case studies of three oligarchic Wisconsin cities. Then they examine the impact of voting behavior on municipal policy and expenditures. Throughout they claim that a "community's economic base is the most important determinant of its social and political structure as well as its political process." Thus they conclude that "socioeconomic variables clearly shaped public policy," whereas such electoral variables as voter turnout, form of election, and competitiveness of electoral contests had "very little systematic effect on the level of expenditures."[15] Yet their methodological artillery actually slays few historical myths, and some of the intellectual spoils of their campaign are less than brilliant. For example, they conclude that there was a correlation between the level of municipal expenditures and the community's per capita wealth. In other words, communities with more money spent more than communities with less money. No one ever seriously doubted such a relationship.

One is left with a new appreciation of the aridity of theory and quantification divorced from an adequate understanding of the empirical and qualitative context. But Anderson and Hollingsworth and Hollingsworth also suggest exciting possibilities for future investigation. They eschew past interpretations and emphasize that the economic facts of life were important in city government. Perhaps the morality and social biases of urban politicians were of minor significance compared to the economic realities that fixed the limits of municipal action. Anderson and the Hollingsworths have asked pertinent and stimulating questions, even if their answers have fallen short.

Recently a group of social scientists has delved further into the history of financing American city government. Their tentative conclusions appear in a book edited by Terrence J. McDonald and Sally K. Ward, *The Politics of Urban Fiscal Policy*.[16] The contributors emphasize that the well-publicized battle between boss and reformer had little impact on the level of municipal expenditures. Working-class bosses were not invariably spendthrifts, and upper-class reformers were not consistent tightwads. Moreover, McDonald and his colleagues are not willing to accept the stance of Anderson and the Hollingsworths that municipal fiscal policy was dependent simply on underlying economic factors such as land costs or per capita wealth. In the minds of the McDonald-Ward authors, neither the social nor economic structure alone can explain the fiscal evolution of the municipality.

Instead these scholars recognize the influence of ideology and institutional structure on the financial history of city government. In his article on the fiscal politics of San Francisco in the late nineteenth century, McDonald argues that a bipartisan commitment to fiscal conservatism was the most important factor in determining the level of city expenditures. Both Boss Christopher Buckley and his reform foes shared this commitment to low taxes, pay as you go, and minimal expenditures, and this ideological restraint is the key to understanding municipal government in the California metropolis. These essays also emphasize the importance of the institutional constraints of the budgetary process. Each year department heads submitted budget estimates to the city comptroller, who then adjusted the figures and presented them to the city council for passage. At each stage of the process, next year's estimate depended largely on this year's expenditures. Consequently there were few sudden shifts in spending policy; the pattern of expenditures was stable and did not rise or fall sharply in response to changing political administrations.

Although each of the McDonald-Ward authors makes use of sophisticated quantitative techniques, their essays argue that nonquantifiable factors were most significant in determining municipal policy. The fashion for social history in the 1970s had shunted ideas and institutions into the scholarly closet, where only a few atavistic pedants continued to ponder these unfashionable topics. Now, however, the quantifiers in the McDonald-Ward book are arguing for a renewed consideration of ideology and institutional structure. The structure of city government might well affect the nature of municipal policy, and decision makers might act not only in response to unthinking social biases but also on the basis of well-considered political positions. In recognizing these facts, McDonald and his colleagues have made a signal contribution to the study of city government, and their essays are among the most stimulating published on the history of urban rule.[17]

The McDonald-Ward book is one of a series sponsored by the Social Science History Association, and it reflects the thinking of those enamored with the idea of applying social science methodology and theory to the study of history. Another group of historians also has looked to the social sciences for a new approach to understanding urban rule. This second group, including most notably David C. Hammack and Carl V. Harris, has followed the lead of sociologists and political scientists of the 1950s and 1960s who sought to map the community power structure. For these social scientists of the mid-twentieth century the formal structure of government consisting of the mayor, comptroller, and council was of little interest or importance. The important question was who really governed. Who, in fact, told the mayor and council what to do? Such scholars as Floyd Hunter and Robert Dahl wrestled with the question twenty-five years ago, and in the 1970s and 1980s, Hammack and Harris have similarly sought to diagram the actual distribution of power and decision-making influence in the city.[18]

In *Power and Society: Greater New York at the Turn of the Century*, Hammack tackles the nation's largest metropolis during the years 1886 to 1903. To discover who exercised power at this time, he analyzes four major areas of decision making. First he examines the selection of mayoral nominees and then proceeds to the struggle to unite New York City, Brooklyn, Queens, and Staten Island into Greater New York. Next he discusses the battle over the construction of New York's subway, and finally he investigates the clash over the centralization of school government and the abolition of ward school boards. According to Hammack, each of these areas of controversy affected a broad range of New Yorkers, was deemed highly significant by city residents, and stimulated heated debate for a number of years. Thus Hammack believes that analysis of these areas offers guideposts in charting the distribution of power in late nineteenth-century New York City.

Hammack concludes that "power was concentrated not in one or two but in several distinct economic, social, and political elites" that "engaged in a shifting complex of alliances, bargained with one another, and sometimes made important concessions to secure the support of other elites and of wider publics."[19] He claims that power was less dispersed than in the mid-twentieth century, but he surmises that by the 1880s and 1890s, the city was already moving in the direction of a wider distribution of power. No monolithic power elite ruled, but neither was New York City a model of perfect pluralism with power rationed equally among its citizenry.

One cannot take serious exception to Hammack's superb description of the four areas of conflict in late nineteenth-century New York. No other historian has written a better, more thorough account of the city's mayoral politics in the 1880s and 1890s, and anyone interested in the creation of Greater New York, the planning of the subway, or school reform should turn to Hammack's excellent chapters. Yet one might question whether Hammack has adequately described the exercise of power and the process of decision making in New York City. Despite the seeming conceptual sophistication of his work, his overall approach suffers from serious flaws. His narrow focus on controversies of general interest leads him to ignore issues and decisions that were highly salient to a smaller segment of New York City's population. Who had the power to make these decisions vital to some but not necessarily of interest to the whole?

The city's disposition of sidewalk space, for example, was probably a more salient issue to thousands of small vendors who sold their wares on the public walkways than was the consolidation of New York City and Brooklyn. New York City's aldermen made scores of grants of sidewalk space to vendors each year, and these governmental decisions were indicative of the small-time retailers' power within the system and their ability to get what they wanted from government. Yet Hammack ignores these decisions because they were not of citywide significance in the eyes of elite New Yorkers blind to these concerns.

Hammack also fails to consider issues that were highly salient to a limited segment of the business community. What power did the fire insurance interests have over decision making with regard to fire protection? The quality of fire-fighting services was a more significant issue for those whose insurance companies depended on efficient fire protection than was the reform of school government. But Hammack considers only his major areas of conflict and draws his conclusions from this special class of issues. Perhaps, as Hammack notes, no historian can deal with every decision made by New York City's government. Yet by limiting himself to only one category of decisions (those arousing general interest), Hammack offers a narrow, one-dimensional study of power in the metropolis. It would have been wiser to present examples of decisions of high salience to certain segments of the population, as well as examples of controversies stimulating general interest. Analysis of a more diverse variety of decisions would have more accurately illustrated the complex, multidimensional nature of power in New York City.

In *Political Power in Birmingham, 1871–1921*, Carl V. Harris does not adopt Hammack's strategy of investigating a few major controversies but instead examines interest group contention over the whole expanse of municipal activity, including everything from conflict over license taxes to the enforcement of vagrancy law. Harris provides a rich catalog of information describing which groups fought for which policies, and he demonstrates an admirable command of the nuances of Birmingham politics during the late nineteenth and early twentieth centuries. Because he deals with the broad scope of municipal endeavor, Harris offers greater insight than does Hammack into the variety of factors, participants, and interests confronting municipal decision makers. But this sweeping approach leaves Harris' book with a fragmentary, disjointed organization, for he must quickly touch on one area of municipal concern after another. He presents two pages on the regulation of smoke, then seven pages on the regulation of railroad crossings, followed by two pages on building and sanitation codes, and a scant half-page paragraph on weight and measure inspection. In each category he attempts to identify who dominated the regulatory process before moving on and repeating the question of who governed for the next area of endeavor. In the end, he offers the less-than-startling conclusion that "within each broad government function and each policy area, the consistent pattern was that among the groups which found the issues highly salient, greater political success went to groups of greater economic power."[20]

By focusing on interest group contention in the decision-making process, community power studies like those of Harris and Hammack tend to underestimate the significance of the institutional structure of city government. Community power studies conceive of government as a dependent variable responsive to whichever external interests push the hardest. Yet as the McDonald-Ward essays recognize, institutional structures may not be inert factors in the policy reaction between competing interest groups. Instead institutional procedures and customs may add an element to the compound of external interests. Thus the budget process may predestine a stable, incremental spending policy and thwart interests seeking sharp shifts in expenditures. Similarly the tradition of aldermanic courtesy, whereby each alderman is solely responsible for municipal business dealing exclusively with his district, might stymie the implementation of citywide standards or policies. Historians should recognize that institutional inertia is itself a force in the decision making process and that the system may be an actor in the drama of who governs.

If this is the case, historians need to devote more attention to this system. From the studies of public services and the McDonald-Ward essays on city finances, it is evident, for example, that the municipal bureaucracy merits more serious consideration than it has previously received. Officials in city departments drafted the budget estimates each year, and the city comptroller adjusted these estimates. Who were these persons? How did they influence decision making? Did they act to preserve the status quo, or did they foist reforms on city government? Robert Caro's biography of New York's Robert Moses describes how one appointed public servant manipulated the decision-making process in order to enhance his power within the governmental system.[21] Were there other characters like Robert Moses in cities across the nation during the nineteenth as well as the twentieth century? In *The Unheralded Triumph*, I identify a large corps of professionals employed by major American municipalities in the late nineteenth century.[22] They and their twentieth-century successors should be the subject of further research.

From this discussion of recent works on the structure of city rule, it is also evident that historians should turn their attention to the suburban municipality. The twentieth-century suburb has been an object of relative neglect, although by the 1970s the United States had become a predominantly suburban nation. How did the structure of municipal government adapt to suburbia? Who governed the suburbs as opposed to the central city? What institutions and interests molded the governmental destinies of suburban cities? A few historians have already explored these and related questions. In *City and Suburb: The Political Fragmentation of Metropolitan America*, I describe the rending of metropolitan America into rival governmental units and consider the factors contributing to this split. Thus I discuss the American tradition of permissive incorporation laws, the heated annexation battles of the nineteenth and twentieth centuries, and the futile attempts to create new federative models of metropolitan rule.[23] Moreover, Zane Miller's *Suburb: Neighborhood and Community in Forest Park, Ohio, 1935–1976*, examines the history of a planned Cincinnati suburb, recounting how residents developed community organizations and eventually fashioned a formal governmental structure.[24]

Another example of the emerging suburban genre is Carol O'Connor's *A Sort of Utopia: Scarsdale, 1891–1981*. Focusing on a posh New York suburb, O'Connor describes how Scarsdale's government of the wealthy, for the wealthy, and by the wealthy fashioned policy to satisfy its privileged constituency. Providing the finest in public services, Scarsdale was a model for other upper middle-class suburbs and a symbol of what suburbia offered to those who could afford it. O'Connor's excellent book says much about the adaptation of local government structure to the preferences and predilections of the upper middle class.[25] But more work is needed on the evolution of suburban government. The suburb is today the most significant element of local government. It is imperative that historians recognize this and apply themselves to rediscovering the suburban past.

The time is also ripe for historians to delve deeper into the period after 1930 when the federal government assumed new importance in the structure of urban rule. Mark I. Gelfand's *A Nation of Cities* chronicles the evolution of federal urban policy from 1933 to 1965, and Charles H. Trout's *Boston, the Great Depression, and the New Deal* discusses the impact of the Roosevelt administration on one aging northeastern city. More recently in *The Contested City* political scientist John H. Mollenkopf has viewed federal urban policy as a product of partisan self-interest with Democrats feeding the coffers of old Democratic central cities and Republicans bestowing federal largesse on the sunbelt and suburbia.[26] These works represent an admirable beginning, but more is needed on the actual implementation of federal programs in American cities after 1945. What was the impact of such notable programs as urban renewal and Model Cities on the local political structure, and what, in turn, was the impact of the local political structure on these federal schemes? In the past, historians of urban government have focused their primary attention on that great era of bossism and reform stretching from 1865 to 1930. Now scholars should move on to the troublesome years of the mid-twentieth century.

The investigations of the past decade have strengthened the historical profession's understanding of municipal rule, but they also have left much unsaid. Community power studies, essays on fiscal policy, and books that recognize the central significance of municipal services in the history of city government have contributed new insights, altering and enhancing the worthy findings of the boss-reformer studies of the 1960s. Today historians have a much sharper picture of the municipal past than they did in 1970. But the post–World War II era deserves added attention, the history of suburban government remains only partially charted, and the municipal bureaucracy is a subject of rich potential for future historical investigation. Although the study of local government long ago fell from its place of prominence on the historian's agenda, in the 1980s as in the 1880s it remains a topic that promises much in the coming years.

Notes

1. See Charles H. Levermore, "The Town and City Government of New Haven," *Johns Hopkins University Studies in Historical and Political Science* 4 (October 1886): 441–543; Edward P. Allinson and Boies Penrose, "City Government of Philadelphia," *Johns Hopkins University Studies in Historical and Political Science* 5 (January–February 1887): 1–72; James M. Bugbee, "City Government of Boston," *Johns Hopkins University Studies in Historical and Political Science* 5 (March 1887): 73–133; Marshall S. Snow, "The City Government of Saint Louis," *Johns Hopkins University Studies in Historical and Political Science* 5 (April 1887): 135–74; Bernard Moses, "The Establishment of Municipal Government in San Francisco," *Johns Hopkins University Studies in Historical and Political Science* 7 (February–March 1889): 71–153; William W. Howe, "Municipal

History of New Orleans," *Johns Hopkins University Studies in Historical and Political Science* 7 (April 1889): 155–87.

2. See, for example, Herman Kogan and Lloyd Wendt, *Big Bill of Chicago* (Indianapolis: Bobbs-Merrill, 1953), and their *Lords of the Levee: The Story of Bathhouse John and Hinky Dink* (Indianapolis: Bobbs-Merrill, 1943).

3. Ernest S. Griffith, *The Modern Development of City Government in the United Kingdom and the United States*, 2 vols. (London: Oxford University Press, 1927); *History of American City Government: The Colonial Period* (New York: Oxford University Press, 1938); *History of American City Government: The Conspicuous Failure, 1870–1900* (New York: Praeger, 1974); *History of American City Government: The Progressive Years and Their Aftermath, 1900–1920* (New York: Praeger, 1974).

4. Samuel P. Hays, "The Politics of Reform in Municipal Government in the Progressive Era," *Pacific Northwest Quarterly* 55 (October 1964): 157–69.

5. Alexander Callow, *The Tweed Ring* (New York: Oxford University Press, 1966); Zane Miller, *Boss Cox's Cincinnati: Urban Politics in the Progressive Era* (New York: Oxford University Press, 1968); Melvin G. Holli, *Reform in Detroit: Hazen S. Pingree and Urban Politics* (New York: Oxford University Press, 1969).

6. John M. Allswang, *Bosses, Machines, and Urban Voters: An American Symbiosis* (Port Washington, N.Y.: Kennikat Press, 1977); Martin Shefter, "The Electoral Foundations of the Political Machine: New York City, 1884–1897," in Joel H. Silbey et al., eds., *The History of American Electoral Behavior* (Princeton: Princeton University Press, 1978), pp. 263–98.

7. Eugene J. Watts, *The Social Bases of City Politics: Atlanta, 1865–1903* (Westport, Conn.: Greenwood Press, 1978).

8. Ronald P. Formisano and Constance K. Burns, eds., *Boston 1700–1980: The Evolution of Urban Politics* (Westport, Conn.: Greenwood Press, 1984).

9. Examples of the recent literature on municipal public works are: the special public works issue of *Journal of Urban History* 5 (May 1979); Louis P. Cain, *Sanitation Strategy for a Lakefront Metropolis: The Case of Chicago* (De Kalb: Northern Illinois University Press, 1978); Martin V. Melosi, ed., *Pollution and Reform in American Cities, 1870–1930* (Austin: University of Texas Press, 1980); Eugene P. Moehring, *Public Works and the Patterns of Urban Real Estate Growth in Manhattan, 1835–1894* (New York: Arno, 1981); Fern L. Nesson, *Great Waters: A History of Boston's Water Supply* (Hanover, N.H.: University Press of New England, 1983); Stanley K. Schultz and Clay McShane, "To Engineer the Metropolis: Sewers, Sanitation, and City Planning in Late-Nineteenth-Century America," *Journal of American History* 65 (September 1978): 389–411.

10. Jon C. Teaford, *The Unheralded Triumph: City Government in America, 1870–1900* (Baltimore: Johns Hopkins University Press, 1984).

11. Estelle F. Feinstein, *Stamford in the Gilded Age: The Political Life of a Connecticut Town, 1868–1893* (Stamford, Conn.: Stamford Historical Society, 1973).

12. Harold L. Platt, *City Building in the New South: The Growth of Public Services in Houston, Texas, 1830–1910* (Philadelphia: Temple University Press, 1983).

13. Alan D. Anderson, *The Origin and Resolution of an Urban Crisis: Baltimore, 1890–1930* (Baltimore: Johns Hopkins University Press, 1977), p. 8.

14. J. Rogers Hollingsworth and Ellen Jane Hollingsworth, *Dimensions in Urban History: Historical and Social Perspectives on Middle-Size American Cities* (Madison: University of Wisconsin Press, 1979), p. 7.

15. Ibid., pp. 29, 154.

16. Terrence J. McDonald and Sally K. Ward, eds., *The Politics of Urban Fiscal Policy* (Beverly Hills: Sage Publishing Co., 1984).

17. For a further critique of the social historians' neglect of politics and power relations in urban government, see Terrence McDonald's neo-Marxist "Comment," *Journal of Urban History* 8 (August 1982): 454–62. Additional neo-Marxist interpretations by non-historians are found in William K. Tabb and Larry Sawers, eds., *Marxism and the Metropolis: New Perspectives in Urban Political Economy* (New York: Oxford University Press, 1978), and Michael Dear and Allen J. Scott, eds., *Urbanization and Urban Planning in a Capitalist Society* (New York: Methuen, 1981).

18. Floyd Hunter, *Community Power Structure: A Study of Decision Makers* (Chapel Hill: University of North Carolina Press, 1953); Robert A. Dahl, *Who Governs? Democracy and Power in an American City* (New Haven: Yale University Press, 1961).

19. David C. Hammack, *Power and Society: Greater New York at the Turn of the Century* (New York: Russell Sage Foundation, 1982), p. 304.

20. Carl V. Harris, *Political Power in Birmingham, 1871–1921* (Knoxville: University of Tennessee Press, 1977), p. 270.

21. Robert A. Caro, *The Power Broker: Robert Moses and the Fall of New York* (New York: Alfred A. Knopf, 1974).

22. Teaford, *Unheralded Triumph*, pp. 132–73.

23. Jon C. Teaford, *City and Suburb: The Political Fragmentation of Metropolitan America, 1850–1970* (Baltimore: Johns Hopkins University Press, 1979). For an earlier account of annexation politics, see Kenneth T. Jackson, "Metropolitan Government Versus Political Autonomy: Politics on the Crabgrass Frontier," in Kenneth T. Jackson and Stanley T. Schultz, eds., *Cities in American History* (New York: Knopf, 1972), pp. 442–62.

24. Zane Miller, *Suburb: Neighborhood and Community in Forest Park, Ohio, 1935–1976* (Knoxville: University of Tennessee Press, 1981).

25. Carol A. O'Connor, *A Sort of Utopia: Scarsdale, 1891–1981* (Albany: State University of New York Press, 1983).

26. Mark I. Gelfand, *A Nation of Cities: The Federal Government and Urban America, 1933–1965* (New York: Oxford University Press, 1975); Charles H. Trout, *Boston, the Great Depression, and the New Deal* (New York: Oxford University Press, 1977); John H. Mollenkopf, *The Contested City* (Princeton: Princeton University Press, 1983). For other works dealing with the relationship between the New Deal and city hall, see Bruce M. Stave, *The New Deal and the Last Hurrah: Pittsburgh Machine Politics* (Pittsburgh: University of Pittsburgh Press, 1970); Lyle W. Dorsett, *Franklin D. Roosevelt and the City Bosses* (Port Washington, N.Y.: Kennikat Press, 1977); Roger Biles, *Big City Boss in Depression and War: Mayor Edward J. Kelly of Chicago* (De Kalb: Northern Illinois University Press, 1984).

6 ———— From Waterfront to Metropolitan Region: The Geographical Development of American Cities

EDWARD K. MULLER

Whether due to the investment incentives of recent tax laws or nostalgia for an imaginary romantic past, Americans are restoring and conserving the history of their cities at an unprecedented pace. They attach historical significance not only to buildings with special architectural characteristics or direct associations with famous people or events but also to entire districts with the ambience of past periods and social groups. This careful attention to the past has been shown to stimulate rather than hinder commercial development, attracting visitors and additional investment.

Ironically, at the very time that the public is expressing an increased awareness of a city's historical buildings and landscapes, urban historians are being admonished to integrate geographical perspectives and analyses into their studies of cities. The spatial configuration of the city and the built environment were more than passive settings for events. They were intricately interwoven with the livelihoods, life-styles, and organizations of urban life. A city's geography responded to changes in work, technology, and society and reciprocally affected the character of events, as well as the texture of urban life.

In the early years of scholarly inquiry into the history of the city, the 1940s and 1950s, historians generally treated the physical city as a site where events occurred. Despite a rich spatial tradition in the writings of urban-oriented social scientists, historians remained largely unconcerned with the city's past geography.[1] Conversely, social scientists ignored the city's history with the exception of a few scholars who compared contemporary residential patterns, usually termed its social ecology, with the classical descriptions of early twentieth-century cities produced often by University of Chicago sociologists.[2] Although this work involved temporal comparisons, it was not expressly historical in purpose or methodology. At about the same time American geographers were examining the population growth of cities and their economic roles in the development of regions and urban systems, but the few geographers with historical inclinations usually studied rural settlement patterns.[3]

In the 1960s historians discovered the city's geographical past. Seminal works by a few historians and geographers and the related emergence of the new urban and social history established the importance of understanding a city's changing geography. Richard Wade's monographs on urban growth in the Ohio Valley frontier and slavery in antebellum southern cities included the spatial themes of residential patterning and segregation, while Sam Bass Warner, Jr.'s, studies of Philadelphia and suburban growth around nineteenth-century Boston explored the spatial patterns of residential expansion, the processes of land development, and the social composition of different areas and neighborhoods.[4] Concurrently, historians were reading the books of geographers Allan Pred, whose work on urban industrial growth included a chapter on the location of manufacturing in early nineteenth-century New York City, and David Ward, who offered an interpretation of the changing geography of industrializing cities.[5] In significant review essays, Roy Lubove urged fellow historians to concentrate on the "city building process," and Warner proposed that the changing organization of work, associated residential environments, and the overall social geography of the city held important implications for understanding the political and social aspects of urban history.[6]

These exhortations fit comfortably with the directions in which proponents of the new urban and social history were moving.[7] With interests in common people and social issues, social theory and quantitative analysis, and interdisciplinary and international exchange, these historians often enthusiastically adopted the theoretical perspectives and spatial methodology of social ecologists and geographers. Although nongeographical questions motivated this historical scholarship, after 1970 most studies incorporated, though not always successfully, some consideration of a city's geography, and a few directly addressed the problems of changing spatial patterns and processes.[8] Moreover, the new urban historians interacted frequently with a small cadre of urban historical geographers.[9]

The publication of *From Downtown to No Town* in 1979 seemed to ensure a central place for geography in urban historical studies. In this popular text, David Goldfield and Blaine Brownell emphasized spatial themes as a means of integrating the diverse phenomena occurring in the city.[10] Their presentation represented a general consensus about the typical American city's geographical structure at different periods in the urban past. Skeptics of the new subdiscipline frequently charged that urban historians errantly included all that occurred within a city under the urban history rubric. Advocates pointed to the existence of distinctive urban politics and political institutions, urban behavior, social institutions, and now urban built environments and spatial patterns, all of which have a history in need of understanding and interpretation. By the late 1970s, conference programs, professional journals, and monographs routinely incorporated spatial themes without special acknowledgment.

In 1978, however, an early proponent of the new urban history, Theodore Hershberg, concluded that conceptual confusion persisted in urban history because historians had failed to clarify the relationships between environment (that is, the ecological or geographical context) and behavior in the city. As a consequence, they had not distinguished what was distinctively urban from what was common to other social trends and, accordingly, did not capture the importance of the city.[11] Recalling the themes of Lubove and Warner, Hershberg emphasized the fundamental importance of the changing character, location, and interrelation of work and residence in shaping the urban experiences of families and groups. In a recent review of studies of Detroit and Hamilton, Maris Vinovskis also wondered why so few scholars have adopted a spatial analysis of cities.[12] While applauding the geographical perspective of one author, Vinovskis nevertheless admonished him for advancing potentially simplified ecological explanations for social behavior. Thus, after nearly twenty years of examining the changing geography of American cities, some historians are questioning the significance of our geographical understanding. They urge colleagues to go beyond the superficial level of spatial context and search for the meaning of past geographies for urban life. In recent separate review essays that extend this critique, historical geographers David Ward and John Radford question the consensus view of past geographical structures and stress the need to explore the more complex and differentiated spatial patterns embedded in the socioeconomic diversity of American life.[13]

During the nineteenth century, a variety of social, economic, and technological developments dramatically transformed the geographical structure of American cities. Functioning primarily as centers of commerce, cities before the 1830s were small in area, focused on central wharves and merchants' countinghouses, and marked by a heterogeneous mixture of land uses, at least as seen from a modern perspective. In the decades following the 1830s, cities were transformed by industrial capitalism, mass transportation, and extensive foreign-born immigration. By the early twentieth century, America's big cities had expanded miles beyond the narrow confines permitted by pedestrian movement, displayed dynamic high-rise downtowns, and contained districts of specialized economic land uses and distinctive social compositions. Moreover, this transformation seemingly turned the city inside out as the wealthy and middle classes moved to the new suburban periphery, abandoning older central neighborhoods to lower-income migrants. The restructuring of urban space involved processes of geographical expansion and intensification, although for some activities, these processes may be more accurately conceived as decentralization and centralization. At the same time, processes of land use specialization and social differentiation contributed to the new configuration of the twentieth-century industrial metropolis.

Historians originally conceptualized this spatial transformation in terms of a simple dichotomous shift from a preindustrial to an industrial society.[14] The early twentieth-century classical models of economic rent and social ecology purported to describe the city's geography that resulted from industrialization and were couched, often explicitly, in a context of dramatic change from an older, preindustrial world.[15] More recent research into eighteenth-century America has emphasized the prevalence of liberal individualistic values and commercial motivations, particularly in towns and cities, and traced the roots to an emergent capitalism in Western Europe. In this view of long-term modernization, American cities are seen as the colonial outposts of vigorous trans-Atlantic mercantile economies and European commercial societies.[16] A preindustrial conceptualization simply fails to convey the functional complexity, demographic diversity, and social divisions of these small cities.[17]

If we must recognize that the increasing scale, density, and heterogeneity of nineteenth-century urban life really occurred as part of a gradual modernizing process of capitalist development, then we must also alter our conception of unilinear industrial change in America by acknowledging its occurrence in different forms and places. For example, large-scale factory organizations dominated the New England textile industry by the middle nineteenth century, while smaller, diverse proprietary forms characterized Philadelphia's textile industry well into the mid-twentieth century.[18] Most nineteenth-century industries involved similar combinations of old, new, and transitional forms of production. Each form of production held different implications for evolving social and political institutions, as well as associated aspects of the city's geography.[19] Further, the mix of economic activities and rate of industrialization varied enormously from city to city.

Recognition of modernizing tendencies in early America and the complexity of industrialization—its long duration, social and economic diversity, and spatial variability—calls into question the general applicability of accepted urban geographical patterns, the timing of spatial change, and the interpretations of these patterns and processes. The remainder of this chapter incorporates aspects of both revisionist interpretations into an overview of the historical geography of the American city. Because the description of geographical patterns and change rests on too few studies that used longitudinal and disaggregated methodologies of spatial analysis and explicitly focused on the historical geography of the city, this chapter proceeds with the recognition that opportunities for research abound and a great deal of work remains to be done.

The chapter is divided into separate discussions of nonresidential and residential spatial patterns, though their interrelationships are both significant and partly at issue. Further, the discussion that follows employs a convenient chronology of commercial (pre–1830), transitional (1830s–1870s), and industrial (1880s–1920s) city eras, which roughly correspond to other familiar periodizations such as mercantile, industrial, and corporate capitalism or early, mid-, and late Victorian. All periodizations clumsily ignore the differential timing of urban development across North America. Indeed, such common conceptual schemes may well present the greatest barriers to rethinking our generalizations. By the 1920s, elements of a fourth era can be readily evidenced, and with the socioeconomic trends and governmental policies associated with the Great Depression and New Deal, World War II, and the immediate postwar years, the mid-twentieth-century city fully blossomed and captured the attention of the media, policymakers, and everyday citizens. Although this fourth era is beyond the scope of this chapter, its emerging elements in the last industrial era will be identified and a brief summarizing description presented as part of the conclusion. Social scientists, planners, and journalists commented extensively on the "modern" city developing around them, but historians and historical geographers have only begun to assess the era.

Nonresidential Patterns

Although the earliest planting of towns in North America often reflected administrative or military motivations, most colonial centers developed and functioned within the unfolding economy of the trans-Atlantic mercantile world. Thus, early American cities pursued commerce as either connecting points between the mother country and developing colonial hinterlands or points within the hinterlands of these seaboard centers and along trade routes to interior frontier settlements. With each succeeding phase of development as Americans marched across the continent in the nineteenth century, commercial cities arose to connect the new regional economies with the national trading system.[20]

This pursuit of commerce was the primary function of most cities, but during the second half of the eighteenth century, some merchants also initiated investment in manufacturing activities in order to satisfy expanding domestic markets. By the middle nineteenth century, industrial production began to replace commerce as the primary foundation of urban growth in many, especially older, cities. The emergence of corporate capitalism in the early twentieth century added substantial managerial and professional service dimensions to the city's traditional commercial and manufacturing activities.

Each functional period with its attendant organization of capital broadly framed the changing geography of American cities. Evolving technologies of transportation, construction, and power, various organizational forms of industrial production, and characteristics of the labor force shaped specific patterns of commercial and industrial land use within a system that valued land largely in economic terms.[21] Although some cities began as industrial investments and others on far western frontiers arose after urban industrial patterns were already established, most larger cities still initially grew as commercial centers and subsequently added manufacturing to their extant commercial structure. Thus, the sequence of land use change that proceeds from commerce has broad applicability despite differences in city site, age, and size that affected arrangement, density, and complexity of phenomena.

The Commercial City

With trade as its lifeblood, the inception point of the commercial city was a suitable wharf site alongside an estuarial bay, river, or lake, even for most western cities that also enjoyed rail service from their beginning. At the wharving area, both long-distance trade and the provision of goods and services for local residents converged and formed the city's focus. In a largely pedestrian city, when the circulation of people was by foot and of goods by wagon, access to the focus was important to residents and businessmen. Minimizing the costs of transshipments and reflecting the limited specialization of business prior to 1830, merchants combined office, showroom, and warehousing functions in one building located adjacent or close to the wharves. During trading seasons, the waterfront presented a picture of intense activity and confusion, dotted with piles of goods and storage sheds, clogged with drays, wagons, animals, and people, and framed by a mass of ships of all manner. Services for shippers and travellers located among the merchant and warehousing quarters. Nearby, or sometimes centered at the docks, a local marketplace housed purveyors of foodstuffs and artisan wares and attracted other retailers and artisans to the vicinity. Although residences fanned outward a few blocks from this waterfront center, shopkeepers, artisans, merchants, and laborers frequently lived at their workplaces amid the confusion of commerce and business in the central area. The combination of workplace and residence in one location also spread nonresidential activities throughout residential areas.[22]

Order among the chaotic concentration of activities came about as a result of the original physical plans and, ironically, further rapid economic growth. Unplanned irregular development along both the waterfront and intersecting overland routeways in America's earliest towns (such as Boston) contrasted with the regular geometry of bastide town plans used in many New England towns and the exhausting uniformity of the speculator's rectangular gridiron plan, for which Philadelphia was reknown and probably the American model aped by town builders across America. Elaborate renaissance and baroque designs gracefully shaped the development of only a few cities (e.g., Williamsburg and Washington, D.C.). Urban plans established precedence for market, wharving, and business locations, but the predominance of commerce and the profit motive for land valuation concentrated activity near the waterfront and frequently undercut original designs.[23]

The small colonial towns of North America's first century blossomed into large seaports and river cities during the decades of emerging political independence and new nationhood. Trans-Appalachian frontier expansion, industrializing European economies, and successful agricultural exports created tremendous commercial opportunities for American merchants and, accordingly, fostered rapid urban growth. The basic geography of the American port city did not change greatly during this golden era of commerce; however, an incipient specialization of commercial functions and land uses became evident. General commission merchants trading in a variety of goods and markets still located throughout the central wharving area. Others profited by concentrating on specific commodities or markets and, along with related artisanal services, located their warehouses near similar establishments, forming small, identifiable concentrations of leather, iron, food, or spirits merchants. Brokers without stock on hand and commercial services such as maritime insurance agents gravitated toward the new commodities exchanges, customs houses, and post offices that serviced the increased levels of trade. Built a few blocks away from the congested goods-handling wharving area, these institutions anchored an embryonic financial district. Artisanal trades continued to exist throughout business and residential areas, though in a few larger cities, a specific trade such as weaving or shoemaking sometimes characterized an adjacent residential quarter as a cottage-style industry.[24]

Despite the growing spatial order among some commercial activities, retail merchants devoted to ladies' needs and high-priced specialty items escaped the chaos and congestion of the central wharving district and formed an exclusive carriage trade street. Similarly, lawyers, other professionals, and elite citizens moved their offices and residences out of this burgeoning business district but rarely more than a few blocks away. Only the land or waterpower requirements of commodity processing, shipbuilding, and building materials manufacturing broke the centripetal pull of the central focus. Shipyards, ropewalks, iron foundries, slaughterhouses, brickyards, and flour mills dotted the urban and waterfront peripheries, while waterpower sites beyond the urban fringe attracted the larger textile and processing mills with their associated residential villages.[25]

The Transitional City

The successive adoption of steamboats, canals, and railroads after the 1820s greatly enhanced marketing opportunities for urban merchants. Once again, trade expanded rapidly, and merchants further specialized in specific markets. Big city populations soared past 200,000 by the end of the transitional era in 1880. The elaborated transportation network also gave urban manufacturers improved access to regional markets and raw materials. Manufacturers met the potential for expanded production in different ways with corresponding implications for the city's spatial structure. Older artisanal and commerce-serving manufactures persisted well into the late nineteenth century, but newer forms of production increasingly predominated and by the Civil War created distinctive employment districts within the urban area.

Iron foundries and rolling mills, makers of tools, locomotives, and agricultural implements, textile manufacturers, and even some resource processing turned to steampower, machines, the factory system, and railroad transportation to expand production. These industries located at the edge of built-up areas where large land sites and rail service were available for factories. If successful, they often attracted imitators, small associated shops, and services such as liveries and teamsters for local hauling. The resulting industrial district, in turn, spawned a small complex of consumer and personal services. Hundreds and thousands of workers, sometimes disproportionately male and ethnically specific, worked, and with their families lived, in these distinctive industrial sections contiguous with the expanding built-up area but a mile or two away from the city's original core.[26]

The product focus and labor force characteristics of the newly emerging industrial districts contrasted markedly with the continued diversity of employment in the central area. Some industries, such as ready-wear garments and shoe-making, expanded output by subdividing the production process and using cheap labor, made available by mushrooming immigration, for the less skilled tasks. While some of these manufacturers collected their work force at inside shops, others put out the work for families to complete in their residences.[27] Either way, the workshops of these manufacturers used inexpensive central warehousing spaces where they maintained access to the merchant's capital, marketing information, and transportation. These central warehouse-workshop areas expanded into older residential quarters, provided work for a large work force including young women, and sometimes subdivided into specialized product clusters along with associated wholesalers and merchants. Together with traditional wholesaling activities around the waterfront, the central warehouse-workshop quarters provided a great variety of employment opportunities for unskilled laborers, carters, teamsters, and semiskilled manufacturing workers in the heart of the city.[28]

Amid the clutter of this central workshop and warehousing district emerged the American downtown—that area of modernity and fashion that contained the city's premier retailing, office, and entertainment activities. Horsecars, omnibuses, and steam railroads enhanced the downtown's centrality in the expanding city and encouraged the removal of residences. Land values at the core sky-rocketed, and reasonably well-articulated subdistricts formed around the retail and financial embryos of the previous commercial era.[29]

The integration of markets across regions affected not only manufacturing production but also the way of transacting business.[30] Although proprietors and partners of manufacturing firms closely supervised their factories in the city, they increasingly depended on salesmen, manufacturer's representatives, bankers, and investment counselors to assist with nonproduction aspects of their business and with their private investments. Financial markets burgeoned as capital investment flowed into transportation (especially railroad stocks), land (the trans-Mississippi West), resources (coal, oil, timber, and precious minerals), and commodities (cattle ranching and bonanza wheat farming). Like their merchant predecessors, these financiers, agents, and brokers required face-to-face communications with investors and the status of prestigious addresses. They converted former merchant houses into offices, built solid masonry banks, and erected impressive cast iron fronted office buildings. From new residential areas outside downtown, these businessmen commuted daily to the new financial districts from which they developed and serviced the frontiers of their urban areas, their regions, and America as settlement swept across the continent.

Women from these same social classes also journeyed into the downtown of the transitional era city, but they came to shop, not to work. Retail merchants recognized the potential market of the growing affluent classes, encouraged a consumer behavior, and competed for such trade with advertising, stylish shops, and fashionable addresses. The fancy women's and specialty shops of the former carriage trade street multiplied and spread into nearby blocks away from the expanding office and wholesaling districts and along the transportation lines that served their middle-class customers. The resplendent tone of the new retail district was set by the emergence of the department store. In the 1860's a few enterprising merchants in Boston, New York, Philadelphia, and Chicago collected several retail functions under one roof in dazzling emporiums. Glittering from gas lighting, polished marble, glass display counters, and cast-iron fronts, department stores became shopping events. Attracting urban shoppers as well as tourists, they anchored the radiant retail district in downtown opposite the more staid but powerful financial district.[31]

By the end of the transitional era in the 1880s, the smallish, weakly differentiated city of America's commercial period had grown twofold or threefold in both population size and areal extent and subdivided into distinctive geographical sections. The vast opportunities for trade, investment, and manufacturing in industrializing nineteenth-century America not only employed new technologies but also spawned growing specialization of functions. While the burgeoning central business area sprawled over a goodly portion of the older city, it also became organized into distinctive cores of activity, reflecting the energy, complexity, and power of America after one hundred years of nationhood. But the central area and its related residential quarters shared the urbanized area with contiguous, semi-autonomous industrial districts linked loosely to the central core by financial and other economic relationships.

The Industrial Metropolis

The Twelfth Census of the United States (1900) advanced manufacturing districts as new geographical units for the collection of data, recognizing that the traditional political boundaries of cities no longer reasonably captured their extent and complexity. The city of the early twentieth century was indeed an industrial metropolitan region. The corporate organization of capital and new technologies of communication, energy, production, and construction extended the land use patterns of the transitional city outward several miles and additionally created satellite communities, separate and distant from the traditional core but still integrated closely with it. Long distances, more effective means of communication, large organizations, and unprecedented economic and social specialization differentiated this region into distinctive functional zones. By the Great Depression of the 1930s, the metropolitan region resembled an octopus (to use contemporary novelist Frank Norris' metaphor)—a single body with identifiable parts run by a central nerve complex and distinguished by several long arms with separate nodes giving it influence and control over the proximate area.[32]

The land requirements of production sites and wholesaling activities were significantly greater in the industrial metropolis than they had been in the nineteenth century. Electrical power, integration of formerly separate functions at one site, and continuous assembly processes emphasized horizontality that demanded enormous land assemblages. At the same time, shippers erected bulk goods terminals and massive railyards to handle the rapidly increasing flow of staple commodities, raw materials, and finished products. Peripheral locations became more attractive and feasible as truck transportation and telephones relaxed for some producers the severe constraints of communication and handling materials that had formerly supported agglomeration economies in the city's central area. The resulting decentralization of some firms and location of new ones along railroads and outlying waterfronts extended older districts into industrial corridors of factories, terminals, and power plants, dramatic for their spatial extent, vibrance, and technology. In every metropolitan region, some corporations leapfrogged the expanding urban area and built satellite industrial communities, often tied by both capital and managerial control to head offices in the central city but isolated from the destabilizing influences of big city populations.[33]

Decentralization of employment opportunities about the region in the initial third of the twentieth century did not, however, end the core-dominated metropolis. Although the proportion of metropolitan manufacturing employment working in the central city fell between 1900 and 1930, the central city still contained a majority of such workers in most metropolises. Older industrial districts from the previous era retained their prominence. In some traditional product lines, such as garments, workshop production expanded. Wholesalers and manufacturers of goods for the city market still needed the central location of the radially focused transportation network. In turn, the new electric trolleys provided access to the region's largest labor market, while fixed capital assets and established agglomeration economies exacted additional inertia.[34] As in the past, lofts and converted residences offered cheap sites, but many owners also demolished these older structures and erected block-size, multistory industrial buildings with the modern features of extensive window ventilation and lighting, reinforced concrete construction, and truck loading docks in addition to railroad sidings. The wharves and warehouses of the city's original commercial area became obsolete and blighted in the face of competition from bulk terminals and the construction of centralized, wholesaling cooperatives at inner-city railyards.

Although the tendency of producers and handlers of specific goods and com- modities to locate near each other provided a perceptual order to the vast central city, a closer examination of land use reveals a persistent intermixture of activ- ities, which concerned urban planners in coming decades. Nevertheless, large satellite industrial sites, new industrial corridors, older industrial districts, blighted central wharves, and specialized goods-handling areas established rec- ognizable land use zones in the industrial metropolis.

If mammoth, horizontal factory complexes represented the industrial character of the metropolis, then downtown and especially the skyscraper symbolized its sophistication and power. Initially banks and then industrial corporations erected buildings of a dozen or so stories at the turn of the century; by the 1930s corporate towers soared to dozens of floors. Piercing the urban skyline once dominated by shipmast, smokestack, and steeple, skyscrapers presented a visual focus for the city, which embodied the centralization processes of corporate capitalism. From these central offices, banks and corporations controlled or influenced through finance and management the development and economic destinies of activities within their region, throughout the continent, and in some cases even overseas (foreshadowing the post–World War II future). The sheer mass of tall terra-cotta and stone-faced towers proclaimed the awe-inspiring power of the new corporations, while the elegant architecture and lavishly styled interior spaces expressed the era's urbanity.[35]

Skyscrapers were not just built for prestige. They were also profitable in- vestments that capitalized on the major forces of industrialization. The corporate organization of business brought forth a white-collar work force of clerks, ste- nographers, and middle-level managers. Headquarters office buildings collected these administrative workers efficiently under one roof and also provided pres- tigious rental space for the burgeoning professionals of the industrial age: ar- chitects, engineers, investment brokers, and accountants. These professional, bureaucratic, and centralizing trends aggravated the scarcity of space in down- towns, and building upward offered a solution. Steel skeleton frames and ele- vators provided the technology for skyscraper construction, while mass transportation by trolleys and rapid transit by subway and elevated railways facilitated the ingress and egress of massive numbers of downtown workers. Bank towers transformed the narrow streets of the financial district into steep- sided canyons, while corporate headquarters were built on adjacent blocks, cre- ating together an office area within downtown.

With extensive trolley networks reaching out to consumers and the captive market of white-collar workers, downtown retailers enjoyed unprecedented op- portunities. At the same time, mass production fueled the mass consumption of goods formerly not seen as necessities. Five-and-dime variety outlets shared downtown retail space with more elegant department stores and specialty shops. The retail district expanded and subdivided by product and consumer class. The allure of downtown was enhanced by the mass entertainment of vaudeville, motion pictures, and in the 1920s, the popularity of jazz. Midday matinees and high-style restaurants catered to female shoppers, while travelling businessmen, tourists, and customer entertainment supported a flourishing hotel trade near new grand railroad terminals that now found room in downtown. Skyscrapers, department stores, theaters, hotels, and railroad stations epitomized the functional districts of downtown. Individual blocks within these districts catered to more specific markets, such as women's shoes, jewelry, or low-brow entertainment.[36]

Downtown reached its apogee in the industrial metropolis. Its dynamism, spatial specialization, and dominance over metropolitan functions were never greater. Major secondary retail centers arose to service residential sectors of the urban area, but they did not rival downtown.[37]

Residential Patterns

The transformation of the social geography of the American city has been variously described and explained in terms of functional-structural forces, cultural imperatives in our plural society, and the social relations of the changing mode of production.[38] Clearly rapid growth and changing technologies, evolving familial values and successive waves of immigration, and the changing organization of work significantly shaped residential patterns. The emphasis of one set of factors, however, belies the close interrelationships of all three sets. The peculiarly American configuration that unfolded reflected the operation of these various factors within the context of an evolving capitalistic economy, a persistent allegiance to the values of privatism, and a laissez-faire perception of government's role that was buffered by a recurrent liberal temperament. The resulting social geography was complex, often contradictory, and at times openly contentious.

The Commercial City

The interspersal of functions, social groups, and classes distinguished the social geography of the commercial city from that of later urban eras.[39] During the colonial years, there was a minimal geographical separation of functions and few, if any, employers large enough to impose a clustering of workers. At a time when people walked to work and spent long hours at their jobs, artisans, shopkeepers, and other proprietors frequently combined work and residence under one roof and sheltered dependent workers such as apprentices on their premises. Although the waterfront and marketplace attracted a large number of businesses, the dense development of small two- and three-story buildings on narrow lots and often winding streets forced many proprietors to locate their shops, and thus their homes, widely about the city. Without either significant divisions among the laboring classes of this artisanal system or overt ethnic antagonism, the scattered distribution of shops and workplaces fostered a mixed residential pattern of social groups.[40] Social cohesion formed around the interdependencies of family, workshop, and religion. As an exception to the general pattern, wealthy merchants, landowners, and colonial administrators congregated near their workplaces adjacent to the central wharves. This central location appropriately situated these leaders amid the nexus of culture and power in the small colonial city.

Rapid demographic and economic growth during the late eighteenth and early nineteenth centuries, together with the liberal ideology of the revolutionary age, produced ebullient commercial cities of markedly increased size, greater complexity, and some initial differentiation in social geography. Most well-to-do merchants capitalized on rising land values and fled the congested, chaotic wharving area for serene, exclusive quarters several blocks away but still within the city's central core. A few of the wealthiest citizens established country estates well outside the city. In the 1820s and 1830s, during the last years of the commercial city area, a few elites were attracted by the nation's earliest real estate developers to suburban sites on the city's periphery, where the steam ferry or omnibus provided transportation.[41]

The expansion of artisanal production and manufactories occurred incrementally away from the traditional colonial core, forming working-class quarters separate from the central elite blocks. Despite growing labor tensions, these quarters continued to display little ethnic clustering except for a crude patterning where concentrations of specific textile, leather, iron, or other trades created a coarse differentiation. The sharpest distinctions occurred at the fringes of the built-up area where poor and socially undesirable residents were relegated amid similarly undesirable industries, such as slaughtering and tanning. Although low-income families also found shelter in crannies and alleys throughout the central area of the city, their shanties and "disorderly houses" joined with the new institutions of the urban poor and transient—the asylum and workhouse—to define an ill-favored living space at the city's edge.[42]

The spatial gradient from a prosperous core to a less dense, poorer fringe reflected long-standing European urban patterns. In America, however, rapid growth and burgeoning economic opportunities induced increasing functional specialization and incipient social differentiation. It is instructive that the emerging social separation accompanied emerging reform efforts designed to cope with poverty, disorderliness, crime, transience, and independent work behavior.

The Transitional City

Although cities shaped by the preponderance of commerce persisted well past the mid-nineteenth century, especially west of the Mississippi River, the rise of industrial capitalism, in conjunction with increased immigration, ascendant domestic values among the middle classes, and an intraurban transport network, fashioned a new social geography by the time of the national centennial in 1876 when America celebrated its industrial progress. No one form of production prevailed in the city. Artisanal shops, mechanized and jobbing workshops, and the factory system existed side by side, creating a complex pattern of employment centers and associated residential areas. By diminishing the prevalence of independent artisans and employing wage labor more extensively, industrial capitalism generally separated the workplace from residence, severed paternalistic ties, and forced many workers into the general housing markets. An inadequate housing supply, relatively expensive transportation, and low incomes constrained housing choices for workers and emphasized proximity to employment locations in a city that had grown beyond the confines of older pedestrian limits.[43] Thus, employment centers, housing values, and incomes primarily differentiated the residential landscape, although other social divisions and persistent patterns from the commercial era complicated a simple class- or employment-based social geography.

The enormous growth of the central business area, a clearer separation of economic functions, and the emergence of downtown indicated substantial changes in the city's core, but at first glance some older central neighborhoods looked much like they had in the earlier commercial era. The fashionable blocks of the earlier merchants' community frequently resisted the encroachment of downtown, remaining an enclave amid the commotion of the transitional city. Similarly, some mixed neighborhoods of middling shopkeepers, proprietors, and artisans endured by virtue of their convenience to downtown employment and the strength of established social institutions. Nevertheless, the influx of immigrants and expansion of central commercial functions challenged the integrity of these central neighborhoods, while concomitantly new centers of employment and residential developments on the city's periphery offered alternative attractions for housing and work.

Workshops, warehouses, and downtown stores threatened central neighborhoods by not only their spatial expansion but also the substantial employment opportunities they extended to unskilled and semiskilled workers. The central business area provided the city's single greatest locus of jobs for day laborers, carters, cleaners, piece-workers, and handicraft workers in warehouse-workshops, among others. The low wages, insecure tenure, and long hours of these jobs created a propertyless class that soon overwhelmed many adjacent housing markets. Former single-family residences and artisan shops were subdivided and rented to families. Boardinghouses for single males and working women also developed, and frequently families took in lodgers. With this growing congestion and the inadequate development of sanitation services, living conditions deteriorated; and where poverty concentrated, slums emerged.[44] Thus, while some central neighborhoods of the wealthy and middle classes endured into the late nineteenth century, increasingly the working classes, including poor families and single persons, inhabited residential areas adjacent to the central business district.

The separate districts of industrial employment that formed along the waterfront beyond the central business area or beside railroad lines at the city's edge spawned adjacent working-class residential areas. Concentrations of specific industries, such as textiles, shipbuilding, leatherworking, or iron foundries and metalworking, distinguished one employment district from another, and consequently the trades and occupations of the dominant industry influenced the composition of the neighborhoods. In industries where specific immigrant groups dominated particular occupations and controlled the hiring networks, the adjacent communities developed old country overtones. Despite the flowering of ethnic churches, shops, and newspapers, the neighborhoods were rarely ethnically exclusive because the congeries of jobs from the many firms and services of an industrial district provided opportunities for a great variety of workers.[45] The most homogeneous social clustering of workers occurred beyond the edge of the city with the establishment of a large industrial plant. While some of these sites were only the older waterpowered mill villages of an early industrial era, many heralded the next era's industrial satellite towns where the owners of a new steampowered factory complex found it necessary to build housing for its large work force.

Thus the primary force behind the residential distribution of the laboring classes was the location of jobs, especially in the central business area and the peripheral industrial districts. The growing immigration of British, Irish, and German nationals after 1830 (and French Canadians to New England) added a new dimension to the city's social geography. However, ethnic clustering operated within the basic geographical framework of jobs, except in those few cities such as Milwaukee where unusually high levels of immigration fostered rapid ethnic concentration.[46] The ethnic division of occupations associated with specific industries produced ethnic neighborhoods, not exclusive ghettos, which sometimes attained enough local identity to attract pejorative names such as Dutchtown or Corktown. Over the decades, general patterns of economic mobility for a group— for example, moving from unstable, unskilled occupations to more secure skilled trades and petty shopkeeping or to rising middle-class occupations—strengthened ethnic concentration as in the former case or weakened it as in the latter. Regardless, during these transitional-era years, working-class neighborhoods, especially in the central city, more frequently contained a variety of immigrant groups both mixed among each other and clustered in adjacent pockets of a few blocks, forming a rich mosaic of plebeian life. The great variety of employment opportunities, scarcity of housing, and high rates of residential mobility or turnover mitigated against large and exclusive ethnic concentrations. Religious, social, craft, and political organizations provided a strong, interrelated network of community institutions and services in these teeming, mixed-heritage neighborhoods.[47]

The rapid growth of American cities during the second and third quarters of the nineteenth century required the construction of new housing at successively greater distances from the central business area. At distances of two miles or more, pedestrian access to downtown was no longer viable and certainly not desirable. The introduction of the horse-drawn omnibus between 1830 and 1850 provided a means of commuting for those few who could afford the time and expense of its slow and uncomfortable movement along congested streets. The main impetus for residential growth at the city's edge came from the rapid adoption of horse-drawn street railways in many cities after 1855. The cheaper, faster, and more comfortable transportation of the horsecar facilitated land development up to four and five miles from downtown offices and stores. By the 1880s, dozens (even hundreds) of miles of horsecar track radiated outwardly from the core to the new neighborhoods of the middle and upper classes. Surviving ridership records make it clear that the working classes lacked the income and flexible schedules necessary for regular commuting on the horsecars.[48]

The development of wealthy residential communities beyond the built-up limits of the city indicated that more than housing pressures and available transportation powered early suburbanization. Steam ferries and, after 1830, railroads carried businessmen to and from scattered suburban towns at distances from five to fifteen miles beyond the city. This suburban movement reflected an ambivalent attitude toward the city. While impressed by the economic opportunity, power, and modernity of the city, many also abhorred the congestion and chaos, growing foreign-born population, and perceived threats from crime and poverty. Withdrawal from the central city at mid-century and afterward not only offered opportunities for home ownership in socially homogeneous and safe neighborhoods but also coincided with growing romantic sentiments for rural virtues and an ideology that linked the family and home together as a moral bulwark against the evils of urban industrialism. Books and magazines idealized the private home on a separate lot encircled by a yard, where the housewife nurtured the moral development of the family. Although real estate developers and contractors built party-wall blocks with architecturally individualized houses throughout this period, freestanding villas and cottages in contemporary Victorian architectural styles increasingly characterized suburban residences.[49]

The suburban compromise for urban residents reflected American middle-class values and increasingly differentiated the city along class lines. The wealthy continued to form exclusive quarters, but now middling groups could consider separating themselves from the working classes and petty shopkeepers who remained tied to their work locations. Allegiances to traditional urban living and specific neighborhoods, the inadequacies of intraurban transportation and the housing market, and the rapid growth of population prevented suburbanization from fully transforming the city's spatial structure and maintained neighborhoods of mixed social composition. However, the allure of the private home in a pastoral setting was firmly implanted in the perception of the American city by the 1880s.

The Industrial Metropolis

Looking back over the previous two or three decades of his adult life, the denizen of a typical American city in the 1880s would have been impressed by how large the city had become. By comparison, a city resident in the 1920s, reflecting back to the waning years of the nineteenth century, would have been awed by the city's new population size and spatial extent. Whereas the population of the median large city in 1880 was nearly 125,000, in 1920 it was over 400,000.

The radius of the built-up periphery from the city's recognized center had increased from four to ten miles, encompassing a great variety of suburban and satellite communities. Further, the communities of this metropolis were far more socially and economically differentiated from each other than they had been at the end of the transitional era. The city resident of 1920 probably did not realize, however, that despite the unprecedented dimensions of the new city, its social geography bore a direct lineage to trends unfolding in the preceding urban era. The new wave of urban migrants, rise of corporate capitalism, and changes in transportation and the supply of housing accelerated the economic selectivity of suburbanization and segregative tendencies within the social plurality of American society.

Similar to the earlier transitional era, the pathbreaking communities beyond the city in the metropolitan regions were surfacially opposites—the industrial milltown and wealthy suburb—that were, in fact, linked at least abstractly through the management of capital in downtown corporate offices. Corporations constructed large factory complexes that brought small satellite towns into existence in a few years. Dominated by the plant's physical presence, production rhythms, labor policies, and tax revenues, these working-class towns projected distinctive images in the metropolitan region. They usually displayed a mixed ethnic composition and subtle social hierarchy, based on occupational differentiation in the factory and the composition of the local business community.[50]

If the large, noisy, and smoky factory proclaimed its dominance over the life of the milltown, the small railroad station, bucolic village, and adjacent cottages of gardeners and servants understated the pervasive presence of wealthy industrialists in fashionable suburbs like the northern shores of Lake Michigan and Long Island or Philadelphia's Main Line. Once the zone of manorial estates, cool summer villas, and weekend retreats beyond the congested city, these new suburbs attracted wealthy, year-around residents after the 1880s in sufficient numbers to build an elite society centered about the country club for social and recreational pursuits. These rural-feeling communities inspired the development of emulous upper middle-class suburbs, closer to the city but astride the same commuter railroads, that employed both community design controls and restrictive deed convenants to create the desired ambience and social exclusivity.[51]

While well-heeled suburbs and industrial milltowns led the invasion of the metropolitan countryside, the main bulk of urban expansion again occurred incrementally at the built-up edge, following the electric streetcar after the 1890s and the automobile in the 1920s. The significantly higher speeds and lower fares of the trolley extended the range of commuting and opened vast new areas of cheap land for the development of middle- and working-class housing.[52] At the same time, innovations in the building materials and construction industries, a new architectural interest in the common house, especially with the bungalow style, and more accessible financing arrangements greatly increased the supply of houses. While small real estate developers and builders dominated the conversion of rural land to residential neighborhoods, some large developers who integrated the entire development process were active in most cities. In some cases, trolley owners were also the developers of new tracts that transportation had made ripe for conversion. By the twentieth century, municipalities and private utilities accelerated the expansion by providing services in advance of construction.[53]

Despite the enormous growth of population during the industrial metropolis era, most large cities increased their housing stock at a faster rate than they attracted new residents. Correspondingly, the number of persons per dwelling actually decreased by 1930. With the notable exception of housing in New York City, single-family and duplex dwellings dominated the housing stock; generally less than 10 percent of all dwellings contained three or more families.[54] In these new tracts of inexpensive homes, city leaders and reformers saw the solution to older, crowded neighborhoods of the inner city.

Upward social mobility among older ethnic groups and growing numbers of middle-class families fueled the demand for the new housing. Corporate capitalism ballooned the number of salaried workers in managerial, administrative, professional, and clerical occupations, while public bureaucracies and municipal services provided vast new employment opportunities. By most indications, wages rose for tradesmen and skilled workers. Developers and reformers encouraged working-class families to pursue home ownership, often at considerable family sacrifice. Indeed, between 1890 and 1930, the rate of home ownership rose to between 30 and 50 percent in most large cities, and in many instances home ownership was higher for ethnic groups than for native-born Americans.[55]

The new neighborhoods spread out along radial trolley lines in a star-shaped fashion, although areas between the trolley spokes beyond walking distance from the lines remained weakly developed. Housing values, overall density, and landscaping appointments in different communities reflected the general income levels of prospective buyers at the outset, but in time rising land values and housing demand in more accessible inner suburban areas often led to increasing densities from both the subdividing of houses and multifamily construction. Even apartment buildings were built along major streetcar lines in these dense inner suburbs. During the 1920s, the adoption of the automobile for commuting by some middle-class residents extended suburban growth beyond the trolley's limits and initiated growth of the undeveloped interstitial areas passed over in the trolley era. While different levels of income, resulting from the more complex differentiation of labor, primarily distinguished these neighborhoods from each other, the reconcentration of an ethnic group or attraction of religious institutions with their associated schools and social organizations often provided distinctive cultural orientations.[56]

Despite the apparently pervasive character of commuting in the industrial metropolis, between one-quarter and one-third of a city's workers still walked to work at the time of the Great Depression. Laborers, cleaners, counter clerks, unskilled factory workers, and helpers of all kinds did not earn enough to join the suburban movement and remained close to the major employment centers in the industrial corridors or the central business area. Black migrants from the South as well as Southern and Eastern European immigrants poured into these older inner-city neighborhoods. Although a few well-heeled central areas persisted, suburbanization left in its wake a lot of housing that filtered down to these lower-income workers. Nevertheless, the old housing stock still could not accommodate the massive influx. Absentee landlords and immigrants themselves subdivided older houses and packed in tenants. Housing codes were hesitantly enforced as inspectors were easily corrupted or recognized that evicted residents had few alternatives for shelter. In some cities, most notoriously New York, speculators built multistory tenements with inadequate ventilation and sanitation.[57]

Slums of unprecedented size and deprivation emerged wherever labor migrants, impoverished and often immigrant families, and speculative investment in anticipation of land use conversion coincided. Overcrowding, deplorable housing, and an unsanitary environment appalled middle-class observers and reformers. Many were additionally alarmed at the exotic character of the immigrant and racial inhabitants. Poverty and discrimination forced many of these new urban migrants to cluster together in ghettos where they could provide mutual support, adapt to the ways of their new environment, and establish separate institutions.[58]

Southern blacks formed the most exclusive residential concentrations in older neighborhoods near downtowns where unskilled service jobs abounded or in communities adjacent to wealthier neighborhoods in which they found employment as domestics, cooks, and laundresses. Small numbers of free blacks in southern and northern cities alike had always lived separately in pockets and enclaves in alleys, back streets, or the city's fringes. The cityward migration of blacks after the Civil War increased the numbers, first in southern cities and later in border and finally after 1890 in northern cities, such that subsequent overt discrimination diminished employment opportunities and engendered a separate black community mentality. The initial racial ghettos of this early twentieth-century era developed small black-owned business bases and separate social institutions. However, marginal economic links to the larger city constrained many blacks in their attempts to establish a stable community, and the influx of migrants during and after World War I overwhelmed meager community resources. Resistant white neighborhoods grudgingly yielded small chunks of territory to black middle-class inhabitants, while the migrants crowded into the limited housing of the ghetto. Under conditions of poverty, these barriers to expansion turned the ghettos into slums.[59]

The experiences of European immigrant groups in American cities were as varied as their origins. The economic growth, employment structure, geographical distribution of jobs, and ethnic composition of the population of individual cities affected the social geography in complex ways. Where large employers and clear-cut employment centers predominated, immigrant clustering proceeded rapidly, and stable ethnic neighborhoods endured past the depression. Where small industries and a more plural ethnic mixture existed, social patterning was less clear-cut. In either case, the ghetto rarely was exclusive and often did not contain a majority of a specific immigrant group in the city. Members moved in and out as job locations and kinship needs required, but the ghetto did provide the institutional focus for the group, even long after many members had dispersed to working- and middle-class suburbs. Over time, the success of a specific group in particular economic niches of a city and the propensity to resist or embrace assimilation influenced the proclivity to buy homes and develop stable, sometimes stagnant, residential communities or to participate in the residential mobility of suburban expansion.[60]

By the 1930s, the industrial metropolis contained an array of neighborhoods that displayed distinctive economic and social characteristics. While the distribution and stratification of the labor market provided an overall framework for the city's social geography, the expanded housing stock and improved transportation offered a greater freedom of choice in residential location, which encouraged either social clustering or individuation. Dense inner-city slums and ethnic and racial ghettos were flanked by working- and lower middle-class streetcar neighborhoods, sometimes with a specific ethnic and religious character of their own. Low-density middle- and upper middle-class suburbs stretched out along trolley lines and highways into the countryside, while the wealthy maintained some older city neighborhoods and established newer graceful, bucolic communities at distant railroad stops. The density gradient declining outwardly from the city core was complicated by the localized industrial communities of manufacturing corridors and satellite milltowns. As a result, the industrial metropolis was extensive, polynuclear, and highly differentiated.

Beyond the Industrial Metropolis

Even as the geography of the industrial metropolis seemed reasonably well established, new technologies and persistent problems were challenging municipal leaders, urban planners, and social reformers to find solutions and influence patterns of growth. Bold planning and more prosaic tinkering with city infrastructure during the century's initial three decades had effected only limited solutions. Old warehousing and wharving areas in the central city had grown obsolete and blighted and often cast a dark shadow over the adjacent downtowns that were facing the competition of suburban businesses and automotive mobility. Inner-city slums worsened during the decade-long depression of the 1930s, and then wartime labor migrations overwhelmed the aging and inadequate housing supply. Black migrants especially suffered as discriminatory real estate practices and federal housing policy kept blacks confined to the ghettos. Continued black migration to the cities after the war exacerbated racial segregation and living conditions. During the 1950s, the diminution of housing units from abandonment, housing code enforcement, and urban renewal in the older ghetto neighborhoods spurred the movement of blacks into adjacent areas that soon became as segregated as the original ghettos. The construction of public housing on slum clearance sites provided some new housing but also maintained segregated patterns. Further, superblock developments and poor design often combined with tenant selection policies to concentrate the worst problems in the projects and dash the enlightened social goals of these rebuilt environments.[61]

Partially in response to the growing blight of inner-city areas and the expansion of racial ghettos, white residents of the city resumed the trek to the suburbs. Other factors than the threat of racial mixing also encouraged this movement. The federal government enhanced access by automobile with subsidization of high-speed expressways. Automobile usage was further encouraged by cheap petroleum energy policies. Federal tax laws and support of mortgage financing made home ownership in approved areas available to a much greater proportion of the public. In short, governmental policy directly fostered the accelerated decentralization of urban life.[62]

Jobs followed people to the suburbs. First retailers and personal services sought the suburban market, but office builders, factory owners, and wholesalers soon took advantage of tax benefits, highway accessibility, and the new labor market of the suburbs. While thousands continued to commute to downtown, many suburbs developed sufficient employment, retail, and entertainment centers to support a network of behavior independent of the central city.[63]

The challenge to the hegemony of downtown in the metropolitan region heightened the sense of urgency among municipal offices and businessmen to rejuvenate downtown facilities, accessibility, and image. Commercial redevelopment frequently converted older waterfronts to parking lots and massive expressways, bulldozed adjacent slums for office and expensive apartment projects, and campaigned for central sports and entertainment complexes.

The broad outlines of this postwar urban restructuring are generally recognized. The white suburbs increasingly encircled a growing black, impoverished inner city and challenged the older downtown interests to revitalize and adapt to a more limited functional role. By the 1960s, the suburbs, viewed as an entity, exhibited a complex, differentiated geography in their own right. In the largest metropolises, separate urban realms were evolving within the larger metropolitan region, which functioned independently of both each other and the older central city.[64]

Historians and geographers have only begun to explore the post–World War II era of urban growth. During the period, social scientists, journalists, and urban professionals wrote extensively about the changing city. Despite this voluminous literature, important themes still must be addressed for this period as well as for the preceding ones. Our present understanding of past geographies is based on a mixture of spatial scales and cross-sectional approaches. Closer inspection of nonresidential and residential patterns through finer-grain disaggregation and longitudinal studies of phenomena will continue to raise new questions about the composition and meaning of urban space.

The resulting reinterpretations of spatial patterns will have to confront the effects on geographical development of political power and powerful individuals in both public and private capacities. Individuals also stood at the intersection between local developments and the intercity institutional and personal networks through which urban innovations, fashions, and solutions diffused. Thus, local political situations and personalities mediated the relationship between macro-levels of urban change and more specific patterns of individual cities.[65]

Not only do we know too little about such topics, though studies of national urban planning and reform movements shed some light on them, but the implications of sectional (southern, western, midwestern) and regional cultural variations for urban geographies are also weakly addressed at best. Recognition of southern racial differences in the nineteenth century, sunbelt growth experiences in the twentieth century, and contrasts with Canadian cities whet the appetite for more cultural and comparative work.[66] The literature also remains markedly silent on the importance of women, the complexities of the evolving middle class, and the related patterns of twentieth-century ethnic assimilation in new suburbs for urban spatial structure. While historians turned to geography twenty years ago to develop a new dimension for their study of the city, students of the city's historical geography today must draw from history the insights that will lead to a richer, more satisfying understanding of past geographies.

Notes

1. Several city histories and review essays might be cited here; however, the early urban history texts reveal this lack of concern for spatial patterning. See, for instance, Charles N. Glaab and A. Theodore Brown, *A History of Urban America* (New York: Macmillan, 1967). For a review of the early urban history literature, see Bruce M. Stave, *The Making of Urban History: Historiography through Oral History* (Beverly Hills: Sage Publications, 1977), pp. 13–30.

2. Robert E. Park, Ernest W. Burgess, and Roderick D. McKenzie, *The City* (Chicago: University of Chicago Press, 1925); Robert E. Faris, *Chicago Sociology: 1920–1932* (San Francisco: Chandler Publishing Co., 1967); Leo F. Schnore, *The Urban Scene: Human Ecology and Demography* (New York: Free Press, 1965); Amos Hawley, *Human Ecology: Theory of Community Structure* (New York: Ronald Press, 1950).

3. Michael P. Conzen, "Analytical Approaches to the Urban Landscape," in Karl W. Butzer, ed., *Dimensions in Human Geography: Essays on Some Familiar and Neglected Themes*, University of Chicago Department of Geography Research Paper No. 186 (Chicago: University of Chicago Press, 1978), pp. 128–65.

4. Richard C. Wade, *The Urban Frontier: Pioneer Life in Early Pittsburgh, Cincinnati, Lexington, Louisville, and St. Louis* (1959; Chicago: University of Chicago Press, 1964) and *Slavery in the Cities: The South, 1820–1860* (New York: Oxford University Press, 1964); Sam Bass Warner, Jr., *Streetcar Suburbs: The Process of Growth in Boston, 1870–1900* (Cambridge, Mass.: Harvard University Press, 1962) and *The Private City: Philadelphia in Three Periods of Its Growth* (Philadelphia: University of Pennsylvania Press, 1968).

5. Allan R. Pred, *The Spatial Dynamics of U.S. Urban-Industrial Growth, 1800–1914* (Cambridge, Mass.: MIT Press, 1966), and David Ward, *Cities and Immigrants:*

A Geography of Change in Nineteenth-Century America (New York: Oxford University Press, 1971).

6. Roy Lubove, "The Urbanization Process: An Approach to Historical Research," *Journal of the American Institute of Planners* 33 (January 1967): 33–39, and Sam Bass Warner, Jr.,"If All The World Were Philadelphia: A Scaffolding for Urban History, 1774–1930," *American Historical Review* 74 (October 1968): 26–43.

7. Stephan Thernstrom and Richard Sennett, eds., *Nineteenth-Century Cities: Essays in the New Urban History* (New Haven: Yale University Press, 1968).

8. See, for example, Kathleen Neils Conzen, *Immigrant Milwaukee, 1830–1860: Accommodation and Community in a Frontier City* (Cambridge, Mass.: Harvard University Press, 1976), and Stuart M. Blumin, *The Urban Threshold: Growth and Change in a Nineteenth-Century American Community* (Chicago: University of Chicago Press, 1976).

9. A high point in this interdisciplinary interaction came at the conference entitled "Historical Urbanization in North America" held at York University, Toronto, in January 1973.

10. David R. Goldfield and Blaine A. Brownell, *Urban America: From Downtown to No Town* (Boston: Houghton Mifflin, 1979).

11. Theodore Hershberg, "The New Urban History: Toward an Interdisciplinary History of the City," *Journal of Urban History* 5 (November 1978): 3–40, and reprinted with minor revisions in Theodore Hershberg, ed., *Philadelphia: Work, Space, Family, and Group Experience in the 19th Century* (New York: Oxford University Press, 1981), pp. 3–35.

12. Maris A. Vinovskis, "Searching for Classes in Urban North America: Review Essay," *Journal of Urban History* 11 (May 1985): 353–60.

13. David Ward and John P. Radford, *North American Cities in the Victorian Age: Two Essays*, Historical Geography Research Series, 12 (Norwich, U.K.: Geo Books, 1983).

14. Samuel P. Hays, *The Response to Industrialism: 1885–1914* (Chicago: University of Chicago Press, 1957).

15. Ernest W. Burgess, "The Growth of the City," in Park, Burgess, and McKenzie, *The City*, pp. 47–62; Robert M. Haig, *Major Economic Factors in Metropolitan Growth and Arrangements* (New York: Regional Plan of New York and Environs, 1927); and Gideon Sjoberg, *The Pre-Industrial City* (New York: Free Press, 1960).

16. James E. Vance, Jr., *The Merchant's World: The Geography of Wholesaling* (Englewood Cliffs, N.J.: Prentice-Hall, 1970), and Richard D. Brown, *Modernization: The Transformation of American Life, 1600–1865* (New York: Hill and Wang, 1976).

17. See, for example, Gary B. Nash, *The Urban Crucible: Social Change, Political Consciousness, and the Origins of the American Revolution* (Cambridge, Mass.: Harvard University Press, 1979).

18. Philip Scranton, "Milling About: Family Firms and Urban Manufacturing in Textile Philadelphia, 1840–1865," *Journal of Urban History* 10 (May 1984): 259–94.

19. The burgeoning historical literature of American working-class life and Marxian interpretations of American capitalism has demonstrated the importance of the changing division of labor and forms of production for the city's geography. See David Harvey, *Social Justice and the City* (London: Edward Arnold, 1973), and Richard A. Walker, "The Transformation of Urban Structure in the Nineteenth Century and the Beginnings

of Suburbanization," in Kevin R. Cox, ed., *Urbanization and Conflict in Market Societies* (Chicago: Maaroufa Press, 1978), pp. 165–211.

20. Vance, *Merchant's World*, pp. 80–95.

21. James E. Vance, Jr., "Land Assignment in the Precapitalist and Postcapitalist City," *Economic Geography* 47 (April 1971): 101–20.

22. The dearth of locationally specific surveys, directories, censuses, and other listings for cities prior to 1800 makes the reconstruction of colonial geographical patterns difficult and impressionistic. Nevertheless, imaginative and painstaking research can yield important evidence of colonial spatial patterns. Warner, *Private City*, pp. 3–21; Nash, *Urban Crucible*, pp. 3–25; and Sherry H. Olson, *Baltimore: The Building of an American City* (Baltimore: Johns Hopkins University Press, 1980), pp. 10–40.

23. James E. Vance, Jr., *This Scene of Man: The Role and Structure of the City in the Geography of Western Civilization* (New York: Harper and Row, 1977), pp. 245–69, and John W. Reps, *The Making of Urban America: A History of City Planning in the United States* (Princeton: Princeton University Press, 1965).

24. Martyn J. Bowden, "The Internal Structure of the Colonial Replica City: San Francisco and Others," (paper presented at the Sixty-eighth Annual Meeting of the Association of American Geographers, Kansas City, 1972); Ian Davey and Michael Doucet, "The Social Geography of a Commercial City, ca. 1853," in Michael B. Katz, *The People of Hamilton, Canada West* (Cambridge, Mass.: Harvard University Press, 1975), pp. 319–42; Edward K. Muller, "Spatial Order before Industrialization: Baltimore's Central District, 1833–1860," Working Papers, Regional Economic History Research Center, Vol. 4, Nos. 1 and 2 (Wilmington, Del.: Eleutherian Mills-Hagley Foundation, 1980), pp. 100–40; and Glenn Porter and Harold C. Livesay, *Merchants and Manufacturers* (Baltimore: Johns Hopkins University Press, 1971).

25. Henry C. Binford, *The First Suburbs: Residential Communities on the Boston Periphery, 1815–1860* (Chicago: University of Chicago Press, 1985), pp. 17–44; and Allan R. Pred, "Manufacturing in the American Mercantile City: 1800–1840," *Annals of the Association of American Geographers* 56 (June 1966): 307–88.

26. Edward K. Muller and Paul A. Groves, "The Emergence of Industrial Districts in Mid-Nineteenth Century Baltimore," *Geographical Review* 69 (April 1979): 159–78; Raymond L. Fales and Leon N. Moses, "Land-Use Theory and the Spatial Structure of the Nineteenth-Century City," *Papers of the Regional Science Association* 28 (1972): 49–80; and Stephanie W. Greenberg, "Industrial Location and Ethnic Residential Patterns in an Industrializing City: Philadelphia, 1880," in Hershberg, *Philadelphia*, pp. 209–14.

27. William H. Mulligan, Jr., "Mechanization and Work in the American Shoe Industry: Lynn, Massachusetts, 1852–1883," *Journal of Economic History* 41 (March 1981): 59–63, and Edward K. Muller and Paul A. Groves, "The Changing Location of the Clothing Industry: A Link to the Social Geography of Baltimore in the Nineteenth Century," *Maryland Historical Magazine* 71 (Fall 1976): 403–20.

28. Ward, *Cities and Immigrants*, pp. 85–103. Far too few studies have used disaggregated data to reconstruct industrial distributional patterns, and fewer still have tried to connect employment centers with workers. See Hershberg, *Philadelphia*, pp. 128–73, and, for a recent example of an excellent disaggregated study, Philip Scranton, *Proprietary Capitalism: The Textile Manufacture at Philadelphia, 1800–1885* (New York: Cambridge University Press, 1983).

29. Martyn J. Bowden, "Downtown Through Time: Delimitation, Expansion, and

Internal Growth,'' *Economic Geography* 47 (April 1971): 121–35, and "Growth of Central Districts in Large Cities,'' in Leo F. Schnore, ed., *The New Urban History* (Princeton: Princeton University Press, 1975), pp. 75–109; David Ward, "The Industrial Revolution and the Emergence of Boston's Central Business District,'' *Economic Geography* 42 (April 1966): 152–71; and Edward K. Muller, "Distinctive Downtown,'' *Geographical Magazine* 53 (August 1980): 747–55. As in the case of industrial activities, the paucity of detailed studies on downtowns leaves an inadequate empirical basis for these generalizations and room for refinement.

30. Glenn Porter, *The Rise of Big Business, 1860–1910* (Arlington Heights, Ill.: Harlan Davidson, 1973), and Alfred A. Chandler, *The Visible Hand: The Managerial Revolution in American Business* (Cambridge, Mass.: Belknap Press of Harvard University Press, 1977).

31. Gunther Barth, *City People: The Rise of Modern City Culture in Nineteenth-Century America* (New York: Oxford University Press, 1980), pp. 110–47.

32. Frank Norris, *The Octopus: A Story of California* (New York: Doubleday, Page & Co., 1901).

33. Few recent studies have reconstructed the complex industrial patterns of industrial metropolises, and our knowledge rests often on contemporary industrial surveys. See Edward E. Pratt, *Industrial Causes of Congestion of Population in New York City* (New York: Longmans, Green & Co., 1911); Graham Romeyn Taylor, *Satellite Cities: A Study of Industrial Suburbs* (New York: D. Appleton and Co., 1915); John R. Stilgoe, *Metropolitan Corridor: Railroads and the American Scene* (New Haven: Yale University Press, 1983), pp. 73–132; Stanley Buder, *Pullman, An Experiment in Industrial Order and Community Planning, 1880–1930* (New York: Oxford University Press, 1967); Edgar M. Hoover and Raymond Vernon, *Anatomy of a Metropolis* (New York: Doubleday, 1962), pp. 21–73; and the *Economic and Industrial Survey* and *Regional Survey of New York and Its Environs*, multivolumes (New York: Committee on Regional Plan of New York and Its Environs, 1924–1933). Some important historical land use information can be gleaned from the recent preparation of historic district nominations for the National Register of Historic Places and of environmental and cultural resource impact assessments required for federally subsidized construction projects.

34. Glenn E. McLaughlin, *Growth of American Manufacturing Areas: A Comparative Analysis with Special Emphasis on Trends in the Pittsburgh District* (Pittsburgh : Bureau of Business Research, University of Pittsburgh, 1938), p. 129, and Leon Moses and Harold F. Williamson, Jr., "The Location of Economic Activity in Cities,'' *American Economic Review* 57 (May 1967): 211–22.

35. Carl Condit, *The Rise of the Skyscraper* (Chicago: University of Chicago Press, 1952); Christopher Tunnard and Henry Hope Reed, *American Skyline* (New York: New American Library, 1956), pp. 155–62; and Paul Goldberger, *The Skyscraper* (New York: Alfred A. Knopf, 1981).

36. Bowden, "Downtown Through Time''; Ward, "Emergence of Boston's Central Business District''; and Muller, "Distinctive Downtown.''

37. Michael P. Conzen and Kathleen Neils Conzen, "Geographical Structure in Nineteenth-Century Urban Retailing: Milwaukee, 1836–90,'' *Journal of Historical Geography* 5 (January 1979): 45–66. While Martyn Bowden's work on downtown San Francisco represents the disaggregated approach necessary for reconstructing spatial patterns and understanding processes, only Conzen and Conzen have extended the approach to commercial activities throughout the city.

38. John P. Radford, "The Social Geography of the Nineteenth Century U.S. City," in D. T. Herbert and R. J. Johnston, eds., *Geography and the Urban Environment: Progress in Research and Applications* (London: John Wiley & Sons, 1981), 4: 257–93.

39. Kenneth T. Jackson, *Crabgrass Frontier: The Suburbanization of the United States* (New York: Oxford University Press, 1985), pp. 12–19. As with nonresidential activities, our picture of the colonial city's social geography depends locationally on impressionistic, imprecise, or unsystematic information.

40. David Montgomery, "The Working Classes of the Pre-Industrial American City, 1780–1830," *Labor History* 9 (Winter 1968): 3–22; Walker, "Transformation of Urban Structure," pp. 173–79; Warner, *Private City*, pp. 3–21; Nash, *Urban Crucible*, pp. 3–25; and Richard W. Bernard, "A Portrait of Baltimore in 1800: Economic and Occupational Patterns in an Early American City," *Maryland Historical Magazine* 69 (Winter 1974): 341–60.

41. Jackson, *Crabgrass Frontier*, pp. 20–33, and Edward Pessen, "The Social Configuration of the Antebellum City: An Historical and Theoretical Inquiry," *Journal of Urban History* 2 (May 1976): 267–306.

42. Gwendolyn Wright, *Building the Dream: A Social History of Housing in America* (Cambridge, Mass.: MIT Press, 1981), pp. 24–40; Norman J. Johnston, "The Caste and Class of the Urban Form of Historic Philadelphia," *Journal of the American Institute of Planners* 32 (November 1966): 334–49; Jackson, *Crabgrass Frontier*, pp. 12–19; Bernard, "Portrait of Baltimore in 1800"; and Binford, *First Suburbs*.

43. James E. Vance, Jr., "Labor-Shed, Employment Field, and Dynamic Analysis in Urban Geography," *Economic Geography* 36 (July 1960): 182–220, and "Housing the Worker: The Employment Linkage as a Force in Urban Structure," *Economic Geography* 42 (October 1966): 294–325; Walker, "Transformation of Urban Structure," pp. 200–203; and David Ward, "Social Structure and Social Geography in Large Cities of the U.S. Urban-Industrial Heartland," in Ward and Radford, *North American Cities*, pp. 1–31.

44. David Ward, "The Victorian Slum: An Enduring Myth?" *Annals of the Association of American Geographers* 66 (June 1976): 323–36, and his *Cities and Immigrants*, pp. 105–23; John M. Marshall, "Residential Expansion and Central-City Change," in James F. Blumstein and Benjamin Walter, eds., *Growing Metropolis: Aspects of Development in Nashville* (Nashville: Vanderbilt University Press, 1975), pp. 34–63; and Paul E. Groth, "Forbidden Housing: The Evolution and Exclusion of Hotels, Boarding Houses, Rooming Houses, and Lodging Houses in American Cities, 1880–1930" (Ph.D. diss., University of California, Berkeley, 1983).

45. John T. Cumbler, "The City and Community: The Impact of Urban Forces on Working Class Behavior," *Journal of Urban History* 3 (August 1977): 427–42; Quoc Thuy Thach, "Social Class and Residential Mobility, The Case of the Irish in Montreal, 1851–1871," *Shared Spaces*, Department of Geography, McGill University, No. 1 (1985); Robert D. Lewis, "The Segregated City: Class and Occupation in Montreal, 1861–1901," *Shared Spaces*, Department of Geography, McGill University, No 3 (1985); and Peter G. Goheen, *Victorian Toronto, 1850–1900*, Department of Geography Research Paper No. 127 (Chicago: University of Chicago Press, 1970).

46. Conzen, *Immigrant Milwaukee*.

47. Alan N. Burstein, "Immigrants and Residential Mobility: The Irish and Germans in Philadelphia, 1850–1880," in Hershberg, *Philadelphia*, pp. 174–203; Francis G. Couvares, *The Remaking of Pittsburgh: Class and Culture in an Industrializing City*,

1877–1919 (Albany: State University of New York Press, 1984), pp. 1–61; and Stephan Thernstrom, *The Other Bostonians: Poverty and Progress in the American Metropolis, 1880–1970* (Cambridge, Mass.: Harvard University Press, 1973).

48. Glen E. Holt, "The Changing Perception of Urban Pathology: An Essay on the Development of Mass Transit in the United States," in Kenneth T. Jackson and Stanley K. Schultz, eds., *Cities in American History* (New York: Alfred A. Knopf, 1972), pp. 324–43; George Rogers Taylor, "The Beginnings of Mass Transportation in Urban America," *Smithsonian Journal of History* 1 (Summer and Autumn, 1966): 31–54; and Theodore Hershberg, Harold E. Cox, Dale B. Light, Jr., and Richard R. Greenfield, "The 'Journey-to-Work': An Empirical Investigation of Work, Residence and Transportation," in Hershberg, *Philadelphia*, pp. 128–73.

49. Wright, *Building the Dream*, pp. 96–113; Richard Sennett, *Families Against the City* (Cambridge, Mass.: Harvard University Press, 1970); Richard A. Walker, "A Theory of Suburbanization: Capitalism and the Construction of Urban Space in the United States," in Michael Dear and Allen J. Scott, eds., *Urbanization and Urban Planning in Capitalist Society* (London: Methuen & Co., Ltd., 1981), pp. 383–429; and Jackson, *Crabgrass Frontier*, pp. 45–86.

50. Buder, *Pullman*; Margaret F. Byington, *Homestead: The Households of a Mill Town* (New York: Russell Sage Foundation, 1910); Taylor, *Satellite Cities*; and Wright, *Building the Dream*, pp. 177–92.

51. Jackson, *Crabgrass Frontier*; Homer Hoyt, *The Structure and Growth of Residential Neighborhoods in American Cities* (Washington, D.C.: U.S. Government Printing Office, 1939).

52. Jackson, *Crabgrass Frontier*, pp. 103–15; Joel A. Tarr, *Transportation Innovation and Changing Spatial Patterns in Pittsburgh, 1850–1934* (Chicago: Public Works Historical Society, 1978); and John S. Adams, "Residential Structure of Midwestern Cities," *Annals of the Association of American Geographers* 60 (March 1970): 37–62.

53. Michael J. Doucet and John C. Weaver, "Material Culture and the North American House: The Era of the Common Man, 1870–1920," *Journal of American History* 72 (December 1985): 560–87, and Michael J. Doucet, "Urban Land Development in Nineteenth Century North America: Themes in the Literature," *Journal of Urban History* 8 (May 1982): 299–342.

54. Robert G. Barrows, "Beyond the Tenement: Patterns of American Urban Housing, 1870–1930," *Journal of Urban History* 9 (August 1983): 395–420.

55. Ibid., pp. 415–16; Jackson, *Crabgrass Frontier*, pp. 132–33; and Roger D. Simon, "The City-Building Process: Housing and Services in New Milwaukee Neighborhoods, 1880–1910," *Transactions of the American Philosophical Society* 68 (July 1978).

56. A great deal of research needs to be done on the changing composition of suburbs between 1900 and 1950. Warner, *Streetcar Suburbs*, passim; David Ward, "A Comparative Historical Geography of Streetcar Suburbs in Boston, Massachusetts and Leeds, England," *Annals of the Association of American Geographers* 54 (December 1964): 477–89; Jackson, *Crabgrass Frontier*, pp. 116–37; and Milton Gordon, *Assimilation in American Life: The Role of Race, Religion and National Origins* (New York: Oxford University Press, 1964).

57. Roy Lubove, *The Progressives and the Slums: Tenement House Reform in New York City, 1890–1917* (Pittsburgh: University of Pittsburgh Press, 1962); James Ford, *Slums and Housing*, 2 vols. (Cambridge, Mass.: Harvard University Press, 1936), and

Housing Conditions in Baltimore (Baltimore Federated Charities, 1907); Walter Firey, *Land Use in Central Boston* (Cambridge, Mass.: Harvard University Press, 1947).

58. Jacob Riis, *How the Other Half Lives: Studies among the Tenements of New York.* (New York: Charles Scribner's Sons, 1890); David Ward, "The Emergence of Central Immigrant Ghettos in American Cities, 1840–1920," *Annals of the Association of American Geographers* 58 (June 1968): 343–59, and his "The Ethnic Ghetto in the United States: Past and Present," *Transactions*, Institute of British Geographers, n.s. 7, 3 (1982): 257–75.

59. Wade, *Slavery in the Cities*; Gilbert Osofsky, *Harlem: The Making of a Ghetto: Negro New York, 1890–1930* (New York: Harper & Row, 1966); Allan H. Spear, *Black Chicago: The Making of a Negro Ghetto, 1890–1920* (Chicago: University of Chicago Press, 1967); Kenneth L. Kusmer, *A Ghetto Takes Shape: Black Cleveland, 1870–1930* (Urbana: University of Illinois Press, 1976); Paul A. Groves and Edward K. Muller, "The Evolution of Black Residential Areas in Late Nineteenth-Century Cities," *Journal of Historical Geography* 1 (April 1975): 169–91; and John Kellogg, "Negro Urban Clusters in the Post-bellum South," *Geographical Review* 67 (July 1977): 310–21.

60. David Ward, "The Internal Spatial Structure of Immigrant Residential Districts in the Late Nineteenth Century," *Geographical Analysis* 4 (October 1969): 337–53; Thomas Kessner, *The Golden Door: Italian and Jewish Immigrant Mobility in New York City, 1880–1915* (New York: Oxford University Press, 1977); Howard P. Chudacoff, *Mobile Americans: Residential and Social Mobility in Omaha, 1880–1920* (New York: Oxford University Press, 1973); John Bodnar, Roger Simon, and Michael Weber, *Lives of Their Own: Blacks, Italians and Poles in Pittsburgh, 1900–1960* (Urbana: University of Illinois Press, 1982); Josef J. Barton, *Peasants and Strangers: Italians, Rumanians, and Slovaks in an American City, 1880–1950* (Cambridge, Mass.: Harvard University Press, 1975); and Olivier Zunz, *The Changing Face of Inequality: Urbanization, Industrial Development and Immigrants in Detroit, 1880–1920* (Chicago: University of Chicago Press, 1982).

61. Lawrence M. Friedman, *Government and Slum Housing: A Century of Frustration* (Chicago: Rand McNally, 1968); Arnold R. Hirsch, *Making the Second Ghetto: Race and Housing in Chicago, 1940–1960* (Cambridge: Cambridge University Press, 1983); John F. Bauman, *Public Housing, Race and Renewal: Urban Planning in Philadelphia, 1920–1974* (Philadelphia: Temple University Press, 1987); Eugene P. Ericksen and William L. Yancey, "Work and Residence in Industrial Philadelphia," *Journal of Urban History* 5 (February 1979): 147–82; and Roy Lubove, *Twentieth Century Pittsburgh* (New York: John Wiley and Sons, 1969).

62. Mark I. Gelfand, *A Nation of Cities: The Federal Government and Urban America, 1933–1965* (New York: Oxford University Press, 1975); Jackson, *Crabgrass Frontier*, pp. 190–282; and Jon C. Teaford, *City and Suburb: The Political Fragmentation of Metropolitan America, 1850–1970* (Baltimore: Johns Hopkins University Press, 1979).

63. James E. Vance, Jr., *This Scene of Man* (New York: Harper & Row, 1977), pp. 402–17, and Peter O. Muller, *Contemporary Suburban America* (Englewood Cliffs, N.J.: Prentice-Hall, 1981).

64. James E. Vance, Jr., *Geography and Urban Evolution in the San Francisco Bay Area* (Berkeley: Institute for Governmental Studies, 1964), and Jon C. Teaford, *The Twentieth-Century American City: Problem, Promise, and Reality* (Baltimore: Johns Hopkins University Press, 1986), pp. 151–56.

65. See, for example, Robert A. Caro, *The Power Broker: Robert Moses and the Fall of New York* (New York: Random House, 1975); Lubove, *Twentieth Century Pittsburgh*;

and Mel Scott, *American City Planning since 1890* (Berkeley: University of California Press, 1969).

66. John P. Radford, "Race, Residence and Ideology: Charleston, South Carolina in the Mid-Nineteenth Century," *Journal of Historical Geography* 2 (October 1976): 329–46, and "Regional Ideologies and Urban Growth on the Victorian Periphery: Southern Ontario and the U.S. South," in Ward and Radford, *North American Cities*, pp. 32–57; Frederic Cople Jaher, *The Urban Establishment: Upper Strata in Boston, New York, Charleston, Chicago, and Los Angeles* (Urbana: University of Illinois Press, 1982); E. Digby Baltzell, *Puritan Boston and Quaker Philadelphia: Two Protestant Ethics and the Spirit of Class Authority and Leadership* (Boston: Beacon Press, 1979); and the many books edited by Alan F.J. Artibise and Gilbert A. Stelter on Canadian urban history.

7 —————— Design, Process, and Institutions: Planning in Urban History

EUGENIE LADNER BIRCH

Although many Anglo-American social historians would like to believe that they have invented planning history, their assumption is incorrect.[1] The field has deeper roots. Its earliest practitioners—architects, archaeologists and classicists—engaged in questions of urban design, the origin of cities, and urbanization. They frequently, but not always, concentrated on the preindustrial periods. They fashioned an inquiry that focused on the physical artifact, the city or urban element, and its changes over time.[2] Additionally, they evaluated individuals, usually architects or planners of national stature. They established a scholarly tradition that is thriving today, particularly in the works of John W. Reps, Norma Evenson, Norman J. Johnston, Thomas S. Hines, and Carl W. Condit.[3]

Although Anglo-American social historians did not invent planning history, they certainly transformed it. In the 1970s, they turned their attention to planning as one of the phenomena shaping the modern city. Drawn in part by the flowering of urban history a decade earlier, they set the parameters of their studies by concentrating on the process and context of planned urban development. In so doing, they expanded the definition of planning to include not only design but also more generalized land use patterns. These authors had a dramatic influence on the field. While they did not forget about the city as a physical artifact, they documented the decisions, people, and events that created the artifact. As they concentrated on the modern period, they assumed a more critical or evaluative stance than their predecessors. An essential part of their work was to question who benefited from planning. Representative of this group are Anthony Sutcliffe, Jon A. Peterson, Blaine A. Brownell, David R. Goldfield, Zane L. Miller, and Daniel Schaffer.[4]

At about the same time, a third group of planning historians emerged. Largely drawn from the profession, they were occupied with establishing a systematic study of institutionalized planning. They focused on its roots, practitioners, internal organization, accomplishments, and failures. Driven in part by a desire to restore a collective memory to a field that had rejected its past, they also sought to interpret the place of planning in American society. They synthesized the approaches of the others, incorporating the design consciousness of the architectural historian and the process orientation of the social historian, yet they rarely strayed from their institutional focus. Some participants here are Donald A. Krueckeberg, Laurence C. Gerckens, Peter Marcuse, Marc A. Weiss, Roger Montgomery, and Eugenie L. Birch.[5]

These three approaches, however different their backgrounds, are currently linked by two themes: their common definition of the field and their focus on the modern period. They are concerned with the collective and conscious decisions that have created comprehensive land use and spatial patterns or special use areas in a city or region, usually in pursuit of an ideal physical environment. They are illuminating the heritage of these decisions in today's world.

Clearly these three traditions—the design based, process oriented, and institution concerned—have shaped current offerings. While these streams are now developing not so much independently as in parallel fashion, they have influenced each other. For example, design-based authors are providing richer contextual material, process-oriented contributors are integrating more design in their analyses, and institution-concerned authors are incorporating design and process into their interpretations.[6] The result is a literature rich in quantity as well as in scope.

Planning History Surveys

A healthy general survey literature has developed over time. Some of this work carries on the tradition of Pierre Lavedan, A. E. J. Morris, and Erwin A. Gutkind.[7] Primarily concerned with assessing the physical attributes of cities and placing metropolitan growth in a chronological context, Leonardo Benevolo, Mark Girouard, and John W. Reps answer the questions of how much, what kind, and where planning existed. Their output, encyclopedic and documentary in character, favors description over analysis. These authors treat the American experience within the time frame and scope of their own studies. Benevolo, in his sweeping *The History of the City*, for example, pays scant attention to the United States, for his view spans prehistory to the present. In contrast, Girouard's *Cities and People*, a narrower Western civilization survey starting with the

Middle Ages, selects cities that "at the time [had] a star quality." Thus New York, Chicago, and Los Angeles dominate the latter part of his narrative. Finally, John W. Reps, with a sole focus on the United States, yields reference-quality description of American cities from the eighteenth to twentieth centuries. His latest survey is *Cities of the American West: A History of Frontier Urban Planning*.[8]

Ideology underlines some recently published surveys of an interpretative nature. Following Manuel Castells, Giorgio Ciucci, David Harvey, and Josef W. Konvitz question the economic and political basis of city development. In a series of four essays, Ciucci and his co-authors advance the Marxian argument that architecture and city planning are agents of the American capitalist system. Their well-documented treatment of city beautiful schemes, park designs, regional planning, Broadacre City, and the rise of the skyscraper, however, is marred by their turgid political arguments. Harvey, in his two-volume work, relates urbanization and capitalism. Konvitz, in concentrating on growth and development, labeled "the city building process," assesses urban adaptability to changing social, economic, and cultural trends over time. He concludes that the modern period is inflexible.[9] Similar to this work, but not so ideological, is Jane Jacobs' *Cities and the Wealth of Nations*. Polemical and assertive as is her wont, Jacobs argues that national growth is dependent on the economic health of cities, not the opposite, and she uses historical cases to bolster this point.[10]

The survey genre also includes what might be called the intellectual or cultural history of planning. Studies such as Anthony Sutcliffe's *The Metropolis, 1980– 1940*, designed to assess the impact of urbanization and its effects on planning, have come a long way since Morton White and Lucia White's *The Intellectual versus the City* and Thomas Bender's *Toward an Urban Vision: Ideas and Institutions in Nineteenth Century America*.[11] This new work, which includes Andrew Lees' *Cities Perceived* and William Sharpe and Leonard Wallock's *Visions of the Modern City*, shows how the dynamism of the urban environment, the rise and fall of metropolises, and the growth of slums and city pathologies have helped create the mental framework around which planners, policymakers, and the general public have formed their basic prescriptive outlook toward reform, change, and improvement in the urban arena.[12] According to these authors, nineteenth-century urbanization and technological advances led contemporary observers to call for progress, conquest, and control as they optimistically asserted that the modern city could be planned, organized and placed in the service of society. Such sentiments found expression in architecture, the arts, and literature and indeed fueled the growth of institutionalized planning.

Professional Development and Institutionalized Planning

That the modern industrial city, of a size and complexity unknown in history, led to conflicts between the free market economies that spawned them and the individuals who lived in them is well documented.[13] That many professions

found their roots in relieving the resulting tensions is also reasonably well illustrated.[14] Until recently, however, the growth of the planning profession has
not received a full measure of attention. An official history commissioned by
the American Institute of Planning in 1969, Mel Scott's encyclopedic *American
City Planning since 1890*, provides a detailed outline of the evolution of the
field. Laurence C. Gerckens' more concise "Historical Development of American City Planning" summarizes the landmarks. Neither gives voice and flesh
to individual planners, interpretive substance to their plans, or an understanding
of how their ideas have been transferred, accepted, or rejected in different times
and places in America.[15] Others have taken on these tasks.

Recent biographies of planners and urban theoreticians have centered on evaluating their influence on the field. For example, in *The American Planner,
Biographies and Recollections*, editor Donald A. Krueckeberg restricts his scope
to subjects whose careers span the teens to the immediate postwar period.[16] He
illuminates how practitioners defined their work by emphasizing the issues they
attacked and attempted to resolve. Although focused on activists who participated
in a rather narrow band of planning projects, his portraits treat the evolution of
zoning, housing reform, and regional planning. Although his book is not comprehensive—it neglects transportation planners, for example—its coverage of
John Nolen, Alfred Bettman, Edith Elmer Wood, Harland Bartholomew, Charles
Eliot, and Charles Abrams provides a chronological framework for planning
thought and practice. Like other works, such as Michael Simpson's *Thomas
Adams*, it shows that the field was ever changing and constrained by external
events and public opinion.[17]

Several authors employ biographies to address how public opinion has limited
the field. David R. Hill's "Lewis Mumford's Ideas on the City" uses the decline
of Mumford's influence on planning practice and education to illustrate this
theme.[18] Underscoring Mumford's reliance on the regional city concept (a rejection of contemporary settlement patterns in favor of a restructuring of metropolitan areas according to garden city principles), Hill argues that Mumford's
vision was too utopian to capture the popular imagination. Further, he asserts
that Mumford's proposals, based on physical determinism and ignorant of political reality, did not fit practitioners' needs for workable strategies. Mark I.
Gelfand's "Rexford Tugwell and the Frustration of Planning in New York City"
shows a similar failure on the part of the New Deal economist known for his
advocacy of urban resettlement programs and instituting planning as a fourth
power of government.[19] He demonstrates how Tugwell, as the first head of the
New York City Planning Commission, failed to create his envisioned model
agency, apolitical, autonomous, and powerful enough to guide municipal capital
decisions and urban development. In attributing this defeat to popular attitudes
that thoroughly rejected this scheme, Gelfand highlights the precarious position
of planning when extended beyond socially accepted bounds. Robert A. Caro's
The Power Broker, with its focus on Robert Moses, an enemy of institutionalized

planning, tells the other side of the Tugwell story. Further, essays on Roosevelt's Greenbelt towns by Daniel Schaffer, and Joseph A. Eden and Arnold A. Alanen on Greendale and sections of Zane L. Miller's *Suburbs, Neighborhood and Community in Forest Park, Ohio*, confirm that the American public was not ready to accept direct government intervention in town building efforts despite its advocacy by planning theorists and practitioners.[20] By the same count, John Robert Mullin in "Henry Ford and Field and Factory: An Analysis of the Ford Sponsored Village Industries Experiment in Michigan, 1918–1941" shows how privately sponsored forays into population dispersion were equally unsuccessful.[21] Their failure resulted not only from popular opposition but also from their economic impracticality.

While biographers have focused on individuals and their impact on the field, others have analyzed the substance of planning. They seek to reveal its essential nature and to show the transferral of ideas among planners in America and Western Europe. For example, Daniel Schaffer in *Garden Cities for America: The Radburn Experience* traces the attempt to transplant English town planning to the United States, while contributors to *The Rise of Modern Urban Planning, 1800–1914*, edited by Anthony Sutcliffe, and *Shaping an Urban World*, edited by Gordon E. Cherry, demonstrate the common reform traditions embodied in the profession throughout the world.[22] All demonstrate the strong strain of physical determinism, largely drawn from the garden city ideal and city beautiful format, underlying pioneering efforts.

Many researchers have documented the roots of this physical determinism. They add subtlety to earlier interpretations, which tend to overemphasize the importance of the Chicago World's Fair as the sole source of city beautiful schemes. Particularly useful in this regard are two essays by Jon A. Peterson. Although Peterson does not treat planning per se, he lays out popular and professional antecedents that were to set the stage for the public acceptance of planning. Further, he demonstrates the development of the ideals of civic beauty that would be later embedded in zoning, subdivision regulation, and downtown development schemes.[23]

Taking the city beautiful literature beyond the usual urban design analysis and its stress on beautification, new contributions focus on the planning process surrounding the adoption and execution of the monumental schemes of the early twentieth century. In "The Ideology, Aesthetics and Politics of the City Beautiful Movement" William H. Wilson reveals the more mundane concerns of its proponents—flood control and drainage—and the grass-roots marketing strategies used to implement the programs. Robert L. Wrigley, Jr.'s, discussion of the 1909 Chicago plan investigates many of the same questions, exposes the intensive campaigning for public acceptance, and demonstrates its results. Finally, Jon A. Peterson's treatment of the McMillan Plan for Washington, D.C., charts the behind-the-scenes action that yielded the components of the influential scheme for the capital.[24] All three of these articles are particularly useful for their disclosure of the controversy and compromise surrounding the programs. Earlier work, in ignoring this aspect of planning, conveyed a rather misleading view of the political nature of the field.

Another group of writers shows how planners extended their promotion of model environments to encompass neighborhoods, shopping centers, transportation schemes, and regional development. For example, resolving fragmented social identities, heightening community participation, and organizing irrational and chaotic land use were some of the aims of the neighborhood unit concept (the arrangement of a residential area around a school), a basic tenet of city planning practice. Both Christopher Silver and Howard Gillette, Jr., trace the origin and subsequent transformation of this idea.[25] While arguing that it ultimately incorporated a far different scheme than first envisioned by its original popularizer, Clarence Perry, they uncover its complicated lineage and contradictory strains. For example, they contrast its segregationist consequences with its city building potential. Finally they carefully document important challenges to its wholesale use. A modern assessment, *Beyond the Neighborhood Unit: Residential Environments and Public Policy* by Tridib Banerjee and William C. Baer, continues the dissenting tradition and attests to the continuing strength of this idea in planning dogma.[26]

Howard Gillette's study of planned shopping centers provides another example of the dominance of physical determinism in the profession. He demonstrates how planners used malls to provide "an exciting environment without its usual attendant nuisances" in the suburbs and later in downtowns. In this work, as well as in his earlier neighborhood unit research, he exposes a theme critical to understanding the history of the profession: the internal struggle among practitioners to shape policies designed to serve the public interest. As Gillette and others illustrate, however, differing interpretations of the public interest by planners, contemporary critics, and today's historians muddy the evaluative waters.[27]

While these students cannot divorce themselves completely from their personal value systems as they judge professional activity, some do attempt to be more objective by employing other standards of assessment. Sometimes they apply a general sort of cost-benefit analysis to gauge the results of a given planning program. At other times, several scholars will look at the same project or policy but measure different factors. Thus, as they lend different weight to their answers, the determination of the success or failure of planning in a given situation is not always clear.

This dilemma is particularly evident in the evaluation of one of the most massive regional planning projects in American history, the Tennessee Valley Authority development. Here, for example, Andrew Isserman, a favorably disposed observer, in "Dare to Plan," is pitted against Nancy Grant, a critic, in "Blacks, Regional Planning and the TVA."[28] Since they construct the public interest component in far different terms—service delivery versus economic displacement—they arrive at opposite conclusions.

Scholarship focusing on the responses of planners to the popularization of the automobile also reflects a division of opinion. Some simply point to professionals' seemingly rapid acceptance of cars as a self-serving device. Mark Foster in *From Streetcar to Superhighway* and Martin Wachs in "Autos, Transit, and the Sprawl of Los Angeles" argue that planners sought to legitimize their profession by becoming expert in traffic management.[29] Others, such as Blaine A. Brownell, reveal the internal conflicts among different practitioners who envisioned many uses for the automobile—an agent of population deconcentration or downtown stabilization.[30] His accurate conclusion that the profession did not operate in a vacuum but within the socioeconomic milieu of the country is confirmed by Kenneth T. Jackson in *The Crabgrass Frontier*. Jackson starts his analysis of transportation policy in the early nineteenth century and argues that advances in transportation certainly enabled population dispersion, but the change in cultural values favoring country living was the driving force behind the twentieth-century growth of suburbs. Planners, he asserts, simply followed popular currents and used their trade to assuage demand. The street, under their direction, switched from being a recreational open space to a vehicular artery. Mark Rose in *Interstate: Express Highway Politics*, a survey of the postwar period, demonstrates the increasing importance of highways in urban renewal schemes advanced by planners. Here, practitioners reasserted their mastery of traffic problems to plot courses to enhance economic development and thus improve the fiscal and physical health of decaying central cities.[31]

While case studies based on elements of planning doctrine usefully explore disparate aspects of the field, few focus on the one principle planners claimed essential to their expertise: the comprehensive vision. Employed in the effort to distinguish their profession from their forebearers—architecture, engineering, and later the individual social sciences—practitioners attested to their ability to view a city or metropolitan region holistically. Two recent studies explore this theme. Further, they trace how the idea changed drastically over time. Robert B. Fairbanks' study of downtown redevelopment in Cincinnati and Dallas shows planners replacing their prewar vision of well-balanced regions of stable neighborhoods and strong central business districts interlaced by rational transportation systems with more limited schemes featuring strong downtowns in the period following the passage of urban renewal legislation.[32] Looking at Washington, D.C., Howard Gillette, Jr., outlines what components changed: circumferential freeways replaced radial parkways; urban business-based redevelopment supplanted carefully designed urban neighborhoods and suburban subdivision. Although planned recentralization, not population decongestion, became the bywords, the planners' basic strategy remained the same: to manipulate a whole metropolitan area.[33]

Many retrospective studies condemn postwar urban policy favoring downtowns and middle-class residential development over slum clearance and public housing. They look to planners' activities to document a misalliance between planners and housers and to blame both for the sorry results of public housing and urban renewal programs. Piece by piece, they construct a picture of conflicting purposes. Peter Marcuse traces the primary separation between the two groups in the early years of the twentieth century, asserting that planners were concerned not with housing problems but with order, public health, and economic stability.[34] Robert B. Fairbanks explains their reunion in the mid-twenties in a common vision of rebuilt neighborhoods.[35] In a special issue of the *Journal of Urban History*, "The Early Years of Public Housing," Rosalie Genevro, Ann Buttenweisser, Peter Marcuse, and Joel Schwartz examine the interwar period to expose deep conflicts among housers and planners over site location, tenant selection, citizen participation, and development goals.[36] John F. Bauman confirms the continuation of the separation of the two groups with their divergent visions—rehousing slum dwellers versus downtown revitalization—and argues that their joining behind urban renewal at the local level would be doomed to failure.[37] In fact, Marc A. Weiss holds that housers made a strategic mistake in supporting the Housing Act of 1949 with its slum clearance legislation because their allies, the planners, had no interest in low-cost shelter, only district replanning.[38] Evaluating the implementation of urban programs, Arnold R. Hirsch indicts planners for employing segregationist policies in site location.[39] Roger Montgomery tempers a similar view with an appreciation of the forces of external events, and Kenneth T. Jackson focuses only on socioeconomic conditions without acknowledging the role of planners at all.[40] All would agree, however, that these urban programs directly contributed to racial unrest, the wholesale discrediting of traditional planners and their plans, and the rise of advocacy planning. Allan David Heskin documents the professional alienation and redefinition in the 1960s in his discussion of some practitioners' disillusionment with contemporary programs.[41]

While metropolitan-centered land use planning flourished through the first half of the twentieth century, so did national planning. Both Otis L. Graham, Jr., and Mark I. Gelfand relate the story of an expanded role for the federal government.[42] Their account of the ten-year life of the National Resources Planning Board exemplifies this phenomenon. Phillip J. Funigiello outlines the application of the latest planning techniques under federal sponsorship.[43] He points to important innovations—expansion of physical planning to integrate social and economic concerns, neighborhood conservation, and urban redevelopment—as rooted in this work. In contrast, an eyewitness account, Carl Feiss' "Foundations of Federal Planning Assistance," states that the board had little impact on planning.[44] Marion Clawson's *New Deal Planning: The National Resources Planning Board* provides still another interpretation.[45] Supplementing these evaluative studies are personal accounts of the experience from participants Albert Lepawsky and Charles W. Eliot II.[46]

To capture the essence of planning as a field of knowledge without establishing causal relationships between outside events and planning practice and de-emphasizing individual participants and their backgrounds is Christine Boyer's approach in *Dreaming the Rational City*.[47] A subscriber to the French philosopher Michel Foucault's teachings, which call for the examination of the discourse of a field—that is, looking at "everything that is said"—Boyer employs a historian's meticulous examination of primary resources to provide a chronology of the field through the documents and teaching of its practitioners. She alludes to external (national or local events) conditions but focuses on internal developments (the adoption of zoning or the promulgation of the neighborhood unit) to portray the advance of the profession. She does not write history—she acknowledges this—but uses history to frame a critique of planning from a Marxist perspective. The result is an interesting book. Some might call it a testimonial to the youth of the 1960s and their disillusionment. It bears witness to that generation who entered planning (and many other professions) to make the world a better place. Once there, they found their values and ideals compromised. Their chosen profession could not or would not accomplish what they hoped. In response, they turned to history to discover what went wrong. Along the way they framed their search in class arguments. The dialectics they produced provide clear reading and give a seemingly systematic understanding to the past. They place their predecessors' actions in simple, uncompromising terms. Yet in the process, they lose the craft of conjecture and logic that their less doctrinaire associates convey in more traditional historical narrative.

Politics, Planning, and Urban Growth

In turning from a narrow focus on institutional planning to a more general look at urban growth, a series of recent studies in local history refines the political science–based debate on the nature of power. Although these works deal with different eras and distinct places, they are unified by their common quest to investigate decision making by examining the relationship between politics and planning. They ask critical questions about who is determining the use and distribution of land, public investment, and the delivery of municipal services. They also speculate about the beneficiaries of various policies. Their provocative answers outline the political environment and social conditions surrounding the city building activities defined as planning. For these scholars, the scenario is broader than the institutional framework laid out by the authors discussed in the previous section. Their scope lies within a more extensive urban growth model. Their planners are not only the professionals but also a larger group of political actors.

Taking the broadest possible view of planning, David R. Goldfield in "Urban Growth in the Old South" uses an unrepresentative region and period to argue that even in the antebellum years, businessmen constituted a closed, self-serving elite who directed public investments to serve their own interest: rapid urban growth.[48] David C. Hammack challenges this interpretation in his study of greater New York.[49] He argues that such decisions as municipal consolidation and transportation planning were in the hands of not one elite but several competing groups differentiated by distinct social, economic, and cultural values. Confirming the pluralistic model advanced by political scientists Wallace Sayre, Herbert

K. Kaufman, and Robert A. Dahl, Hammack asserts that the presence of different groups resulted in a failure to agree on a common set of initiatives.[50] Thus when Andrew H. Green, an influential activist, repeatedly called for a comprehensive plan to determine the city's infrastructure and open space patterns, he received no support.

Despite wide differences among nineteenth-century leaders, American municipal governments did manage to plan and provide a higher standard of public services—water, light, parks, public transportation—than their counterparts abroad. Additionally, as Jon C. Teaford maintains in *The Unheralded Triumph*, they did not accomplish this without some highly trumpeted failures—corruption and devastating political infighting. But they did indeed work out a practical mode of operation: "a system of compromise and accommodation, a balancing act among elements of society that shared no mutual respect."[51] One facet of the compromise is most important for planning historians: the growing importance of the professional in this political arena. The civil engineer or the landscape architect, for example, had the expertise to plan a sewer or park. As an unassailable bureaucrat or highly respected consultant, he directed the course of urban development with little need to enter into the political fray. The political boss, uneducated in technological matters but savvy in negotiation, took care of that part of the deal. Teaford's clear analysis of this process illuminates that later posture of the early twentieth-century planners who cast themselves as politically disinterested technicians.

The close linkage of politics and planning in the twentieth century is exposed in three surveys: of Richmond, Virginia, by Christopher Silver, of Portland, Oregon, by Carl Abbott, and of Chicago by Arnold Hirsch.[52] These authors reject distinctions between public and private spheres in policy analysis and assert that for planning, at least, the two are the same. They view planning as a reflection of dominant corporate and institutional values. Consequently it is pro-growth and conservative. It blindly pursues a self-serving course at the expense of minority needs. These characteristics, they argue, are clearly exhibited in postwar planning activities: the levels and type of expenditures, the location of downtown renewal projects, public housing, and highway systems. A particularly pernicious aspect, outlined by Silver and Hirsch, is its institutionalized racism. Hirsch's careful plotting of the location of public housing and clearance projects in Chicago during the crucial 1940 to 1960 period shows the same patterns as Silver's analysis in Richmond: clear-cut residential segregation. Further evidence comes from J. Anthony Lukas in his Pulitzer Prize–winning account of Boston, *Common Ground: A Turbulent Decade in the Lives of Three American Families*.[53] He delineates the conflicts inherent in municipal housing policies—gentrification, 221 (d) 3 subsidies, site programs—and their relationship to the school busing crisis. While these authors acknowledge that the problems of competition for space in a highly restricted environment certainly had deeper roots than the postwar period, they show how the planners' subscription to private practices limiting black mobility and their use of public funds to contain newcomers within ghetto areas would sow the seeds of deep discontent and disillusionment among the black population.[54]

Politics and planning are clearly linked in the pursuit of another pro-growth goal: capturing military expenditures. Roger W. Lotchin's "The City and the Sword in Metropolitan California, 1919–1941" demonstrates the unquestioned popular acceptance of the use of comprehensive planning for harbor development and transportation to attract the defense dollar booty to several cities.[55] During World War II, however, politicians bypassed established planning to meet short-term housing crises and other emergencies, according to Carl Abbott's account of Portland. Here the power structure (the mayor, city council and business interests) did not have the time or need to co-opt planners into promoting their programs.

In *The Contested City*, John H. Mollenkopf finds this analysis of the relationship between planning and politics too parochial.[56] He looks elsewhere for explanations of planning decisions. While he admits the existence of local pro-growth coalitions, he sees their roots in national New Deal politics and the rise of Democratic liberalism. From his study of Boston and San Francisco, he holds that support for urban redevelopment was not the creature of private interests but the offspring of the pragmatic "political entrepreneurs," clever, risk-taking politicians who forged disparate interests into unbeatable power bases. The federal government cemented this process, funneling well-funded, carefully directed programs to the local leaders. This partnership fell apart, however, in the 1970s when national demographic and economic trends transformed American cities and disturbed earlier arrangements. His argument that political logic, not private initiatives, shaped the course of planning policy is rather startling in the light of previous analyses.

In another interesting corrective, Joel Schwartz's study of redevelopment in New York City looks beyond party politics to examine the part of liberals, radicals, and leftists in forming the urban policy.[57] He argues that these groups failed to temper the segregationist, private sector dominance of the projects for several reasons, including an inability to agree on a proper course and disparate, selfish motivations.

Town Site, Urban Design, and Utopian Planning

Physical planning has generated its own rather separate literature. Its most prolific and wide-ranging author is John W. Reps. Surveying American city development for the past twenty years, he has uncovered enough evidence of European design precedents, colonial new town policies, gridiron arrangements, and religious and utopian schemes to convince even the most skeptical observer that the United States has a strong and vital town site planning tradition.[58] His most recent work, *Cities of the American West, A History of Frontier Urban Planning*, disputes the Turner thesis, which held that rural settlement preceded urbanization on the frontier. He demonstrates that, contrary to the Turnerian vision, western cities did not develop incrementally but were laid out as wholly planned communities.[59] Consequently, he argues, the western city shaped frontier life, not the reverse.

Recent works by architectural historians demonstrate the range of inquiry covered by historians of physical planning. For example, Dora P. Crouch, Axel I. Mundigo, and Daniel Garr's *Spanish City Planning in North America* shows the enduring strength of the Laws of the Indies in shaping Spanish colonial cities in North America, while John S. Garner's *The Model Company Town* demonstrates that planning is not only a public sector activity.[60] Other authors, such as John Archer, describe how design ideals are transferred from place to place, a thesis held by architect Robert A. M. Stern in his accounts of suburbs. Finally, a special issue of *Public Interest* discusses public space in America by looking at parks, streets, and civic buildings.[61] The authors here provide more than a stylistic analysis by probing deeply into the motivations of the sponsors.

Investigations of the utopian strains of planning usually focus on physical designs for whole communities. Robert Fishman's *Urban Utopias of the Twentieth Century* treats the schemes of Ebenezer Howard, Frank Lloyd Wright, and Le Corbusier. Herbert Muschamp's *Man about Town* deals only with Wright but does it very well,[62] while William H. Wilson's "Moles and Skylarks" contrasts idealistic and pragmatic thinkers in a cleverly written essay.[63]

A refreshing contribution to the traditional utopian literature is Dolores Hayden's *The Grand Domestic Revolution*.[64] Assembling a collection of unknown schemes, Hayden's provocative account demonstrates a planning counterculture calling for a radical restructuring of the physical environment to make it suitable for women in the modern industrial age. Other surveys of domestic architecture and design that have some treatment of utopian schemes are David P. Handlin's *The American Home* and Gwendolyn Wright's *Moralism and the Model Home* and *Building the Dream*.[65]

Basic Documents and Other Resources

No bibliographic essay on the history of planning would be complete without reference to the growing but scattered body of resources. Anthony Sutcliffe's *The History of Urban and Regional Planning: An Annotated Bibliography* provides a thorough account of American and European writing through 1980.[66] Donald A. Krueckeberg's reference list in *Introduction to Planning History* is more up-to-date and focuses on the United States. John W. Reps' bibliographies accompanying his books are especially authoritative. Of particular note are his citations in *Cities of the American Frontier*.

There are three types of sources for documentary evidence of American urbanization and planning. The first, exemplified by Reps' *Views and Viewmakers of Urban America*, demonstrates the wide variety of maps available. Here nineteenth-century growth and public investment can be charted.[67] The second, represented by Peter Bacon Hales' *Silver Cities: The Photography of American*

Urbanization, 1839–1915, indicates the power of the picture.[68] Offerings like Hales' are valuable for their analysis of how photographers used their medium to provide a message about city life and urban problems. The third, private papers, is illustrated by *Creating Central Park*, the third volume of the Frederick Law Olmsted papers, edited by Charles E. Beveridge and David Schuyler.[69] The editors' careful annotations and selections as well as their publication of the full park plan make this resource more readily accessible. Very few such collections are published, however. Researchers must depend on library collections, such as the vast assemblage of planning papers at Cornell's Olin Library, whose holdings were recently surveyed in a fine exhibition. Its catalog is available on request.[70]

Finally, the appearance of oral histories and reminiscences of some of the major actors in the modern planning movement has provided useful material. Donald A. Krueckeberg's *The American Planners, Biographies and Recollections* and the *Journal of the American Planning Association* have several. Of particular note are Robert C. Weaver's "The First Twenty Years of HUD" and "Between the Housers and the Planners: The Recollections of Coleman Woodbury."[71] For an excellent view of the 1920s and 1930s, see *Findings and Keepings* by Lewis Mumford and Carl Sussman's *Planning the Fourth Migration*.[72]

Planning History Today and Tomorrow

As this assessment of the development of planning history demonstrates, the field is alive and healthy, benefiting from the contributions of three types of scholars: the design based, process oriented, and institution concerned. While some observers question the legitimacy of planning history, its prolific output stands as testimony to its existence.[73] Further, the firming of its definition, its scope, and its format serves to guarantee it as a focused and expandable area of inquiry.

Clearly social historians have had a dramatic impact on planning history. This group, with their societal outlook, has broadened the definition of planning to include nonprofessionals as well as practitioners. They have extended the field's scope beyond the examination of urban physical artifacts to a more comprehensive regard of the city. While at times they downplay the built environment in analysis, others (design-based and institution-concerned scholars) stand by to correct them. Additionally, they have circumscribed the time frame of their inquiries to focus on the modern period. Although their view is somewhat narrow, they do concentrate on the relationship between urbanization and industrialization, an important theme. Finally, they have added a strong evaluative dimension. This flows naturally from their interest in process. Not content merely to record metropolitan change, they seek to explain how and why it has occurred. This aspect adds great interest to the literature and lends to the imposition of value judgements in interpretation. All is not perfect in planning history, yet it is more defined and has more potential than ever before. Planning history is a field of accomplishment as well as promise. It has produced surveys, biographies, case studies, and documentary collections. The current growth of interest in the area indicates an intriguing future.

Notes

1. See, for example, Anthony Sutcliffe, ed., *The Rise of Modern Urban Planning, 1800–1914* (New York: St. Martin's Press, 1980), pp. 1–10.

2. Christopher Tunnard and Henry Hope Reed, *American Skyline: The Growth and Form of Our Cities and Towns* (New York: New American Library, 1955); R. E. Wycherly, *How the Greeks Built Cities* (New York: Doubleday, 1969); V. Gordon Childe, *What Happened in History* (Baltimore: Penguin Books, 1964).

3. See, for example, John W. Reps, *Cities of the American West: A History of Frontier Urban Planning* (Princeton: Princeton University Press, 1979); Norma Evenson, *Paris: A Century of Change, 1878–1978* (New Haven: Yale University Press, 1979); Norman J. Johnston, *Cities in the Round* (Seattle: University of Washington Press, 1983); Thomas S. Hines, *Burnham of Chicago: Architect and Planner* (New York: Oxford University Press, 1974); Carl W. Condit, *The Port of New York: A History of the Rail and Terminal System from the Beginnings to Pennsylvania Station* (Chicago: University of Chicago Press, 1980).

4. See, for example, Anthony Sutcliffe, *The Autumn of Central Paris: The Defeat of Town Planning, 1850–1970* (London: Edward Arnold, 1970); Jon A. Peterson, "The Nation's First Comprehensive City Plan: A Political Analysis of the McMillan Plan for Washington, D.C., 1900–1902," *Journal of the American Planning Association* 51 (Spring 1985): 134–50; Blaine A. Brownell and David R. Goldfield, *The City in Southern History: The Growth of Urban Civilization in the South* (Port Washington, N.Y.: Kennikat Press, 1977); David R. Goldfield and Blaine A. Brownell, *Urban America: From Downtown to No Town* (Boston: Houghton Mifflin, 1979); Zane L. Miller, *Suburb: Neighborhood and Community in Forest Park, Ohio, 1935–1976* (Knoxville: University of Tennessee Press, 1981); and Daniel Schaffer, *Garden Cities for America: The Radburn Experience* (Philadelphia: Temple University Press, 1982).

5. See, for example, Donald A. Krueckeberg, ed., *Introduction to Planning History in the United States* (New Brunswick: Center for Urban Policy Research, 1983); Laurence C. Gerckens, "Bettman of Cincinnati," in Donald A. Krueckeberg, ed., *The American Planner: Biographies and Recollections* (New York: Methuen, 1983), pp. 120–48; Peter Marcuse, "Housing Policy and City Planning: The Puzzling Split in the United States, 1893–1931," in Gordon E. Cherry, ed., *Shaping an Urban World* (New York: St. Martin's Press, 1980), pp. 23–58; Marc A. Weiss, "The Origins and Legacy of Urban Renewal," in J. Paul Mitchell, *Federal Housing Policy and Programs, Past and Present* (New Brunswick: Center for Urban Policy Research, 1985), pp. 253–76; Roger Montgomery, "Pruitt-Igoe: Policy Failure or Societal System," in Barry Checkoway and Carl V. Patton, eds., *The Metropolitan Midwest, Policy Problems and Prospects for Change* (Urbana: University of Illinois Press, 1985), 229–43; and Eugenie L. Birch, "Advancing the Art and Science of Planning, Planners and Their Organizations," *Journal of the American Planning Association* 46 (January 1980): 22–49.

6. Mark Girouard, *Cities and People* (New Haven: Yale University Press, 1985); Kenneth T. Jackson, *Crabgrass Frontier: The Suburbanization of the United States* (New

York: Oxford University Press, 1985); Marc A. Weiss, *The Rise of the Community Builder: American Real Estate Developers, Urban Planners and the Creation of Modern Residential Subdivisions* (New York: Columbia University Press, forthcoming).

7. Pierre Lavedan, *Histoire de l'urbanisme*, 3 vols. (Paris: H. Laurens, 1928–1953); Erwin A. Gutkind, *International History of City Development*, 5 vols. (New York: Harcourt, Brace and World, 1961); and A. E. J. Morris, *History of Urban Form* (New York: John Wiley, 1974).

8. Leonardo Benevolo, *The History of the City* (Cambridge, Mass.: MIT Press, 1980); Girouard, *Cities and People*; Reps, *Cities of the American West*.

9. Manuel Castells, *The Urban Question* (Cambridge, Mass.: MIT Press, 1979); Giorgio Ciucci, Francesco Dal Co, Mario Manieri-Elia, and Manfredo Tafuri, *The American City: From the Civil War to the New Deal* (Cambridge, Mass.: MIT Press, 1979); David Harvey, *Consciousness and the Urban Experience: Studies in the History and Theory of Capitalist Urbanization* and *The Urbanization of Capital: Studies in the History and Theory of Capitalist Urbanization* (Baltimore: Johns Hopkins University Press, 1985); Josef W. Konvitz, *The City Building Process from the Early Middle Ages to the Present* (Carbondale: Southern Illinois University Press, 1985).

10. Jane Jacobs, *Cities and the Wealth of Nations: Principles of Economic Life* (New York: Random House, 1984).

11. Anthony Sutcliffe, ed., *Metropolis: 1890–1940* (Chicago: University of Chicago Press, 1984); Morton White and Lucia White, *The Intellectual Versus the City* (New York: Mentor Books, 1964); Thomas Bender, *Toward an Urban Vision: Ideas and Institutions in Nineteenth-Century America* (Lexington: University Press of Kentucky, 1975).

12. Andrew Lees, *Cities Perceived: Urban Society in European and American Thought, 1820–1940* (New York: Columbia University Press, 1985); William Sharpe and Leonard Wallock, eds., *Visions of the Modern City*, Proceedings of the Heyman Center for the Humanities (New York: Columbia University, 1983).

13. See, for example, Paul Boyer, *Urban Masses and Moral Order in America, 1820–1920* (Cambridge, Mass.: Harvard University Press, 1978); Robert H. Bremner, *From the Depths: The Discovery of Poverty in the United States* (New York: New York University Press, 1956); Blake McKelvey, *The Urbanization of America, 1860–1915* (New Brunswick: Rutgers University Press, 1963); Zane L. Miller, *The Urbanization of Modern America: A Brief History* (New York: Harcourt Brace Jovanovich, 1973).

14. See Roy Lubove, *The Professional Altruist: The Emergence of Social Work as a Career, 1880–1930* (Cambridge, Mass.: Harvard University Press, 1965); idem, "I. N. Phelps Stokes, Tenement Architect, Economist, Planner," *Journal of the Society of Architectural Historians* 23 (May 1964): 89–100; Arthur Mann, *Yankee Reformers in an Urban Age: Social Reform in Boston 1880–1900* (New York: Harper & Row, 1954); Allen F. Davis, *Spearheads for Reform: The Social Settlements and the Progressive Movement, 1890–1914* (New York: Oxford University Press, 1967); Clarke A. Chambers, *Paul U. Kellog and the Survey: Voices for Social Welfare and Social Justice* (Minneapolis: University of Minnesota Press, 1971).

15. Mel Scott, *American City Planning since 1890* (Berkeley: University of California Press, 1969); Laurence C. Gerckens, "Historical Development of American City Planning," in Frank S. So, ed., *The Practice of Local Government Planning* (Washington, D.C.: International City Management Association, 1979), pp. 21–60.

16. Krueckeberg, *American Planner*.

17. Michael Simpson, *Thomas Adams* (London: Mansell, 1985).

18. David R. Hill, "Lewis Mumford's Ideas on the City," *Journal of the American Planning Association* 51 (Autumn 1985): 407–21.

19. Mark I. Gelfand, "Rexford Tugwell and the Frustrations of Planning in New York City," *Journal of the American Planning Association* 51 (Spring 1985): 151–60.

20. Robert A. Caro, *The Power Broker: Robert Moses and the Fall of New York* (New York: Vintage Books, 1975); Daniel Schaffer, "Resettling Industrial America: The Controversy over FDR's Greenbelt Town Program," *Urbanism Past and Present* 8 (Winter-Spring 1983): 18–32; Joseph A. Eden and Arnold R. Alanen, "Looking Backward at a New Deal Town: Greendale, Wisconsin, 1935–1980," *Journal of the American Planning Association* 49 (Winter 1983): 40–58; Miller, *Suburbs*. See also Joseph L. Arnold, *The New Deal in the Suburbs: A History of the Greenbelt Town Program, 1935–1954* (Columbus: Ohio State University Press, 1971).

21. John Robert Mullin, "Henry Ford and Field and Factory: An Analysis of the Ford Sponsored Village Industries Experiment in Michigan, 1918–1941," *Journal of the American Planning Association* 48 (Autumn 1982): 419–31.

22. Schaffer, *Radburn*; Sutcliffe, *Rise of Modern Planning*; and Cherry, *Shaping an Urban World*.

23. Jon A. Peterson, "The Impact of Sanitary Reform upon American Urban Planning, 1840–1890" *Journal of Social History* 13 (Fall 1979): 83–103, and "The City Beautiful Movement: Forgotten Origins and Lost Meanings," *Journal of Urban History* 2 (August 1976): 415–34. Also in Krueckeberg, *Introduction to Planning History*, pp. 13–57.

24. William H. Wilson, "The Ideology, Aesthetics and Politics of the City Beautiful Movement," in Sutcliffe, *Rise of Modern Planning*, pp. 166–98; Robert L. Wrigley, Jr., "The Plan of Chicago," in Krueckeberg, *Introduction to Planning History*, pp. 58–72; and Peterson, "Nation's First Comprehensive City Plan."

25. Christopher Silver, "Neighborhood Planning in Historical Perspective," *Journal of the American Planning Association* 51 (Spring 1985): 161–74; Howard Gillette, Jr., "The Evolution of Neighborhood Planning: From the Progressive Era to the 1949 Housing Act," *Journal of Urban History* 9 (August 1983): 421–44.

26. Tridib Banerjee and William C. Baer, *Beyond the Neighborhood Unit: Residential Environments and Public Policy* (New York: Plenum Press, 1984).

27. Howard Gillette, Jr., "The Evolution of the Planned Shopping Center in Suburb and City," *Journal of the American Planning Association* 51 (Autumn 1985): 449–60.

28. Nancy Grant, "Blacks, Regional Planning and the TVA" (Ph.D. diss., University of Chicago, 1978); Andrew M. Isserman, "Dare to Plan," *Town Planning Review* 56 (October 1985): 483–91. Another more extensive review of the TVA is Erwin C. Hargrove and Paul K. Conklin, eds., *TVA: Fifty Years of Grass-Roots Bureaucracy* (Urbana: University of Illinois Press, 1983).

29. Mark S. Foster, *From Streetcar to Superhighway: American City Planners and Urban Transportation, 1900–1940* (Philadelphia: Temple University Press, 1981); Martin Wachs, "Autos, Transit, and the Sprawl of Los Angeles: The 1920's," *Journal of the American Planning Association* 50 (Summer 1984): 297–310.

30. Blaine A. Brownell, "Urban Planning, the Planning Profession and the Motor Vehicle in Early Twentieth-Century America," in Cherry, *Shaping an Urban World*, pp. 59–78.

31. Mark H. Rose, *Interstate: Express Highway Politics, 1941–1956* (Lawrence: Regents Press of Kansas, 1979); Kenneth T. Jackson, *Crabgras Frontier: The Suburbanization of the United States* (New York: Oxford University Press, 1985).

32. Robert B. Fairbanks, "Metropolitan Planning and Downtown Redevelopment: The Cincinnati and Dallas Experience" (paper presented at the Annual Meeting of the Organization of American Historians, April 11, 1986).

33. Howard Gillette, Jr., "A National Workshop for Urban Policy: The Metropolitanization of Washington, 1946–1968," *The Public Historian* 7 (Winter 1985): 7–27. For a comprehensive study of planning in Washington, D.C., see Frederick Gutheim, *Worthy of the Nation: The History of Planning for the National Capital* (Washington, D.C.: Smithsonian Press, 1977).

34. Peter Marcuse, "Housing Policy and City Planning: The Puzzling Split in the United States," in Cherry, *Shaping an Urban World*, pp. 23–58.

35. Robert B. Fairbanks, "From Better Dwellings to Better Community: Changing Approaches to the Low Cost Housing Problem, 1890–1925," *Journal of Urban History* 11 (May 1985): 314–34.

36. Deborah Gardner, ed., "The Early Years of Public Housing," special issue of the *Journal of Urban History* 12 (August 1986). Included are the following articles: Ann L. Buttenwieser, "Shelter for What and for Whom? On the Route Toward Vladeck Houses, 1930 to 1940"; Rosalie Genevro, "Site Selection and the New York Housing Authority, 1934–1939"; Joel Schwartz, "Tenant Unions in New York City's Low-Rent Housing, 1933–1949"; and Peter Marcuse, "The Beginnings of Public Housing in New York."

37. John F. Bauman, "Visions of a Post-War City: A Perspective on Urban Planning in Philadelphia and the Nation," in Krueckeberg, *Introduction to Planning History*, pp. 170–88. See also William R. Barnes, "The Origins of Urban Renewal: The Public Housing Controversy and the Emergence of a Redevelopment Program in the District of Columbia, 1942–1949" (Ph.D. diss., Syracuse University, 1972); Mary Susan Cole, "Catherine Bauer and the Public Housing Movement" (Ph. D. diss., George Washington University, 1975); Eugenie Ladner Birch, "Edith Elmer Wood and the Genesis of Liberal Housing Thought, 1910–1945" (Ph.D. diss., Columbia University, 1975); and Robert B. Fairbanks, "Better Housing Movements and the City: Definitions of and Responses to Cincinnati's Low Cost Housing Problem, 1910–1954" (Ph.D. diss., University of Cincinnati, 1981).

38. Weiss, "The Origins and Legacy of Urban Renewal," pp. 253–77.

39. Arnold R. Hirsch, *Making the Second Ghetto: Race and Housing in Chicago, 1940–1960* (Cambridge: Cambridge University Press, 1983).

40. Montgomery, "Pruitt-Igoe" pp. 229–43.

41. Alan David Heskin, "Crisis and Response, A Historical Perspective on Advocacy Planning," *Journal of the American Planning Association* 46 (January 1980): 50–63.

42. Otis L. Graham, Jr., *Toward a Planned Society, From Roosevelt to Nixon* (New York: Oxford University Press, 1976); Mark I. Gelfand, *A Nation of Cities: The Federal Government and Urban America, 1933–1965* (New York: Oxford University Press, 1975).

43. Phillip J. Funigiello, "City Planning in World War II: The Experience of the National Resources Board," in Krueckeberg, *Introduction to Planning History*, pp. 152–69.

44. Carl Feiss, "The Foundations of Federal Planning Assistance: A Personal Account of the 701 Program," *Journal of the American Planning Association* 51 (Spring 1985): 177.

45. Marion Clawson, *New Deal Planning: The National Resources Planning Board* (Baltimore: Johns Hopkins University Press, 1981).

46. Albert Lepawsky, "The Planning Apparatus: A Vignette of the New Deal," *Journal*

of the American Institute of Planners 42 (January 1975): 16–32; Donald A. Krueckeberg, "From the Background Garden to the Whole U.S.A.: A Conversation with Charles W. Eliot, 2nd," *Journal of the American Planning Association* 46 (October 1980): 449–56.

47. M. Christine Boyer, *Dreaming the Rational City: The Myth of American City Planning* (Cambridge, Mass.: MIT Press, 1983).

48. David R. Goldfield, "Urban Growth in the Old South," in Sutcliffe, *Rise of Modern Urban Planning*, pp. 11–30.

49. David C. Hammack, *Power and Society: Greater New York at the Turn of the Century* (New York: Russell Sage Foundation, 1982).

50. Wallace Sayre and Herbert K. Kaufman, *Governing New York City: Politics in the Metropolis* (New York: Russell Sage Foundation, 1960); Robert A. Dahl, *Who Governs? Democracy and Power in an American City* (New Haven: Yale University Press, 1961).

51. Jon C. Teaford, *The Unheralded Triumph: City Government in America, 1870–1900* (Baltimore: Johns Hopkins University Press, 1984).

52. Christopher Silver, *Twentieth-Century Richmond: Planning, Politics, and Race* (Knoxville: University of Tennessee Press, 1984); Carl Abbott, *Portland: Planning, Politics and Growth in a Twentieth-Century City* (Lincoln: University of Nebraska Press, 1983); Arnold R. Hirsch, *Making the Second Ghetto: Race and Housing in Chicago, 1940–1960* (Cambridge: Cambridge University Press, 1983). See also Alonzo N. Smith, "Blacks and the Los Angeles Municipal Transit System," *Urbanism Past and Present* 6 (Winter-Spring 1981): 25–31.

53. J. Anthony Lukas, *Common Ground: A Turbulent Decade in the Lives of Three American Families* (New York: Alfred A. Knopf, 1985).

54. For information on the making of the ghetto in an earlier period, see Thomas L. Philpott, *The Slum and the Ghetto: Neighborhood Deterioration and Middle Class Reforms, Chicago, 1880–1930* (New York: Oxford University Press, 1978); Allan H. Spear, *Black Chicago: The Making of a Negro Ghetto, 1890–1920* (Chicago: University of Chicago Press, 1967); Gilbert Osofsky, *Harlem: The Making of a Ghetto: Negro New York, 1890–1930* (New York: Harper & Row, 1966); and Kenneth L. Kusmer, *A Ghetto Takes Shape: Black Cleveland, 1870–1930* (Urbana: University of Illinois Press, 1976).

55. Roger W. Lotchin, "The City and the Sword in Metropolitan California, 1919–1941," *Urbanism Past and Present* 7 (Summer-Fall 1982): 1–16; see also Lotchin, *The Martial Metropolis: U.S. Cities in War and Peace* (New York: Praeger, 1984), in particular, the chapter by Robert B. Fairbanks and Zane L. Miller, "Housing, Planning, and Race in Cincinnati, 1940–1955," pp. 191–222.

56. John H. Mollenkopf, *The Contested City* (Princeton: Princeton University Press, 1983).

57. Joel Schwartz, "Tenant Radicals, Urban Liberals and Redevelopment in New York City, 1937–1953" (paper presented at the Annual Meeting of the Organization of American Historians, April 11, 1986).

58. Reps' work includes: *The Making of Urban America: A History of City Planning in the United States* (Princeton: Princeton University Press, 1965); *Monumental Washington: The Planning and Development of the Capital Center* (Princeton: Princeton University Press, 1967).

59. *Cities of the American West: A History of Frontier Urban Planning* (Princeton: Princeton University Press, 1979). For an earlier revisionist view, see Richard C. Wade,

The Urban Frontier: The Rise of Western Cities, 1790–1830 (Cambridge, Mass.: Harvard University Press, 1959).

60. Dora P. Crouch, Axel I. Mundigo, and Daniel Garr, *Spanish City Planning in North America* (Cambridge, Mass.: MIT Press, 1982); John S. Garner, *The Model Company Town: Urban Design through Private Enterprise in Nineteenth-Century New England* (Amherst: University of Massachusetts Press, 1984).

61. John Archer, "Country and City in the American Romantic Suburb," *Journal of the Society of Architectural Historians* 62 (May 1983): 139–56; Robert A. M. Stern and John Montagne Massengale, eds., " The Anglo American Suburb," *Architectural Design* 50 (June 1981); Robert A. M. Stern assisted by Thomas Mellins and Raymond Gastil, *Pride of Place: Building the American Dream* (New York: Houghton Mifflin, 1986). In *Public Interest* 74 (Winter 1984), the following articles dealt with the topic: J. B. Jackson, "The American Public Space," pp. 52–76; Donlyn Lyndon, "Public Buildings: Symbols Qualified by Experience," pp. 77–97; Michael A. Scully, "The Triumph of the Capital," pp. 99–115.

62. Robert Fishman, *Urban Utopias of the Twentieth Century* (New York: Basic Books, 1977); Herbert Muschamp, *Man about Town: Frank Lloyd Wright in New York City* (Cambridge, Mass.: MIT Press, 1983).

63. William H. Wilson, "Moles and Skylarks," in Krueckeberg, *Introduction to Planning History*, pp. 88–121.

64. Dolores Hayden, *The Grand Domestic Revolution: A History of Feminist Designs for American Homes, Neighborhoods, and Cities* (Cambridge, Mass.: MIT Press, 1981), p. 198.

65. David P. Handlin, *The American Home: Architecture and Society, 1815–1915* (Boston: Little, Brown, 1979); Gwendolyn Wright, *Moralism and the Model Home: Domestic Architecture and Cultural Conflict in Chicago, 1873–1913* (Chicago: University of Chicago Press, 1980), and *Building the Dream: A Social History of Housing in America* (New York: Pantheon, 1981).

66. Anthony Sutcliffe, *The History of Urban and Regional Planning: An Annotated Bibliography* (New York: Facts on File, 1981).

67. John W. Reps, *Views and Viewmakers of Urban America: Lithographs of Towns and Cities in the United States and Canada* (Columbia: University of Missouri Press, 1984). See also idem, *Panoramas of Promise: Pacific Northwest Cities and Towns in Nineteenth-Century Urban Lithographs* (Seattle: Washington State University Press, 1985), and *Cities on Stone: Nineteenth-Century Lithograph Images of the Urban West* (Fort Worth: Amon Carter Museum, 1976).

68. Peter Bacon Hales, *Silver Cities: The Photography of American Urbanization, 1839–1915* (Philadelphia: Temple University Press, 1984).

69. Charles E. Beveridge and David Schuyler, eds., *Creating Central Park*, vol. 3 of *Papers of Frederick Law Olmsted* (Baltimore: Johns Hopkins University Press, 1983).

70. Elaine D. Engst and H. Thomas Hickerson, *Urban America: Documenting Planners* (Exhibition at the John M. Olin Library, Cornell University, Ithaca, N.Y., October 21–December 31, 1985).

71. Robert C. Weaver, "The First Twenty Years of HUD," *Journal of the American Planning Association* 51 (Autumn 1985): 463–74; Donald A. Krueckeberg, "Between the Housers and the Planners: The Recollections of Coleman Woodbury," in Krueckeberg, *American Planner*, pp. 323–49.

72. Lewis Mumford has been slowly releasing his edited version of his papers in

preparation for the full-scale biography. To date, he has published: *Findings and Keepings: Analects for an Autobiography* (New York: Harcourt Brace Jovanovich, 1975); *My Works and Days: A Personal Chronicle* (New York: Harcourt Brace Jovanovich, 1979); and *Sketches from Life: The Autobiography of Lewis Mumford: The Early Years* (New York: Dial Press, 1982). Carl Sussman, *Planning the Fourth Migration: The Neglected Vision of the Regional Planning Association of America* (Cambridge, Mass.: MIT Press, 1976).

73. Seymour J. Mandelbaum, "Historians and Planners: The Constructions of Pasts and Futures," *Journal of the American Planning Association* 51 (Spring 1985): 185–88.

8 ———— Architecture and the City

RICHARD LONGSTRETH

Architecture has always comprised the major portion of the urban fabric in the United States—and everywhere else. This stuff of the city stands not just as a material deposit but as a varied, complex, and ever-changing record of commerce, institutions, industry, and residence; of regulations and their absence; of economic imperatives, individual causes, collective concerns, and political maneuverings; of aspirations, achievements, and failures. Yet American architecture's urban dimensions are just emerging as a serious subject of scholarship.[1] While much has been written about the architecture of a given district, community, or region, the traditional focus of this work has been on individual buildings, their designers, or, less often, their clients. Similarly, urban histories that incorporate aspects of physical development in much depth have been the exception, and ones analyzing specific architectural qualities in relation to broader phenomena are rare. No doubt many factors have contributed to this gap, not the least of which are the pronounced differences in the roots of architectural history and urban history as academic disciplines. The former emerged from art history, with its long-standing concern for analysis of the material qualities and symbolic content of seminal efforts in the visual arts. On the other hand, the study of urban history stems from the social sciences and allied pursuits wherein scant attention has been paid to the tangible world. This portrayal oversimplifies the picture, but it helps to explain why what might appear to be a natural correlation of interests has only begun to occur in recent years as both fields of study have come into their own and have been broadening their respective realms.

A marked change has indeed taken place over the past two decades. Architectural historians have greatly expanded their parameters of investigation, and scholars from a number of other disciplines, including urban history, are now adding much to our knowledge of architecture. Were this chapter written even a decade ago, at least half the citations would be absent.[2] Given this rapid, ongoing state of change, criticism of earlier efforts from a current viewpoint seems unnecessary. The aim of this chapter is to offer a reference guide, which at the same time indicates the progress that has been made and suggests some subject areas where further probing can yield beneficial results.

Studies of architecture by place—district, community, or region—can be especially valuable as a means of correlating divergent subjects into a holistic framework. Through such accounts, there is the potential to learn not only about houses and residential patterns, for example, but also about how these precincts relate to educational facilities, shopping districts, industrial quarters, parks, and many other components of the urban fabric. The broader is the coverage, the less detail on any one aspect may be included. Nevertheless, this genre of study affords an ideal instrument for understanding places as totalities and the complex relationships of their constituent parts.

During the first half of the twentieth century, books on the architecture of American cities were for the most part antiquarian in tone, concentrating on individual buildings from the colonial and early Republic periods. Their texts focus primarily on individual buildings; sometimes on materials, construction techniques, and designers; and on associated occupants and events.[3] A more inclusive approach in its temporal and topical dimensions began in the 1950s with the publication of books on Providence, Richmond, and Philadelphia.[4] Other cities were covered in the following decade, and there has been a veritable onslaught of books produced since 1970. Some of these studies attempt to cover work from the time of earliest settlement to the present, but a greater number limit themselves to an era, an architectural phase,[5] selected parts of the city,[6] or certain thematic spheres.[7] Since the 1950s, there has been a clear trend in these books to address an ever greater range of building types, to examine vernacular as well as high-style examples, to depict architecture's impact on the character of precincts and the city as a whole, and to consider in some detail social, political, economic, and other external forces that have figured in shaping the environment.

From an architectural perspective, the most important American cities have been New York, Philadelphia, Boston (beginning in the colonial period), Chicago (beginning in the 1880s), San Francisco, and Los Angeles (beginning around 1900). Most seminal tendencies in design, construction, and the development of building types have occurred in those places, and most of the country's renowned architects have practiced there or in nearby communities.[8] There are notable exceptions, such as Detroit's once-leading role in the design of factories or Frank Lloyd Wright's choice of rural Wisconsin as his home base from the 1910s to the end of his long career. Yet such cases are minor when placed in the context of patterns that define the whole of America's urban architecture. Thus the significance of work in these six cities derives not only from the prominence of the places themselves but from the influence they had on architecture in many other parts of the country. The Federal row houses of Philadelphia, the Victorian mercantile buildings of that city and of New York, the skyscrapers of New York and Chicago, the eighteenth- and early twentieth-century ecclesiastical work of Boston, the suburban architecture of Philadelphia and San Francisco, and the automobile-oriented buildings of Los Angeles are some obvious examples of types that have had an enormous impact on shaping the American landscape.

No architectural counterpart to Harold Mayer and Richard Wade's extraordinary and still unmatched urban history of Chicago exists for any of these cities.[9] However, several recent books have made significant contributions to understanding architecture in Chicago and New York, especially. Carl Condit has written a hard-hitting critique of twentieth-century commercial, institutional, and public projects in Chicago. The voluminous study by Robert Stern and his associates of New York architecture between 1890 and 1915 marshals copious documentation to generate a sense of the energy, innovation, and sheer extent of high-quality design that left an indelible imprint on that city. Christine Boyer takes a very different approach, using architecture to clarify the complex, unregulated patterns of urban development in New York between 1850 and 1900.[10]

As valuable as such efforts may be, they represent only a beginning. Much more remains to be studied in each of these cities. But probably an even greater lacuna stems from the fact that, with few exceptions, this whole genre of architectural history is parochial, lacking profound comparative analysis of work in other places, large and small, at home and abroad. The literature on New York architecture alone constitutes a small library, but precious few pages analyze how patterns there were similar to or different from those in Boston or Los Angeles, London or Vienna, or how they may have influenced those in St. Louis and Denver, Grand Rapids, and Charlotte.[11]

The need for comparative study is at least equally desirable in works devoted to the architecture of other cities, irrespective of their size. Recent books on St. Louis, Milwaukee, Minneapolis, and Dallas stand among the best examples of how buildings can provide insight on the myriad factors that have shaped the metropolis.[12] Yet one is generally left to speculate as to the degree such places echo bigger or older settlements and the degree to which they may differ by virtue of location, size, economic base, demographic composition, planning initiatives, and many additional factors. And have much smaller cities—the Lynchburg, Virginias, and Wilmington, North Carolinas, of the United States—developed in substantially different ways from those many times their size, or are they merely miniature metropolitan centers?[13] Most such books are written primarily for a local audience and therefore tend to cover various periods and types of building in more or less equal measure. The resulting documentation can serve local purposes admirably and often can be useful to scholars as well. But one unfortunate by-product of this approach is to give less than adequate attention to aspects of major consequence, such as the extensive park system and network of garden suburbs in Kansas City.

Specialness has generated studies on the architecture of towns. The industrial enclave and fashionable resort have elicited interest precisely because they appear quite different from most other places.[14] Several good books on more representative towns have also been published, yet the collective results are meager when compared to those for larger settlements.[15] Coverage of individual communities will no doubt remain limited, for few scholars worthy of the task find such projects appealing, and equally few publishers find them economically justifiable. Where opportunities do exist is in undertaking thematic studies on towns in one or more regions. For several decades, urban historians have analyzed the diffusion of the impulse to create urban centers across the nation. This drive for city building provided the conceptual and physical matrices for thousands of towns—places that wanted to but never did become cities. Aspirations of urbanity can be found in town architecture as well, but the subject remains to be explored in depth. Once again, one must ask the extent to which towns are abbreviated cities or whether the relationship must be considered the other way around. Additional topics such as the existence of regional distinctions and differences that occur due to functional orientation, size, periods of growth, or ethnicity beg for no less attention. The few thematic studies conducted to date, focusing on such dissimilar subjects as early preservation efforts[16] and elements common to various types of settlement,[17] reveal the rich possibilities in this realm.

Two other publication formats on communities constitute important sources of information. One is the architectural inventory, which is generally prepared under the auspices of a municipal agency, historical society, or state preservation office. Books of this type tend to provide material on a large number of buildings, far more than often can be found in local histories. But the best products distill the collected data into one or more essays. The first to be published was on Charleston in 1944,[18] but most belong to the last two decades. The multivolume inventories of Cambridge, Massachusetts, and New Orleans offer unparalleled documentation of urban development.[19] A number of others, varying in quality, have been written on communities[20] and districts.[21] The preservation offices in Rhode Island,[22] North Carolina,[23] and Maryland[24] have embarked on ambitious publication programs that are projected eventually to cover all communities and rural areas in those states.

The other format is the architectural guidebook, which has become a popular means to present work in communities during the past two decades.[25] American guides of this type constitute a distinctive genre. In most cases, buildings and other sites are individually listed, each with accompanying data and often a concise descriptive text. Entries are grouped by area, and there is generally an introductory essay that seeks to lend some historical perspective to the contents. Paralleling what has occurred with local histories, guides have tended to become ever more inclusive in the selection of examples and in what is written about them. Guides now exist for most large American cities[26] and for many less populous communities as well.[27] In most instances, entries are limited to those found within municipal boundaries, which may preclude giving a sense of the metropolitan region. However, two guides have been written exclusively on work in outlying areas of major cities.[28] Several other guides encompass the whole, or a very large part of a state, but this approach generally leads to less coverage of any one community.[29]

The great strength of these guidebooks is a structure facilitating quick retrieval of information on a particular subject and finding the corresponding sites. No better means exists for aiding in the firsthand discovery of a place than a good architectural guide. At the same time, their compartmentalized format resists presenting many physical aspects of a district or a community as a whole.[30] The focus tends to be on buildings and some prominent structures such as bridges; streets, open spaces, public fixtures such as street lights, monuments, or rapid transit systems are less frequently mentioned. In recent years, new approaches have been tried. One series concentrates on detailed observations about a selective group of sites in order to convey a greater sense of the city's character.[31] Other guides have a topical focus allowing one aspect of the urban fabric to be examined in greater depth.[32]

The study of building types—that is, buildings classified according to their functions—constitutes another basic approach by which architecture can be explored in its urban context. An analysis that focuses on railroad stations, courthouses, libraries, or any other functional type may not lead to a synoptic view of a community; however, it can yield a rich core sample of more detailed information on factors that have been instrumental in shaping the form and character of settlement.

While type studies may concentrate on buildings and little else, such treatment affords an incomplete picture, leaving function narrowly defined and presented in somewhat of a vacuum. Public schools, for example, represent key markers in community in both its tangible and intangible dimensions. Schools can also suggest the nature of that community, for important differences often are to be found between those in cities and towns and their rural counterparts. Little scholarly analysis of these buildings exists in print, but they afford a good basis for delineating the sort of inquiry that can be undertaken to shed new light on the urban scene.

Public schools are not wished into existence; they are constructed through allocation of government funds in response to a variety of actual and perceived needs. When, where, and how schools were built can reveal much about the local political system, the emphasis placed on public improvements, attitudes toward education at various levels and among various constituencies, residential growth patterns, and demographic composition, among many other things.

Schools situated in affluent enclaves may be designed quite differently from those in working-class districts, and there may be more or less of them per capita in a given precinct depending on the role played by various types of private institutions. Schools may have very prominent locations—on a hill, at a major intersection—and may be designed as landmarks. Or they may be unobtrusive components of the urban fabric in siting and appearance. The degree to which the school is rendered as a monument to civic pride or as a utilitarian necessity may indicate the prosperity of the populace, the whims or dedication of public officials and their boards, the importance placed on different age groups, and numerous additional factors, which in turn can contribute to understanding the specifics of the community's physical and social character.

Additional questions are sure to follow. Were schools exemplary in their standards of construction and technical features, or did they represent a minimal investment? Were school sites carefully planned, or was selection a matter of expediency? Did the building of schools keep apace of residential development or lag far behind? To these considerations can be added a temporal matrix, for all facets of school building can vary from one period to the next. This is by no means an exhaustive list of factors, but it is sufficient to underscore how type studies can provide myriad insights on the community itself.

The very extent of pertinent factors poses problems, however. Examining schools from a holistic perspective in a major city, or even a minor one, and for a period of say seventy-five years can necessitate extensive research and may result in a substantial volume. The product might reveal many particulars but lack a comparative base. To what extent, for example, was school design in this community a localized phenomenon, and how much did it depend on regional or national tendencies? Sometimes school design as it developed in one locality became influential in many other places, but did the process of diffusion always occur in this way? Rather than concentrating on one place, would it be more productive to focus the inquiry on a subtype, such as late nineteenth- and early twentieth-century industrial schools in large cities, or to address a broader topical question such as the city beautiful movement's impact on school design? Would any such study lend sufficient insight on the subject without the existence of an overall history of American public school buildings? In reality, each of these pursuits can make a substantive contribution, for the amount of material published on building types in the United States remains meager. Only a few scholarly surveys exist.[33] From an urban historian's viewpoint, the most valuable material is more detailed and quite narrow in the geographic area and chronological period investigated. The richness of findings in these essays suggests how fruitful further exploration can be as type studies emerge from their current nascent stage.

By far the most frequently examined building type is the house. Several good surveys now exist on houses and housing; all of them in different ways place their subject in a broader cultural framework and, with one exception, integrate urbanistic considerations in their texts.[34] These books address a number of general thematic areas, such as company towns, reform in tenement house design, town improvement initiatives, and the subdivision communities created by mid-twentieth-century merchant builders. Treatment of each topic is necessarily generalized but affords a valuable overview.

City dwellings—row houses, attached houses, or freestanding ones in a form that distinguishes them from counterparts in suburbs, towns, and rural areas—have long been investigated. But until recent decades, these studies tended to concentrate on documenting early, high-style residences and the lives of their occupants.[35] A decisive break in this approach came in 1967 with Bainbridge Bunting's *Houses of Boston's Back Bay*, which set a new standard in the analysis of city dwellings, Victorian and early twentieth-century architecture, and pertinent urban factors.[36] The topographical development of Boston, the planning of this ambitious new quarter, and the impact of building codes, among other aspects, are used to paint a vivid picture of the Back Bay and much of the rest of the old city as well. Bunting's remarkable effort was soon followed by Charles Lockwood's *Bricks and Brownstone* (1972), which encompasses the development of the attached house on Manhattan Island for over a century and a half.[37] Although aimed at a popular audience, this book is even more an urban history, chronicling such facets as the growth and decline of key residential neighborhoods, speculative development practices, and the complexion of local building trades. Betsy Blackmar's essay on housing in New York at the turn of the nineteenth century adds greater depth to this documentation. Architecture becomes a means for examining real estate history, its impact on social patterns, and its role in the emergence of the single-family house as a middle-class status symbol.[38] Jay Cantor has examined the genesis of that city's palatial residences and how the prototypical work of this genre became closely identified with the accomplishments of its owner and also stood as a public monument.[39]

More modest dwellings, which often comprise a major portion of the metropolitan fabric, are beginning to receive no less careful attention. The pioneering essay in this regard is Margaret Tinkom's study of Southwark, the oldest extant working-class neighborhood in Philadelphia and perhaps in the United States.[40] Tinkom analyzes houses not only in their original form but as they have been modified over time, and she correlates patterns of residential development to the location of workplaces nearby. Mary Ellen Hayward investigates the evolution of Baltimore's Federal Hill as a district and also as a composite of house forms that were frequently derived from those found in more affluent sectors of the city.[41] Another approach is exemplified in Anne Bloomfield's history of a major speculative building firm in San Francisco, delineating the contribution of one business to the city's growth patterns during the post–Civil War era.[42]

These focused case studies afford many insights, but they comprise only an initial step in presenting a substantive picture of urban habitation. Much still needs to be done in exploring residential patterns citywide, the physical and social relationships of precincts occupied by various groups, and the geographic ties between dwelling and places of employment.[43] Bunting and Lockwood among others investigate interior spaces and how they are used; nevertheless, much more can be done to delineate how the organization and embellishment of rooms reflected living patterns particular to the city as opposed to those associated with suburban, country, or resort life.[44] Comparing work in different cities has yet to be undertaken. In their external appearance, urban dwellings in Boston, New York, Philadelphia, Washington, Chicago, and San Francisco, to cite some obvious cases, are often conspicuously dissimilar. Throughout the nineteenth and twentieth centuries, local conventions flourished in this sphere of design, providing a sharp contrast to patterns that affected many forms of suburban and rural houses across the country. Do the differences that exist between one metropolitan center and another stem from personal tastes harbored by the designers of city houses or their clients, or do these differences embody varying attitudes toward their respective places and the ways of life there? Why were row houses so common to working-class portions of cities such as Philadelphia and Baltimore and multiple-family dwellings endemic to comparable areas in cities such as Providence? Why were row and other forms of attached houses the dominant pattern in Washington, D.C., from the mid-nineteenth through the early twentieth centuries, and then almost completely rejected for freestanding houses of suburban character? As a sequel to John Reps' exhaustive treatment of the diffusion of orthogonal grid street plans, much could be learned from a study of the widespread use of the attached house as an emblem of city building in developing portions of the Middle Atlantic region and the Midwest during the first half of the nineteenth century.[45]

Freestanding house types that can be found in suburbs of large cities and in many sectors of smaller cities and towns rank among the most extensively discussed of American buildings. Yet accounts that analyze the urban context of such dwellings are rare. Among the reasons for this paradox is the long-standing, and indeed lingering, tendency to depict both the architecture and its setting in generalized terms. Stereotypes such as the picturesque villa, bungalow, and ranch house become easy molds in which to cast the residence, just as Riverside, Illinois; Forest Hills Gardens, New York; and Levittown, Pennsylvania, are often depicted as normative surburban developments. The far more complex historical reality began to be explored by urban historians in the 1960s. The seminal research of Sam Bass Warner, Jr., Richard Wade, and geographer Harold Mayer reveals that the process of suburban growth was an intricate, multifaceted phenomenon encompassing different segments of the populace and numerous residential forms, including row houses and apartment buildings.[46] Since that time, there has been a steadily mounting literature on suburbs, but only a few essays have explored the connections between architecture and development in any depth.[47] The wealth of insights to be gained from such inquiry is suggested by Douglass Tucci's work on suburban Boston, in which he has expanded upon Warner's thesis to document why affluent enclaves were so densely developed with large, freestanding houses during the late nineteenth century.[48] In analogous fashion, Roger Miller and Joseph Siry have documented portions of West Philadelphia as they evolved between 1850 and 1880. Again using architecture as an index, they have shown the varieties of suburbanization that occurred sometimes in sequence, sometimes simultaneously, and have probed the implications of imagery and the choice of specific locales for building.[49] As a given precinct may include many sizes and forms of house, so some of those forms, when used extensively in a metropolitan area, can become important contributors to its character. Daniel Prosser focuses on one such form, the bungalow, examining the factors that made it so popular among Chicago's speculative builders.[50]

Each good case study raises a host of new questions. Just as row houses were erected in suburbs, so freestanding forms, such as the bungalow, were employed extensively in dense urban settings, in small towns, and in rural areas. Yet little is known about why this form was so pervasive or why it carried associations that varied from region to region. In the Midwest and South, bungalows often were sought by affluent, if not rich, citizens. In the Northeast, however, the bungalow could be more closely identified with the working class and assumed pejorative connotations among other groups. In a more general vein, was suburban architecture the primary spawning ground for forms later employed in towns, and, if so, did these forms carry metropolitan connotations when they were applied elsewhere? On the other hand, were certain house forms adopted in city and town at more or less the same time and hence become neutral in their associations? Perhaps even more important, why was so much of the residential architecture in suburbs and towns nearly identical though both the physical context and living patterns could be quite different?

One type that is especially conducive to use as a focus for investigating such issues is the apartment house. Long ignored by scholars, these buildings have become the subject of considerable interest during the last decade. Most Americans regarded multiunit residences in negative terms during the nineteenth century. Acceptance among the rich and middle class occurred only gradually in the decades following the Civil War. Apartment living gained momentum in cities toward the century's close, and then greatly accelerated after 1900. By the 1920s, it was a widespread phenomenon in metropolises and many smaller cities as well. Yet an ambivalence toward this type persisted; with the exception of a few very dense urban centers such as Manhattan, apartment houses seldom seem to have acquired widespread stature as a positive emblem of city life. Studying the type thus affords valuable insights on social attitudes toward habitation, as well as on changes in economic structure, development and transportation patterns, and building technology. A provocative overview of the subject has been written by John Hancock, and there are now a number of essays on Boston, Chicago, and New York.[51] Richard Plunz has analyzed how a variety of external forces have had a decisive influence in shaping multiunit housing in New York.[52] Carroll Westfall and others have investigated how image and spatial configurations were developed to render the apartment house acceptable as a living place.[53] While concentrating on work in one city, each of these essays tends to be introductory in nature. Much remains to be learned from case studies

on topics such as the evolution of a precinct from an enclave of single-family
residences to one much more densely occupied.[54]

Apartment house construction was often resisted in residential areas, the buildings and even their tenants seen as unwanted intruders. The proliferation of the
type during the early twentieth century fostered the adoption of zoning ordinances
and other controls, a process about which we still know little in detail. And one
can only guess as to why the imagery of moderate-income apartment houses
differed in so many places and the degree to which local developers may have
generated those images. Did the construction of high-rise apartment houses in
localities where land values remained relatively low stem from associations of
urbanity and social status? How much did apartment buildings satisfy the housing
needs of some segments of the populace that heretofore had not been adequately
met? The suburbanization of the type beginning in the 1920s has yet to be
scrutinized. In places such as southern California, apartment complexes sometimes assumed unprecedented forms, yet much remains to be learned about the
reasons for such departures.[55] Most studies concentrate on major examples. The
more pervasive vernacular forms of apartment house design have been neglected,
with the exception of an engaging essay on mid-twentieth-century infill units in
Los Angeles.[56]

Multiunit housing built for the working class and poor has, of course, been
the subject of countless publications about contemporary planning and social
issues, yet scholarly analyses relating architectural and urbanistic aspects remain
scarce. Some attention has been given to nineteenth-century dwellings of New
England textile mill employees, which rank among the earliest forms of planned
industrial housing in the United States. This is the subject of James Vance's
exemplary probe into how the complexion of the work force affected the nature
of their places of residence. Richard Horowitz has sought to reveal how the
boardinghouse in these manufacturing centers was viewed relative to the traditional concept of home.[57] The most extensive treatment of mill housing and of
its physical environment has been written by John Garner, who demonstrates
how important domestic architecture can be to understanding the nature of
community.[58]

In recent years, considerable attention has been given to low-cost housing in
major cities. Eugenie Birch and Deborah Gardner provide a useful overview of
philanthropic initiatives. Cynthia Zaitzevsky has written a much more detailed
study of Boston's seminal philanthropic projects and their debt to British pro-
totypes.[59] Anthony Jackson examines both public and private housing efforts in
New York, which he argues has always been in the forefront of addressing the
problem despite the fact that the need for adequate shelter among low-income
persons has never been successfully met.[60] Among the best accounts of early
public housing campaigns is by John Bauman, who analyzes several Philadelphia
projects in terms of planning objectives, politics, and divergent attitudes toward
urban development. Richard Pommer looks at key work from the 1930s in
Philadelphia, Cleveland, and New York, comparing it to European examples

and demonstrating the major influence American street patterns and planning principles had on the solutions.[61]

Public and institutional buildings make ideal candidates for the study of architecture in relation to its urban context. More often than not, these edifices are landmarks in every sense of that term: they house key functions of an organized society and hence can reflect its values both in terms of achievement and aspiration. Even when a populace cannot afford to reveal these values fully in places of residence, it often finds the means to manifest ideals in work, such as the courthouse, school, church, or asylum. The symbolic role of this work may be expressed in a variety of ways, including prominent location, embellishment, fine materials and workmanship, landscaping, and sheer mass. Given these attributes, it is surprising how little public architecture has been carefully examined. Among the few general studies on major types, the subject tends to be treated in isolation.[62] More has been done with courthouses, and Edward Price's now-classic essay on courthouse squares underscores the importance of urban configuration in analyzing such work.[63] But almost nothing has been written about even more ubiquitous public buildings such as post offices, schools, and libraries.[64] By far the most ambitious study in this realm is Rebecca Zurier's on firehouses, which begins to integrate technical, symbolic, and political factors into the overview of the type's development.[65]

The study of institutional types, such as hospitals, asylums, and the myriad facilities developed by social organizations, remains virtually uncharted territory.[66] Much the same can be said about churches in their urban context, although one essay on rural houses of worship shows how worthwhile it would be to pursue the topic further.[67] Equally needed are studies that examine the emergence of public and private institutional buildings as essential contributors to the idea of community. With some exceptions, this institutional presence was quite limited in the colonial period, with one or two religious and civic buildings fulfilling a spectrum of collective needs. A multitude of facilities, each serving a discrete purpose and conspicuously marked on the urban landscape, is a development that occurred for the most part during the nineteenth and early twentieth centuries. These buildings, and their locational relationships, afford a wealth of clues not only on the changes in social structure but on those affecting the very concept of urban life, be it in a city, suburb, or town.

American institutions of higher learning have always tended to evolve as communities unto themselves; however, ample reasons exist for investigating them in a broader urban context. The existence of even a small college in a town could figure significantly in that place's development, and during the nineteenth century these institutions often became instruments used to further growth.[68] Around 1900 campus design itself had an impact of furthering the objectives of the city beautiful movement.[69] The campus in effect became a laboratory where large-scale planning techniques could be tested. More recently, this relationship has assumed another form, with new university complexes offering models for efforts to revive the urban core as a multifunctional center.[70] Parallel developments have occurred in the design of large correctional facilities and military bases, which, like university campuses, beg attention to their own right and as indicators of patterns existing or intended in the urban matrix.

If many institutions lend themselves to study as singular places in the landscape, commercial buildings often must be examined as parts of a greater whole, comprising the essential stuff that defines a city or town center. Well before the advent of the skyscraper, Victorian banks, office blocks, retail establishments, hotels, theaters, railroad stations, and other types came to signify the individualism of their enterprises and the collective thrust toward intensifying the core area as a place of business. Densely packed along crowded streets, these buildings transformed the dynamics and character of American communities. Commercial precincts emerged as aggressively conspicuous and ornate, but no less pragmatic, places. As a subject unto themselves, commercial centers are just beginning to be analyzed in depth. Karen Luehrs and Timothy Crimmins examine the morphological development of downtown Atlanta, delineating its persistent role as the image of the city over a fifty-year period. Perry Duis has studied the changing social functions of Chicago's core.[71] Several portions of New York have been investigated, as have two principal phases of growth in downtown Portland.[72] Much less has been written on comparable precincts in smaller communities.[73]

For many years scholarly attention focused on one commercial building form, the skyscraper, which was analyzed in its expressive and technical aspects as a key contributor to twentieth-century modernism.[74] A broader perspective is now commonly held, yet numerous topical areas related to the skyscraper have only begun to be addressed. Very little is known about these buildings as functional components of the city, for example.[75] And while New York and Chicago long served as the principal incubators for new developments in skyscraper design, the rapid acceptance of the form in other places awaits detailed study. By the early 1890s, tall buildings were being planned in a number of cities, and by the 1910s this form was seen as an essential mark of urban progress irrespective of whether economic pressures in a given locality dictated its use.[76]

Several instructive case studies now exist on commercial building types. Department stores comprise the most popular subject matter, with written essays on these emporia as agents for transforming city centers into places appealing to women and of generating new patterns of consumption.[77] The impact some major facilities have had on perceptions of scale and character appropriate to the metropolitan core also has been explored.[78] Deborah Andrews has written on nineteenth-century Philadelphia banks, correlating architectural image with the development of financial institutions.[79] Others have examined office buildings, hotels, and theaters, but the key role these places had in determining urban character and urban life is just beginning to be understood.[80] And work in this sphere, as with other building types, tends to concentrate on examples in a few major centers. Far less is known about counterparts in smaller cities and towns.

Some of the best type studies have been done on railroad stations. Carl Condit's volumes on Cincinnati and New York examine terminal facilities as integral parts of railroad systems providing a new perspective on urban history through his detailed chronicle of these transportation networks.[81] Elliot Willensky has analyzed Grand Central Station as an agent for the redevelopment of midtown Manhattan, and Jeffrey Roberts has provided an excellent analysis of how terminal location affected growth patterns in Philadelphia.[82] Stations in smaller cities have received less attention; however, considerable work has been done on examples in towns, documenting the prominence the depot enjoyed in those communities.[83]

Much has been written in recent years on architecture designed to accommodate the motorist, but this research has concentrated more on buildings than on their physical context.[84] Likewise, essays on the automobile strip landscape generally consider architecture only in passing.[85] The best synthesis of these topics is Chester Liebs' study of morphological changes that have occurred in twentieth-century retail zones, linking shifts in architectural form and image to those of a landscape organized in response to the widespread use of cars. Thomas Schlereth's case history of U.S. Route 40 in Indiana offers a vivid picture of the highway as a multifaceted and constantly changing landscape.[86] The social implications of the automobile's impact on hostelries have been studied by Warren James Belasco. Essays by Meredith Clausen, Howard Gillette, Jr., and myself have begun to explore the regional shopping center—as much a product of an automobile-oriented society as can be found—and its instrumental role in reshaping patterns of retail development in both the urban periphery and center.[87] While the automobile's impact on settlement form and on almost every conceivable building type has long been recognized, the historian's work of delineating the process and its effect has just begun. With the exception of railroad depots, little work has been done on the architecture of twentieth-century transportation facilities, and broader issues central to understanding the structure of the twentieth-century landscape still await preliminary investigation.[88]

One other sphere of commercial development merits note: complexes created for expositions and amusement parks. At first, the two may seem entirely different entities. World's fairs, of course, are international events—short-lived but serious endeavors that more often than not have marshaled some of the country's leading designers to create a singular, idealized, and stunning ensemble that always elicits widespread attention and frequently achieves considerable influence on ideas about the urban environment, if not on what is actually accomplished. The amusement park, by contrast, is a local or at best a regional facility, designed by persons whose names have long been forgotten and regarded as an anecdotal world of fantasy and escape. Yet both types are largely self-contained compounds built for commercial purposes and reflect idealized notions of the built environment. Since the late nineteenth century, world's fairs and amusement parks have in various ways affected ideas about urban life, not only in its physical dimension but in terms of how that life might be ordered. For such reasons, it is understandable that the former had a marked influence on the design of the latter for at least several decades after 1900, and similar relationships may well exist between more recent expositions and contemporary theme parks. No one has explored this connection in the depth that it deserves, but a growing number of scholars have analyzed individual world's fairs within their urban context.[89] While much less has been written about amusement parks, a few essays indicate how much about the city and its culture may be gleaned from the topic.[90]

Since the early nineteenth century, industrial complexes have had a major role in determining the physical structure, demographic base, economic complexion, and indeed the culture of communities of all sizes and in many parts of the United States.[91] However, the obvious does not necessarily induce substantive investigation, as is all too evident by the dearth of studies made on this very rich subject. Among specialists, such work has tended to be of interest primarily from the standpoint of the technology employed in the buildings and their manufacturing equipment. Others have admired industrial architecture purely on formal grounds, as embodying a utilitarian aesthetic that contributed to the development of modernism beginning in the 1910s.[92] Few historians concerned with architecture have given much attention to industrial buildings in a broader context. As with workers' housing, much of the pertinent scholarship in this regard has focused on the antebellum New England textile industry.[93] Other forms of production have fared less well. Only in several cases has the architecture of industry been examined in relation to matters of community development and life.[94]

Probably the oldest historigraphical form to address American architecture is the monograph devoted to the individual architect. Since the 1880s, books have been written about distinguished figures in the field, and, as with other topical areas, the corpus of literature in this one has recently swelled.[95] Sometimes these monographs are biographies, but more often the work itself is the focus of attention. Texts tend to rely heavily on descriptive analysis, noting circumstances that helped determine the design of important projects and, less often than should be the case, placing the subject in a broader artistic context. Salient aspects of the architect's career are generally woven into this matrix; however, the locality of practice seldom receives more than passing notice. This omission is unfortunate since the specifics of place may have a decisive effect upon the nature of the product.[96] The types of buildings designed, the concerns of clients, climate, topography, social habits, business practices, cultural concerns, economic structure, materials available and practical for use, and the presence of strong traditions or the lack thereof are among the factors that can be essential to understanding the product fully. Conversely, work by one architect or a group of them designing in a more or less similar way can reveal much about the place in which they work. Charles Bulfinch and Henry Hobson Richardson in Boston; McKim, Mead & White in New York; Burham & Root in Chicago; Bernard Maybeck in the San Francisco Bay Area—in each case, and many others could be cited, the architect has left a decisive imprint upon the area, both through his own efforts and those of others inspired by his example.[97]

The physical dimension provides a springboard for addressing other issues.

One could no doubt learn much about business practices in Chicago by studying the office buildings there by Holabird & Roche, education in suburban San Francisco from the schools of Ernest Kump, changes in retailing strategies in New York from the stores of Victor Gruen, resort life in Palm Beach from the houses of Addison Mizner, values cherished by the East Coast middle class from the more modest dwellings of Royal Barry Wills. The legacy of major figures is of undisputable importance in this regard. At the same time there are hundreds of other architects—competent expositors of current tendencies in design rather than innovators—who could be studied to provide insights on the mainstream of professional practice.[98]

In many cities and towns, one or several firms has been responsible for a large portion of buildings erected during a given period, and collectively this work may yield as much information about that place as any single source can provide. Consider the case of Eckel & Mann in St. Joseph, Missouri. Established in 1872, the firm continues today and has several thousand projects to its credit, the majority of them in that city and its environs. Banks, stores, hotels, schools, auditoria, churches, government buildings, factories, clubs, and houses are among the many types it produced. The scope and quantity of this work combine to present a cross-section of St. Joseph's development for over a century: a profile of its businesses and institutions, residential districts and recreational pursuits, periods of prosperity and stagnation or decline, political patronage and civic initiatives, and no doubt much more.[99] The special value of such inquiry is that it affords the potential to correlate diverse facets of the urban scene with buildings, which can be one of the most tangible and telling indicators of society's values.[100]

No less productive an approach would be to study a generation of architects, and for that matter builders, in a given community. Where these people came from, the nature of this experience, the types of work they did and for whom: such matters can elucidate the dynamics of a locality as much as its physical character. The great influx of people talented in the building art that moved to the Midwest during the first half of the nineteenth century, for example, was no accident. Skilled persons locate where a demand exists for their services, where there is sufficient growth, sufficient resources, and sufficient recognition of that talent. These people, in turn, can become central agents in concretizing the agendas of development. Generalities are easy enough to postulate. What is needed are detailed investigations that probe particular circumstances. To continue the midwestern example, in an emerging city or prosperous town, how many designers were trained architects and how many trained in the artisan tradition? How sophisticated were their technical abilities? Was a sizable portion from one other part of the United States or abroad, or was this segment of the populace cosmopolitan? How much did their work retain characteristics of that which they knew before, and how much was adaptation? Did a cooperative spirit, fragmentation, or even factionalism prevail once settled in their new home? Were many of these people transients, moving on after several months or years, or did the majority establish roots and leave a sustained legacy? How many of them were outsiders and how many part of larger migration patterns? In pursuing such questions, there is abundant opportunity to provide a fresh perspective on the community itself.[101]

The categories of place, type, and architect are used here as an instrument of convenience in order to divide a large amount of material in such a way that it may be readily consulted for reference. Numerous methodological approaches have been used, and had the aim of this chapter been primarily analytical, method could well have provided the organizational framework. But no form of categorical division and no register of methods employed should be construed as defining the boundaries of exploration. Much to their credit, some recent studies enter new topical realms and thereby underscore the continued need for fresh thinking.[102] As efforts of this type mature, let us hope for a closer alliance between the disciplines that have sought meaning in the visual arts and those that have sought to explain social, economic, and political phenomena. Scholarship published during the past decade especially has made great progress, and not the least of its accomplishments has been to reveal how much more ground there is to be covered in learning what architecture can tell us about urban settlement and populace.

Notes

1. In order to keep the scope of this survey managable, the term *architecture* refers to buildings of all types but excludes many other things that are often of concern to the architectural historian: nonhabitable structures (bridges, watertowers, etc.), public embellishments (monuments, fountains, etc.), and parks, cemeteries, and other forms of landscape design. *Urban* refers to concentrated forms of settlement, ranging from major metropolises to small towns.

2. Most of the citations are to works that in one way or another shed light on aspects of urbanism; however, additional references are sometimes noted in the event they may prove useful sources for specialized study. Survey texts are not included in most instances, although some contain good general information relating architecture to its urban context. These books also may prove an instructive starting point for the historian who knows little about American architecture. The best single-volume survey is Leland M. Roth, *A Concise History of American Architecture* (New York: Harper & Row, 1979). See also Alan Gowans, *Images of American Living: Four Centuries of Architecture and Furniture as Cultural Expression* (Philadelphia: J. B. Lippincott, 1964), and Vincent Scully, *American Architecture and Urbanism* (New York: Frederick A. Praeger, 1969). Much more detailed coverage is given in the four-volume series, American Buildings and Their Architects, the first two by William H. Pierson, the second two by William H. Jordy (Garden City, N.Y.: Doubleday, 1970, 1972, 1978). Carl Condit's two-volume *American Building Art* (New York: Oxford University Press, 1960, 1961) remains the indispensable reference work on the history of architectural technology in the United States.

3. See, for example, Harold Donaldson Eberlein and Horace Mather Lippincott, *The Colonial Homes of Philadelphia and Its Neighbourhood* (Philadelphia: J. B. Lippincott, 1912); Alice R. and D. E. Huger Smith, *The Dwelling Houses of Charleston,*

South Carolina (Philadelphia: J. B. Lippincott, 1917); and Nathaniel Cortlandt Curtis, *New Orleans: Its Old Houses, Shops and Public Buildings* (Philadelphia: J. B. Lippincott, 1933).

4. John Hutchins Cady, *The Civic and Architectural Development of Providence, 1639–1950* (Providence: Book Shop, 1957); Mary Wingfield Scott, *Old Richmond Neighborhoods* (1950; Richmond: Valentine Museum, 1975); Luther P. Eisenhardt, ed., *Historic Philadelphia from the Founding until the Early Nineteenth Century* (Philadelphia: American Philosophical Society, 1953). Scott's book remains antiquarian in approach and excludes work realized after the Civil War but is unusual for the period in its breadth and district-based organization. *Historic Philadelphia* is a collection of essays focusing on an even earlier time frame, which helped to establish a high standard of scholarship for local studies. The essays devoted to building types are especially relevant to urban historians. See also the companion volume: Harry M. Tinkom et al., *Historic Germantown from the Founding to the Early Part of the Nineteenth Century* (Philadelphia: American Philosophical Society, 1955).

5. David Gebhard and Harriette Von Breton, *L.A. in the Thirties, 1931–1941* (Santa Barbara and Salt Lake City: Peregrine Smith, 1975); Carol Newton Johnson et al., *Tulsa Art Deco: An Architectural Era, 1925–1942* (Tulsa: Junior League of Tulsa, 1980); Hans Wirz and Richard Striner, *Washington Deco: Art Deco in the Nation's Capital* (Washington, D.C.: Smithsonian Institution Press, 1984); Gideon Bosker and Lena Leneck, *Frozen Music: A History of Portland Architecture* (Portland: Western Imprints, Press of the Oregon Historical Society, 1985). References to works that are broader in their chronological scope are cited in the notes below.

6. Studies devoted to the earliest district of a city include: Clay Lancaster, *Old Brooklyn Heights* (Rutland, Vt.: Charles E. Tuttle, 1961); *Plan and Program for the Preservation of the Vieux Carre* (New Orleans: Bureau of Governmental Research, 1968); and Byron A. Johnson et al., *Old Town Albuquerque, New Mexico: A Guide to Its History and Architecture* (Albuquerque: City of Albuquerque, 1980). On rare occasions, a street or square has provided the basis for the area examined: Joseph Jackson, *America's Most Historic Highway: Market Street, Philadelphia* (Philadelphia and New York: John Wanamaker, 1926); Francis James Dallett, *An Architectural View of Washington Square, Philadelphia* (Frome and London: Butler & Tanner, 1968). None of these books is as valuable as it could be from an urbanistic perspective. More germane studies in this regard focus on precincts with one dominant function (commerce, residence, or the like) and are cited in the notes on building types.

7. Beginning with Nathan Silver, *Lost New York* (Boston: Houghton Mifflin, 1967), a number of books have been published on buildings and other components of the urban fabric that have been destroyed. Among them, Jane Holtz Kay, *Lost Boston* (Boston: Houghton Mifflin, 1980), is especially instructive. See also James M. Goode, *Capital Losses: A Cultural History of Washington's Destroyed Buildings* (Washington, D.C.: Smithsonian Institution Press, 1979), and Mary Cable, *Lost New Orleans* (New York: American Legacy Press, 1980).

8. These circumstances are implicit in the literature of American architecture, but the topic has never been studied in the detail that it deserves. Emphasizing the importance of these six cities in no way obviates the value of rural building traditions, which have existed in the United States since the earliest period of settlement. Knowing urban architecture is by no means synonymous with knowing all of American architecture.

9. Harold M. Mayer and Richard C. Wade, *Chicago: Growth of a Metropolis*

(Chicago: University of Chicago Press, 1969). Another landmark study of this type, albeit one employing different historigraphical methods, is Walter Muir Whitehill, *Boston: A Topographical History* (Cambridge, Mass.: Belknap Press of Harvard University Press, 1958; rev. ed., 1968). A fine sequel to Whitehill's book, concentrating more on architecture, is Douglass Shand Tucci, *Built in Boston: City and Suburb* (Boston: New York Graphic Society, 1978). George B. Tatum, *Penn's Great Town: 250 Years of Philadelphia Architecture* (Philadelphia: University of Pennsylvania Press, 1961), set the standard for many subsequent local studies. Paul Gleye et al., *The Architecture of Los Angeles* (Los Angeles: Rosebud Books, 1981), is introductory in nature. Reyner Banham, *Los Angeles: The Architecture of Four Ecologies* (New York: Harper & Row, 1971), departs from the norm in its thematic structure and broad-based view of the environment but concerns itself more with current observations than with historical analysis. Works on New York and Chicago are cited below.

10. Carl W. Condit, *Chicago 1910–29: Building, Planning and Urban Technology* (Chicago: University of Chicago Press, 1974). A good cultural perspective on nineteenth-century Chicago work is afforded by Perry Duis, *Chicago: Creating New Traditions* (Chicago: Chicago Historical Society, 1976). Robert A. M. Stern et al., *New York 1900: Metropolitan Architecture and Urbanism 1890–1915* (New York: Rizzoli, 1983); M. Christine Boyer, *Manhattan Manners: Architecture and Style, 1850–1900* (New York: Rizzoli, 1985). See also Charles Lockwood, *Manhattan Moves Uptown: An Illustrated History* (Boston: Houghton Mifflin, 1976), and Thomas Bender and William R. Taylor, "Culture and Architecture: Some Aesthetic Tensions in the Shaping of Modern New York City," in William Sharpe and Leonard Wallock, eds., *Visions of the Modern City*, Proceedings of the Heyman Center for the Humanities (New York: Columbia University, 1983), pp. 185–215. The New York books are devoted mostly, sometimes exclusively, to Manhattan. The other boroughs have no comparable studies; however, David Ment et al., *Building Blocks of Brooklyn: A Study of Urban Growth* (Brooklyn: Brooklyn Educational & Cultural Alliance, 1979), is a solid introductory piece for one of them.

11. John Zukowsky et al., *Chicago and New York: Architectural Interactions* (Chicago: Art Institute of Chicago, 1984), takes a step in this direction.

12. Lawrence Lowic, *The Architectural Heritage of St. Louis 1803–1891: From the Louisiana Purchase to the Wainwright Building* (St. Louis: Washington University Gallery of Art, 1982); Randy Garber, ed., *Built in Milwaukee: An Architectural View of the City* (Milwaukee: Landscape Research, 1980); John R. Borchert et al., *Legacy of Minneapolis: Preservation amid Change* (Bloomington, Minn.: Voyageur Press, 1983); William L. McDonald, *Dallas Rediscovered: A Photographic Chronicle of Urban Expansion, 1870–1925* (Dallas: Dallas Historical Society, 1978). See also Edmund B. Chapman, *Cleveland: Village to Metropolis* (Cleveland: Western Reserve Historical Society and Western Reserve University Press, 1964); Eric Johannesen, *Cleveland Architecture, 1876–1976* (Cleveland: Western Reserve Historical Society, and Western Reserve University Press, 1979); W. Hawkins Ferry, *The Buildings of Detroit: A History*, rev. ed. (Detroit: Wayne State University Press, 1980); George Ehrlich, *Kansas City, Missouri: An Architectural History 1826–1976* (Kansas City: Historic Kansas City Foundation, 1979); Robert C. Peters, ed., *A Comprehensive Program for Historic Preservation in Omaha* (Omaha: Landmarks Heritage Preservation Commission, 1980). Washington, D.C., still lacks a comparable study but does have a history of its physical development: National Capital Planning Commission and Frederick Gutheim, *Worthy of the Nation: The History of Planning for the National Capital* (Washington, D.C.: Smithsonian Institution Press,

1977). Thomas Vaughan and Virginia Guest Ferriday, eds., *Space, Style and Structure: Buildings in Northwest America*, 2 vols. (Portland: Oregon Historical Society, 1974), is a unique and copious regional study filled with information on a part of the United States generally ignored by scholars of architecture. Yet the contents are comprised of essays by different authors, and among the cities, Portland is by far the most extensively covered, with the result that little of the potential for comparisons is realized.

13. Martin Dibner, ed., *Portland* (Portland, Me.: Greater Portland Landmarks, 1972); S. Allen Chambers, Jr., *Lynchburg: An Architectural History* (Charlottesville: University Press of Virginia, 1981); Tony P. Wrenn, *Wilmington, North Carolina: An Architectural and Historical Portrait* (Charlottesville: University Press of Virginia, 1984); Marlys A. Svendsen et al., *Davenport, Where the Mississippi Runs West* (Davenport, Iowa: City of Davenport, 1982); Laurence Lafore, *American Classic* (Iowa City: Iowa State Historical Department, 1975); Roxanne Kuter Williamson, *Austin, Texas: An American Architectural History* (San Antonio: Trinity University Press, 1973); Arthur A. Hart, *Historic Boise: An Introduction to the Architecture of Boise, Idaho, 1863–1938* (Boise: Historic Boise, 1980); Mark Reinberger et al., *Auburn Illustrated: A History in Architecture* (Auburn, N.Y.: Schweinfurth Memorial Art Center, 1983). As a group, these books tend to give less attention to urbanistic concerns than those on larger cities.

14. Factory towns, especially those associated with the New England textile industry, have received considerable attention, beginning with John Coolidge's pioneering book, *Mill and Mansion: A Study of Architecture and Society in Lowell, Massachusetts, 1820–1865* (New York: Columbia University Press, 1942). More recent studies include Richard M. Candee, "New Towns of the Early New England Textile Industry," in Camille Wells, ed., *Perspectives in Vernacular Architecture* (Annapolis, Md.: Vernacular Architecture Forum, 1982), pp. 31–50; and John S. Garner, *The Model Company Town: Urban Design Through Private Enterprise in Nineteenth-Century New England* (Amherst: University of Massachusetts Press, 1984). Works concerning other types of industrial communities include: Garner, "LaClaire, Illinois: A Model Company Town (1890–1934)," *Journal of the Society of Architectural Historians* 30 (October 1971): 219–27; Leland M. Roth, "Three Industrial Towns by McKim, Mead & White," *Journal of the Society of Architectural Historians* 38 (December 1979): 317–47; Richard M. Candee, *Atlantic Heights: A World War I Shipbuilder's Community* (Portsmouth, N.H.: Peter E. Randall, 1985); and C. Eric Stoehr, *Bonanza Victorian: Architecture and Society in Colorado Mining Towns* (Albuquerque: University of New Mexico Press, 1975). See also Anthony F. C. Wallace, *Rockdale: The Growth of an American Village in the Early Industrial Revolution* (New York: Alfred A. Knopf, 1978), and James B. Allen, *The Company Town in the West* (Norman: University of Oklahoma Press, 1966).

Concerning resort communities see Antoinette F. Downing and Vincent J. Scully, Jr., *The Architectural Heritage of Newport, Rhode Island, 1640–1915* (Cambridge, Mass.: Harvard University Press, 1952; rev. ed., New York: Charles N. Potter, 1967); and George E. Thomas and Carl Doebley, *Cape May: Queen of the Seaside Resorts* (Philadelphia: Art Alliance Press, 1976).

15. Among the most thorough analyses of town architecture and urban development are Robert Brugemann, *Benecia: Portrait of an Early California Town* (San Francisco: 101 Publications, 1980); Christopher Weeks, *The Building of Westminster in Maryland* (Annapolis: Fishergate, 1978); and Susan E. Maycock, *An Architectural History of Carbondale, Illinois* (Carbondale: Southern Illinois University Press, 1983). See also Constance Greiff et al., *Princeton Architecture: A Pictorial History of Town and Campus*

(Princeton: Princeton University Press, 1967); Rebecca M. Rogers, *Hudson, Ohio: An Architectural and Historical Study* (Hudson: The Council, Village of Hudson, 1973); Peter J. Schmitt, *Kalamazoo: Nineteenth-Century Homes in a Midwestern Village* (Kalamazoo: Kalamazoo City Historical Commission, 1976); Royster Lyle, Jr., and Pammela Hemenway Simpson, *The Architecture of Historic Lexington* (Charlottesville: University Press of Virginia, 1977); Christopher A. Cain et al., eds., *The Burlington Book: Architecture, History, Future* (Burlington: University of Vermont, Historic Preservation Program, 1980); William R. Mitchell, Jr., *Landmarks: The Architecture of Thomasville and Thomas County, Georgia, 1820–1980* (Thomasville, Ga.: Thomasville Landmarks, 1980). Frank E. Sanchis, *American Architecture: Westchester County, New York, Colonial to Contemporary* (Croton-on-Hudson, N.Y.: North River Press, 1977), offers voluminous coverage of work in outlying communities of a metropolitan area but little on urbanism. Stephen W. Jacobs, *Wayne County: The Aesthetic Heritage of a Rural Area* (Lyons, N.Y.: Wayne County Historical Society, 1979), provides excellent analysis of small farm communities, which are discussed by type (crossroads, town, canal town, port, township center, etc.). See also Gregory Ramsey et al., *Historic Buildings of Centre County, Pennsylvania* (University Park, Pa.: Keystone Books, 1980).

16. Two essays have been written on how sentiment for a lost, and to a degree imaginary, heritage induced complete transformations in the character of the respective communities. See David Gebhard, *Santa Barbara—The Creation of a New Spain in America* (Santa Barbara: University of California, Santa Barbara Art Museum, 1982), and William Butler, "Another City upon a Hill: Litchfield, Connecticut, and the Colonial Revival," in Alan Alexrod, ed., *The Colonial Revival in America* (New York: W. W. Norton, 1985), pp. 15–51. Another study reveals how sentiment for the past induced a desire for continuity and saving key landmarks: David Chase, "Notes on the Colonial Revival in Newport: Escaping the 'Vandalism of Civilization,' " *Newport History* 55 (Spring 1982): 38–62. See also Charles B. Hosmer, Jr., *Preservation Comes of Age: From Williamsburg to the National Trust, 1926–1949*, 2 vols. (Charlottesville: University Press of Virginia, 1981); and Nathan Weinberg, *Preservation in American Towns and Cities* (Boulder, Colo.: Westview Press, 1979).

17. Richard V. Francavigla, *The Mormon Landscape: Existence, Creation, and Perception of a Unique Image in the American West* (New York: AMS Press, 1978), scrutinizes the subtle particularities that can distinguish certain towns from others; however, some of the findings have been disputed. John A. Jakle, *The American Small Town: Twentieth-Century Places Image* (Hamden, Conn.: Archon Books, 1982), is more generalized and offers an instructive matrix for analyzing physical features and the forces that shaped them in midwestern towns. Anthony N. B. Garvan, *Architecture and Town Planning in Colonial Connecticut* (New Haven: Yale University Press, 1951), was unusually broad in its scope at the time of publication but does not integrate the material presented about these two spheres.

18. Samuel Gaillard Stoney, *This Is Charleston* (Charleston: Carolina Art Association, 1944; rev. ed., 1960). See also Leopold Adler II et al., *Historic Savannah* (Savannah: Historic Savannah Foundation, 1968; rev. ed., Mary L. Morrison, ed., 1979).

An enormous amount of unpublished material, varying in quality, has been compiled in the course of such surveys at the local and state levels, as well as for nominations to the National Register of Historic Places. Work of this sort done for historic districts can be especially useful.

19. Bainbridge Bunting et al., *Survey of Architectural History in Cambridge, Report*

One: East Cambridge (Cambridge: Cambridge Historical Commission, 1965); Antoinette F. Downing et al., *Survey . . . Report Two: Mid-Cambridge* (Cambridge: Cambridge Historical Commission, 1967); Bainbridge Bunting et al., *Survey . . . Report Three: Cambridgeport* (1971); Bainbridge Bunting et al., *Survey . . . Report Four: Old Cambridge* (1973); and Arthur Krim et al., *Survey . . . Report Five: Northwest Cambridge* (1977). On New Orleans: Samuel Wilson et al., *New Orleans Architecture*, Vol. 1: *The Lower Garden District* (Gretna, La.: Pelican Publishing, 1971); Mary Louise Christovich et al., Vol. 2: *The American Sector (Faubourg St. Mary)* (1972); Marie Louise Christovich et al., Vol. 3: *The Cemeteries* (1974); Samuel Wilson et al., Vol. 4: *The Creole Faubourgs* (1974); Marie Louise Christovich et al., Vol 5: *The Esplanade Ridge* (1977); and Roulac Toledano and Mary Louise Christovich, Vol 6: *Faubourg Tremé and the Bayou Road* (1980).

20. Among the finest of these are Julie Cook Guice et al., *The Buildings of Biloxi: An Architectural Survey* (Biloxi: City of Biloxi, 1976), and Landscape Research, *Beyond the Neck: The Architecture and Development of Somerville, Massachusetts* (Somerville: Office of Planning and Community Development, 1982). See also *Nineteenth Century Mobile Architecture: An Inventory of Existing Buildings* (Mobile: Mobile City Planning Commission, 1974); Robert E. Samuelson et al., *Architecture: Columbus* (Columbus, Ohio: Columbus Chapter American Institute of Architects, 1976); *Historic Preservation Inventory and Planning Guidelines: City of Las Vegas* (San Francisco: Charles Hall Page and Associates, 1978); Charles Hall Page and Associates and Robert R. Frankeberger, *Phoenix Historic Building Survey* (Phoenix: City of Phoenix, 1979); and Charles Hall Page and Associates, *Amarillo Historic Building Survey & Preservation Program Recommendations* (Amarillo: City of Amarillo, 1981). See also Richard J. Webster, *Philadelphia Preserved: Catalog of the Historic American Buildings Survey* (Philadelphia: Temple University Press, 1976), the one urban-focused book on the contents of this vast, ongoing federal survey project.

21. Michael R. Corbett, *Splendid Survivors: San Francisco's Downtown Architectural Heritage* (San Francisco: California Living Books, 1979), stands among the finest works of its type. See also Robert P. Winthrop, *Architecture in Downtown Richmond* (Richmond, Va.: Junior Board of Historic Richmond Foundation, 1982); *Hartford Architecture*, Vol. 1: *Downtown* (Hartford, Conn.: Hartford Architectural Conservancy, 1978); Merle Kummer, ed., *Hartford Architecture*, Vol. 2: *South Neighborhoods* (Hartford: Hartford Architectural Conservancy, 1980); Shirley de Fresne McArthur, *North Point Historic Districts—Milwaukee* (Milwaukee: North Point Historical Society, 1981); Larry K. Hancks et al., *Strawberry Hill: A Neighborhood Study* (Kansas City, Kans.: City of Kansas City, 1978); John S. McCormick, *The Historic Buildings of Downtown Salt Lake City* (Salt Lake City: Utah Historical Society, 1982); and Karl T. Haglund and Philip F. Notarianni, *The Avenues of Salt Lake City* (Salt Lake City: Utah Historical Society, 1980).

22. James H. Gibbs, *East Greenwich, Rhode Island* (Providence: Rhode Island Historical Preservation Commission, 1974); Elizabeth S. Warren, *Warren, Rhode Island* (1975); James H. Gibbs and Pamela Kennedy, *The West Side, Providence* (1976); Richard Longstreth, *East Providence, Rhode Island* (1976); David Chase, *Woonsocket, Rhode Island* (1976); John F. A. Herzan, *The West Broadway Neighborhood, Newport, Rhode Island* (1977); Robert O. Jones, *Narragansett Pier, Narragansett, Rhode Island* (1978); Pamela A. Kennedy, *Central Falls, Rhode Island* (1978); Leslie J. Volmert, *South Providence* (1978); Robert O. Christiensen, *Elmwood, Providence* (1979); Ellen Weiss,

North Kingston, Rhode Island (1979); John F. A. Herzan, *The Southern Thames Street Neighborhood in Newport* (1980); Robert Eliot Freeman, *Cranston, Rhode Island* (1980); Wm. McKenzie Woodward, *Smith Hill, Providence* (1980); Wm. McKenzie Woodward, *Downtown Providence* (1981); Lisa C. Fink, *Providence Industrial Sites* (1981); Robert O. Jones, *Warwick, Rhode Island* (1981); Pamela A. Kennedy, *Lincoln, Rhode Island* (1982); Ancelin V. Lynch, *Foster, Rhode Island* (1982).

23. Ruth Little-Stokes, *An Inventory of Historic Architecture, Caswell, County, North Carolina* (Yanceyville: Caswell County Historical Association, 1979); Diane E. Lee and Claudia Roberts, *An Architectural and Historical Survey of Tryon, North Carolina* (Raleigh: North Carolina Division of Archives and History, 1979); Carl Lounsbury, *The Architecture of Southport* (Southport, N.C.: Southport Historical Society, 1979); David E. Black, ed., *Historic Architectural Resources of Downtown Asheville, North Carolina* (Asheville: City of Asheville, 1979); Diane E. Lea and Claudia P. Roberts, *An Architectural and Historical Survey, Central Lumberton, North Carolina* (Raleigh: North Carolina Division of Archives and History, 1980); Thomas A. Greco, *Historic Architecture of Selma, North Carolina* (Selma: Town of Selma, 1980); Peter R. Kaplan, *The Historic Architecture of Cabarrus County, North Carolina* (Concord: Historic Cabarrus, City of Concord, and Cabarrus County, 1981); Laura A. W. Phillips, *Reidsville, North Carolina: An Inventory of Historic and Architectural Resources* (Reidsville: Reidsville Historic Properties Commission, 1981); Douglas Swaim, ed., *Cabins and Castles: The History and Architecture of Bucombe County, North Carolina* (Asheville: City of Asheville, 1981); Gwynne Stephens Taylor, *From Frontier to Factory: An Architectural History of Forsyth County* (Winston-Salem: Winston-Salem/Forsyth County Historic Properties Commission and City-County Planning Board of Forsyth County and Winston-Salem, 1981); Dru Gatewood Haley and Raymond A. Winslow, Jr., *The Historic Architecture of Perquimans County, North Carolina* (Hertford, N. C.: Town of Hertford, 1982); Claudia P. Roberts et al., *The Durham Architectural and Historic Inventory* (Durham: City of Durham and Historic Preservation Society of Durham, 1982).

24. Christopher Weeks et al., *Where Land and Water Intertwine: An Architectural History of Talbot County, Maryland* (Baltimore: Johns Hopkins University Press, 1984); and Christopher Weeks, ed., *Between the Nanticocke and the Choptank: An Architectural History of Dorchester County, Maryland* (Baltimore: Johns Hopkins University Press, 1984).

25. Many types of guides have long included architecture, but the first to focus on this subject was a series sponsored by local chapters of the American Institute of Architects in conjunction with that organization's annual meetings. Most of these books placed considerable emphasis on recent work and have now themselves become valuable documents of the past. See Hunson Jackson, *New York Architecture, 1650–1952* (New York: Reinhold, 1952); Victor Steinbrueck, *Seattle Architecture, 1850–1953* (New York: Reinhold, 1953); Henry-Russell Hitchcock, *Boston Architecture, 1637–1954* (New York: Reinhold, 1954); Douglas Honnold, *Southern California Architecture 1769–1956* (New York: Reinhold, 1956); Washington-Metropolitan Chapter American Institute of Architects, *Washington Architecture, 1791–1957* (New York: Reinhold, 1957); Cleveland Chapter, American Institute of Architects, *Cleveland Architecture, 1796–1958* (New York: Reinhold, 1958); and Samuel Wilson, Jr., *A Guide to the Architecture of New Orleans, 1699–1959* (New York: Reinhold, 1959). Many subsequent guides have been initiated under the same auspices, and the Institute deserves much credit for popularizing this genre of publication.

26. Michael and Susan Southworth, *The Boston Society of Architects' A.I.A. Guide to Boston* (Chester, Conn.: Globe Pequot Press, 1984); Elizabeth Mills Brown, *New Haven: A Guide to Architecture and Urban Design* (New Haven: Yale University Press, 1976); Norvel White and Elliot Willensky, *AIA Guide to New York City*, rev. ed. (New York: Macmillan, 1978); Paul Malo, *Landmarks of Rochester and Monroe County: A Guide to Neighborhoods and Villages* (Syracuse: Syracuse University Press, 1974); Francis R. Kowsky et al., *Buffalo Architecture: A Guide* (Cambridge, Mass.: MIT Press, 1981); Edward Teitelman and Richard Longstreth, *Architecture in Philadelphia: A Guide* (Cambridge, Mass.: MIT Press, 1974); Foundation for Architecture, *Philadelphia Architecture: A Guide to the City* (Cambridge, Mass.: MIT Press, 1984); Walter C. Kidney, *Landmark Architecture of Pittsburgh and Allegheny County* (Pittsburgh: Pittsburgh History and Landmarks Foundation, 1985); John Dorsey and James D. Dilts, *A Guide to Baltimore Architecture*, rev. ed. (Centreville, Md.: Tidewater Publication, 1981); Warren J. Cox et al., *A Guide to the Architecture of Washington, D.C.*, rev. ed. (New York: McGraw-Hill, 1974); Paul S. Dulaney, *The Architecture of Historic Richmond* (Charlottesville: University Press of Virginia, 1968); Kermit B. Marsh, *The American Institute of Architects Guide to Atlanta* (Atlanta: Atlanta Chapter, American Institute of Architects, 1975); Arlene R. Olson, *A Guide to the Architecture of Miami Beach* (Miami: Dade Heritage Trust, 1978); Marjorie Longenecker White, ed., *Downtown Birmingham: Architectural and Historical Walking Tour Guide* (Birmingham: Birmingham Historical Society, 1980); Albert C. Ledner et al., *A Guide to New Orleans Architecture* (New Orleans: New Orleans Chapter, American Institute of Architects, 1974); Rick A. Ball et al., *Indianapolis Architecture* (Indianapolis: Indiana Architectural Foundation, 1975); Katherine Mattingly Meyer, ed., *Detroit Architecture: A.I.A. Guide*, rev. ed. (Detroit: Wayne State University Press, 1980); Ira J. Bach, ed., *Chicago's Famous Buildings*, rev. ed. (Chicago: University of Chicago Press, 1980); Ira J. Bach, *Chicago on Foot: Walking Tours of Chicago Architecture*, rev. ed. (Chicago: Rand McNally, 1977); Joseph J. Korom and Gary W. Cotterell, *Look Up Milwaukee: Eastside/Westside, All Around Downtown* (Milwaukee: Franklin Publishers, 1979); Bonnie Richter, ed., *Saint Paul Omnibus: Images of the Changing City* (Saint Paul: Old Town Restorations, 1979); James Allen Scott, *Duluth's Legacy*, vol. 1: *Architecture* (Duluth: Department of Research and Planning, City of Duluth, 1974); George McCue, *The Building Art in St. Louis: Two Centuries*, rev. ed. (St. Louis: St. Louis Chapter, American Institute of Architects, 1981); James Anthony Ryan et al., *Kansas City: A Place in Time* (Kansas City: Landmarks Commission of Kansas City, Missouri, 1977); Joan L. Michalak et al., *Kansas City* (Kansas City: Kansas City Chapter, American Institute of Architects, 1979); Allan R. Sumner, ed., *Dallasights: An Anthology of Architecture and Open Spaces* (Dallas: Dallas Chapter, American Institute of Architects, 1978); Peter C. Papademetriou et al., *Houston: An Architectural Guide* (Houston: Houston Chapter, American Institute of Architects, 1972); Langdon E. Morrris, Jr., *Denver Landmarks* (Denver: Charles W. Cleworth, 1979); Central Arizona Chapter, American Institute of Architects, *A Guide to the Architecture of Metro Phoenix* (Layton, Utah: Peregrine Smith Books, 1986); John Henderson et al., *AIA Guide to San Diego* (San Diego: San Diego Chapter, American Institute of Architects, 1977); David Gebhard and Robert Winter, *Architecture in Los Angeles: A Compleat Guide* (Layton, Utah: Peregrine Smith Books, 1985); Sally B. Woodbridge and John M. Woodbridge, *Architecture San Francisco: The Guide* (San Francisco: San Francisco Chapter, American Institute of Architects, 1982); Thomas Vaughan and George A. McMath, *A Century of*

Portland Architecture (Portland: Oregon Historical Society, 1967); Caroline Tobin, *Downtown Seattle Walking Tours* (Seattle: City of Seattle, 1985).

27. Byrant F. and Carolyn K. Tolles, *Architecture in Salem: An Illustrated Guide* (Salem, Mass.: Essex Institute, 1983); Robert Bell Rettig, *Guide to Cambridge Architecture: Ten Walking Tours* (Cambridge, Mass.: MIT Press, 1969); Stephen S. Prokopoff et al., *The Nineteenth-Century Architecture of Saratoga Springs* (New York: New York State Council of the Arts, 1970); Daniel R. Snodderly, *Ithaca and Its Past: The History and Architecture of the Downtown*, rev. ed. (Ithaca: DeWitt Historical Society of Tompkins County, 1984); Virginia B. Kelly et al., *Wood and Stone: Landmarks of the Upper Mohawk Region* (Utica: Central New York Community Arts Council, 1972); Nancy S. Shedd, *An Architectural Study of the Ancient Borough of Huntington* (Huntington, Pa.: n.p., 1976); Ethelyn Cox, *Historic Alexandria, Virginia, Street by Street: A Survey of Existing Early Buildings* (Alexandria: Historic Alexandria Foundation, 1976); *A Guide to Historic Beaufort* (Beaufort, S.C.: Historic Beaufort Foundation, 1970); Ed Polk Douglas, *Architecture in Clairborne County, Mississippi: A Selective Guide* (Jackson: Mississippi Department of Archives and History, 1974); Camille Wells, *Architecture of Paducah and McCracken County* (Paducah, Ky.: Image Graphics, 1981); William A. Brenner, *Downtown and the University: Youngstown, Ohio* (Youngstown: Author, 1976); Geoffrey Blodgett, *Oberlin Architecture, College and Town: A Guide to its Social History* (Oberlin: Oberlin College, 1985); Jeanette S. Fields, ed., *A Guidebook to the Architecture of River Forest* (River Forest, Ill.: River Forest Community Center, 1981); *Building and People: Guidelines for Historic Preservation: Moorhead, Minnesota* (Moorhead: Moorhead Community Development Department, 1979); Larry Hanks and Meredith Roberts, *Roots: The Historic and Architectural Heritage of Kansas City, Kansas* (Kansas City, Kans.: City of Kansas, 1976); John Chase, *The Sidewalk Companion to Santa Cruz Architecture* (Santa Cruz, Calif.: Santa Cruz Historical Society, 1975); Southwestern Chapter, American Institute of Architects, *Style and Vernacular: A Guide to the Architecture of Land County, Oregon* (Salem: Oregon Historical Society, 1983).

28. Carole Rifkind and Carol Levine, *Mansions, Mills, and Main Streets: Buildings and Places to Explore within Fifty Miles on New York City* (New York: Schocken Books, 1975); Ira J. Bach, *A Guide to Chicago's Historic Suburbs on Wheels and on Foot* (Chicago and Athens, Ohio: Swallow Press and Ohio University Press, 1981). Neither of these books explores urbanistic features in much detail.

29. Bryant F. and Carolyn K. Tolles, *New Hampshire Architecture: An Illustrated Guide* (Hanover, N.H.: University Press of New England, 1979); David Gebhard and Tom Martinson, *A Guide to the Architecture of Minnesota* (Minneapolis: University of Minnesota Press, 1977); David Gebhard and Robert Winter, *A Guide to Architecture in Los Angeles and Southern California* (Santa Barbara and Salt Lake City: Peregrine Smith, 1977); David Gebhard et al., *The Guide to Architecture in San Francisco and Northern California* (Layton, Utah: Peregrine Smith Books, 1986); Sally B. Woodbridge and Roger Montgomery, *A Guide to Architecture in Washington State* (Seattle: University of Washington Press, 1980).

30. Among the several guides devoted to a single district, see A. McVoy McIntyre, *Beacon Hill: A Walking Tour* (Boston: Little, Brown, 1975); and Ellen Fletcher Rosebrock, *Walking around in South Street: Discoveries in New York's Old Shipping District* (New York: South Street Seaport Museum, 1974).

31. Donlyn Lyndon, *The City Observed: Boston; A Guide to the Architecture of the Hub* (New York: Vintage Books, 1982); Paul Goldberger, *The City Observed: New York;*

A Guide to the Architecture of Manhattan (New York: Random House, 1979); Charles Moore et al., *The City Observed: Los Angeles: A Guide to Its Architecture and Landscapes* (New York: Vintage Books, 1984).

32. Two guides exist focusing on work from a single period: Ada Louise Huxtable, *Classic New York: Georgian Gentility and Greek Elegance* (Garden City, N.Y.: Doubleday, 1964); and Pauline Chase Harrell and Margaret Supplee Smith, eds., *Victorian Boston Today: Ten Walking Tours* (Boston: New England Chapter, Victorian Society in America, 1975). One guide is devoted to the properties of a single institution: Nancy Lurie Salzman, *Buildings and Builders: An Architectural History of Boston University* (Boston: Boston University, 1985). There is a copious guide to sculpture and a much briefer one on landscape design in Washington, D.C.: James M. Goode, *The Outdoor Sculpture of Washington, D.C.: A Comprehensive Historical Guide* (Washington, D.C.: Smithsonian Institution Press, 1974); and James Matthew Evans, *The Landscape Architecture of Washington, D.C.: A Comprehensive Guide* (Washington, D.C.: Landscape Architecture Foundation, 1981). See also Ira J. Bach and Mary Lackritz Gray, *A Guide to Chicago's Public Sculpture* (Chicago: University of Chicago Press, 1983); Dennis Alan Nawrocki and Thomas J. Holleman, *Art in Detroit Public Places* (Detroit: Wayne State University Press, 1980); and Esther M. Klein, *Fairmount Park: A History and a Guidebook* (Bryn Mawr, Pa.: Harcum Junior College Press, 1974). Among the finest specialized guides is Marjorie Longenecker White, *The Birmingham District: An Industrial History and Guide* (Birmingham, Ala.: Birmingham Historical Society, 1981). See also Charles K. Hyde, *Detroit: An Industrial History Guide* (Detroit: Detroit Historical Society, n.d.).

33. Most of the studies done on American types do not match counterparts on work abroad. See, for example, Carol Herselle Krinsky, *Synagogues of Europe: Architecture, History, Meaning* (New York and Cambridge, Mass.: Architectural History Foundation and MIT Press, 1985); and Johann Friedrich Geist, *Arcades: The History of a Building Type,* trans. Jane O. Newman and John H. Smith (Cambridge, Mass.: MIT Press, 1983). Several other excellent books focus on types in Great Britain, including Stefan Muthesius, *The English Terraced House* (New Haven: Yale University Press, 1982); Colin Cunningham, *Victorian and Edwardian Town Halls* (London: Routledge & Kegan Paul, 1981); Malcolm Seaborne, *The English School: Its Architecture and Organization, 1370–1870* (Toronto: University of Toronto Press, 1971); and Malcolm Seaborne and Roy Lowe, *The English School: Its Architecture and Organization, vol. 2: 1870–1970* (London: Routledge & Kegan Paul, 1977).

34. Jan Cohn, *The Palace or the Poorhouse: The American House as a Cultural Symbol* (East Lansing: Michigan State University Press, 1979); David P. Handlin, *The American Home: Architecture and Society, 1815–1915* (Boston: Little, Brown, 1979); Gwendolyn Wright, *Moralism and the Model Home: Domestic Architecture and Cultural Conflict in Chicago, 1873–1913* (Chicago: University of Chicago Press, 1980); Gwendolyn Wright, *Building the Dream: A Social History of Housing in America* (Cambridge, Mass.: MIT Press, 1981). Despite its title, Wright's *Moralism* places less emphasis on in-depth case histories than it does introducing a wide range of related material that is pertinent to a number of places in addition to the Chicago metropolitan area.

35. After World War II, such studies focused almost entirely on buildings but remained antiquarian in tone; see, for example, Carl J. Weinhardt, Jr., "The Domestic Architecture of Beacon Hill, 1800–1850," *Proceedings of the Bostonian Society,* (1958), pp. 11–32; Scott, *Old Richmond Neighborhoods;* and Lancaster, *Old Brooklyn Heights.*

Marcus Whiffen, *The Eighteenth-Century Houses of Williamsburg* (Williamsburg: Colonial Williamsburg, 1960), presents an unusually meticulous account of the building art as well as of the buildings themselves. Grant Miles Simon's brief "Houses and Early House Life in Philadelphia," in Eisenhardt, *Historic Philadelphia*, was unusual at that time in depicting a more general picture of the residential landscape and living patterns. By the 1960s, Victorian city houses began to be studied, but initial accounts stress more the legitimacy of the topic than analyze either the architecture or its urban context. See Theodore M. Brown and Margaret M. Bridwell, *Old Louisville* (Louisville: University of Louisville, 1961); and Henry H. Glassie, "Victorian Homes in Washington," *Records of the Columbia Historical Society of Washington, D.C., 1963–1965*, (1966), pp. 320–65.

36. Bainbridge Bunting, *Houses of Boston's Back Bay: An Architectural History, 1840–1917* (Cambridge, Mass.: Belknap Press of Harvard University Press, 1967). See also Lewis Mumford and Walter Muir Whitehill, *Back Bay Boston: The City as a Work of Art* (Boston: Museum of Fine Arts, 1969). A more modest book concerning a somewhat comparable district in Philadelphia is Bobbye Burke et al., *Historic Rittenhouse: A Philadelphia Neighborhood* (Philadelphia: University of Pennsylvania Press, 1985).

37. Charles Lockwood, *Bricks and Brownstone: The New York Row House, 1783–1929; An Architectural and Social History* (New York: McGraw-Hill, 1972). Work done after 1875 is treated in a cursory fashion. See also Lockwood, *Manhattan Moves Uptown*.

38. Betsy Blackmar, "Re-walking the 'Walking City': Housing and Property Relations in New York City, 1810–1840," *Radical History Review* 21 (Fall 1979): 131–48. See also Peter A. Coclanis, "The Sociology of Architecture in Colonial Charleston: Pattern and Process in an Eighteenth-Century Southern City," *Journal of Social History* 18 (Summer 1985): 607–23, which seeks to demonstrate how the architectural character of that city was determined by a combination of social and economic forces.

39. Jay E. Cantor, "A Monument of Trade: A. T. Stewart and the Rise of the Millionaire's Mansion in New York," *Winterthur Portfolio* 10 (1975): 165–97. Other essays on Stewart are cited in note 78. The case study approach, focusing on one pivotal work, is also used for William C. Shopsin et al., *The Villard Houses: Life Story of a Landmark* (New York: Viking Press and Municipal Art Society of New York, 1980); and George B. Tatum, *Philadelphia Georgian: The City House of Samuel Powel and Some of Its Eighteenth-Century Neighbors* (Middletown, Conn.: Wesleyan University Press, 1976). Good general studies of New York's city houses after 1850 include Boyer, *Manhattan Manners,* and Stern, *New York 1900.* (Many of the local histories cited in the notes contain information on a variety of building types; only some of those that are especially informative in this regard cited again here and in the notes that follow.) See also Sarah Bradford Landau, "The Row Houses of New York's West Side," *Journal of the Society of Architectural Historians* 34 (March 1975): 19–36.

40. Margaret B. Tinkom, "Southwark, A River Community: Its Shape and Substance," *Proceedings of the American Philosophical Society* 114 (August 1970): 327–42. See also William John Murtagh, "The Philadelphia Row House," *Journal of the Society of Architectural Historians* 16 (December 1957): 8–13. A similar study on Spanish colonial settlement is Albert Manucy, *The Houses of St. Augustine* (St. Augustine: St. Augustine Historical Society, 1962).

41. Mary Ellen Hayward, "Urban Vernacular Architecture in Nineteenth-Century Baltimore," *Winterthur Portfolio* 16 (Spring 1981): 67–86. See also Robert L. Alexander, "Baltimore Row Houses of the Early Nineteenth Century," *American Studies* 16 (Fall

1975): 65–76; and Natalie W. Shivers, *Those Old Placid Rows: The Aesthetic and Development of the Baltimore Rowhouse* (Baltimore: Maclay & Associates, 1981). Although they do not focus on architecture per se, James Borchert's studies of alley dwellings in Washington, D.C., afford insight on both developmental and social patterns. See his "Alley Landscapes in Washington," *Landscape* 23 (Spring 1979): 3–10, reprinted in Dell Upton and John Michael Vlach, eds., *Common Places: Readings in American Vernacular Architecture* (Athens: University of Georgia Press, 1986), pp. 281–91; and James Borchert, *Alley Life in Washington: Family, Community, Religion, and Folklore in the City, 1850–1970* (Urbana: University of Illinois Press, 1980).

42. Anne Bloomfield, "The Real Estate Associates: A Land and Housing Developer of the 1870s in San Francisco," *Journal of the Society of Architectural Historians* 37 (March 1978): 13–33.

43. The Cambridge and New Orleans survey volumes (n. 19) take an important step in this direction, presenting some of the most extensive material on housing patterns available for any community in the United States. The Rhode Island, Somerville, and Biloxi surveys (nn. 22, 20) and histories such as Borchert, *Legacy of Minneapolis*, and Garber, *Built in Milwaukee*, are also valuable in this regard. An excellent essay focusing on urban development is Roger D. Simon, "The City-Building Process: Housing and Services in New Milwaukee Neighborhoods 1880–1910," *Transactions of the American Philosophical Society* 68 (July 1978): 5–64.

44. To date, some of the best analyses of urban residential interiors include Tatum, *Philadelphia Georgian*; Rodris Roth, "Interior Decoration of City Houses in Baltimore: The Federal Period,"*Winterthur Portfolio* 5 (1969): 59–86; Kenneth L. Ames, "Meaning in Artifacts: Hall Furnishings in Victorian America," *Journal of Interdisciplinary History* 9 (Summer 1978): 19–46, reprinted in Upton and Vlach, *Common Places*, pp. 240–60; and Lizabeth A. Cohen, "Embellishing a Life of Labor: An Interpretation of the Material Culture of American Working-Class Homes, 1885–1915," *Journal of American Culture* 3 (Winter 1980): 752–75, reprinted in Upton and Vlach, *Common Places*, pp. 261–78. Sally McMurry, "City Parlor, Country Sitting Room: Rural Vernacular Design and the American Parlor, 1840–1900," *Winterthur Portfolio* 20 (Winter 1985): 261–80, takes a significant step in comparing interiors of town and country but does not focus on distinctly urban houses.

45. John W. Reps, *The Making of Urban America: A History of City Planning in the United States* (Princeton: Princeton University Press, 1965).

46. Sam Bass Warner, Jr., *Streetcar Suburbs: The Process of Growth in Boston, 1870–1900* (Cambridge, Mass.: Harvard University Press, 1962); Mayer and Wade, *Chicago*.

47. A catalog of well-known planned developments is Robert A. M. Stern and John Montague Massengale, eds., *The Anglo-American Suburb* (London: Architectural Design, 1981). The best recent essay on the emergence of the picturesque suburb in the United States is John Archer, "Country and City in the American Romantic Suburb," *Journal of the Society of Architectural Historians* 42 (May 1983): 139–56. Case studies have been written on early and, for their time, highly unusual developments; see James B. Davies, "Llewellyn Park in West Orange, New Jersey," *Antiques* 107 (January 1975): 142–58; Theodore Turak, "Riverside: Roots in France," *Inland Architect* 25 (November-December 1981): 12–19; and Walter L. Creese, *The Crowning of the American Landscape* (Princeton: Princeton University Press, 1985), pp. 219–40. The development of a somewhat similar suburb in the late nineteenth century is presented in Margaret Sammartino

Marsh, "Suburbanization and the Search for Community: Residential Decentralization in Philadelphia, 1880–1900," *Pennsylvania History* 44 (April 1977): 99–116. Mark H. Rose, " 'There Is Less Smoke in the District': J. C. Nichols, Urban Change, and Technological Systems," *Journal of the West* 25 (January 1986): 44–54, focuses on the role of the developer in creating the Country District in Kansas City, one of the nation's most extensive planned suburban areas. Albert Fein has examined the transformation of a country seat into a suburban enclave of the rich, a process that probably occurred in a number of places around large eastern cities; see his *Wave Hill, Riverdale, and New York City: Legacy of a Hudson River Estate* (Bronx, N.Y.: Wave Hill, 1979). A good model for chronicling suburban growth and subsequent change in a concise format is afforded by Michael J. McCleer, *Woodbridge: A History of the Woodbridge Historic District, Detroit, Michigan* (Detroit: Woodbridge Citizens District Council, 1980). See also Ernest R. Sandeen, *St. Paul's Historic Summit Avenue* (St. Paul, Minn.: Macalester College Living Historical Museum, 1978); David A. Landgran and Ernest R. Sandeen, *The Lake District of Minneapolis: A History of the Calhoun-Isles Community* (St. Paul, Minn.: Macalester College Living Historical Museum, 1979); George W. McDaniel et al., *Images of Brookland: The History and Architecture of a Washington Suburb*, GW Washington Studies 10 (Washington, D.C.: George Washington University, 1982); Ann Mc-Corquodale Burkhardt and Alice Meriwether Bowsher, eds., "Town within a City: The Five Points South Neighborhood, 1880–1930," *Journal of the Birmingham Historical Society* 7 (November 1982): whole issue; Timothy J. Crimmins and Dana F. White, "Urban Structure Atlanta," *Atlanta Historical Journal* 26 (Summer-Fall 1982): whole issue; Michael H. Ebner, " 'In the Suburbes of Toun': Chicago's North Shore to 1871," *Chicago History* 11 (Summer 1982): 66–77; Ronald Dale Karr, "Brookline and the Making of an Elite Suburb," *Chicago History* 13 (Summer 1984): 36–47; and Catherine W. Bishir and Lawrence S. Earley, eds., *Early Twentieth-Century Suburbs in North Carolina: Essays on History, Architecture and Planning* (Raleigh: North Carolina Division of Archives and History, 1985). Some studies contain useful information on suburban development and residents but tend to discuss architecture merely in terms of stylistic motifs; see Samuel W. Thomas and William Morgan, *Old Louisville: The Victorian Era* (Louisville: Data Courier, 1975); Jean F. Eberle et al., *Urban Oasis: 75 Years in Parkview, a St. Louis Private Place* (St. Louis: Boar's Head Press, 1979); and Bruce Maston, *An Enclave of Elegance: A Survey of the Architecture Development and Personalities of the General Electric Realty Plot Historic District* (Schenectady, N.Y.: GERPA Publications, 1983).

Concerning alternative planned residential communities developed between the two world wars, see Wright, *Building the Dream*, pp. 193–214; Joseph L. Arnold, *The New Deal in the Suburbs: A History of the Greenbelt Town Program* (Columbus: Ohio State University Press, 1971); and Daniel Schaffer, *Garden Cities for America: The Radburn Experience* (Philadelphia: Temple University Press, 1982).

48. Tucci, *Built in Boston*.

49. Roger Miller and Joseph Siry, "The Emerging Suburb: West Philadelphia, 1850–1880," *Pennsylvania History* 47 (April 1980): 99–145. W. Edward Orser, "The Making of a Baltimore Rowhouse Community: The Edmondson Avenue Area, 1915–1945," *Maryland Historical Magazine* 80 (Fall 1985): 203–27, is another good case study documenting how, in that city, an urban house form was adapted as part of a suburban development package, and analyzes the social structure as well as the physical character of the precinct. See also Jean F. Block, *Hyde Park Houses, An Informal History, 1856–*

1910 (Chicago: University of Chicago Press, 1978); and Haglund, *Avenues of Salt Lake City*. Barbara Rubin, "A Chronology of Architecture in Los Angeles," *Annals, Association of American Geographers* 67 (December 1977): 521–37, seeks to demonstrate how suburban houses provide an index to the city's growth. The essay helps to establish a basis for inquiry but is undermined in its interpretation of architecture as a succession of superficial styles, a flaw that borders on an epidemic in recent literature. Richard Fusch and Larry R. Ford, "Architecture and the Geography of the American City," *Geographical Review* 73 (July 1983): 324–40, correlates basic house forms with period and precinct in Columbus and San Diego with findings that are useful though not profound. Robert W. Bastian, "Architecture and Class Segregation in Late Nineteenth-Century Terre Haute, Indiana," *Geographical Review* 65 (April 1975): 166–79, examines houses as a means of identifying class and income; and John A. Jakle, "Twentieth Century Revival Architecture and the Gentry," *Journal of Cultural Geography* 4 (Fall-Winter 1983): 28–43, depicts how historical references used in the design of houses in Urbana, Illinois, can be interpreted as symbols of status. Both accounts suffer from a lack of understanding the architecture they discuss, however. John Chase, *Exterior Decoration: Hollywood's Inside-out Houses* (Los Angeles: Hennessey & Ingalls, 1982), takes an unconventional topic, modest yet elaborately remodeled houses in West Hollywood, to explore architecture's cultural and locational implications. See also James S. Duncan, Jr., "Landscape Taste as a Symbol of Group Identity: A Westchester County Village," *Geographical Review* 63 (July 1973): 334–55.

50. Daniel J. Prosser, "Chicago and the Bungalow Boom of the 1920s," *Chicago History* 10 (Summer 1981): 86–95. See also Wim de Wit, "Apartment Houses and Bungalows: Building the Flat City," *Chicago History* 12 (Winter 1983-1984): 18–29. Anthony D. King, *The Bungalow: The Production of a Global Culture* (London: Routledge & Kegan Paul, 1984), considers urban factors in discussing this form but only in very broad terms based on the research of others. Robert Winter, *The California Bungalow* (Los Angeles: Hennessey & Ingalls, 1980), briefly considers why this form became so popular in southern portions of the state but does not explore the matter of physical context in depth. More instructive in this regard is Laura Chase, "Eden in the Orange Groves: Bungalows and Courtyard Houses of Los Angeles," *Landscape* 25, no. 3 (1981): 29–36. A cursory examination of this form in a Florida community is provided by James M. Ricci, "The Bungalow: A History of the Most Predominant Style of Tampa Bay," *Tampa Bay History* 1 (Fall-Winter 1979): 6–13. An excellent introduction to the bungalow as an idea is Richard Mattson, "The Bungalow Spirit," *Journal of Cultural Geography* 1 (Spring-Summer 1981): 75–92.

51. John Hancock, "The Apartment House in Urban America," in Anthony D. King, ed., *Buildings and Society: Essays on the Social Development of the Built Environment* (London: Routledge & Kegan Paul, 1980), pp. 151–89. See also Wright, *Building the Dream*, pp. 135–57; and Handlin, *American Home*, pp. 377–85. Concerning New York, see Robert A. M. Stern, "With Rhetoric: The New York Apartment House," *Via* 4 (1980): 78–111; Stern, *New York 1900*; Boyer, *Manhattan Manners*; Condit, *Chicago 1930–70*; de Wit, "Apartment Houses." See also nn. 52–53.

52. Richard Plunz, "Institutionalization of Housing Form in New York City, 1920–1950," in Richard Plunz, ed., *Housing Form and Public Policy in the United States* (New York: Praeger, 1980), pp. 157–200.

53. Carroll William Westfall, "Home at the Top: Domestic Chicago's Tall Apartment Buildings," *Chicago History* 14 (Spring 1985): 20–39; Celia Howard, " 'Rent Reasonable

to the Right Parties': Gold Coast Apartment Buildings, 1906–1929," *Chicago History* 8 (Summer 1979): 66–77; Tucci, *Built in Boston*. Dolores Hayden, *The Grand Domestic Revolution: A History of Feminist Designs for American Homes, Neighborhoods, and Cities* (Cambridge, Mass.: MIT Press, 1981), explores apartment design as part of feminist reform efforts.

54. A noteworthy exception is Jean A. Follett, "The Hotel Pelham: A New Building Type for America," *American Art Journal* 15 (Autumn 1983): 58–73.

55. Stefanos Polyzoides et al., *Courtyard Housing in Los Angeles: A Typological Analysis* (Berkeley and Los Angeles: University of California Press, 1982), provides an introduction to some of the more elaborate examples in that city.

56. John Beach and John Chase, "The Stucco Box," in Charles W. Moore et al., eds., *Home Sweet Home: American Domestic Vernacular Architecture* (New York: Rizzoli: 1983), pp. 118–29.

57. James E. Vance, Jr., "Housing the Worker: The Employment Linkage as a Force in Urban Structure," *Economic Geography* 42 (October 1966): 294–325; Richard Horowitz, "Architecture and Culture: The Meaning of the Lowell Boarding House," *American Quarterly* 25 (March 1973): 64–82. See also Coolidge, *Mill and Mansion*; William H. Pierson, Jr., *American Buildings and Their Architects: Technology and the Picturesque, The Corporate and Early Gothic Styles* (Garden City, N.Y.: Doubleday, 1978), chap. 2; and Wright, *Building the Dream*, pp. 58–72, 177–92.

58. Garner, *Model Company Town*. See also Candee, *Atlantic Heights*. Another popular New England workers' housing form, known as the three decker, is discussed in Tucci, *Built in Boston*. Arthur J. Krim, "The Three Decker as Urban Architecture in New England," *Monadnock* 44 (June 1970): 45–55, discusses the diffusion of this form in southern New England industrial centers. See also Garber, *Beyond the Neck*, and the Cambridge and Rhode Island surveys (nn. 19, 22).

59. Eugenie Ladner Birch and Deborah S. Gardner, "The Seven-Percent Solution: A Review of Philanthropic Housing, 1870–1910," *Journal of Urban History* 7 (August 1981): 403–38; Wright, *Building the Dream*, pp. 114–34; Handlin, *American Home*, pp. 197–214, 363–77; Cynthia Zaitzevsky, "Housing Boston's Poor: The First Philanthropic Experiments," *Journal of the Society of Architectural Historians* 42 (May 1983): 157–67. See also Peter Marcuse, "Housing in Early City Planning," *Journal of Urban History* 6 (February 1980): 153–76.

60. Anthony Jackson, *A Place Called Home: A History of Low-Cost Housing in Manhattan* (Cambridge, Mass.: MIT Press, 1976). See also Plunz, "Institutionalization of Housing Form"; Wright, *Building the Dream*, pp. 220–39; Devereux Bowly, Jr., *The Poorhouse: Subsidized Housing in Chicago, 1895–1976* (Carbondale: Southern Illinois University Press, 1978); and Condit, *Chicago, 1930–70*.

61. John F. Bauman, "Public Housing in the Depression: Slum Reform in Philadelphia Neighborhoods in the 1930s," in William W. Cutler III and Howard Gillette, Jr., eds., *The Divided Metropolis: Social and Spatial Dimensions of Philadelphia, 1800–1975* (Westport, Conn.: Greenwood Press, 1980), pp. 227–48; Richard Pommer, "The Architecture of Urban Housing in the United States during the Early 1930s," *Journal of the Society of Architectural Historians* 37 (December 1978): 235–64.

62. Lois Craig et al., *The Federal Presence: Architecture, Politics, and Symbols in United States Government Building* (Cambridge, Mass.: MIT Press, 1978), provides a compendium of data on federal architecture of all types. Henry-Russell Hitchcock and William Seale, *Temples of Democracy: The State Capitols of the U.S.A.* (New York:

Harcourt Brace Jovanovich, 1976), provides a well-written chronicle of the buildings themselves. William L. Lebovich, *America's City Halls* (Washington, D.C.: Preservation Press, 1984), includes a brief introductory history of the type followed by a catalog of selected examples. Marcus Whiffen, *The Public Buildings of Williamsburg, Colonial Capital of Virginia* (Williamsburg: Colonial Williamsburg, 1958), presents a detailed and unique survey of government and institutional buildings in this eighteenth-century community.

63. Edward T. Price, "The Central Courthouse Square in the American County Seat," *Geographical Review* 58 (January 1968): 29–60, reprinted in Upton and Valch, *Common Places*, pp. 124–45. See also Marian M. Ohman, "Diffusion of Foursquare Courthouses to the Midwest 1785–1885," *Geographic Review* 72 (April 1982): 171–89. Richard Pare, ed., *Court House; A Photographic Document* (New York: Horizon Press, 1978), is a superb pictorial study with supplementary essays. The most detailed examination of the subject on a statewide basis is Willard B. Robinson, *The People's Architecture: Texas Courthouses, Jails, and Municipal Buildings* (Austin: Texas Historical Commission and University of Texas Center for Studies in Texas History, 1983). See also *100 Courthouses: A Report on North Carolina Judicial Facilities,* 2 vols. (Raleigh: North Carolina State University, School of Design, 1978); Marian H. Ohman, *Encyclopedia of Missouri Courthouses* (Columbia: University of Missouri-Columbia, Extension Division, 1981); and Julie A. Wortman and David P. Johnson, *Legacies: Kansas' Older County Courthouses* (Topeka: Kansas State Historical Society, 1981). Donald F. Dosch, *The Old Courthouse: Americans Build a Forum on the Frontier* (St. Louis: Jefferson National Expansion Historical Association, 1979), is an excellent case study, which examines the building's symbolic and political factors, as well as how its functional requirements were accommodated over time. See also C. Ross Bloomquist, "Planning and Building a Courthouse for Foster County, 1907–1912," *North Dakota History* 49 (Spring 1982): 12–21; and Calvin F. Schwartzkopf, "The Rush County-Seat War," *Kansas Historical Quarterly* 36 (Spring 1970): 40–61.

On city halls, Howard Gillette, Jr., "Philadelphia's City Hall: Monument to a New Political Machine," *Pennsylvania Magazine of History and Biography* 97(April 1973): 233–49, reveals the insights public buildings can provide on municipal politics. See also John Maass, "Philadelphia City Hall—Monster or Masterpiece?" *AIA Journal* 54 (February 1965): 23–30. Glen E. Holt, " 'Will Chicago's Itinerant City Hall Be Moved Once More?' " *Chicago History* 6 (Fall 1977): 155–66, indicates the complex, often tempestuous histories of large nineteenth-century public buildings. Charles T. Goodsell, "The City Council Chamber: From Distance to Intimacy," *Public Interest* 74 (Winter 1984): 116–31, correlates physical character with governmental practices. Samuel Wilson, Jr., and Leonard V. Huber, *The Cabildo on Jackson Square* (Gretna, La.: Pelican Publishing Company, 1973), provides a meticulous account of New Orleans' governmental center from its inception.

64. Harold N. Cooledge, "Samuel Sloan and the 'Philadelphia Plan,' " *Journal of the Society of Architectural Historians* 23 (October 1964): 151–54, documents the origins of an important early development of a widely used nineteenth-century school form. Andrea R. Andrews, "The Baltimore School Building Program, 1870–1900: A Study in Urban Reform," *Maryland Historical Magazine* 70 (Fall 1975): 260–74, analyzes the political system but not the architecture. Helen Lefowitz Horowitz, *Culture and the City: Cultural Philanthropy in Chicago from the 1880s to 1917* (Lexington: University Press of Kentucky, 1976), provides a somewhat hypothetical analysis of buildings such as the

Chicago Public Library as an embodiment of patronage and class status. Patronage, typological development, and a detailed examination of the fabric of Boston's Public Library are included in William H. Jordy, *American Buildings and Their Architects: Progressive and Academic Ideals at the Turn of the Twentieth Century* (Garden City, N.Y.: Doubleday, 1972), chap. 7. Useful studies exist of two other public building types: David Glassberg, "The Design of Reform: The Public Bath Movement in America," *American Studies* 20 (Fall 1979): 5–21; and Robert A. Sauder, "Municipal Markets in New Orleans," *Journal of Cultural Geography* 2 (Fall-Winter 1981): 82–95. See also Stern, *New York 1900*, and Condit, *Chicago 1910–29*.

65. Rebecca Zurier, *The American Firehouse: An Architectural and Social History* (New York: Abbeville Press, 1982).

66. However, David J. Rothman, *The Discovery of the Asylum: Social Order and Disorder in the New Republic* (Boston: Little, Brown, 1971), is an excellent cultural history of hospitals, prisons, and several other institutional types.

67. Robert C. Ostegren, "The Immigrant Church as a Symbol of Community and Place in the Upper Midwest," *Great Plains Quarterly* 1 (Fall 1981): 225–38. See also Terry G. Jordan, "A Religious Geography of the Hill Country Germans of Texas," in Frederick C. Luebke, ed., *Ethnicity on the Great Plains* (Lincoln: University of Nebraska Press, 1980), pp. 109–28.

68. Daniel J. Boorstin, *The Americans: The National Experience* (New York: Vintage Books, 1965), pp. 152–61; Richard Longstreth, "From Farm to Campus: Planning, Politics, and the Agricultural College Idea in Kansas," *Winterthur Portfolio* 20 (Summer-Autumn 1985): 149–79.

69. Paul Venable Turner, *Campus: An American Planning Tradition* (New York and Cambridge, Mass.: Architectural History Foundation and MIT Press, 1984), pp. 163–213. Turner's book provides an excellent overview of collegiate architecture and planning. See also Richard Longstreth, *On the Edge of the World: Four Architects in San Francisco at the Turn of the Century* (New York and Cambridge, Mass.: Architectural History Foundation and MIT Press, 1983), pp. 244–51; Francesco Pessanti, "The Design of Columbia in the 1890s: McKim and His Client," *Journal of the Society of Architectural Historians* 36 (May 1977): 69–84; Loren W. Partridge, *John Galen Howard and the Berkeley Campus: Beaux-Arts Architecture in the "Athens of the West"* (Berkeley: Berkeley Architectural Heritage Association, 1978); Buford Pickens and Margaretta J. Darnall, *Washington University in St. Louis: Its Design and Architecture* (St. Louis: Washington University School of Architecture, 1980); Stephen Fox, *The General Plan of the William M. Rice Institute and Its Architectural Development* (Houston: Rice University School of Architecture, 1980); and *Caltech, 1910–1950: An Urban Architecture for Southern California* (Pasadena: Baxter Art Gallery, 1983).

70. Turner, *Campus*, chap. 7; Reyner Banham, *Megastructure: Urban Futures of the Recent Past* (New York: Harper & Row, 1976), pp. 135ff.

71. Karen Luehrs and Timothy J. Crimmins, "In the Mind's Eye: The Downtown as Visual Metaphor for the Metropolis," *Atlanta Historical Journal* 26 (Summer-Fall 1982): 177–98; Perry Duis, "Whose City? Public and Private Places in Nineteenth Century Chicago," *Chicago History* 12 (Spring 1983): 2–27.

72. Boyer, *Manhattan Manners*; Lockwood, *Manhattan Moves Uptown*; Lois Severini, *The Architecture of Finance, Early Wall Street* (Ann Arbor: UMI Research Press, 1983); Ellen W. Kramer, "Contemporary Descriptions of New York City and Its Public Architecture ca. 1850," *Journal of the Society of Architectural Historians* 27 (December

1968): 264–80. See also Stern, *New York 1900*, and Winston Weisman, "Commercial Palaces of New York: 1845–1875," *Art Bulletin* 36 (December 1954): 285–302. On Portland, see William John Hawkins III, *The Grand Era of Cast-Iron Architecture in Portland* (Portland, Ore.: Binford & Mort, 1976); and Virginia Guest Ferriday, *Last of the Handmade Buildings: Glazed Terra Cotta in Downtown Portland* (Portland: Mark Publishing Company, 1984). See also Condit, *Chicago 1910–29*; Garber, *Built in Milwaukee*; Lowic, *St. Louis*; Corbett, *Splendid Survivors*; Winthrop, *Downtown Richmond*; Christovich, *New Orleans Architecture*, vol. 2; Woodward, *Downtown Providence*; McCormick, *Downtown Salt Lake City*; and Winston Weisman, "Philadelphia Functionalism and Sullivan," *Journal of the Society of Architectural Historians* 20 (March 1961): 3–19. Neal O. Hines, *Denny's Knoll: A History of the Metropolitan Tract of the University of Washington* (Seattle: University of Washington Press, 1980), gives a detailed account of a small portion of Seattle's business center. Timothy J. Noel, *Denver's Larimer Street: Main Street, Skid Row and Urban Renaissance* (Denver: Historic Denver, 1981), is a popular account of that city's former principal artery.

73. The basic introductory study, containing superb illustrations, is Carole Rifkind, *Main Street: The Face of Urban America* (New York: Harper Colophon Books, 1977). See also Jakle, *American Small Town*, and *Main Street: Mirror of Change* (Bowling Green: Western Kentucky University Museum, 1980). Local histories such as Brugemann, *Benecia*; Weeks, *Westminster*; Maycock, *Carbondale*; and surveys such as Landscape Research, *Beyond the Neck*, and those for Cambridge (n. 19) and Rhode Island (n. 22) are also valuable in this regard. Richard Mattson, "Store Front Remodeling on Main Street," *Journal of Cultural Geography* 3 (Spring-Summer 1983): 41–55, outlines general tendencies in commercial modernization that have occurred in many towns since the mid–1930s.

74. See, for example, Frank A. Randall, *History of the Development of Building Construction in Chicago* (Urbana: University of Illinois Press, 1949), and Carl W. Condit, *The Chicago School of Architecture* (Chicago: University of Chicago Press, 1964).

75. Jean Gottmann, "Why the Skyscraper?" *Geographical Review* 56 (April 1966): 190–212, provides a good introduction to this topic. For an overview of skyscraper development, see Paul Goldberger, *The Skyscraper* (New York: Alfred A. Knopf, 1981). Carol Willis, "Zoning and *Zeitgeist*: The Skyscraper City in the 1920s," *Journal of the Society of Architectural Historians* 45 (March 1986): 47–59, explores the impact of zoning ordinances on skyscraper design and urban visions of the period; see also her "Skyscraper Utopias: Visionary Urbanism in the 1920s," in Joseph J. Corn, ed., *Imagining Tomorrow: History, Technology and the American Future* (Cambridge, Mass.: MIT Press, 1986), pp. 164–87. Kenneth Turney Gibbs, *Business Architectural Imagery in America, 1870–1930* (Ann Arbor: UMI Research Press, 1984), offers a preliminary investigation of how skyscrapers reflected attitudes of the business community. Among the most provocative discussions of the skyscraper in its urban context are Thomas A. P. Van Leeuwen, "The Skyward Trend of Thought: Some Ideas on the History of the Methodology of the Skyscraper," in David G. De Long et al., eds., *American Architecture: Innovation and Tradition* (New York: Rizzoli, 1986), pp. 59–81; Mario Manieri-Elia, "Toward an 'Imperial City': Daniel H. Burham and the City Beautiful Movement," and Manfredo Tafuri, "The Disenchanted Mountain: The Skyscraper and the City," both in Giorgio Ciucci et al., *The American City: From the Civil War to the New Deal*, trans. Barbara Luigia La Penta (Cambridge, Mass.: MIT Press, 1979), pp. 1–142, 389–528. See also Stuart Cohen, "The Tall Building Urbanistically Reconsidered," *Threshold* 2 (Autumn 1983): 6–13;

Paul Goldberger, "Skyscrapers and the City," *Chicago History* 12 (Winter 1983–1984): 6–17; and a personal, engaging interpretation, Rem Koolhas, *Delirious New York: A Retrospective Manifesto for Manhattan* (New York: Oxford University Press, 1978). Two excellent case studies have been written about one of the nation's most ambitious skyscraper complexes: Carol Herselle Krinsky, *Rockefeller Center* (New York: Oxford University Press, 1978), and Alan Balfour, *Rockefeller Center: Architecture as Theater* (New York: McGraw-Hill, 1978). Two popular accounts have also been written about major New York landmarks: Theodore James, Jr., *The Empire State Building* (New York: Harper & Row, 1975); and Sy Rubin and Jonathan Mandell, *Trump Tower* (Secaucus, N.J.: Lyle Stuart, 1984).

76. Larry Ford, "The Diffusion of the Skyscraper as an Urban Symbol," *Association of Pacific Coast Geographers Yearbook* 34 (1973): 49–60, provides an introductory case study of Ohio during the 1920s.

77. Russell Lewis, "Everything under One Roof: World's Fairs and Department Stores in Paris and Chicago," *Chicago History* 12 (Fall 1983): 28–47; Boyer, *Manhattan Manners*; Stern, *New York 1900*; Susan Porter Benson, "Palace of Consumption and Machine for Selling: The American Department Store, 1880–1940," *Radical History Review* 21 (Fall 1979): 199–221; William R. Leach, "Transformations in a Culture of Consumption: Women and Department Stores, 1890–1925," *Journal of American History* 71 (September 1984): 319–42. A good introduction to the type is given in Daniel J. Boorstin, *The Americans: The Democratic Experience* (New York: Vintage Books: 1973), pp. 101–9.

78. Ann Lorenz Van Zanten, "The Marshall Field Annex and the New Urban Order of Daniel Burnham's Chicago," *Chicago History* 11 (Fall-Winter 1982): 130–41; James F. O'Gorman, "The Marshall Field Wholesale Store: Materials toward a Monograph," *Journal of the Society of Architectural Historians* 37 (October 1978): 175–94. See also Harry E. Resseguie, "A. T. Stewart's Marble Palace—The Cradle of the Department Store," *New York Historical Society Quarterly* 48 (April 1964): 131–62; and Resseguie, "Alexander Turney Stewart and the Development of the Department Store, 1823–1876," *Business History Review* 39 (Autumn 1965): 301–22.

79. Deborah C. Andrews, "Bank Buildings in Nineteenth-Century Philadelphia," in Cutler and Gillette, *Divided Metropolis,* pp. 57–83. See also Severini, *Architecture of Finance.*

80. Francis Duffy, "Office Buildings and Organizational Change," in King, *Buildings and Society,* pp. 256–80, is the only essay focusing on this important aspect of commercial building design. Kym S. Rice, *Early American Taverns: For the Entertainment of Friends and Strangers* (Chicago: Regnery Gateway, 1983), discusses factors such as location and use of both urban and rural examples. See also Robert Earle Graham, "The Taverns of Colonial Philadelphia," in Eisenhardt, *Historic Philadelphia,* pp. 318–25.

Concerning hotels, see Ivan D. Steen, "Palaces for Travelers: New York City's Hotels in the 1850's as Viewed by British Visitors," *New York History* 51 (April 1970): 269–86; Boyer, *Manhattan Manners*; and Stern, *New York, 1900.* Boorstin, *The Americans,* provides a good overview of the type in the nineteenth century. Several popular accounts have been written, including Jefferson Williams, *The American Hotel: An Anecdotal History* (1930; New York: Arno Press, 1975); Richard A. Van Orman, *A Room for the Night: Hotels of the Old West* (Bloomington: Indiana University Press, 1966); Sandra Dallas, *No More Than Five to a Bed: Colorado Hotels in the Old Days* (Norman:

University of Oklahoma Press, 1967); and Oscar Lewis and Carroll D. Hall, *Bonanza Inn: America's First Luxury Hotel* (New York: Alfred A. Knopf, 1939). Concerning resort hotels, see Thomas, *Cape May*.

The best account of theater architecture in its urban context is Tucci, *Built in Boston*. Mary C. Henderson, *The City and the Theatre: New York Playhouses from Bowling Green to Times Square* (Clifton, N.J.: James T. White & Company, 1973), examines the city's legitimate houses as a component of urban history. See also Boyer, *Manhattan Manners*, and Stern, *New York 1900*. Edgar B. Young, *Lincoln Center: The Building of an Institution* (New York: New York University Press, 1980), is a detailed official history that places its subject within the context of New York's urban renewal efforts of the post–World War II era. Most accounts offer little in this regard; see, for example, Brooks McNamara, *The American Playhouse in the Eighteenth Century* (Cambridge, Mass.: Harvard University Press, 1969); Arthur Hobson Quinn, "The Theatre and Drama in Old Philadelphia," in Eisenhardt, *Historic Philadelphia*, pp. 313–17; Toni Young, *The Grand Experience: A History of the Grand Opera House* (Watkins Glen, N.Y.: American Life Foundation, 1976); Charlie H. Johnson, Jr., *The Central Opera House: A 100 Year History* (Colorado Springs: Little London Press, 1980). Popular histories of movie theaters include Ben M. Hall, *The Best Remaining Seats: The Story of the Golden Age of the Movie Palace* (New York: Bramhall House, 1961); David Naylor, *American Picture Palaces: The Architecture of Fantasy* (New York: Van Nostrand Reinhold, 1981); Preston J. Kaufmann, *Fox—The Last Word . . . Story of the World's Finest Theatre* (Pasadena: Showcase Publications, 1979); George D. Bushnell, "Chicago's Magnificent Movie Palaces," *Chicago History* 6 (Summer 1977): 99–106; and *Jewel of Joliet* (Joliet, Ill.: Will County Cultural Arts Association, 1977).

81. Carl W. Condit, *The Railroad and the City: A Technological and Urbanistic History of Cincinnati* (Columbus; Ohio State University Press, 1977), *The Port of New York: A History of the Rail and Terminal System from the Beginnings to Pennsylvania Station* (Chicago: University of Chicago Press, 1980), and *The Port of New York: A History of the Rail and Terminal System from the Grand Central Electrification to the Present* (Chicago: University of Chicago Press, 1981). See also Condit, *Chicago 1910–29*. John R. Stilgoe, *Metropolitan Corridor: Railroads and the American Scene* (New Haven: Yale University Press, 1983), discusses some components of the railroad landscape as it developed during the late nineteenth and early twentieth centuries. The basic history of railroad stations themselves remains Carroll L. V. Meeks, *The Railroad Station: An Architectural History* (New Haven: Yale University Press, 1956).

82. Elliot Wellinsky, "Grand Central: Shaper of a City," in Deborah Nevins, ed., *Grand Central Terminal: City within a City* (New York: Municipal Art Society, 1982), pp. 85–108; see also William D. Middleton, *Grand Central . . . the World's Greatest Railway Terminal* (San Marino, Calif.: Golden West Books, 1977). Jeffrey P. Roberts, "Railroads and the Downtown: Philadelphia 1830–1900," in Cutler and Gillette, *Divided Metropolis*, pp. 27–55. See also Kenton Forest and Charles Albi, *Denver's Railroads: The Story of Union Station and the Railroads of Denver* (Golden: Colorado Railroad Museum, 1981). Sally Kitt Chappell, "Railroad Terminals and Urban Life: Examples in the Works of Graham, Anderson, Probst, and White," *Threshold* 3 (1985): 36–48, discusses the idea of the railroad station's role in efforts to reorder the city. There are also useful popular histories of subways and commuter railroad lines: Benson Bobrick, *Labyrinths of Iron: A History of the World's Subways* (New York: Newsweek Books,

1981); and Lawrence Grow, *On the 8:02: An Informal History of Commuting by Rail in America* (New York: Main Street Press, 1979).

83. Keith L. Bryant, Jr., "Cathedrals, Castles, and Roman Baths; Railway Station Architecture in the Urban South," *Journal of Urban History* 2 (February 1976): 195–230, offers little beyond basic documentation. Studies on railroad depots in towns are far more useful. See H. Roger Grant and Charles W. Bohi, *The Country Railroad Station in America* (Boulder, Colo.: Pruett Publishing Company, 1978), and Stilgoe, *Metropolitan Corridor*.

84. An excellent introduction to the subject is Barbara Rubin, "Aesthetic Ideology and Urban Design," *Annals of the Association of American Geographers* 69 (September 1979): 339–61, reprinted in Upton and Vlach, *Common Places*, pp. 482–508. Type studies include Bruce A. Lohof, "The Service Station in America: The Evolution of a Vernacular Form," *Industrial Archaeology* 11 (Spring 1974): 1–13; Richard J. S. Gutman, "Diner Design: Overlooked Sophistication," *Perspecta* 15 (1975): 41–53; Paul Hirshorn and Steven Izenour, *White Towers* (Cambridge, Mass.: MIT Press, 1979); Daniel I. Vierya, *"Fill'er Up": An Architectural History of America's Gas Stations* (New York: Collier Books, 1979); John A. Jakle, "Motel by the Roadside: America's Room for the Night," *Journal of Cultural Geography* 1 (Fall-Winter 1980): 34–49; Keith A. Sculle, "The Vernacular Gasoline Station: Examples from Illinois and Wisconsin," *Journal of Cultural Geography* 1 (Spring-Summer 1981): 56–74; John A. Jakle, "Roadside Restaurants and Place-Product-Packaging," *Journal of Cultural Geography* 3 (Fall-Winter 1982): 76–93; Alan Hess, *Googie: Fifties Coffee Shop Architecture* (San Francisco: Chronicle Books, 1985); and Philip Langdon, *Orange Roofs, Golden Arches: The Architecture of American Chain Restaurants* (New York: Alfred A. Knopf, 1986).

85. See, for example, Thomas J. Baerwald, "The Emergence of a New 'Downtown,' " *Geographical Review* 68 (July 1978): 308–18; Alvin W. Urguhart, "Stripping the Urban Landscape," *Association of Pacific Coast Geographers Yearbook* 43 (1981): 7–21; and John Fraser Hart, "The Bypass Strip as an Ideal Landscape," *Geographical Review* 72 (April 1982): 218–23.

86. Chester H. Liebs, *Main Street to Miracle Mile: American Roadside Architecture* (Boston: New York Graphic Society, 1985); Thomas J. Schlereth, *U.S. 40: A Roadscape of the American Experience* (Indianapolis: Indiana Historical Society, 1985). See also Elisabeth Walton, "Auto Accommodation," in Vaughan and Ferriday, *Space, Style and Structure*, pp. 518–41. The classic study on the contemporary strip, written from a designer's perspective yet of value to anyone investigating the topic, is Robert Venturi et al., *Learning from Las Vegas* (Cambridge, Mass.: MIT Press, 1972).

87. Warren James Belasco, *Americans on the Road: From Auto-camp to Motel, 1910–1945* (Cambridge, Mass.: MIT Press, 1979); Meredith Clausen, "Northgate Regional Shopping Center—Paradigm from Provinces," *Journal of the Society of Architectural Historians* 43 (May 1984): 144–61; Howard Gillette, Jr., "The Evolution of the Planned Shopping Center in Suburb and City," *Journal of the American Planning Association* 51 (Autumn 1985): 449–60; Richard Longstreth, "J. C. Nichols, the Country Club Plaza, and Notions of Modernity," *Harvard Architecture Review* 5 (1986): 121–35.

88. Some useful introductory studies in this regard include Joseph Interrante, "You Can't Go to Town in a Bathtub: Automobile Movement and the Reorganization of Rural American Space, 1900–1930," *Radical History Review* 21 (Fall 1979): 151–68; Joseph Interrante, "The Road to Autopia: The Automobile and the Spatial Transformation of

American Culture," *Michigan Quarterly Review* 19–20 (Fall 1980-Winter 1981): 502–17; Folke T. Kihlstedt, "The Automobile and the Transformation of the American House, 1910–1935," *Michigan Quarterly Review* 19–20 (Fall 1980-Winter 1981): 555–70; Jakle, *American Small Town*, pp. 119–66; J. B. Jackson, *The Southern Landscape Tradition in Texas* (Fort Worth: Amon Carter Museum, 1980), pp. 25–35; and J. B. Jackson, "The Vernacular City," *Center* 1 (1985): 27–43.

89. By far the most studied fair is the World's Columbian Exposition in Chicago; see David J. Burg, *Chicago's White City of 1893* (Lexington: University of Kentucky Press, 1976); Thomas S. Hines, *Burnham of Chicago: Architect and Planner* (New York: Oxford University Press, 1974), pp. 92–138; Mario Manierie-Elia, "Toward an 'Imperial City,' "; and M. Christine Boyer, *Dreaming the Rational City: The Myth of American City Planning* (Cambridge, Mass.: MIT Press, 1983), pp. 46ff. A good account of the city politics involved in sponsoring one such exposition is Marjorie M. Dobkin, "A Twenty-Five-Million-Dollar Mirage," in Burton Benedict et al., *The Anthropology of World's Fairs: San Francisco's Panama Pacific International Exposition of 1915* (London and Berkeley: Scholar Press, 1983), pp. 66–93. The urbanistic implications of that fair's midway are discussed in Rubin, "Aesthetic Ideology." See also Karal Ann Marling, *The Colossus of Roads: Myth and Symbol along the American Highway* (Minneapolis: University of Minnesota Press, 1984). Folke T. Kihlstedt, "Utopia Realized: The World's Fairs of the 1930s," in Corn, *Imagining Tomorrow*, pp. 97–118, analyzes the influence of these events on visions of the metropolis of the future. A good account of the 1933 Century of Progress Exposition is in Condit, *Chicago, 1930–70*, pp. 3–19. For accounts of other fairs, see John Maass, *The Glorious Enterprise: The Centennial Exhibition of 1876 and H. J. Schwarzmann, Architect-in-Chief* (Watkins Glen, N.Y.: American Life Foundation, 1973); Helen A. Harrison et al., *Dawn of a New Day: The New York World's Fair, 1939/40* (New York: Queens Museum, 1980); and George McMath, "Lewis and Clark Exposition," in Vaughan and Ferriday, *Space, Style and Structure*, pp. 311–23.

90. See, for example, Robert E. Snow and David E. Wright, "Coney Island: A Case Study in Popular Culture and Technical Change," *Journal of Popular Culture* 9 (Spring 1976): 960–75; and John F. Kasson, *Amusing the Million: Coney Island at the Turn of the Century* (New York: Hill & Wang, 1978). A personal interpretation of this complex is provided in Koolhaas, *Delirious New York*, pp. 21–65. A somewhat analogous account of Disneyland, also written by an architect, is Charles W. Moore, "You Have to Pay for the Public Life," *Perspecta* 9–10 (1965): 57–87. Written for a popular audience, Gary Kyriazi's *The Great American Amusement Parks: A Pictorial History* (Secaucus, N.J.: Citadel Press, 1976), provides an overview of the subject. Popular accounts also have been written on some individual parks; see, for example, Charles J. Jacques, *Kennywood . . . Roller Coaster Capital of the World* (Vestal, N.Y.: Vestal Press, 1982). Among the few scholarly essays not about Coney Island are Millicent Hall, "The Park at the End of the Trolley," *Landscape* 22 (Autumn 1977): 11–18, which discusses the role of street railway companies in developing amusement parks; and Alan Havig, "Mass Commercial Amusements in Kansas City before World War I," *Missouri Historical Review* 75 (April 1981): 316–45. A useful history has been written about an amusement pier: Nancy D. and John S. McCormick, *Saltair* (Salt Lake City: University of Utah Press, 1985). An excellent analysis of the urbanistic aspects of one type of sports arena is Philip H. Bess, "From Elysian Fields to Domed Stadiums: Form, Context, and Character in American Baseball Parks," *Threshold* 2 (Autumn 1983): 116–27.

91. John R. Stilgoe, *Common Landscape of America, 1580 to 1845* (New Haven: Yale

University Press, 1982), pp. 265–336, provides a good analysis of earlier industrial sites and some of the reasons why they stood isolated from traditional communities.

92. The best study of the subject is Reyner Banham, *A Concrete Atlantis: U.S. Industrial Building and European Modern Architecture 1900–1925* (Cambridge, Mass.: MIT Press, 1986), which includes some analysis of the work itself.

93. See note 14.

94. Good studies in this regard include Fink, *Providence Industrial Sites*; Larry D. Lankton and Charles K. Hyde, *Old Reliable: An Illustrated History of the Quincy Mining Company* (Hancock, Mich.: Quincy Mine Hoist Association, 1982); and White, *Birmingham District*. A rare account of the early twentieth-century industrial landscape is provided in Stilgoe, *Metropolitan Corridor*, pp. 77–103. Lewis L. McArthur, "Industrial Building," in Vaughan and Ferriday, *Space, Style and Structure*, pp. 161–69, 391–403, 542–52, 673–83, offers a valuable perspective on a region's industrial development. Brief accounts of industrial complexes are given in some inventories including reports 3 and 5 for Cambridge (n. 19); Landscape Research, *Beyond the Neck,* and several of the Rhode Island and North Carolina volumes (nn. 22–23). Much valuable documentary information has been gathered in reports published under the aegis of the Historic American Engineering Record, including Robert M. Vogel, ed., *A Report of the Mohawk-Hudson Area Survey* (Washington, D.C.: Smithsonian Institution Press, 1973); Charles K. Hyde, *The Lower Peninsula of Michigan: An Inventory of Historic Engineering and Industrial Sites* (Washington, D.C.: Office of Archeology and Historic Preservation, National Park Service, 1976); Charles K. Hyde, *The Upper Peninsula of Michigan: An Inventory of Historic Engineering and Industrial Sites* (Washington, D.C.: Office of Archeology and Historic Preservation, National Park Service, 1976); Charles K. Hyde, *The Upper Peninsula of Michigan: An Inventory of Historic Engineering and Industrial Sites* (Washington, D.C.: Office of Archeology and Historic Preservation, 1978); Gary Kulik et al., *Rhode Island: An Inventory of Historic Engineering and Industrial Sites* (Washington, D.C.: Office of Archeology and Historic Preservation, 1978); and Daniel M. Bluestone, ed., *Cleveland: An Inventory of Historic Engineering and Industrial Sites* (Washington, D.C.: Office of Archeology and Historic Preservation, 1978).

95. The initial monographs of this type were biographies of celebrated contemporary figures, each written shortly after its subject's premature death: Mariana Griswold Van Rensselaer, *Henry Hobson Richardson and His Works* (1888; New York: Dover, 1969), and Harriet Monroe, *John Wellborn Root: A Study of His Life and Work* (1896; Park Forest, Ill.: Prairie School Press, 1966). After 1900, monographs began to be published on historical figures, for example: Sidney Fiske Kimball, *Thomas Jefferson, Architect* (1916; New York: Da Capo Press, 1968). Several more ambitious studies were released during the next two decades, but their number remained small until after 1950.

96. To my knowledge, only one study has been made concentrating on the impact a community had on an architect's work: Herbert Muschamp, *Man about Town: Frank Lloyd Wright in New York City* (Cambridge, Mass.: MIT Press, 1983).

97. Among recent monographs, Robert A. M. Stern, *George Howe: Toward a Modern American Architecture* (New Haven: Yale University Press, 1975), devotes more than the usual amount of attention to the social milieu and the physical setting in which the architect worked. Leland M. Roth, *McKim, Mead & White, Architects* (New York: Harper & Row, 1983), affords numerous insights on the partners' view of New York City, how it affected their work, and how their work helped to alter the complexion of the metropolis. I have sought to provide a similar analysis of the San Francisco Bay Area in *On the Edge*

of the World. Tucci, *Built in Boston,* uses the work of several key architects as a reference point in discussing whole episodes of the city's development. See also Hines, *Burnham of Chicago;* Donald Hoffmann, *The Architecture of John Wellborn Root* (Baltimore: Johns Hopkins University Press, 1973); Thomas S. Hines, *Richard Neutra and the Search for Modern Architecture: A Biography and History* (New York: Oxford University Press, 1982); Bainbridge Bunting, *John Gaw Meem: Southwestern Architect* (Albuquerque: University of New Mexico Press, 1983); and Donald W. Curl, *Mizner's Florida: American Resort Architecture* (New York and Cambridge, Mass.: Architectural History Foundation and MIT Press, 1984).

98. Historical studies focusing on the architect's practice are few and tend to concentrate on leading figures; see Bernard Michael Boyle, "Architectural Practice in America, 1865–1965—Ideal and Reality," in Spiro Kostof, ed., *The Architect: Chapters in the History of the Profession* (New York: Oxford University Press, 1977), pp. 309–44; and Andrew Saint, *The Image of the Architect* (New Haven: Yale University Press, 1983). An exception is Judith R. Blau, *Architects and Firms: A Sociological Perspective on Architectural Practice* (Cambridge, Mass.: MIT Press, 1984). Case studies have great potential for expanding the scope of our knowledge on the subject, as is indicated in George Ehrlich and Peggy E. Schrock, "The A. B. Cross Lumber Company," *Missouri Historical Review* 60 (October 1985): 14–32, which discusses the impact of conditions in a nascent city on establishing a practice.

99. I am indebted to Dennis Domer for bringing some important facts concerning the firm's career to my attention. To date, studies of important local or regional firms have not addressed these matters, as is evident in Thomas J. Holleman and James P. Gallagher, *Smith, Hinchman & Grylls: 125 Years of Architecture and Engineering, 1853–1978* (Detroit: Wayne State University Press, 1978); Lloyd C. and June-Marie F. Engelbrecht, *Henry C. Trost, Architect of the Southwest* (El Paso: El Paso Public Library Association, 1981); and Robert C. Broward, *The Architecture of Henry John Klutho: The Prairie School in Jacksonville* (Jacksonville: University of North Florida Press, 1983).

100. George E. Thomas, "Architectural Patronage and Social Stratification in Philadelphia between 1840 and 1920," in Cutler and Gillette, *Divided Metropolis,* pp. 85–123, offers a unique analysis of how prominent old families and the nouveaux riches settled in different precincts of the city, chose different architects, and how these class allegiances affected physical character in each instance.

101. David P. Handlin, "New England Architects in New York, 1820–40," *American Quarterly* 19 (Winter 1967): 681–95, seeks to address some of these topics. Despite the fact that the views expressed on architecture are often dated, the approach merits attention. Several compendia of architects who have practiced in a city exist and can be very useful reference sources. See, for example, Beatrice St. Julien Ravenel, *Architects of Charleston,* rev. ed. (Charleston: Carolina Art Association, 1964); *Albany Architects: The Present Looks at the Past* (Albany: Historic Albany Foundation, 1978); and Penny Morrill, *Who Built Alexandria? Architects in Alexandria, 1750–1900* (Alexandria: Northern Virginia Regional Park Authority, 1979). By far the most ambitious work of this nature is Sandra L. Tatman and Roger W. Moss, *Biographical Dictionary of Philadelphia Architects: 1700–1930* (Boston: G. K. Hall, 1985).

102. See, for example, Peter Hales, *Silver Cities: The Photography of American Urbanization, 1839–1915* (Philadelphia: Temple University Press, 1984), concerning how photographs have manifested changing attitudes toward the city; Egon Verheyen, " 'The

Splendor of Its Empire'; Reconsidering Jefferson's Role in the Planning of Washington,'' in Erich Hubala and Gunter Schweikhart, eds., *Festschrift Herbert Siebenhuner* (Wurzburg, Germany: Ferdinand Schoningh, 1978), pp. 183–206, concerning ties between views of the presidency and architecture; and Samuel E. Bleecker, *The Politics of Architecture: A Perspective on Nelson A. Rockefeller* (New York: Rutledge Press, 1981), concerning a politician-philanthropist's role in shaping several major urban schemes.

9 ———— Patterns in the Development of the Urban Infrastructure

JOEL A. TARR AND JOSEF W. KONVITZ

Technology is critical to cities, but it is only within the last decade or so that historians have begun to pay serious attention to its important role.[1] Urban infrastructure provides what may be called the vital technological sinews of the modern city: its road, bridge and transit networks; its water and sewer lines and waste disposal facilities; and its power and communications systems. These sinews permit urban functioning and facilitate urban economic development.[2] The city-building process, however, is highly selective, attentive to certain features and treating others as of marginal importance. Implicit in city building are judgments about what can be done and what should or should not be done. These judgments are largely a matter of routine, of accepting conventional wisdom and of applying proven techniques. Occasionally, however, the costs of maintaining the status quo are outweighed by the benefits of change and produce a transition in the city-building process from one set of conventions to another. It is around such transitions that we have organized this chapter.

We have attempted to provide a general scaffolding for comprehending the origins and development of the urban capital infrastructure in the United States during the nineteenth and twentieth centuries. The chapter is divided into three sections: 1790–1880, 1880–1920, and 1920–1986. This periodization corresponds generally to the periods of the walking or pedestrian city; the networked or wired, piped, and tracked city; and the development of the automobile-oriented, decentralized metropolis. The first period can be viewed as a period of foundations, the second as that of the construction of the core infrastructure, and the third as that of the extension of infrastructure throughout an extended urbanized area with a concomitant decline of the central city.

History, of course, does not fall into neat compartments, and any division risks oversimplification, for there were important lags and overlaps in different sectors. Infrastructure itself has often been extremely slow to change, lagging behind other urban technological and demographic developments. Infrastructure consists essentially of structures and networks, which provide shelter and channels for people, substances, and machines. As David P. Billington has observed, structures change very slowly compared to the so-called breakthroughs of technology.[3] The same point can be made in regard to networks, especially those located underground. Infrastructure, therefore, can act as a force for development in one time period, but the same structures can provide a barrier to urban change in a later period.

Although economic factors and technological innovation were obviously of great importance in the development of the infrastructure, we believe that a rigid technological determinism or a sole focus on an economic demand model distorts the pattern of its evolution. History suggests that the preferences and perceptions of different actors such as business leaders, politicians, and public health and engineering professionals in a particular city at a particular time may be more important in the timing of the city-building process than a generalized set of forces that relates to all cities.[4] How and why innovations spread throughout the urban network, however, is also an extremely important subject for investigation.

The Era of the Pedestrian City, 1790–1880

During the period 1790–1880, the urban population grew from approximately 202,000 to over 14 million. In 1790 there was no city with a population over 50,000; in 1880, thirty-five exceeded that figure, with three between 500,000 and a million and one over a million. Until the last decades of this period, most cities could be called pedestrian or walking cities. Except for the largest urban areas, most cities had relatively compact spatial areas, dense population and land use densities, mixed patterns of land use, and no large separation, if at all, between workplace and residence.

Until the 1850s, the means of public transportation were minimal. Horse-drawn buses called omnibuses appeared in a few cities, such as New York, Philadelphia, and Baltimore, in the 1820s and 1830s; commuter railroads first carried passengers in Boston in the 1830s; and the street railway, with horses as the means of motive power, received its initial systematic development in New York in 1852. These innovations spread to the larger cities in this period, with the streetcar becoming a relatively ubiquitous part of the urban infrastructure by 1880. In addition, elevated railways and cable-driven systems appeared in the largest cities in the 1870s. Growing numbers of urbanites utilized these various transport forms, although the large majority of working-class urbanites probably continued to walk to work up through the last decade of the century.[5]

Government on many levels—federal, state, county, and city—constructed or financed transportation infrastructure in this period, stimulating urbanization and economic development. State aid to public works projects was especially important in the construction of canals and railroads to link together eastern coastal ports with western cities in the 1820s and 1830s. The depressions of 1837 and 1857, however, caused a reaction against such spending, and many state legislatures enacted constitutional limitations on borrowing. For several decades following, municipalities and counties, convinced that they were doomed economically without access to a railroad line or a canal, filled the infrastructure investment gap.[6]

During these decades, in a shift from the earlier pattern, city governments began to assume many of the service functions currently accepted as their responsibility. While eighteenth-century municipalities provided some infrastructure, such as street paving and lighting, town wells, and docks, their chief concern was with the regulation and protection of commercial activities. In addition, many services that later became a municipal responsibility were handled by volunteer groups or remained an individual responsibility.[7] These patterns changed gradually in the nineteenth century. Structural changes in city government permitted the development of the service orientation, as states granted municipalities new charters and authorized the revision of old ones.[8] By the 1840s and 1850s, in the larger municipalities, functions such as firefighting had been assumed by professional fire departments; organized police forces had taken the place of the night watch and constables; and urban governments had enlarged their activities in matters involving public health and sanitation.[9] In a number of cases, these functions were made the responsibility of newly created executive departments rather than committees of the city council. Diffusion of the more modern governmental forms through the urban network, however, took place at a relatively slow pace, with the older and larger cities initially adopting the innovations.[10]

The forces underlying the changes in city government, especially increased infrastructure construction, were relatively complex. It is clear that much infrastructure construction and municipal delivery of urban services was related to commerce and development.[11] In this regard, government was serving the same role as it did in providing support for internal improvements; that is, it acted to aid the private economy, especially business interests and real estate developers. A second set of forces driving change stemmed from considerations that related not only to development but also to concerns about the public order and the public health (preventing the spread of epidemic disease). The actors who reflected this set of views included a number of commercial elites, professionals, and sanitarians.[12] Third, the 1840s and 1850s saw the rise of a new type of urban political professional who based his career on appeals to the recently enlarged electorate. In this context, the delivery of public works improvements and of services was often a response to voting constituencies or the needs of specific interest groups.[13] The role of such political organizations in constructing infrastructure was particularly apparent in the post–Civil War decades in cities such as New York and Washington, D.C.[14]

The interaction of the various forces driving infrastructure construction is clearly illustrated with regard to three areas of importance in the walking city: streets, water supply, and sewers. All three involved networks and flows of different sorts on the surface and underneath the ground. Streets related to the circulation and flow of traffic, freight, and pedestrians throughout the urban environment, while water and sewer pipes, themselves utilizing the streets above and below the surface, involved the metabolism of the city. Water was critical for household uses such as drinking, cooking and cleaning, for cleansing the streets, for fighting fires, and for industrial use. Sewers made possible the removal of human and household wastewater from the vicinity of the home and from businesses, as well as the removal of stormwater from the streets, permitting traffic to circulate. Because they utilized the largely publicly owned streets, all three required the approval of the municipal legislative body or city council before construction. Funding might be provided by the municipality itself or by abutters who made the decision to receive the service.

City councils often spent a majority of their time considering street-related matters, such as financing, openings, maintenance, and cleaning. They normally responded quickly to requests for street openings or improvements that served commerce and related to the flow of traffic in the principal business section. Downtown streets were usually paved first, while most secondary streets remained unpaved. While rough pavements such as cobblestones were commonly used in initial paving, a preference for smoother road surfaces resulted in a shift to macadam, trap blocks, or other smooth pavements.[15] In residential neighborhoods, abutters decided when and how streets would be paved by petitioning the municipal government. Not surprisingly, paving was more common in wealthy neighborhoods and less common in the poorer areas. The limited amount of paving in residential areas reflected not only citizen reluctance to assume the financial costs but also the desire to protect the social functions of streets, common in the walking city, from disruptive traffic.[16] Once constructed, streets required maintenance and cleaning if they were to serve as proper circulatory mechanisms. These functions were largely a municipal responsibility, but shifts in funding availability and in administrative procedures resulted in a seesaw between the demand for service and the demand for economy and between the private contract system and the municipal scavenging corps. In all communities, however, the normal pattern was clear—priorities in regard to provision and care of the streets were largely determined by commercial needs, by wealth, and by status.[17]

While the quality and extent of the street network was expanding and altering in the changing pedestrian city, important developments were also occurring both on top and underneath its surface in regard to the creation of other networks. Here the initial development was in regard to water supply. Until the last quarter of the nineteenth century, most American urbanites depended on local sources such as wells, ponds, and cisterns for water. Vendors also carried casks of water from private streams and peddled water on the streets. Local supplies, however, proved inadequate to provide for the needs of growing cities. Wells and ponds became visibly polluted, and groundwater levels receded. The desire of urbanites for more copious and cleaner water supplies for household and industrial uses, concern over threats to the public health from polluted local sources and filthy streets, and the insufficiency of water to control fires led to a search for nonlocal sources of supply.[18] Water supply therefore represents a situation in which a number of interests—business and industries, home owners, fire insurance companies, and those concerned with the public health—joined to demand the construction of large public works in order to secure more adequate supplies at a reasonable cost. City boosters considered waterworks as crucial in the competition of municipalities for population, trade, and industry and emphasized their possession in touting their cities.[19]

The first large city to construct a municipal water supply system was Philadelphia (1799–1801), motivated by a severe yellow fever epidemic. Cincinnati installed a water system in the 1820s, New York opened the Croton Aqueduct in 1841, and Boston the Cochituate Aqueduct in 1848. By 1860, the nation's sixteen largest cities had waterworks, with a total of 136 systems: fifty-seven public, seventy-nine private. By 1880 there were 598 systems: 293 public and 305 private.[20] The larger cities were more likely to have publicly owned waterworks and the smaller cities to have privately owned, many with relatively few users. The large capital requirements of the systems and frequent inadequacies of the private companies often resulted in a preference for public ownership. A number of cities that began with private water supply companies, such as New York and Chicago, shifted to public ownership because the private companies refused to provide adequate water for civic purposes such as street flushing and fire hydrants, to eliminate pollution, to enlarge their works in anticipation of population growth, or to service distant districts.[21]

The provision of water supply, therefore, especially in large cities, presents a triumph of technology and administration in the construction of large public works to provide a needed service. A capital-intensive and centralized technological system replaced a decentralized and labor-intensive method of delivery. Progress, however, was far from uniform, and municipalities encountered many problems in the process of development and construction. Cities often functioned with inadequate supplies at a high cost in fire damage and disease long after the technological capability for improved water systems existed, and water systems diffused through the urban network at a relatively slow rate.[22]

A supply of potable water was only part of the city's metabolic system. Human wastes and used water, as well as solid wastes, also had to be disposed of. Ideally they should have been removed from the settled areas, but, in most locales in this period, human wastes and wastewater were disposed of in cesspools and privy vaults located close by residences or even in cellars. By the 1820s and 1830s, most large cities tried to institute periodic vault emptying by private scavengers under city contract or by city employees, but again the experience was similar to that of street cleaning—dissatisfaction with performance under whatever system was in effect and a seesaw between service by municipal employees and the private contract system.[23] Although both private and public underground sewers existed in the larger cities such as New York, Baltimore, and Boston, they were intended for street stormwater drainage rather than for human waste removal. The majority of nineteenth-century cities had no underground drains, and street gutters of wood or stone provided for stormwater and occasionally for human wastes. (Private householders often constructed drains to the street gutter to remove rainwater from cellars.) Municipal governments focused on the removal of stormwater from streets because of the need to keep roadways clean for commerce, the problems of flooded basements, and the belief that standing water gave rise to "miasmas" that endangered the public health.

Urban crowding, especially in the original central cores, resulted in overloaded cesspools and privy vaults that filled alleys and yards with stagnant water and fecal wastes and badly polluted nearby wells.[24] The construction of urban water systems increased the problem; households installed water-using appliances and ran the used water into existing cesspools. Water closets caused the most serious difficulties, and overflowing cesspools filled yards and alleys with fecally polluted wastewater. Householders were offended by the nuisance, and physicians and sanitarians who believed that disease was caused by miasmas generated by filth and decaying organic matter ("anti-contagionists") were concerned about possible epidemics.[25]

Different solutions for these problems, such as the odorless excavator, a vacuum pump for cesspool emptying used in many cities, were attempted, but with limited success. By the 1870s and 1880s, most sanitarians, engineers, and business leaders agreed that the water carriage system of waste removal (sewerage) was the most cost-efficient and effective technology available because it simultaneously provided for collection and transportation. The first planned municipal sewer systems were constructed in Brooklyn and Chicago in the late 1850s, and other cities such as Washington, D.C., and New York followed in the postwar decades, but it was not until the 1880s and 1890s that extensive sewer construction began. Important here was the resolution of certain technical problems, such as the decision between separate and combined sewers, as well as growing public health concerns.[26]

The construction of the planned sewerage systems signified a movement away from the "piecemeal, decentralized approach to city-building characteristic of the 19th century."[27] The unplanned approach was illustrated by the New York sewer system before 1860. The system included elliptical as well as circular sewers, some of stone and others of brick. A number of streets had private sewers that made their own path to the river. A lack of maps or records prevented maintenance, even if municipal authorities had been so inclined.[28] While these haphazard conditions gradually changed, large-scale planning on the scale applied to the major French and German cities in the nineteenth century by Baron Haussmann and German engineers was not practiced in the United States. But if continental cities can be taken as examples of what might have happened to American cities had their infrastructure systems been planned in a similar way at that time, it seems that the advantages of the planned over the unplanned were not great. Planned continental infrastructure systems were usually limited to the central cities, and suburban zones on the periphery developed in an unplanned way. Since planning, as practiced in France and Germany, left little room for the impacts of invention and innovation, planned infrastructure often forced a rigidity on the urban environment. American cities were clearly more haphazard but also more open to dramatic infrastructure innovation.[29]

Financing Infrastructure in the Pedestrian City

Large-scale municipal involvement in the construction of urban infrastructure, such as streets or capital-intensive water supply and sewerage systems, required a resort to new forms of financial instruments.[30] Projects such as street improvements were often financed by assessments on abutters because of a municipal reluctance to become involved in debt. When abutters did not or would not pay, recourse to general tax revenues was necessary. Many capital-intensive infrastructure projects, such as street lighting, schools, water and sewer systems, and various public buildings, were financed with municipal bonds; city tax revenues were usually insufficient to cover capital costs. Large-scale debt financing was new to American cities. When the building of the Croton Aqueduct increased New York City's debt from $500,000 to over $9 million, many citizens anticipated financial disaster.[31] Municipal infrastructure creation plus involvement in various railroad funding schemes increased municipal debt from $25 million in 1840 to $821 million in 1880, or from $1.17 per capita to $16.37 per capita.[32]

Economic cycles had an important effect on infrastructure construction. Some of these cycles produced institutional changes and modifications that affected infrastructure construction for many years after the economic downturn had passed. In the period 1866–1873, for instance, postwar economic prosperity and delayed demand resulted in a large expansion of public works building in a number of cities. Per capita municipal debt more than doubled from 1860 to 1870 ($6.36 to $13.38) at a time when state debt increased only about 12 percent ($8.17 to $9.15). A sharp economic downturn in the early 1870s, however, resulted in many municipal failures; at the peak of the depression in 1873, nearly one-fifth of municipal debt was in default.[33]

The states responded to municipal financial distress by establishing limitations on municipal debt. By 1880, more than half the states had constitutional limitations on city debt, usually a set proportion of the tax base.[34] The widespread urban financial problems in the early 1870s led to what Kenneth Fox calls the "first national urban crisis."[35] The constitutional doctrines of Judge John F. Dillon heavily influenced the scope of financial limitations and the direction of structural reform by affirming that the municipal corporation was a mere creature of state government without independent or implied powers. The Dillon rule, as applied, combined with the debt limitations, resulted in suspension of municipal public works improvements and sharply curtailed municipal services and the construction of infrastructure in a number of cities.[36]

Engineers and Urban Technology

It is customary today to assume that the construction and maintenance of urban infrastructure involves the talents of trained engineers; this was not necessarily true with regard to much of the period from 1790 through 1880. Before the latter part of the century, a relatively small number of engineers had received formal engineering training. Instead, most belonged to the craft tradition and had learned from direct, practical experience, especially on the large public works and railroad projects of the antebellum period. Of those with formal training, some were trained in Europe, and others had gone to the few institutions offering engineering training, such as West Point, Rensselaer Polytechnic Institute, and Stevens Institute. In the years after the Civil War, however, engineering education greatly expanded, providing a body of talent for the explosion of infrastructure construction that occurred after 1890.[37]

Economic historian Nathan Rosenberg has written that technological change in nineteenth-century America depended on the borrowing of the major components—machinery, power, and new materials—from a stock of innovations that had already been developed and employed in Great Britain.[38] Such a situation also existed in regard to urban technologies. British and European cities had accumulated considerable experience over their long histories in dealing with urban problems, and it is not surprising that the relatively new American cities would look to them for information regarding public sector technologies. Technology transfer was vital for the construction of the nineteenth-century urban infrastructure although with modifications for American conditions.[39]

According to historian of technology Brooke Hindle, the basic agents of technology transfer in the antebellum period were individuals—Europeans who learned the technology abroad and carried the knowledge to the United States and Americans who went to Europe to learn about technology.[40] Benjamin Henry Latrobe is often pointed to as the prime example of a trained European who brought his skills and knowledge about advanced English technology to the United States.[41] While European-trained engineers continued to make substantial contributions in America throughout the century, the supply of engineers was increasingly homegrown. Many American civil engineers who secured their training on great state public works projects such as the Erie Canal, the Pennsylvania Main Line Canal, and the railroads were also involved in construction of major structures in the urban infrastructure.[42]

Increasingly, as Rosenberg notes, American engineers acted as initiators in technological innovation rather than as borrowers, although in many areas European examples were critical.[43] Important innovations were made in streetcar systems and other urban transit technologies, building, and construction methods, and materials (such as the balloon frame and cast-iron framing); wooden and iron truss bridges; and wire cables for bridges and inclines. The telegraph was an important American invention that was adapted to urban service delivery systems; municipalities widely adopted it beginning in the 1850s for fire and police alarm systems. These developments combined with other European and British imports, such as street paving, gas lighting, sewers, and omnibuses, to make the technology of the American urban infrastructure a blend of European ideas and adaptations and homegrown inventions and innovations.[44]

Constructing the Core Infrastructure in American Cities, 1880–1920

The 1880–1920 period was one of great city growth in the United States, as millions of immigrants and migrants from rural areas chose urban destinations. Urban population increased from approximately 14 million to over 54 million, and, for the first time, over half of the nation's population had an urban residence. Large cities became relatively commonplace, as the number of cities with more than a 250,000 population grew from eight to twenty-five with twelve of these having over 500,000 population, and three passing the million mark.

The shift of population from country to city, natural increase, and the absorption of immigrants brought about important changes in urban size, changes that produced incentives to introduce new approaches to control the urban environment. Although these changes involved the extensive application of some traditional techniques, such as paving, sewerage systems, and water mains, they were more largely different from than similar to older infrastructure systems. The new systems introduced in the 1880s and after involved the delivery of new services such as telephones and electricity through primary infrastructure networks and the application of such services to other infrastructure systems to provide power and to coordinate and control them.[45] Materials such as glass and steel were available in unprecedented quantities, permitting a revision of traditional notions of building structure and urban form.[46] This period began with a transitional phase characterized by growing critical awareness, and hence intolerance, of existing city-building approaches and by a great deal of experimentation and innovation. By the 1910s, a new set of norms and procedures was being codified.

Perhaps the most important contrast between infrastructures in this period and the preceding one has to do with the latent adaptability of the environment. Most of the urban environment in the nineteenth-century city was composed of wooden structures of modest proportions and of stone buildings that rarely exceeded a half-dozen stories. It was therefore relatively easy, and indeed usually profitable, to modify that environment to accommodate new infrastructure systems. In some cases, such as Chicago and Boston, fire destroyed a large part of the existing built environment, furnishing opportunities for new systems.[47] These new systems provided benefits but also added layers of bureaucratic regulation and limitations on land use that inhibited the further modification of the built environment; they also imposed technological restraints because buildings had to connect to infrastructure systems whose operating capacities were already determined and difficult to adjust.

In providing residential and commercial structures, builders and developers took pains to differentiate their products according to the quality and kind of internal services provided, services such as heat, light, power, and ventilation, which in turn were the product of large-scale infrastructure systems.[48] Public and private land uses were intermingled extensively in the nineteenth-century city; by contrast, the twentieth-century city has far more specialization in land uses and in building types. Finally, it should be emphasized that many infrastructure systems introduced in this period had long life cycles. Their designers, however, failed to foresee that social, economic, and technological change would call existing urban spatial patterns into question. As a result, modern cities have many prematurely obsolete buildings and districts that conform to outdated patterns. Modern cities are considerably more difficult to modernize, adapt, and renew than nineteenth-century cities.[49]

Municipal Provision of Infrastructure

The infrastructure built in the growing cities and suburbs was almost entirely provided at the municipal level and included medium- and smaller-sized cities, as well as larger urban areas. With regard to largely publicly supplied technologies, the number of waterworks increased from 1,878 to 9,850 (1890–1920), the population served by filtered water from 310,000 to 17,291,000 (1890–1914), and the miles of sewers from 6,005 to 24,972 (1890–1909).[50] Federal spending for urban public works was relatively minor, and state government expenditures did not rise significantly until highway expenditures accelerated after 1910 in response to automobile development. More important than direct state spending was the increase in state regulatory functions in infrastructure-related areas, such as public utilities, transportation, and public health.[51]

Urban transit networks, consisting primarily of electrically powered streetcars but also including subways, elevated railways, and commuter railroads, provided the essential framework for the expansion of urban areas and, hence, of infrastructure. From 1890 to 1907, for instance, streetcar mileage (almost all privately supplied) increased from 5,783 to 34,404 miles, most of it electric powered, and annual rides per urban inhabitant jumped from 111 to 250 as the use of public transit far outdistanced population increase. Vast areas surrounding the central cities were opened for residential development. Streetcar suburbs proliferated along the transit routes, and commuter rails transformed small towns into commuter suburbs. In addition to extending the fringe of the urbanized area, public transit, which focused on the downtown, accelerated the transformation of the urban core from an area used for mixed residential, commercial, and industrial purposes into a true central business district (CBD) devoted primarily to commercial and business uses. Work and residence became more sharply separated, and the larger cities developed the modern traffic pattern of a morning and evening flow of commuters to and from the CBD.[52]

In many cities, first priority was given to the provision of improved services to the CBD. This reflected the concern of the downtown business interests with enhancing property values and remaining competitive with other towns, as well as the technological requirements of the new office structures. The steel-frame skyscrapers that altered the skylines of American cities in the late nineteenth and early twentieth centuries could not function without basic infrastructure— water supply and waste removal, energy (electricity) and heat, as well as transportation networks to funnel commuters in and out of the downtown.[53] In addition to the new office buildings, the so-called city beautiful movement resulted in large-scale public improvements that included the widening of streets, the planting of trees and shrubs, the planning of parks, and the building of new public buildings and monuments that enhanced the aesthetic as well as the functional aspects of city centers.[54] The development of the new infrastructure-based CBD, characterized by high-rise office structures and important retail and commercial sectors, was the most obvious manifestation of the rise of the modern networked city at the beginning of the twentieth century.[55]

Infrastructure was also important to residential development, and here patterns varied by function and by income class. In cities in which municipal resources were especially limited, such as in Birmingham, Alabama, priorities dictated the provision of first-class services for the downtown, while residential areas of the city remained deprived.[56] In new middle- and upper-class areas of other cities, builders usually provided services before dwellings were constructed. In Milwaukee, for instance, the developers assumed the cost of installing services in the expectation of recouping the cost in the purchase price.[57] In contrast, in Boston's suburban towns, the city (or new metropolitan authorities) provided water and sewer lines after speculators had furnished rough graded streets. Once the utilities were laid, the city would pave and maintain the streets. Such services were provided below cost as a subsidy to the development process and paid for out of general taxes.[58]

The pattern differed somewhat in areas in which builders did not provide the services. In the more affluent neighborhoods, home owners petitioned the municipality for services immediately after homes were purchased. In the poorer areas, new home owners delayed the acquisition of sewers, piped-in water, and paved streets in order to keep housing expenses low; in these situations, savings in housing costs were often replaced by health expenses as householders exposed themselves and their families to infectious disease stemming from inadequate water and sewage services.[59] Another variation came in the cities with strong ward-based political machines, in which politics could affect the distribution and provision of services. In some cities, such as Baltimore, Chicago and Cincinnati, neighborhood associations at the turn of the century were successful in ensuring equality of service delivery.[60]

In many late nineteenth- and early twentieth-century suburbs, the provision of urban infrastructure as well as urban services was beyond the financial capabilities of the towns. Faced by these deprivations, inhabitants of outlying communities voted to merge with the central city in order to acquire superior services at a lower cost. City boosters concerned with municipal growth encouraged these mergers, and in many cases the cities offered services to the newly annexed areas at low cost in order to ensure a positive suburban voter response.[61]

The rapid infrastructure development in this period rested on a number of society-wide changes. An organizational revolution involving the development of large-scale systems such as corporations, the growth of investment banking, and the development of a national bond market were necessary preconditions.[62] National industry associations shared technical data and coordinated industry policy, accelerating the diffusion of innovations among cities. And various professional organizations, such as the American Public Health Association (1872), the American Water Works Association (1881), and the American Society of Civil Engineers (1852, 1868), used conferences and journals to distribute information and to agitate for boards of health, water supply protection, street construction, and street paving.[63]

On the local level, there were also significant organizational and institutional changes. Voluntary associations, such as chambers of commerce, commercial clubs, and other urban booster-type organizations, pressed for downtown improvements and water and sewer systems in order to outdo rival communities.[64] On the political side, especially in the larger cities, political organizations or machines that assumed control regarded large public works projects as beneficial because they provided patronage, voter loyalty, and contracts. Some of the most important infrastructure projects of this period were constructed while machines were in power.[65]

The implantation of infrastructures brought social and political reformers into coalitions with architects and engineers. While each group viewed the city from a different perspective, they agreed on many aspects of the city-building process. Modern infrastructures, with their regulatory frameworks, improved building and sanitary codes, paved streets, and power systems, played critical roles in these shared urban images. This period was infused with a sense of optimism about city building that emboldened actors in the private and public sectors alike to undertake massive capital-intensive projects. New infrastructures affected lighting, power, heat, and transportation in particular, with results that were felt in the workplace, in the home, and in semi-public, semi-private facilities, such as department stores, arts and entertainment facilities, and railroad stations. The adaptability of work routines in offices, factories, stores, and kitchens to the opportunities offered by improved infrastructure systems contributed to their spread. In many cities in the late nineteenth and early twentieth centuries, politics centered around questions of infrastructure investment. This pattern largely resulted from the fact that cities were in a stage of transition from the older compact, commercial walking city to the new industrial metropolis, with its strong core orientation, spread characteristics, and ring of residential suburbs. Within this context of change, important decisions regarding the quantity, type, and location of infrastructure had to be made. Urban politics therefore was often a struggle over the answers to these questions and the identity of the decision makers.[66]

A number of local institutional changes directly affected infrastructure provision. These changes often emphasized values of efficiency, economy, expertise, and bureaucratic administration.[67] Many cities, for instance, adopted new charters providing for centralization, strong mayors, and at-large rather than ward-elected councils. In the smaller cities, commission and city manager forms of government were popular.[68] The special district government was another institutional development with strong implications for the provision of infrastructure.[69] Reformers argued that these new structures would improve the efficiency of infrastructure and service provision and eliminate political interference. Because city engineers appeared to represent best the values of efficiency, professionalism, and economy that reformers desired, municipalities drew on them extensively as city managers.[70]

By the 1920s, as urban territorial growth slackened, central city populations declined and suburban growth accelerated. Suburbs no longer sought annexation or consolidation with central cities because of a desire for superior municipal services, as strengthened municipal bond markets, improved technology, and relaxed state restrictions on borrowing enabled them to develop their own infrastructure. Special district governments also developed as a means of suburban infrastructure provision and service delivery. Legislation permitting intergovernmental contractual relationships for such projects as joint sewage and water systems provided for more efficient services and furnished a further disincentive for annexation.[71]

Financing Infrastructure

While the 1870s and 1880s were marked by limitations on public spending for public works, such investments accelerated again in the 1890s and especially after the depression of 1893. Driving investment were city boosters, urban reformers, and various professionals who held visions of a new, modern, and sanitary metropolis. The refinement of capital markets and the development of nationwide investment banking provided outlets for municipal bonds, while state legislatures facilitated expansion by granting cities the power to spend on explicit projects, a permissible interpretation of the Dillon rule. In the 1890s, according to Edward C. Kirkland, the growth of American cities became the "new generative factor" in the American economy.[72] This pattern of heavy municipal expenditure on capital improvements continued through 1914, and by this date spending for infrastructure constituted a much larger share of municipal budgets than it had a half-century earlier.[73]

A critical issue involving infrastructure that occupied municipal political agendas in the late nineteenth and early twentieth centuries was the question of the private or public ownership of utilities.[74] During the late nineteenth century, electric light and power, gas, and transit became integrated into the urban fabric and became nearly as important to urban functioning as water supplies. Just as piped-in water supplies had earlier shifted from a luxury to a necessity, so now other utility services made the same transformation. Since the majority of waterworks were publicly owned, this suggested to some that the same course should be followed for the other utilities. Many of the most heated political battles of the late nineteenth and early twentieth centuries occurred over the question of the political influence of public utilities, the terms of franchises, and the wisdom of municipal ownership as a means to improve service delivery and provide income for the city.[75]

The municipal ownership movement had only limited success. The trend toward public ownership of waterworks continued and rose to 70 percent by World War I, while sewers remained virtually wholly publicly owned. Fierce battles over the municipal takeover of transit companies occurred in many cities, but most companies remained private.[76] For other utilities, such as electricity and power, municipal ownership was usually confined to small cities (about 1,500 systems by 1912, generating only about 4 percent of electrical power), although again there were exceptions (Cleveland, Kansas City, Los Angeles, and Seattle had municipal light and power plants). Municipally owned telephone companies were also found only in small cities and towns.[77] There were no clear statistics on the advantages of municipal over private ownership, and disputes usually centered around ideological questions. In order to resolve the controversy, pragmatic reformers shifted toward regulation by state commissioners as a means to ensure service delivery at reasonable rates. Many utilities themselves supported this course.[78]

Engineering and Science Developments

During the late nineteenth and early twentieth centuries, factors such as information availability, a supply of technically competent professionals, and the existence of organizations to facilitate technological innovation generated the diffusion of technologies throughout the urban network. Critical to this diffusion was the supply and quality of engineering. A number of urban public works earlier in the century had failed or operated poorly due to a lack of engineering expertise. In the late nineteenth and early twentieth centuries, however, American engineering education expanded, and universities and technical institutes produced a large supply of trained civil engineers. Municipalities employed a growing number of civil engineers as city engineers and as consultants. In addition, private consulting firms became increasingly important on projects that required specialized skills not available in-house.[79]

On the technological supply side, important advances were made in new and old infrastructure areas. The field of water supply is a good example. Early distribution systems had suffered from pipe deterioration, but by 1860 the development of improved methods of manufacturing cast-iron pipe and of coating their interiors had solved the problem. In addition, after the Civil War, improvements in steam engine design and in pump standardization provided for steady pressure maintenance. Facilitating the distribution of these improved methods throughout the urban network were the marketing practices of the two largest pump manufactures (Holly and Worthington), which offered municipalities an entire water package, including source recommendations, engineering and construction plans, and pumps. These two corporations secured franchises for their systems in thousands of towns and cities.[80]

Similar improvements in materials, technological design, and industrial organization occurred in other areas related to urban public works, such as street paving and construction material, sewer design and pipe materials, and energy and communications systems. As the urban network expanded in the late nineteenth and early twentieth centuries, demand and supply interacted to diffuse urban technologies through the system.[81] The U.S. Bureau of the Census attempted to stimulate this diffusion by presenting, beginning in 1902, comparative statistics on the characteristics of infrastructure systems, such as sewers and the annual operating expenditures for five major municipal functions of cities with more than 30,000 population. This information could be used by cities contemplating service adoption or by those that intended to measure their outlays on a comparative basis. The Census Bureau administrators believed that these comparative statistics would force cities to improve the quality of municipal service delivery and to eliminate graft and confusion in municipal bookkeeping.[82]

As technologies spread throughout the urban network, they often created unforeseen problems, such as pollution or traffic and neighborhood disruption, as well as benefits. Some of these problems were corrected by technological adaptations such as water filtration or sewage treatment, but others were less susceptible to remedy.[83] The larger and more administratively efficient cities attempted to make use of scientific investigation and technical expertise to improve the public health and the quality of the infrastructure by establishing bacterial and testing laboratories.[84] Most cities, however, had neither laboratories nor testing facilities and depended on city engineers or consulting engineers or state agencies for technical and scientific information.

The Automobile Revolution and the Expansion of Federal Intervention, 1920–1986

Two factors, one technological and the other governmental, primarily affected urban infrastructure developments from 1920 through the 1970s. The critical technological innovation was the automobile (along with the motor truck and bus), first made widely available by Henry Ford's assembly-line production techniques. This innovation generated a host of social, spatial, and administrative developments that sharply altered infrastructure priorities and patterns. The crucial expansion of the federal government first took place in the 1930s in the New Deal, continuing in the postwar period at a reduced level of investment, with a rise again in the 1960s and 1970s. Although numerous other technological and administrative innovations affected urban infrastructure during these years, the explosion of automobile usage and the altered role of the federal government are the most critical factors.

The introduction of the automobile between 1910 and 1930 highlights some of the points made so far concerning the inflexibility of infrastructure once constructed. To the extent to which infrastructure systems designed for automobile traffic were more easily built in rapidly growing cities and on the periphery of major urban areas, their construction reveals the declining adaptability of urban space characteristic of city building since the late nineteenth century. The impact of the automobile probably strengthened certain residential suburbs, specialized land uses, and building types and diminished community control over the use of streets.[85] In hindsight the growth of vehicular traffic seems obvious, but it was not obvious at that time. In the 1910s and 1920s, railroad traffic was growing and reached what we now know was its maximum level of service. Planners and administrators were often more concerned about locating rail yards, which consumed huge amounts of land, consolidating terminal service into new, highly automated facilities, and building bridges and grade crossings to separate vehicular and rail traffic than they were with responses to the automobile.[86]

Between 1910 and 1930, the nation's auto registrations rose from 458,000 to nearly 22 million, or from one car to every 201 persons to one car to every 5.3 persons. The development of the motor vehicle occurred at a time of rapid urbanization, and automobiles, trucks, and buses became largely concentrated in cities in the 1920s, although rural areas were also substantially affected. The automobile had a dramatic impact on the urban fabric and infrastructure. It greatly accelerated the process of deconcentration initiated by the streetcar, caused a vast increase in the flow of commuter traffic between the downtown and suburban residential areas, and sharply increased congestion in the downtown cores. This radical innovation promoted massive alterations in the urban infrastructure, primarily the construction and improvement of roads and highways, the development of traffic systems, the building of bridges and tunnels, and the widening and reconstruction of downtown streets.[87]

Planners and members of the new engineering subdiscipline of traffic engineering, developed primarily in response to the automobile, viewed downtown congestion as an engineering problem, requiring both planning and public works construction.[88] Automobile-induced changes in the CBD included the widening and double-decking of streets, the elimination of grade crossings, and the development of a variety of traffic controls. In addition, street surfacing with smooth pavements (mostly asphalt) took place throughout urban areas. Cities and counties built hundreds of bridges and tunnels to facilitate cross-river transportation, while Chicago, New York, Pittsburgh, and Los Angeles constructed limited access roadways into the downtown area.[89]

The outlying areas of cities and their suburbs were the other major areas strongly affected by the automobile. Urban growth along streetcar lines radiating from the CBD often left large tracts of land undeveloped near the periphery. The flexibility of the automobile facilitated development of these areas. In addition, the automobile stimulated extensive development of the urban fringe. The 1920s witnessed the emergence of the modern automobile-dependent residential suburb, with numerous new towns and villages appearing outside large cities and older suburbs undergoing increased growth.[90] In the newer, dispersed cities that lacked strong downtown business districts, such as Los Angeles and Denver, the automobile became the primary shaping element, and the dense patterns of development characteristic of the older eastern cities never materialized.[91]

The needs of the automobile, motor truck, and bus for improved roads and highways, expressed by automobile clubs, business organizations, and engineering associations, resulted in extensive construction. Although total highway mileage increased only slightly in the 1920s, from 235,000 to 250,000, and total national mileage from 3.16 to 3.25 million, the mileage of surfaced roads increased 157 percent and high-grade surfaced roads 776 percent between 1914 and 1929.[92] The Bureau of Public Roads, aided by the American Road Builders' Association, the American Society for Municipal Improvements, and the American Society of Civil Engineers, developed standards and specifications that were often used in designing new roadways and the rebuilding and resurfacing of highways and streets.[93]

The most important automobile-related funding in the 1920s occurred on the state level, where the innovative gasoline tax (Oregon, 1919, all states by 1929) provided funding for highway construction.[94] Municipal expenditures for streets and highways also rose, although cities depended largely on conventional means of financing such as bonds, the property tax, or special assessments to provide improvements. In the 1920s, municipal operating and capital expenditures for streets and highways were exceeded only by spending for education.[95] Cities, counties, and other governmental authorities cooperated to improve transportation infrastructure. In New York's Westchester County, for example, the city authorities joined with the Bronx Parkway Commission to build a limited access parkway and sewer system along the Bronx River.[96] In Pittsburgh, the county embarked on a large bridge-building program and coordinated it with city construction of a limited access roadway connecting the suburbs and downtown.[97]

Infrastructure construction in a number of other areas accompanied the road building boom of the decade. School building construction accelerated in order to accommodate a 41 percent increase in school-age population. Funds committed to sewers and waterworks tripled, while public health and water quality considerations caused the population served by treated water and sewage treatment to more than double. While taxation largely paid for highway construction, a large fraction of other infrastructure development was debt financed. From 1922 to 1932, per capita municipal debt increased from $8.64 to $9.17. But while state and local expenditures for infrastructure advanced rapidly, federal investment reached its lowest point since the Civil War, with the federal share of the cost of total government construction amounting to only 11.2 percent.[98]

The New Deal, World War II, and the Postwar Period

The New Deal evolved as a governmental response to the economic hardships caused by the Great Depression. Cities were especially hard hit by the sharp contraction after 1929, and a number either defaulted or were close to bankruptcy. As a result of the policies of President Franklin D. Roosevelt, the federal government assumed for the first time a vital role in the construction of urban infrastructure. The rationalization for such intervention included the need for federal policies to relieve mass unemployment, the use of public works to provide a yardstick by which to measure the performance of private enterprise, and the use of public construction for pump priming.[99] Federal spending amounted to 60 to 65 percent of all public construction from 1933 to 1938 and nearly a third of total construction.[100]

The federal government constructed a huge range of projects, including roads, sewers, sewage and water treatment plants, waterworks, multiple-purpose dams, bridges, parks, docks, airports, hospitals, and other public buildings and "prevented what would have been near eclipse of an entire generation of public construction projects."[101] The largest federal construction projects were in the mountain, Pacific, and southern states, but Public Works Administration (PWA) projects, which included hospitals, sewers, educational buildings, and water supply, were more concentrated in the urbanized areas of the mid-Atlantic and east north central states.[102] PWA funds, for example, accounted for 35 to 50 percent of all new sewer and water supply construction during the 1930s. By 1938, federal financing had aided in the construction of 1,165 of the 1,310 new municipal sewage treatment plants built in the decade. The population served by sewage treatment increased from 21.5 million in 1932 to more than 39 million by 1939, substantially improving the quality of the waterways used for municipal waste disposal.[103]

In World War II, as in World War I but on a larger scale, the strains of war affected American cities. War production called for a massive expansion of industrial work at many established cities, such as Baltimore and Detroit, and at new locations or at cities that lacked major industry, such as Portland and Oakland. An influx of workers generated enormous pressure on housing and transportation facilities. Federal public works investment was almost entirely for factory plant and equipment, and municipal spending for construction and maintenance was sharply reduced.[104] In the face of wartime demand, however, existing infrastructure systems had to be expanded and modified far more rapidly than ever in peacetime. In the process, new ways of designing factories and housing were introduced, and new styles of management and coordination were adopted. Some professionals hoped that New Deal and wartime innovations would survive and flourish in the postwar era. Their hopes were misplaced. There was a widespread tendency to minimize war-related changes in the belief that war would be short and in the hope that there would be a quick return to prewar normalcy.[105] Massive war-related population shifts raised conflicts over the degree to which the national government should be held financially responsible for ameliorating local (and perhaps temporary) conditions. The war proved nonetheless to influence postwar developments by reinforcing conservative tendencies in city building practices and by habituating people to a greater degree of government intervention in their lives. Part of the strong postwar trend toward suburbanization can be explained by these two tendencies: suburbs rather than the inner city better resembled the kind of improved environment that people had idealized during the war, and they also promised residents greater control over government so that they could enhance and preserve their emotional and financial investment in housing.[106]

The postwar decades witnessed increased suburbanization and the beginnings of central city decline. The effects of this trend were masked for a time by a backlog of war-induced infrastructure needs that produced a period of vigorous growth. By 1945, public construction for infrastructure had a total shortfall of 3.3 years of building at 1940 levels. Public investment for infrastructure resumed after the war, expanding from $2.9 billion in 1946 to $8.6 billion in 1950, to $13.6 billion in 1960 (1957–1959 constant dollars). Construction of sewers and waterworks, school buildings, and roads proceeded at a rapid pace, reflecting the impacts of suburbanization, the automobile, and the baby boom.[107]

Central city decline and suburban proliferation created different sorts of infrastructure pressures. Suburbanization produced an increase in the formation of municipalities in many metropolitan areas. In suburban Saint Louis County, for instance, the number of municipalities grew from twenty-one in 1930 to eighty-three in 1950; in Los Angeles County, the number went from forty-five to sixty-eight in the 1950s. In medium-sized cities of the West and the South after 1945, annexation of adjacent suburbs often occurred, but this route was politically impossible for the older urban centers. The loss of population, industry, and commercial activities by these centers caused a severe weakening of their tax bases. Except in a few cities, attempts to deal with these problems by forming metropolitan governments also failed.[108]

Policymakers often tried to cope with fragmentation by expanding old and creating new special-purpose metropolitan districts.[109] The functions of county government also expanded in the postwar period. By 1972, of the 150 major urban counties, more than half provided public libraries and recreational facilities, over a third sewage disposal, and about a fifth solid waste collection and water supply. Such county activities were advanced by state legislation that permitted the county to act in place of the municipality.[110]

Faced by rapid suburbanization and central city decline, downtown business interests and urban politicians joined in private-public partnerships to attempt to revitalize the CBDs. These city booster coalitions hoped to revive the CBDs, stimulate the return of the middle classes, and improve the economic climate of the central city. Their programs largely involved a combination of private sector investment in office structures with public sector investment in supporting infrastructure. Attempts were also made to improve environmental conditions.[111]

The immediate postwar renewal efforts did not involve large numbers of federal dollars. In those years, there was a reaction against the spending of the New Deal, although federal involvement in the cities and in infrastructure never completely stopped.[112] Federal involvement in other areas, such as sewers, sewage treatment, and water quality, came haltingly, especially compared with the heavy investment of the 1930s. The Federal Water Pollution Control Act of 1948 provided funds for research and planning and for low-interest loans, while the 1956 amendment enlarged federal participation by providing grants to stimulate the construction of municipal sewage treatment facilities. The dollars available for subsidy remained limited, however, due to a belief that federal grants actually retarded the pace of municipal investments. Total spending on new construction for sewer and water systems did not reach the 1930 level in constant dollars until 1951.[113]

The pattern of rapid suburbanization caused spending for highway construction to expand dramatically. Federal dollars were available in limited amounts under the Federal Aid Highway Act of 1944, which allocated funds on a matching basis, but highway needs, in the terms of new roads and repair of old, were immense. A number of states (for example, Illinois, Ohio, and Pennsylvania) constructed toll roads (3,338 miles by 1963) to solve the problem of financing intercity transportation. Leaders of renewal coalitions in cities such as Pittsburgh, New Haven, and St. Paul regarded urban expressways as critical to redevelopment and funded them through state or municipal bond issues.[114] Given the scope of urban and national highway needs, however, some sort of federal involvement was necessary. Urban spokesmen observed that federal financial responsibility for new interstate highways would have the additional benefit of freeing up local and state funds for maintenance and for the construction of secondary and urban road networks.

Throughout the 1950s, truckers' automobile clubs, highway contractors, the automobile industry, engineering associations, and business groups lobbied Congress to provide federal funding for new highway construction. The Advisory Committee on a National Highway Program, headed by retired General Lucius D. Clay, stated that both national security and the health of the economy were dependent on rapid construction of the highway network. Congress finally approved the bill in 1956. The final legislation provided for federal assumption of

90 percent of the costs, with gasoline tax revenues placed in a Highway Trust Fund to prevent diversion.[115]

The 41,000-mile network created by the Interstate Highway Act was the largest single item of infrastructure ever projected. Congress gave little consideration, however, to the effects of its construction on urban areas. The Clay committee had sold the interstate system to Congress as a carrier of long-haul traffic, but municipal leaders visualized the highways as a means to solve traffic congestion problems. Because highway construction through congested urban areas was exceedingly expensive, cities eventually received a large percentage of the total allocations. The interstates, however, although they speeded commuter traffic in some urban areas, also accelerated central city decline by making it easier for residents to move to the suburban fringe and still commute to central city workplaces.[116]

The postwar infrastructure development has also had a major impact on debates about aesthetics. The infrastructures of the period 1880–1920 had been used to fashion powerful images such as skylines and massive bridges (such as the Brooklyn Bridge), and artists and writers sought to include infrastructure elements in their works.[117] Some architects embellished mass transit systems and power generating plants with styles derived from traditional artistic models; others sought a new visual language that enhanced certain features of machines or sought to capture a machine style. These efforts focused on the urban core as the spiritual as well as the material center of the city, thus perpetuating values inherited from the Renaissance. In contrast, suburbs supported industrial uses incompatible with urban values or residences whose appearance consciously avoided reference to urban life.[118]

But in the postwar era, suburbs acquired more of the residential and commercial functions of cities and, hence, some of the traditional urban forms. The growth of suburbs in the postwar era, however, coincided with a time when architects and engineers in America did not seek to elaborate a new style of civic design. As a result, many of the suburban visual design elements with a big impact on ordinary people inhibit a strong sense of place from emerging; the best-designed structures are most often corporate or residential facilities spatially and visually isolated from the rest of the suburban zone. On the one hand, the difficulty of building infrastructures for the automobile in older urban zones enhanced the impression of modernity in suburbs; on the other hand, the indifference of planners and administrators to the design dimensions of infrastructure systems in automobile age suburbs created an impression of uniform environments that retarded the development of a sense of place.[119]

The Rise of the Outer City and Recent Trends Influencing Urban Infrastructure, 1956–1986

Several interrelated demographic, fiscal, and social trends have severely affected urban infrastructure in the decades since the passage of the Interstate

Highway Act. Central city population loss and the movement to the suburbs have continued at a rapid rate. In some cases, this migration has produced metropolitan as well as central city decline. Accompanying central city losses has been a massive regional population shift from the older cities of the Northeast and the Midwest toward the cities of the sunbelt.[120] The most important consequence for the urban infrastructure of these population trends has been a decline in tax revenues to support maintenance and renewal.

While the inner city has often experienced dramatic population declines, the outer city is undergoing a continuing boom. Traditional suburbia as well as exurbia have attracted a mass of urban activities that were formerly a central city monopoly. Most prominent in the outer city are the new multiple-purpose centers (or mini-cities) that provide concentrations of retailing, entertainment, and other employment activities. These are located on or close to the beltways and freeways constructed since the 1956 Interstate Highway Act and are surrounded by residential areas.[121] In addition, by the 1960s, airports had begun to generate a host of traditionally downtown-type activities in their normally outer city locales, including hotels, conference centers, office buildings, retail shops, and distribution centers.[122] In many cases, special purpose authorities that levy user taxes and are better able to absorb the costs of maintenance and construction provide infrastructure, often aided by federal and state funds. These outer city areas are infrastructure dependent but are also quite dispersed, raising important questions concerning the applicability of infrastructure originally developed to fit the needs of a more concentrated environment.[123]

At the same time changing fiscal trends have dramatically affected infrastructure in the 1960s, 1970s, and 1980s. In the sixties and seventies, the federal government returned to the pattern of heavy involvement with the infrastructure that it had followed in the middle of the nineteenth century and during the Great Depression. From 1957 to 1977, federal grants to state and local governments for capital projects increased from about 10 percent of public works investment to about 40 percent. Highways, sewers, and spending for mass transit absorbed the largest amount of federal funds.[124] This reliance on federal dollars, claim some urban authorities, produced a sharp change in the nature of federalism and a skewing of local priorities toward projects for which federal funds have been available. Perhaps most critical for the health of infrastructure was a bias in the legislation in favor of new construction rather than maintenance of existing capital stock.[125]

Beginning in 1979, however, federal funding for infrastructure began to decline in response to pressure on the federal budget from inflation, and this decline has accelerated under the Reagan administration. Municipalities and other institutions have been forced to depend more heavily on their own resources for infrastructure construction. Local governments, however, have experienced revenue shortfalls since the early 1970s that have severely restricted their ability to undertake infrastructure funding.[126] In addition, the privatization philosophy of the Reagan administration has resulted in many tasks that were formerly the responsibility of government now being delegated to the private sector.[127]

Conclusion

By the 1970s, the energy crisis highlighted the lack of synchronization between urban infrastructures on the one hand and social and technological development on the other. The explosive rise in energy costs alone made people aware of the built-in limitations in their buildings, urban spatial patterns, and infrastructure systems. An expensive period of modification began, but the erratic pressure of energy costs and the ability of the economy to absorb increases at progressively higher levels depressed incentives to make major, radical changes in residential building design, transportation, and urban land use patterns. Due in part to recessions associated with but not entirely caused by the energy crisis, governments cut back on essential maintenance of infrastructure systems—just at the point, moreover, when many of them were reaching the end of their useful life cycles.[128]

The high costs of repairing and maintaining current infrastructure systems and of building new ones suggest that everything cannot be done. Some systems will be allowed to decay, and others will be extensively modified. Yet the structure of urban government in the United States, which prevents the federal government from having a coherent urban policy and which distributes power over cities through state government, means that there are no clearly assigned responsibilities for making the necessary decisions about design of and investment in infrastructure renewal. In addition, there is a bias in public opinion and in government in favor of large-scale public works projects as a means of stimulating economic development. This bias in favor of hard solutions commits Whitehead's fallacy of misplaced concreteness, whereby society pursues values such as social justice and prosperity through the provision of structures such that the rate of construction is determined to be a measure of progress toward achieving social goals. "Hard" solutions locate power over the environment in government agencies and private corporations, minimize the extent to which users can provide for their own needs, and politicize environmental decision making. "Soft" solutions would favor individual initiative, improvisation, and importance of aesthetic elements in design, and institutional flexibility.[129]

One theory about current economic conditions emphasizes long cycles in developing technological ideas and in translating them into useful products.[130] From this perspective, it would seem as if the U.S. economy is at a point between cycles; many of the useful products of the future have not yet been invented, and the basic ideas that will feed them are only being elaborated in the 1980s. We need to know more about how urban environments facilitate technological change, but it seems as if infrastructure systems, particularly modern ones that emphasize land use regulations and diminish opportunities for public social and civic life, are not helpful. Soft solutions are not necessarily an expression of anti-technological ideology. Technological innovation might itself favor soft solutions and might proceed more rapidly if they were pursued.[131] If so, we need not another industrial revolution but another Renaissance or Enlightenment—in other words, a period when fundamental ideas about political economy and new kinds of services, organizations, and attitudes develop faster than new forms of power and machinery.

Notes

1. Two excellent recent guides to aspects of technology and the city are Suellen M. Hoy and Michael C. Robinson, eds., *Public Works History in the United States: A Guide to the Literature* (Nashville: Association for State and Local History, 1982), and Eugene P. Moehring, *Public Works and Urban History: Recent Trends and New Directions*, Essays in Public Works History No. 13 (Chicago: Public Works Historical Society, 1982).

2. See the discussion in Mark Aldrich, "A History of Public Works in the U.S., 1790–1970," in CONSAD Corporation, *A Study of Public Works Investment in the United States* (Washington, D.C.: Government Printing Office, 1980). For an argument about the relationship of infrastructure to the process of capital accumulation, see David Harvey, "The Urban Process under Capitalism: A Framework for Analysis," in Michael Dear and Allen J. Scott, eds., *Urbanisation and Urban Planning in Capitalist Society* (London: Methuen, 1981), pp. 91–122; for an interpretation dealing with the relationship among city planning, infrastructure, and surplus capital, see M. Christine Boyer, *Dreaming the Rational City: The Myth of American City Planning* (Cambridge, Mass.: MIT Press, 1983), pp. 33–82.

3. David P. Billington, "Technology and the Structuring of Cities," in Michael Mooney and Florian Stuber, eds., *Small Comforts for Hard Times: Humanists on Public Policy* (New York: Columbia University Press, 1977), p. 183; idem, *The Tower and the Bridge: The New Art of Structural Engineering* (Princeton: Princeton University Press, 1983), pp. 3–24.

4. Roy Lubove, "The Urbanization Process: An Approach to Historical Research," *Journal of the American Institute of Planners* 33 (January 1967): 33–39; Christine Meisner Rosen, "Infrastructural Improvement in Nineteenth-Century Cities: A Conceptual Framework and Cases," *Journal of Urban History* 12 (May 1986): 211–56.

5. Theodore Hershberg, Harold E. Cox, Dale B. Light, Jr., and Richard R. Greenfield, "The 'Journey-to-Work': An Empirical Investigation of Work, Residence and Transportation, Philadelphia, 1850 and 1880," in Theodore Hershberg, ed., *Philadelphia: Work, Space, Family, and Group Experience in the 19th Century* (New York: Oxford University Press, 1981), pp. 128–73; Kenneth T. Jackson, *Crabgrass Frontier: The Suburbanization of the United States* (New York: Oxford University Press, 1985), pp. 20–115.

6. Douglas Booth, "Transportation, City Building, and Financial Crisis: Milwaukee, 1852–1868," *Journal of Urban History* 9 (May 1983): 335–63; Michael F. Holt, *Forging a Majority: The Formation of the Republican Party in Pittsburgh, 1848–1860* (New Haven: Yale University Press, 1969), pp. 220–62; and Sherry H. Olson, *Baltimore: The Building of an American City* (Baltimore: Johns Hopkins University Press, 1980), pp. 156–60.

7. Roger Lane, *Policing the City: Boston, 1822–1885* (Cambridge, Mass.: Harvard University Press, 1967), pp. 6–8; and Jon C. Teaford, *The Municipal Revolution in America: Origins of Modern Urban Government, 1650–1825* (Chicago: University of Chicago Press, 1975).

8. Peter R. Gluck and Richard J. Meister, *Cities in Transition: Social Changes and Institutional Responses in Urban Development* (New York: New Viewpoints, 1979), pp. 43–46.

9. Howard Gillette, Jr., "The Emergence of the Modern Metropolis: Philadelphia in the Age of Consolidation," in William W. Cutler III and Howard Gillette, Jr., eds., *The Divided Metropolis: Social and Spatial Dimensions of Philadelphia, 1800–1975* (Westport, Conn.: Greenwood Press, 1980), pp. 7–14; David R. Goldfield and Blaine A. Brownell, *Urban America: From Downtown to No Town* (Boston: Houghton Mifflin, 1979), pp. 170–80.

10. In New York, the common council resisted the creation of executive departments. See Eugene P. Moehring, *Public Works and the Patterns of Urban Real Estate Growth in Manhattan, 1835–1894* (New York: Arno Press, 1981), pp. 55–56.

11. Goldfield and Brownell, *Urban America*, pp. 168–70.

12. Sam Bass Warner, Jr., *The Private City: Philadelphia in Three Periods of Its Growth* (Philadelphia: University of Pennsylvania Press, 1968), pp. 99–160.

13. Gluck and Meister, *Cities in Transition*, pp. 45–52.

14. Moehring, *Public Works,* pp. 291–324; Constance McLaughlin Green, *Washington: Village and Capital, 1800–1878* (Princeton: Princeton University Press, 1962), pp. 344–55; and William M. Maury, *Alexander "Boss" Shepherd and the Board of Public Works*, George Washington Studies No. 3 (Washington: George Washington University, 1975).

15. Moehring, *Public Works*, pp. 109–14; Ellis L. Armstrong, Michael C. Robinson, and Suellen M. Hoy, eds., *History of Public Works in the United States, 1776–1976* (Chicago: American Public Works Association, 1976), pp. 66–67.

16. Clay McShane, "Transforming the Use of Urban Space: A Look at the Revolution in Street Pavements, 1880–1924," *Journal of Urban History* 5 (May 1979): 270–90.

17. See, for instance, the comments about streets in Olson, *Baltimore*, pp. 56–57, 131–33, and Moehring, *Public Works*, pp. 109–14.

18. Nelson M. Blake, *Water for the Cities: A History of the Urban Water Supply Problem in the United States* (Syracuse: Syracuse University Press, 1956), pp. 3–17, and Moehring, *Public Works*, pp. 23–51.

19. Letty D. Anderson, "The Diffusion of Technology in the Nineteenth Century American City: Municipal Water Supply Investments" (Ph.D. diss., Northwestern University, 1980), pp. 99–103.

20. Armstrong, Robinson, and Hoy, *History of Public Works*, pp. 217–22; Charles Jacobson, Steven Klepper, and Joel A. Tarr, "Water, Electricity, and Cable Television: A Study of Contrasting Historical Patterns of Ownership and Regulation," *Urban Resources* 3 (Fall 1985): 9–18, 64.

21. Anderson, "Diffusion of Technology," pp. 119–24; Stuart Galishoff, "Triumph and Failure: The American Response to the Urban Water Supply Problem, 1860–1923," in Martin V. Melosi, ed., *Pollution and Reform in American Cities, 1870–1930* (Austin: University of Texas Press, 1980), p. 36.

22. Moehring, *Public Works*, pp. 23–32; Olson, *Baltimore*, p. 81; Blake, *Water for the Cities*, pp. 100–247; Anderson, "Diffusion of Technology," pp. 86–125.

23. Joel A. Tarr and Francis C. McMichael, "The Evolution of Wastewater Technology and the Development of State Regulation: A Retrospective Analysis," in Joel A. Tarr, ed., *Retrospective Technology Assessment* (San Francisco: San Francisco Press, 1977), pp. 166–67.

24. Joel A. Tarr, James McCurley, and Terry F. Yosie, "The Development and Impact of Urban Wastewater Technology: Changing Concepts of Water Quality Control, 1850–1930," in Melosi, *Pollution and Reform*, pp. 59–64.

25. Ibid., pp. 61–64.

26. Joel A. Tarr, "The Separate vs. Combined Sewer Problem: A Case Study in Urban Technology Design Choice," *Journal of Urban History* 5 (May 1979): 308–39.

27. Jon A. Peterson, "The Impact of Sanitary Reform upon American Urban Planning," *Journal of Social History* 13 (Fall 1979): 84–89. For studies of the construction of sewerage systems in various cities, see Louis Cain, *Sanitation Strategy for a Lakefront Metropolis: The Case of Chicago* (De Kalb: Northern Illinois University Press, 1978); Geoffrey Giglierano, "The City and the System: Developing a Municipal Service 1800–1915," *Cincinnati Historical Society Bulletin* 35 (Winter 1977): 223–45; and Stuart Galishoff, "Drainage, Disease, Comfort, and Class: A History of Newark's Sewers," *Societas—A Review of Social History* 6 (Spring 1976): 121–38.

28. Moehring, *Public Works*, pp. 87–95.

29. Josef W. Konvitz, *The Urban Millennium: The City-Building Process from the Early Middle Ages to the Present* (Carbondale: Southern Illinois University Press, 1985), pp. 106–30.

30. There is a limited historical literature on questions of urban finance. For a recent study, see Terrence J. McDonald and Sally K. Ward, eds., *The Politics of Urban Fiscal Policy* (Beverley Hills: Sage Publications, 1984).

31. Paul Studenski and Herman E. Krooss, *Financial History of the United States* (New York: McGraw-Hill, 1952), p. 134.

32. Albert M. Hillhouse, *Municipal Bonds: A Century of Experience* (New York: Prentice-Hall, 1936), p. 36.

33. Ernest S. Griffith, *The Conspicuous Failure: A History of American City Government, 1870–1900* (New York: Praeger, 1974), p. 16; Albert M. Hillhouse, "Lessons from Previous Eras of Defaults," in A. Chatters, ed., *Municipal Defaults: Their Prevention and Adjustment,* Publication 35 (Chicago: Municipal Finance Officers Association, 1935); Studenski and Krooss, *Financial History*, p. 197.

34. Griffith, *Conspicuous Failure,* p. 21.

35. Kenneth Fox, *Better City Government: Innovation in American Urban Politics, 1850–1937* (Philadelphia: Temple University Press, 1977), pp. 21–22.

36. For a discussion of the larger implications of the Dillon rule for cities, see Edwin A. Gere, Jr., "Dillon's Rule and the Cooley Doctrine: Reflections of the Political Culture," *Journal of Urban History* 8 (May 1982): 271–98.

37. Daniel H. Calhoun, *The American Civil Engineer: Origins and Conflict* (Cambridge, Mass.: MIT Press, 1960), and Raymond H. Merritt, *Engineering in American Society, 1850–1875* (Lexington: University Press of Kentucky, 1969), pp. 27–62.

38. Nathan Rosenberg, *Technology and American Economic Growth* (White Plains, N.Y.: M. E. Sharpe, 1972), pp. 59–86.

39. For an introductory discussion of technology transfer to American cities in the nineteenth century, see Joel A. Tarr, "Bringing Technology to the Nineteenth-Century

City" (paper delivered at the 1984 Society for the History of Technology annual meeting, Boston).

40. Brooke Hindle, Introduction to Barbara E. Benson, ed., *Benjamin Henry Latrobe and Moncure Robinson* (Wilmington, Del.: Eleutherian Mills Historical Library, 1975), p. 7.

41. See Edward C. Carter II, *Benjamin Henry Latrobe and Public Works: Professionalism, Private Interest, and Public Policy in the the Age of Jefferson*, Essays in Public Works History No. 3 (Washington, D.C.: Public Works Historical Society, 1976), p. 14.

42. See, for instance, the biographies of John B. Jervis, Ellis S. Chesbrough, and Julius W. Adams in American Society of Civil Engineers, *A Biographical Dictionary of American Civil Engineers* (New York: ASCE, 1972); Calhoun, *American Civil Engineer*, p. 47–53.

43. Rosenberg, *Technology and American Economic Growth*, pp. 87–116.

44. Tarr, "Bringing Technology to the Nineteenth Century City"; Merritt, *Engineering in American Society*.

45. For a masterful study of the development of electrical technology, see Thomas P. Hughes, *Networks of Power: Electrification in Western Society* (Baltimore: Johns Hopkins University Press, 1983). There is no equivalent study for the telephone. Several suggestive essays on the impact of the telephone on the city can be found in Ithiel de Sola Pool, ed., *The Social Impact of the Telephone* (Cambridge, Mass.: MIT Press, 1977), pp. 299–370.

46. David P. Billington, *The Tower and the Bridge: The New Art of Structural Engineering* (Princeton: Princeton University Press, 1983).

47. See Christine Rosen, *The Limits of Power: Great Fires and the Process of City Growth in America* (New York: Cambridge University Press, 1986), and her "Infrastructural Improvement in Nineteenth-Century Cities."

48. Ann Durkin Keating, "From City to Metropolis: Infrastructure and Residential Growth in Urban Chicago," in *Infrastructure and Urban Growth in the Nineteenth Century*, Essays in Public Works History No. 14 (Chicago: Public Works Historical Society, 1985), pp. 3–27.

49. Konvitz, *Urban Millennium*, pp. 156–66.

50. Joel A. Tarr, "Building the Urban Infrastructure in the Nineteenth Century: An Introduction," in *Infrastructure and Urban Growth*, pp. 72–73.

51. Robert H. Wiebe, *The Search for Order, 1877–1920* (New York: Hill and Wang, 1967), pp. 164–95.

52. Jackson, *Crabgrass Frontier*, pp. 20–115, furnishes the best summary of these developments; see also James L. Davis, *The Elevated System and the Growth of Modern Chicago* (Evanston: Northwestern University Press, 1965); Clay McShane, *Technology and Reform: Street Railways and the Growth of Milwaukee, 1887–1900* (Madison: Wisconsin State Historical Society, 1974); Sam Bass Warner, Jr., *Streetcar Suburbs: The Process of Growth in Boston, 1870–1900* (Cambridge, Mass.: Harvard University Press, 1962); and Joel A. Tarr, *Transportation Innovation and Spatial Change in Pittsburgh, 1850–1934*. Essays in Public Works History No. 6 (Chicago: Public Works Historical Society, 1978), pp. 1–24.

53. Konvitz *Urban Millennium*, pp. 138–39.

54. James Marston Fitch, *American Building I: The Historical Forces That Shaped*

It (Boston: Houghton Mifflin, 1966), pp. 168–213; Jon A. Peterson, "The City Beautiful Movement: Forgotten Origins and Lost Meaning," *Journal of Urban History* 2 (August 1976): 415–30, and his "The Nation's First Comprehensive City Plan: A Political Analysis of the McMillan Plan for Washington, D.C., 1900–1902," *Journal of the American Planning Association* 51 (Spring 1985): 134–50.

55. Martyn J. Bowden, "Growth of the Central Districts in Large Cities," in Leo F. Schnore, ed., *The New Urban History: Quantitative Explorations by American Historians* (Princeton: Princeton University Press, 1975), pp.75–109.

56. Carl V. Harris, *Political Power in Birmingham, 1871–1921* (Knoxville: University of Tennessee Press, 1977), pp. 149–53.

57. Roger D. Simon, *The City Building Process: Housing and Services in New Milwaukee Neighborhoods 1880–1910* (Philadelphia: American Philosophical Society, 1978), p. 40.

58. Warner, *Streetcar Suburbs*, pp. 154–55.

59. Simon, *City Building Process*, pp. 40–41.

60. Joseph Arnold, "The Neighborhood and City Hall: The Origin of the Neighborhood Associations in Baltimore, 1890–1911," *Journal of Urban History* 6 (November 1979): 3–30, and Keating, "From City to Metropolis," p. 23.

61. Jon C. Teaford, *City and Suburb: The Political Fragmentation of Metropolitan America, 1850–1970* (Baltimore: Johns Hopkins University Press, 1979), pp. 32–63.

62. Wiebe, *Search for Order*, pp. 111–63.

63. Armstrong, Robiinson, and Hoy, *History of Public Works*, pp. 670–90.

64. Harold L. Platt, *City Building in the New South: The Growth of Urban Services in Houston, Texas, 1830–1915* (Philadelphia: Temple University Press, 1983), pp. 3–7, 14–18, 77–84, and John H. Ellis, "Businessmen and Public Health in the Urban South during the Nineteenth Century: New Orleans, Memphis, and Atlanta," *Bulletin of the History of Medicine* 44 (May-June 1970): 354–58.

65. Jon C. Teaford, "Finis for Tweed and Steffens: Rewriting the History of Urban Rule," *Reviews in American History* 10 (December 1982): 137–39, and Moehring, *Public Works*, pp. 291–324.

66. See, for example, Harris, *Political Power in Birmingham,* pp. 146–269, and Platt, *City Building in the New South*, pp. 157–64.

67. These values derived from the modern business corporation as well as from concepts of administrative efficiency developed in Germany. See Samuel P. Hays, "The Changing Political Structure of the City in Industrial America," *Journal of Urban History* 1 (November 1974): 6–38, and Martin J. Schiesl, *The Politics of Efficiency: Municipal Administration and Reform in America: 1880–1920* (Berkeley: University of California Press, 1977).

68. Bradley R. Rice, *Progressive Cities: The Commission Government Movement in America, 1901–1920* (Austin: University of Texas Press, 1977).

69. Louis Cain, *The Search for an Optimum Sanitary Jurisdiction: The Metropolitan Sanitary District of Greater Chicago: A Case Study*, Public Works History Essay No. 10 (Chicago: Public Works Historical Society, 1980); Robert B. Hawkins, Jr., *Self-Government by District: Myth or Reality* (Stanford, Calif.: Hoover Institute Press, 1976), p. 25; Paul Studenski, *The Government of Metropolitan Areas in the United States* (New York: National Municipal League, 1930), pp. 256–62.

70. Schiesl, *Politics of Efficiency*, pp. 181–88; Stanley K. Schultz and Clay McShane,

"To Engineer the Metropolis: Sewers, Sanitation and City Planning in Late-Nineteenth Century America," *Journal of American History* 65 (September 1978): 389–411.

71. Teaford, *City and Suburb*, p. 77.

72. Edward C. Kirkland, *Industry Comes of Age: Business, Labor, and Public Policy, 1860–1897* (New York: Holt, Rinehart and Winston, 1961), p. 237.

73. Studenski and Krooss, *Financial History*, p. 196.

74. For a discussion of this issue from the perspective of contract theory, see Jacobson, Klepper, and Tarr, "Water, Electricity, and Cable Television," pp. 9–18, 63.

75. Kirkland, *Industry Comes of Age*, pp. 247–53. For examples of these city-utility political struggles, see Melvin G. Holli, *Reform in Detroit: Hazen S. Pingree and Urban Politics* (New York: Oxford University Press, 1969), pp. 74–124, and James B. Crooks, *Politics and Progress: The Rise of Urban Progressivism in Baltimore, 1895–1911* (Baton Rouge: Louisiana State University Press, 1968), pp. 108–26.

76. See, for instance, Paul Barrett, *The Automobile and Urban Transit: The Formation of Public Policy in Chicago, 1900–1930* (Philadelphia: Temple University Press, 1983); Charles W. Cheape, *Moving the Masses: Urban Public Transit in New York, Boston, and Philadelphia, 1880–1912* (Cambridge, Mass.: Harvard University Press, 1980); and McShane, *Technology and Reform*.

77. Kirkland, *Industry Comes of Age*, pp. 252–53.

78. Douglas Anderson, "State Regulation of Electric Utilities," in James Q. Wilson, ed., *The Politics of Regulation* (New York: Basic Books, 1980), p. 6.

79. Armstrong, Robinson, and Hoy, *History of Public Works*, pp. 670–86, and Jeffrey K. Stine, *Nelson P. Lewis and the City Efficient: The Municipal Engineer in City Planning during the Progressive Era*, Essays in Public Works History No. 11 (Chicago: Public Works Historical Society, April 1981).

80. Anderson, "Diffusion of Technology," pp. 12–23.

81. Armstrong, Robinson, and Hoy, *History of Public Works*, pp. 670–74; Platt, *City Building in the New South*, pp. 75–118.

82. Fox, *Better City Government*, pp. 63–89.

83. Tarr, McCurley, and Yosie, "Development and Impact of Urban Wastewater Technology," pp. 69–78.

84. Bacterial laboratories were located at Ann Arbor, Cincinnati, Milwaukee, New York City, and Providence. City testing laboratories were created in Cincinnati, Rochester, and Pittsburgh. For bacterial laboratories, see John Duffy, *A History of Public Health in New York City, 1866–1966* (New York: Russell Sage Foundation, 1974), pp. 91–111, and Judith Walzer Leavitt, *The Healthiest City: Milwaukee and the Politics of Health Reform* (Princeton: Princeton University Press, 1982), p. 177; for materials on testing labs, see, for example, Edwin A. Fisher, "Engineering and Public Works in the City of Rochester," in Edward R. Foreman, ed., *Centennial History of Rochester, New York,* vol. 3: *Expansion* (Rochester, N.Y., 1933), pp. 168–69.

85. Jackson, *Crabgrass Frontier*, pp. 157–218, 231–82; McShane, "Transforming the Use of Urban Space," pp. 300–307.

86. Mark S. Foster, *From Streetcar to Superhighway: American City Planners and Urban Transportation, 1900–1940* (Philadelphia: Temple University Press, 1981), pp. 91–115.

87. Jackson, *Crabgrass Frontier*, pp. 157–89, 246–71; Blaine A. Brownell, *The Urban Ethos in the South, 1920–1930* (Baton Rouge: Louisiana State University Press, 1975), pp. 116–24; Foster, *From Streetcar to Superhighway*, pp. 65–115; Robert M.

Fogelson, *The Fragmented Metropolis: Los Angeles 1850–1930* (Cambridge, Mass.: Harvard University Press, 1967), pp. 85–163; and Tarr, *Transportation Innovation and Spatial Change*, pp. 26–28.

88. Barrett, *Automobile and Urban Transit*, pp. 155–63.

89. Carl W. Condit, *Chicago 1910–1929: Building, Planning and Urban Technology* (Chicago: University of Chicago Press, 1973), pp. 249–52; Tarr, *Transportation Innovation and Changing Spatial Patterns*, pp. 25–31; and Marilyn Weingold, *Pioneering in Parks and Parkways: Westchester County, New York, 1895–1945*, Essays in Public Works History No. 9 (Chicago: Public Works Historical Society, 1980).

90. Jackson, *Crabgrass Frontier*, pp. 157–89.

91. Peter O. Muller, *Contemporary Suburban America* (Englewood Cliffs, N.J.: Prentice-Hall, 1981), pp. 19–60.

92. John B. Rae, *The Road and the Car in American Life* (Cambridge, Mass.: MIT Press, 1971), p. 354.

93. Ibid., pp. 50–83; Bruce E. Seely, "Engineers and Government-Business Cooperation: Highway Standards and the Bureau of Public Roads, 1900–1940," *Business History Review* 58 (Winter 1984): 51–77.

94. Aldrich, "History of Public Works," p. F.46; John C. Burnham, "The Gasoline Tax and the Automobile Revolution," *Mississippi Valley Historical Review* 48 (December 1961): 435–56.

95. Aldrich, "History of Public Works," p. F.107.

96. Weingold, *Pioneering in Parks and Parkways*.

97. Tarr, *Transportation Innovation and Spatial Change*, pp. 28–31.

98. Aldrich, "History of Public Works," p. F.47; Hillhouse, *Municipal Bonds*, p. 36.

99. Aldrich, "History of Public Works," p. F.49. For a study of government use of public works to deal with unemployment before the 1930s, see Udo Sautter, "The Use of Public Works before the New Deal," *Journal of American History* 73 (June 1986): 59–86.

100. Aldrich, "History of Public Works," p. F.50; Mark I. Gelfand, *A Nation of Cities: The Federal Government and Urban America, 1933–1965* (New York: Oxford University Press, 1975), pp. 23–105.

101. Aldrich, "History of Public Works," p. F.55; Roger Daniels, *The Relevancy of Public Works History: The 1930s—A Case Study* (Washington, D.C.: Public Works Historical Society, 1975), pp. 2–11.

102. Ibid., pp. 12–17.

103. Joel A. Tarr et al., *Retrospective Assessment of Wastewater Technology in the U.S., 1850–1972: A Report to the National Science Foundation* (Washington, D.C.: National Technical Information Service, 1978), chap. 8, pp. 12–19.

104. John H. Mollenkopf, *The Contested City* (Princeton: Princeton University Press, 1983), pp. 102–9.

105. Philip W. Funigiello, *The Challenge of Urban Liberalism: Federal-City Relationships during World War II* (Knoxville: University of Tennessee Press, 1978).

106. Jackson, *Crabgrass Frontier*, pp. 272–82; Michael N. Danielson and Jameson W. Doig, *New York: The Politics of Urban Regional Development* (Berkeley: University of California Press, 1982), pp. 66–77.

107. Aldrich, "History of Public Works," pp. F.59–71.

108. Teaford, *City and Suburb*, pp. 171–76; Danielson and Doig, *New York*, pp. 71–77.

109. Hawkins, *Self-Government by District*, pp. 171–86.

110. Teaford, *City and Suburb*, pp. 174–75.

111. See Scott Fosler and Renee Berger, eds., *Public-Private Partnership in American Cities* (New York: Lexington Books, 1984).

112. Gelfand, *Nation of Cities*, pp. 205–16.

113. U.S. Department of Commerce, Bureau of the Census, *Historical Statistics of the United States: Colonial Times to 1970* (Washington, D.C.: Government Printing Office, 1975), p. 621; Tarr et al., *Retrospective Assessment of Wastewater Technology*, chap. 7, pp. 22–26.

114. Mark H. Rose, *Interstate: Express Highway Politics, 1941–1956* (Lawrence: Regents Press of Kansas, 1979), p. 65.

115. Ibid., p. 102.

116. Gelfand, *Nation of Cities*, pp. 222–29; Rose, *Interstate*, pp. 70–84.

117. Alan Trachtenberg, *Brooklyn Bridge: Fact and Symbol* (New York: Oxford University Press, 1965); Paul Goldberger, *The Skyscraper* (New York: Knopf, 1981); and Carl W. Condit, *The Chicago School of Architecture: A History of Commercial and Public Building in the Chicago Area, 1875–1925* (Chicago: University of Chicago Press, 1964), pp. 14–142.

118. John Stilgoe, *Metropolitan Corridor: Railroads and the American Scene* (New Haven: Yale University Press, 1983), pp. 267–310, and his "Moulding the Industrial Zone Aesthetic," *Journal of American Studies* 16 (April 1982): 5–24.

119. See, for instance, Vincent Scully, *American Architecture and Urbanism* (New York: Praeger, 1969), and Kevin Lynch, *What Time Is This Place?* (Cambridge, Mass.: MIT Press, 1972).

120. Carl Abbott, *The New Urban America: Growth and Politics in Sunbelt Cities* (Chapel Hill: University of North Carolina Press, 1981), pp. 34–56; Muller, *Contemporary Suburban America*, pp. 119–82.

121. Muller, *Contemporary Suburban America*, pp. 119–82; Gary Schwartz, "Urban Freeways," *Southern California Law Review* 49 (1976). For Los Angeles freeways, see David Brodsly, *L.A. Freeway: An Appreciative Essay* (Berkeley: University of California Press, 1981).

122. Richard DeNeufville, *Airports Systems Planning* (Cambridge, Mass.: MIT Press, 1977); "Airways and Airports," in Armstrong, Robinson, and Hoy, *History of Public Works*, pp. 187–216. For the early development of airports and their impact on cities, see Paul Barrett, "Cities and Their Airports: 1925–1950" (paper delivered at the Organization of American Historians Annual Convention, New York, April 12, 1986).

123. John P. Eberhard and Abram B. Bernstein, *Technological Alternatives for Urban Infrastructure* (Washington, D.C.: National Research Council, 1986), pp. 16–19.

124. CONSAD, *Study of Public Works Investment*, pp. I.80–I.125.

125. Ibid., p. I.125; Roger J. Vaughan, "Financing the Nation's Infrastructure Requirements," in Alan H. Molof and Carl J. Turkstra, eds., *Infrastructure: Maintenance and Repair of Public Works* (New York: New York Academy of Sciences, 1984), pp. 46–47.

126. American Public Works Association, *Revenue Shortfall: The Public Works Challenge of the 1980s* (Chicago: American Public Works Association, 1981).

127. For a discussion of alternative means of supplying public works, see Douglas C.

Henton and Steven A. Waldhorn, "The Future of Urban Public Works: New Ways of Doing Business," in Royce Hanson, ed., *Perspectives on Urban Infrastructure* (Washington, D.C.: National Academy Press, 1984), pp. 178–210.

128. Eberhard and Bernstein, eds., *Technological Alternatives for Urban Infrastructure*, pp. 31–38.

129. See, for instance, the suggestions for innovative approaches in ibid., pp. 39–52.

130. Gerhard Mensch, *Stalemate in Technology: Innovation Overcomes the Depression* (Cambridge, Mass.: Ballinger, 1979).

131. Ibid., pp. 236–37. For a discussion of the possible future impacts of new technology on urban form, see John Brotchie, Peter Newton, Peter Hall, and Peter Nijkamp, *The Future of Urban Form: The Impact of New Technology* (New York: Nichols Publishing Co., 1985).

10 —————— Re-Reading Suburban America: Urban Population Deconcentration, 1810–1980

MICHAEL H. EBNER

Examined from a modern perspective, the basic vocabulary that describes urban America has changed. Key words such as *city*, *suburb*, and *metropolis* have become inadequate. The need exists, as William Sharpe and Leonard Wallock recently observed, for new conventions to read its parts effectively:

> The transfer of basic urban functions from a central city, first to the suburbs, and then to the still larger decentralized "urban field" has required the visual vocabulary of the nineteenth-century city to change. With this transformation, once-significant urban emblems have been deformed, submerged, erased, or dislocated as the city has grown. It is usually claimed that the sheer physical expansion of the nineteenth- and twentieth-century city has led to our present inability to explore and map its intricate systems of exchange and influence.[1]

Kenneth T. Jackson, pre-eminent among students of the suburban experience, offers an important addition—*urban population deconcentration*—to historians' language of metropolitan development. This demographic process constitutes a causal explanation encompassing the vast sweep of American urban history since the beginning of the nineteenth century.[2]

What follows is a chronologically organized analysis of urban population deconcentration from 1810 to 1980. Identifying its successive stages or sequences necessarily leads to categorizing and classifying suburban development. In turn, this yields a systematic understanding of consequential social, economic, and technological benchmarks instructive for situating this process within the cultural context of the American past. Whether one's historical focus is on a specific community, a network of communities, or urban population deconcentration studied regionally or nationally, this essay offers a frame of reference.[3]

Suburban history has a self-consciously urban focus. Write Harold M. Mayer and Richard C. Wade at the outset of their important book, *Chicago: The Growth of a Metropolis*: "The modern metropolis, with its central city, suburbs, and 'satellite cities,' is a single historic and geographic entity."[4] Sam Bass Warner, Jr.'s, *Streetcar Suburbs: The Process of Growth in Boston, 1870–1900*, the first book by an urban historian to examine systematically the suburban tradition, remains the singular example of this approach.[5] And not mincing words in accounting for the inextricable conjuncture of city and suburb is Kenneth Jackson: "This historical dimension of the suburban trend is important because the urban structure we have inherited has been largely shaped by the decisions and impulses of a half-century ago."[6]

Scholarly publishing reflects heightened interest in the suburban tradition's historiography. Among books about aspects of suburban history published since *Streetcar Suburbs*, two were issued in the 1970s and six since 1980.[7] The first anthology was *Suburbia: The American Dream and Dilemma* edited by Philip C. Dolce. Similar in format but geographically localized is *Cities of the Garden State* edited by Joel Schwartz and Daniel Prosser. Urban history textbooks— David R. Goldfield and Blaine A. Brownell, *Urban America: From Downtown to No Town* and Raymond A. Mohl, *The New City: Urban America in the Industrial Age, 1860–1920*—provide a welcome metropolitan focus for studying suburbs. Historical geographer Peter O. Muller has written a textbook, *Contemporary Suburban America*, that commands attention despite its ahistorical title. A highly regarded social history of contemporary America, Richard Polenberg's *One Nation Indivisible: Class, Race, and Ethnicity in the United States since 1938*, contains a useful chapter, "The Suburban Nation." And published in 1985 by Oxford University Press was Kenneth Jackson's much-awaited and influential *Crabgrass Frontier: The Suburbanization of the United States*.[8]

The origins and beginnings of the suburban tradition, which by necessity draw upon English and continental antecedents, informs American research by virtue of chronology as well as cultural differentiation.[9] Often cited is Chaucer's casual reference in *The Canterbury Tales* to the "suburbes of toun."[10] Simultaneously in Central and Eastern European cities of the late Middle Ages, including Gdansk, Prague, Poznan, Lublin, Warsaw, and Riga, the poor often inhabited outlying reaches; some parcels were specifically allocated to Jews for reasons political and cultural rather than economic.[11] When Vienna was assaulted by Ottomans in 1529 and 1683, those living outside its well-fortified defenses found refuge in the city.[12]

But what Lewis Mumford viewed as the embryo of modern suburbs took root in the sixteenth century and evolved over the next 400 years. "As the crowding became more universal," he wrote in *The Culture of Cities*, "the demand to get away became more imperious: if one did not leave of one's own initiative the doctor's orders would prescribe it."[13] Still, a painstaking reconstruction of the evolution of South London from its inception in 1735 affirms that the modern suburb evolved slowly. Into the first half of the 1800s, this district remained largely agricultural despite construction of new bridges and roadways linking it to the central city. It is best appreciated as an extramural settlement, a concept applied by H. J. Dyos, the eminent English urban historian, and now used in settings elsewhere.[14]

The Industrial Revolution altered such arrangements on both sides of the Atlantic Ocean. Kenneth Jackson dates the modern suburb to 1815. The pace of American urban growth, and its attendant pressures, exceeded almost every expectation during the first quarter of the nineteenth century. If congestion, filth, and disease united to exert a significant force prompting better classes to consider alternatives to urban life, perfection of new transportation spawned what came to be known as commuter suburbs.[15] Three corresponding (but not simultaneous) innovations—the steam-powered ferry boat, a variety of horse-drawn conveyances, and the steam locomotive—exerted momentous influence. An English scholar writing about railways (which made their appearance about 1830 in England as well as the United States) captures the result: "they made possible a new kind of life—a life that could be lived in two quite different places at one time."[16]

Several factors account for the type of transport best suited to a metropolis: topography, proximity to navigable waterways, population density, availability of suitable tracts for residential development, and distance from commercial or industrial centers. Brooklyn, often counted as prototypical among commuter suburbs, achieved its distinction as a result of its ferry boat connection across the East River to Manhattan in 1811.[17] San Francisco, the "large-scale Venice of the West," benefitted at mid-century largely because the Bay Area physical configuration allowed a combination of water transportation and surface transit.[18] In Manhattan and Philadelphia, the horse-drawn street omnibus proved dominant into the 1840s by virtue of compact, built-up neighborhoods.[19]

The commuter railway swiftly became the most influential metropolitan conveyance. Here were the origins of the phenomenon that John R. Stilgoe writes of in *Metropolitan Corridor: Railroads and the American Scene*, recasting physical landscape and cultural patterns.[20] It took hold first in Boston. Overcrowded as early as 1820, in part resulting from a scarcity of real estate, rudimentary commuting service became available in 1838. By late 1849, daily passenger trains entering or departing its seven depots numbered 208, 118 of them moving in a fifteen-mile radius[21] A railway was constructed north of Manhattan into Westchester County in the 1840s; seven weekday trains visited Croton Falls, six more stopped at White Plains, and fifteen at Williamsbridge. A combination of steam railways and ferry boats brought residents of several counties in northeastern New Jersey into Manhattan via Jersey City.[22] In Chicago and its environs, a "revolution in social and economic organization" resulted from railroading. In 1848 only ten miles of track entered the city; by 1856 the figure exceeded 3,600 miles as eleven new lines were constructed.[23]

Kenneth Jackson pinpoints the second quarter of the nineteenth century as the time when the North American pattern of spatial change took hold in the larger, established cities, transforming the metropolis. Its principal characteristic was "peripheral affluence and central despair." Such settings fostered what Gunther Barth aptly refers to in *City People: The Rise of Modern City Culture in Nineteenth-Century America* as the "isolationist features of modern city life."[24] New York City's four outlying boroughs nearly doubled their populations during the 1830s, increased 140 percent in the 1840s, and doubled in the 1850s. By 1830, Brooklyn was growing more quickly than Manhattan and would achieve legal status as a city in 1834; at mid-century, a journalist complained about the exodus across the East River, claiming it resulted in the "desertion of the city by its men of wealth." And by the 1850s, Boston had its Chestnut Hill, Philadelphia its Germantown, Chicago its North Shore, and San Francisco its Nob and Russian Hill.[25]

But to appreciate fully the suburban ideal at mid-century, we turn to the romantic influence on physical design fostered by upper-class suburban residents prior to the Civil War. It reflected the long-standing ambivalence of Americans toward their cities, epitomized in the often-mentioned pastoral mentality of the Founding Fathers in general and Thomas Jefferson in particular. Romanticism's emphasis on man-made improvement of the natural landscape was undeniably of English origins, at least in considering suburbs; in the United States, it manifested itself in the guise of rural cemeteries and then urban parks as precursors of the suburb. But it was English locales such as Manchester's Victoria Park and Liverpool's Rock Park (the latter best accessible by ferrying across the Mersey), designed almost simultaneously in the mid-1830s, that came to be regaled on both sides of the ocean as models. Noteworthy American replicas included New Brighton on Staten Island, Evergreen Hamlet north of Pittsburgh, Llewellyn Park in northeastern New Jersey, Glendale near Cincinnati, and Lake Forest and Riverside on the outskirts of Chicago. The landscape architects in the United States responsible for perpetuating the romantic influence were engaged in mediating what one urban historian regards as the "widening gap between the expectations and realities associated with the growth of the metropolis." Foremost was Andrew Jackson Downing and his disciples, among them Calvert Vaux, Frederick Law Olmsted, and Horace W. S. Cleveland.[26]

But in post–Civil War America, the configuration of the metropolis underwent dramatic reordering. Several factors contributed to change: economic forces such as industrialization, ever more massive influxes of European immigrants, significant new developments in communications as well as sanitary engineering, and further advances in the technology of surface transportation. Tellingly, the federal census report of 1880 heralded the advent of the nation's first metropolitan district: New York City and its environs, a two-state region including the autonomous cities of Manhattan, Brooklyn, Jersey City, Hoboken, and Newark. Although the suburbs that evolved were being portrayed in many instances as the latest manifestation of prewar romanticism, now they mostly attracted the urban middle class. In West Philadelphia, once "genteel estates" gave way by 1880 to a pattern of land development premised on the sensitivity of prospective residents to achieving a "uniformity of appearance, of price, and of situation." Walter L. Creese pointedly defines these Victorian suburbs as "not . . . one great house, as on country estates, but a multitude of houses, a set of discrete assertions."[27]

By the second half of the nineteenth century, suburban residents found their communities coveted by the imperialists of the metropolis. This involved designs by the leaders of several major cities to centralize municipal or administrative control over adjacent territories. Jon C. Teaford explains in *City and Suburb: The Political Fragmentation of Metropolitan America, 1850–1970* that pro-annexation campaigns constituted an explicit understanding among urban leaders as to the enviable circumstances of nearby suburbs. The first such effort occurred in Philadelphia, which in one fell swoop in 1854 expanded its municipal boundaries from a mere two square miles to 129. Chicago added 125 square miles to its existing 43 in 1889 by absorbing the entire Southside, including the municipality of Hyde Park, the largest single addition of outlying land in its history. Most noteworthy, however, was the formation in 1898 of greater New York City, wherein its square mileage went from 40 to 300, its population growing instantaneously by 2 million. Now included in New York City was Brooklyn, counted in the census of 1890 as the nation's fourth largest city. Similar accessions occurred in St. Louis, Boston, New Orleans, Baltimore, Minneapolis, Cleveland, Cincinnati, and Pittsburgh, as well as in smaller cities.[28]

Not that urban imperialism proceeded without pause. In some long-established suburbs at the edges of major cities, people prized their local autonomy and distinctive identities. Citizens of Brookline thwarted plans for consolidation with Boston beginning in 1873, a decision now regarded by urban historians as the first significant setback to the annexation mania then sweeping the United States. When other communities—Cambridge (1891) and Somerville (1893) adjacent to Boston or the Chicago suburb of Evanston (1894)—faced similar questions, their citizens voted against consolidation. Then again, some contemporary writers during the 1890s—Adna F. Weber remains the best known—celebrated the prospect of suburbs absorbed into central cities as harbingers of metropolitan democracy. But the firm opposition to imperialist designs within well-established suburbs is evidence that the "closed social cells" associated with modern-day urban life were being set into place.[29]

A technological innovation in transportation—perfection of the electrified street railway in 1888—added to the complexity of metropolitan life as the nineteenth century drew to its conclusion. First launched experimentally at Richmond, Virginia, soon thereafter the West End Railway ran profitably into the suburbs of Boston. This caused a revolution in mass transit that soon attained international proportions. Its instant success has been attributed to economy, cleanliness, speed, and geographic radius. By 1895, 85 percent of all street railways in the United States had been electrified. Although suburban preserves of the elite—Lake Forest and New York City's Tuxedo Park—would continue to rely primarily on steam railroads for commuting, electrified trolleys proved a boon to the middle class.[30]

Sam Bass Warner, Jr., in *Streetcar Suburbs* critically examines the resulting effect on metropolitan residential development. Builders of the new transit lines, faced with their own economic imperatives, laid down track on whatever suburban property became available rather than along well-designed coordinates. Instead of new communities or neighborhoods and the public life associated with them, by 1900 there evolved a fragmented pattern of civic life best defined as centerless. Concludes Warner: "Middle-class families were free to choose among hundreds of possible locations, free to find a neighborhood which suited both their ethnic feelings and their progress up the economic ladder."[31]

Nor did electric street railways win universal approbation, reinforcing the increasingly variegated nature of the metropolis. In Newark's affluent suburbs, a protracted campaign temporarily prevented electric street railway lines from penetrating the long-established communities of Orange, East Orange, and Montclair. These suburban residents, already fearful about influxes of new-stock ethnic inhabitants, created legal obstacles to franchise petitions. Along the North Shore of Chicago substantial opposition prevented the completion of a new line for nine years until 1899. Contributing to this delay was concern over preserving local autonomy, fear of encroachment by people and corporations deemed foreign because of their urban addresses as well as corporate ties, and uncertainty as to how this advance would affect the suburban landscape.[32]

As profound as the influence of the electrified street railway proved during the 1890s, in this decade another revolutionary innovation in transportation— the automobile—first exerted influence. In a recent book about the history of urban transportation from 1900 to 1940, Mark S. Foster observes that by the turn of the century, the relationship between street railway and automobile was shifting, although the tilt was not completed until World War I. A variety of factors contributed to the change: diminishing profits for transit companies, political criticism over fare levels, overcrowded cars, and deteriorating rolling stock.[33] "By 1900," Glen Holt has written, "two or three generations in every large American city had waited for the opportunity to break away from the crowded cars and personal discipline imposed by the necessity of riding on a mass transit system."[34] The alternative was the private automobile. Its effect on the metropolis is readily imaginable.

The relationship (or marriage) between suburb and automobile flourished in the 1920s. Statistics underscore this: car registration reached 8 million as of 1920; in 1927, one car existed for every five persons, and the United States manufactured 85 percent of the world's output; in 1929, 4.8 million cars were produced and 26 million vehicles operated on the nation's roads. Highway and road construction mounted, stimulated in part by federal legislation enacted in 1916 and 1921 that assisted state governments to engage in major improvement programs; in 1925, for the first time, total highway-related construction nationally surpassed $1 billion annually. Key linkages were erected: the Benjamin Franklin Bridge tied Philadelphia and Camden in 1926, the Holland Tunnel joined lower Manhattan and Jersey City in 1927, and the George Washington Bridge did the same for upper Manhattan and Bergen County, New Jersey, in 1931. Although the federal census of 1920 revealed that for the first time more Americans resided in cities (51.4 percent) than in rural locales, the category of city as a place with 2,500 or more inhabitants was loosely defined and obscured what was taking place in the suburbs.[35]

A well-known chronicle of the changing metropolis is found in William E. Leuchtenberg's classic history of that decade, *The Perils of Prosperity, 1914-1932*. Population doubled in the borough of Queens, Detroit's Grosse Point Park grew by 700 percent, Cleveland's Shaker Heights by 1,000 percent, and Los Angeles' Beverly Hills by 2,500 percent.[36] Meanwhile the nation's forty largest industrial counties suffered a net loss of 617,965 jobs at the expense of peripheral locales over a seventeen-year period beginning in 1919. In retailing, highway clutter was becoming common along major arterial roadways leading into cities. Strips of retail businesses catered to suburban consumers, advertising their wares using neon-illuminated signs and billboards.[37]

But the effect of automobiles on suburbanization during the 1920s should not be overestimated. What was happening reflected a process whose social and demographic origins extended into the nineteenth century. The suburban-situated industrial plants (Allis Chalmers established its Norwood, Ohio, operation in 1898 on the northeastern edge of Cincinnati) took hold as management sought to avoid costly land acquisitions and high tax rates; correspondingly, workers found it more convenient to relocate in close proximity to their employment. Retailers also found it essential to decentralize. Between 1910 and 1929, Chicago department stores such as Wieboldts, Sears Roebuck, and Marshall Fields as well as Filene's of Boston established branches. Further contributing to the exodus from the core was the modernization of selected commuter transit lines, making it comfortable for white-collar occupational groups to live in the suburbs and work in cities. As early as 1911, more than 50 percent of all the practicing lawyers in Boston lived beyond its corporate limits; the figure reached 40 percent for Newark, New Jersey, by 1925.[38]

Accompanying the supposed triumph of the American suburb during the 1920s were doubts and outright criticism about its influence. To be sure, Harlan Paul Douglass could write a much-acclaimed book, *The Suburban Trend*, wherein he portrayed his topic (not uncritically) as an integral dimension of "urban civilization." He defined the suburbs in this way: "It is an urban society trying to eat its cake, and keep it, too."[39] The introduction and widespread acceptance of zoning codes, whatever the original intentions of such legislation, contributed to the practice of codifying the restrictiveness of affluent suburbs. Euclid, Ohio, in a landmark policy later sustained by the U.S. Supreme Court, prohibited construction of multiple-family residences.[40]

During the 1920s, Lewis Mumford advocated a very different vision of the suburb's place on the metropolitan landscape. As John L. Thomas suggests in *Alternative America: Henry George, Edward Bellamy, Henry Demarest Lloyd and the Adversary Tradition*, the young Mumford was influenced by decentralist thinkers of the late nineteenth century.[41] His plan was to create new, planned, tightly controlled communities within the metropolis "fully equipped for work, play, and 'living.' " This notion was realized with the development of Radburn, launched during 1928 in Bergen County, New Jersey. During the 1930s, the concept of planned communities on the periphery would be revived, albeit briefly, by the federal government. Although Mumford's idea was never fully achieved either at Radburn or elsewhere, its influence on the American suburban tradition has endured among intellectuals as well as some planners.[42] What is certain, as Daniel Schaffer observes in *Garden Cities for America: The Radburn Experience*, is that its fate foreshadowed the limitations as well as possibilities of the American political economy for spawning community development plans.[43]

The 1930s exacerbated the complex and uneasy relationship between suburb and city. The Great Depression affected the core with particular severity. Unemployment nationwide reached between 12 and 15 percent by 1932, the year that Franklin Delano Roosevelt was first elected president of the United States. In major cities, joblessness soared: 1 million in New York City, 600,000 in Chicago, 298,000 in Philadelphia, 178,000 in Pittsburgh. Some neighborhoods in Boston as of 1934 reported unemployment of between 38 and 43 percent. Still, the gross effects of massive economic dislocation, compelling as they are, do not tell all. Puzzlingly as it initially appears, cities suffered at the expense of suburbs because of New Deal policies! This is curious in that Franklin Roosevelt is widely regarded as a politician whose electoral base was urban.[44]

Two pieces of New Deal housing legislation stand essential to any appreciation of Rooseveltian liberalism. The Home Owners Loan Corporation (HOLC) sought to curtail massive foreclosures of private-home mortgages, and the Federal Housing Administration (FHA) subsidized the home construction industry in upgrading existing dwelling or in initiating new starts. Conventional wisdom once instructed that such laws restored faith and prosperity, but urban and political historians have learned otherwise. The policies of the respective agencies undermined the well-being of housing stock in the core while enhancing circumstances on the periphery. Real estate appraisers employed by HOLC developed the practice known now as redlining, wherein loans are not granted in portions of the city classified as physically or economically deteriorated or in neighborhoods inhabited by Afro-Americans or ethnics. The FHA favored low-risk loans: new units rather than existing dwellings, open spaces rather than built-up locales, white collar rather than working class, whites rather than blacks, native born rather than ethnics. Of course, neither housing agency possessed a legislative mandate to defend or revive central cities. Rather, New Deal housing programs fit the classic New Deal mold: utilizing public funds to induce a return to economic health in the private sector. Whatever the motives of those who designed HOLC and FHA, they would best serve suburban, middle-class home ownership.[45]

After World War II, the suburban trend seemed inevitable, a self-fulfilling prophecy. Housing starts between 1946 and 1955 doubled the figure for the preceding fifteen years. Many new homes were situated on the periphery, constructed inexpensively by tract developers and subsidized by the FHA or the loan program of the Veterans Administration. Highway construction also flourished, reaching $2 billion by 1949 and $4 billion by 1955. When construction began in 1955 on the Long Island Expressway (based on the budget of $500 million), it was anticipated that it would carry 80,000 vehicles daily; by 1963 the figure reached 132,000. The Interstate Highway Act of 1956 projected a transcontinental network of superhighways stretching 42,500 miles and costing $60 billion. Not surprisingly, by 1970 some 14,000 suburban shopping centers—described in functional terms as stores surrounded by immense parking lots—served retail consumers, diverting them from long-established central business districts.[46]

Whether the vantage point is social or economic, the ramifications of the postwar suburban trend affected the nation's older cities. Between 1950 and 1960, cities grew 11 percent, suburbs 46 percent. In the thirty-year period ending in 1980, Detroit's population fell 600,000, St. Louis' 404,000, and Cleveland's 341,000. Among fifteen cities with populations exceeding 1 million, fourteen lost residents in the 1950s; over the thirty-year span 1950-1980, Buffalo lost 38 percent of its residents, Minneapolis 29 percent, and Newark 25 percent. During the 1950s, the twelve largest cities lost 3.6 million whites and gained 4.5 million nonwhites. A brief look at the Afro-American proportions of the total populations in major cities is revealing: Cleveland's increased from 16.2 percent in 1950 to 43.8 percent by 1980, Baltimore's from 23.7 percent to 54.8 percent, and Detroit's from 16.3 percent to 63 percent. Similar shifts occurred in employment opportunities. Between 1948 and 1963, industrial jobs declined 7 percent in the nation's twenty-five largest cities at the same time that suburban jobs rose 61 percent and in trade 122 percent. Suburban-situated jobs, 1970-1977, increased 48 percent in Washington, D.C., 41 percent in Baltimore, 31 percent in St. Louis, and 22 percent in Philadelphia.[47]

But in the new urban America, a phrase coined by Carl Abbott, the city demonstrates its new vitality. The cause was an interregional shift to the nation's sunbelt, the southern and western regions, reflecting the economic and technological realities of the late twentieth century. Between 1940 and 1980, the states situated south of the thirty-seventh parallel experienced a population increase of 112.3 percent as contrasted with 41.9 percent in the Northeast and Midwest. Newer urban centers prosper at the expense of older metropolitan areas in the frostbelt, whether the measure is population, employment opportunities, or capital formation. In sunbelt cities—which lack some of the problems associated with the older urban locales—municipal boundaries have been extended through consolidation and annexation to include peripheral territory, protions of it still undeveloped and with minimal population density. Albuquerque, New Mexico, comprised 11 square miles in 1940 and 92 square miles as of 1975. Between 1945 and 1949, Houston's size doubled to nearly 160 square miles and subsequently grew to 556 square miles. Jacksonville, Florida, comprises 850 square miles, although in population size it compares with Newark, New Jersey, a city of 23 square miles. Phoenix went from 9.6 square miles in 1940 to 187.4 by 1960 and 324.1 by 1980.[48]

From this review of nearly two centuries of suburbanization, we discover yet another unhappy chapter in the urban history of the United States. Brian J. L. Berry, the distinguished geographer, has best identified the process taking place as counterurbanization, or the most recent manifestation of population deconcentration. In the United States during the 1970s, nonmetropolitan growth (1.18 percent) exceeded that of metropolitan areas (0.73 percent). Urban population growth between 1970 and 1980 (0.1 percent, as contrasted to 3.7 percent during the 1960s) was the lowest since 1820. Hence counterurbanization and suburbanization are benchmarks in the continuum of circumstances—Jackson's concept of urban population deconcentration—that reach back into the early nineteenth century.[49] While the future ramifications of counterurbanization await precise calculation, surely the city remains the focus of attention in the American metropolis.

What are the prospects for communities regarded by any objective historical definition as being within the suburban tradition? Their residents may well discover themselves the latest victims of demographic sprawl. Some suburbanites could yet draw the conclusion—disconcerting as this circumstance appears to them at first hearing—that proximity, economies of scale, and cultural tradition link their future well-being to the core rather than to the periphery. What is essential, to return to Sharpe and Wallock, are new definitions that explain the altered circumstances of the suburbs as the twentieth century draws to a close.

Notes

1. William Sharpe and Leonard Wallock, "From 'Great Town' to 'Nonplace Urban Realm': Reading the Modern City," in William Sharpe and Leonard Wallock, eds., *Visions of the Modern City: Essays in History, Art, and Literature*, Proceedings of the Heyman Center for the Humanities (New York: Columbia University, 1983), pp. 7–46, esp. p. 22.

2. Kenneth T. Jackson, "Urban Deconcentration in the Nineteenth Century: A Statistical Inquiry," in Leo F. Schnore, ed., *The New Urban History: Quantitative Explorations by American Historians* (Princeton: Princeton University Press, 1975), pp. 110–42.

3. Sam Bass Warner, Jr., "If All the World Were Philadelphia: A Scaffolding for Urban History, 1774–1930," *American Historical Review* 74 (October 1968): 26–43,

wrote about identifying "the succession of urban environments" and their consequential social, economic, and technological benchmarks. Too much overlooked by historians is Douglas Shand Tucci, *Built in Boston: City and Suburb, 1800–1950* (Boston: Little, Brown, for the New York Graphic Society, 1978). Peter O. Muller, "Everyday Life in Suburbia: A Review of Changing Social and Economic Forces that Shape Daily Rhythms within the Outer City" *American Quarterly* 34 (bibliography issue 1982): 262–77, is a pioneering effort by a historical geographer at classification and categorization.

4. Harold M. Mayer and Richard C. Wade, *Chicago: The Growth of a Metropolis* (Chicago: University of Chicago Press, 1969), p. ix.

5. Sam Bass Warner, Jr., *Streetcar Suburbs: The Process of Growth in Boston, 1870–1900* (Cambridge, Mass.: Harvard University Press 1962), passim.

6. Kenneth T. Jackson, "The Crabgrass Frontier: 150 Years of Suburban Growth in America," in Raymond A. Mohl and James F. Richardson, eds., *The Urban Experience: Themes in American History* (Belmont, Calif.: Wadsworth, 1973), pp. 197ff.

7. Listed chronologically: Joseph L. Arnold, *The New Deal and the Suburbs: A History of the Greenbelt Town Program, 1935–1954* (Columbus: Ohio State University Press, 1971); Jon C. Teaford, *City and Suburb: The Political Fragmentation of Metropolitan America, 1850–1970* (Baltimore: Johns Hopkins University Press, 1979); Zane L. Miller, *Suburb: Neighborhood and Community in Forest Park, Ohio, 1935–1976* (Knoxville: University of Tennessee Press, 1981); Daniel Schaffer, *Garden Cities of America: The Radburn Experience* (Philadelphia: Temple University Press, 1981); Carol O'Connor, *A Sort of Utopia: Scarsdale, 1891–1981* (Albany: State University of New York Press, 1983); and Matthew Edel et al., *Shaky Palaces: Homeownership and Social Mobility in Boston's Suburbanization* (New York: Columbia University Press, 1984). Published in 1985, in addition to Jackson's book, is Henry C. Binford, *The First Suburbs: Residential Communities on the Boston Periphery, 1815–1960* (Chicago: University of Chicago Press, 1985). Gregory E. Singleton, "The Genesis of Suburbia: A Complex of Historical Trends," in Louis E. Masotti and Jeffrey K. Hadden, eds., *The Urbanization of the Suburbs*, vol. 7: *Urban Affairs Annual Review* (Beverly Hills: Sage Publications, 1973), pp. 29–50, and Michael H. Ebner, "Suburban Biography as Urban History," *Reviews in American History* 11 (September 1983): 442–46, assay the urban tradition in suburban historiography.

8. Philip C. Dolce, ed., *Suburbia: The American Dream and Dilemma* (Garden City, N.Y.: Anchor Press/Doubleday, 1976); Joel Schwartz and Daniel Prosser, eds., *Cities of the Garden State: Essays in the Urban and Suburban History of New Jersey* (Dubuque: Kendall-Hunt, 1977); David R. Goldfield and Blaine A. Brownell, eds., *Urban America: From Downtown to No Town* (Boston: Houghton Mifflin, 1979); Raymond A. Mohl, *The New City: Urban America in the Industrial Age, 1860–1920* (Arlington Heights, Ill.: Harlan Davidson, 1985); Peter O. Muller, *Contemporary Suburban America* (Englewood Cliffs, N.J.: Prentice-Hall, 1981); Richard Polenberg, *One Nation Divisible: Class, Race, and Ethnicity in the United States since 1938* (Garden City, N.Y.: Doubleday, 1983), pp. 127–63; and Kenneth T. Jackson, *Crabgrass Frontier: The Suburbanization of the United States* (New York: Oxford University Press, 1985).

9. George Fredrickson, "Comparative History," in Michael Kammen, ed., *The Past Before Us: Contemporary Historical Writing in the United States* (Ithaca: Cornell University Press, 1980), pp. 457–73 offers a thoughtful and sophisticated precis of this genre of scholarship, albeit underestimating the contributions of American urban historians. Asa Briggs, *Victorian Cities* (New York: Harper & Row, 1965), passim, and Eric

E. Lampard, "The Urbanizing World," in H. J. Dyos and Michael Wolff, eds., *The Victorian City, Images and Realities* (London: Routledge & Kegan Paul, 1973), 1: 3–57 represent pre-eminent examples of comparative urban history.

10. H. J. Dyos, *Victorian Suburb: A Study of the Growth of Camberwell* (Leicester: Leicester University Press, 1960), p. 20.

11. Henryk Samsonowicz, " 'Suburbium' in the Late Middle Ages: The Economic and Social Importance of Suburbs in East-Central Europe," *Review* 5 (Fall 1981), p. 312ff.

12. A.E.J. Morris, *History of Urban Form before the Industrial Revolution*, 2nd ed. (New York: John Wiley, 1979), p. 191.

13. Lewis Mumford, *The Culture of Cities* (New York: Harcourt-Brace and Company, 1938), p. 211.

14. H. J. Dyos, "The Growth of a Pre-Victorian Suburb: South London, 1580–1836," *Town Planning Review* 25 (1954): 65–75; Briggs, *Victorian Cities*, pp. 28ff.; and Muller, *Contemporary Suburban America*, p. 23.

15. Jackson, "Urban Deconcentration," pp. 110–42.

16. Jack Simmons, "The Power of the Railway," in Dyos and Wolff, eds., *Victorian City*, 1: 295. Essential to this discussion of urban transportation in the nineteenth-century metropolis are Joel A. Tarr, "The Evolution of the Urban Infrastructure in the Nineteenth and Twentieth Centuries," in Royce Hanson, ed., *Perspectives on Urban Infrastructure* (Washington, D.C.: National Academy Press, 1984), pp. 7ff.; George Rogers Taylor, "The Beginnings of Mass Transportation in Urban America: Part I," *Smithsonian Journal of History* 1 (Summer 1966): 35–50, idem., "The Beginnings of Mass Transportation in Urban America: Part II," *Smithsonian Journal of History* 1 (August 1966): 31–54; and David Ward, *Cities and Immigrants: A Geography of Change in Nineteenth-Century America* (New York: Oxford University Press, 1971), pp. 121–45. An exemplary case study is Joel A. Tarr, "Transportation Innovation and Changing Spatial Patterns in Pittsburgh, 1850–1934," Essays in Public Works History No. 6 (Chicago: Public Works Historical Society, 1976): pp. 1–64; also consult Richard Rhoda, "Urban Transport and the Expansion of Cincinnati, 1858–1934," Essays in Public Works History No. 6 (Chicagao: Public Works Historical Society, 1976): pp. 1–64; also consult Richard Rhoda, "Urban Transport and the Expansion of Cincinnati, 1858–1920," *Cincinnati Historical Society Bulletin* 35 (Summer 1977): 131–43.

17. David Ment, *The Shaping of a City: A Brief History of Brooklyn* (Brooklyn: Brooklyn Rediscovery, 1979), pp. 28–32, and Jackson, "Urban Deconcentration," p. 131.

18. James E. Vance, Jr., *Geography and Urban Evolution in the San Francisco Bay Area* (Berkeley: Institute of Government, University of California, Berkeley, 1964), pp. 33–37.

19. Taylor, "Beginnings of Mass Transportation, Part I," pp. 40ff.

20. John R. Stilgoe, *Metropolitan Corridor: Railroads and the American Scene* (New Haven: Yale University Press, 1983), p. ix.

21. Charles J. Kennedy, "Commuter Services in the Boston Area, 1835–1860," *Business History Review* 36 (Summer 1962): 161ff., and Ronald Dale Karr, "Brookline and the Making of an Elite Suburb," *Chicago History* 13 (Summer 1984): 37.

22. Edward K. Spann, *The New Metropolis: New York City, 1940–1857* (New York: Columbia University Press, 1981), pp. 188ff.

23. William J. Cronon, "To Be the Central City: Chicago, 1848–1857," *Chicago History* 10 (Fall 1981): 130ff.; Carl Abbott, " 'Necessary Adjuncts to Its Growth': The Railroad Suburbs of Chicago, 1854–1875," *Journal of the Illinois State Historical*

Society 73 (Summer 1980): 117–31.

24. Gunther Barth, *City People: The Rise of Modern City Culture in Nineteenth-Century America* (New York: Oxford University Press, 1980), 53.

25. Jackson, "Urban Deconcentration," pp. 131ff.

26. John Archer, "Country and City in the American Romantic Suburb," *Journal of the Society of Architectural Historians* 42 (May 1983): 142–65; also instructive are John Brinkerhoff Jackson, *American Space: The Centennial Years, 1865–1876* (New York: W. W. Norton, 1972), pp. 72–78; Thomas Bender, *Toward an Urban Vision: Ideas and Institutions in Nineteenth-Century America* (Lexington: University Press of Kentucky, 1975); Roy Lubove, "Social History and the History of Landscape Architecture," *Journal of Social History* 9 (Winter 1975): 268–75; Geoffrey Blodgett, "Frederick Law Olmsted: Landscape Architecture as Conservative Reform," *Journal of American History* 62 (March 1976): 869–89; David Schuyler, *The New Urban Landscape: The Redefinition of City Form in Nineteenth-Century America* (Baltimore: Johns Hopkins University Press, 1986); and Spann, *New Metropolis*, pp. 193ff.

27. Walter L. Creese, "Imagination in the Suburb," in U. C. Knoepflmacher and G. B. Tennyson, eds., *Nature and the Victorian Imagination* (Berkeley: University of California Press, 1977), p. 50; Gwendolyn Wright, *Building the American Dream: A Social History of Housing in America* (New York: Pantheon, 1981), p. 99; and Ward, *Cities and Immigrants*, pp. 124–34. Case studies include: Margaret Sammartino Marsh, "Suburbanization and the Search for Community: Residential Decentralization in Philadelphia, 1880–1900," *Pennsylvania History* 44 (April 1977): 99–116; Robert J. Jucha, "The Anatomy of a Streetcar Suburb: A Development History of Shadyside, 1852–1916," *Western Pennsylvania Historical Magazine* 62 (October 1979): 301–19; Roger Miller and Joseph Siry, "The Emerging Suburb: West Philadelphia, 1850–1880," *Pennsylvania History* 47 (April 1980): 99–145; and Timothy J. Sehr, "Three Gilded Age Suburbs of Indianapolis: Irvington, Brightwood, and Woodruff Place," *Indiana Magazine of History* 77 (December 1981): 305–32.

28. Kenneth T. Jackson, "Metropolitan Government Versus Political Autonomy: Politics on the Crabgrass Frontier," in Kenneth T. Jackson and Stanley K. Schultz, eds., *Cities in American History* (New York: Alfred Knopf, 1972), pp. 445–48; and Howard Gillette, Jr., "The Emergence of the Modern Metropolis: Philadelphia in the Age of Consolidation," in William W. Cutler III and Howard Gillette, Jr., eds., *The Divided Metropolis: Social and Spatial Dimensions in Philadelphia, 1800–1975* (Westport, Conn.: Greenwood Press, 1980), pp. 3–25.

29. Karr, "Brookline," pp. 42ff.; Bessie Louise Pierce, *A History of Chicago*, vol. 3: *The Rise of the Modern City, 1871–1893* (New York: Knopf, 1957), pp. 332ff; Louis P. Cain, "To Annex or Not to Annex: A Tale of Two Cities: Evanston and Hyde Park," *Explorations in Economic History* 20 (January 1983): 58–72; Michael H. Ebner, "The Result of Honest Hard Work: Creating a Suburban Ethos for Evanston," *Chicago History* 13 (Summer 1984): 48–65; and Perry R. Duis, *The Saloon: Public Drinking in Chicago and Boston, 1880–1920* (Urbana: University of Illinois Press, 1983), pp. 204–29. Also consult with benefit: Arthur Evans Le Gacy, "Improvers and Preservers: A History of Oak Park, Illinois, 1833–1940" (Ph.D. dissertation, University of Chicago, 1967), pp. 53–124; Michael P. McCarthy, "The New Metropolis: Chicago, the Annexation Movement, and Progressive Reform," in Michael H. Ebner and Eugene M. Tobin, eds., *The Age of Urban Reform: New Perspectives on the Progressive Era* (Port Washington, N.Y.: Kennikat Press, 1977), pp. 43–54; Harry Jebsen, Jr., "Preserving Suburban Identity in an Expanding Metropolis: The Case of Blue Island, Illinois," *Old Northwest* 7 (1981):

139–42; Barbara M. Posadas, "Suburb into City: The Transformation of Urban Identity on Chicago's Periphery—Irving Park as a Case Study, 1870–1910," *Journal of the Illinois State Historical Society* 86 (Autumn 1983): 162–76; Adna F. Weber, *The Growth of Cities in the Nineteenth Century: A Study in Statistics* (New York: Columbia University Press, 1899), pp. 473–75; and Muller, *Contemporary Suburban America*, p. 30.

30. George W. Hilton and John Due, *The Electric Interurban Railways in America* (Stanford: Stanford University Press, 1960), p. 6; Glen E. Holt, "The Changing Perceptions of Urban Pathology: An Essay on the Development of Mass Transit in the United States," in Jackson and Schultz, eds., *Cities in American History*, p. 331; John P. McKay, *Tramways and Trolleys: The Rise of Urban Mass Transit in Europe* (Princeton: Princeton University Press, 1976), pp. 51, 71; Charles W. Cheape, *Moving the Masses: Urban Public Transit in New York, Boston, and Philadelphia, 1880–1912* (Cambridge, Mass.: Harvard University Press, 1980), pp. 118ff.; and Stilgoe, *Metropolitan Corridor*, p. 291.

31. Warner, *Streetcar Suburbs*, pp. 158–61.

32. Joel Schwartz, "Suburban Progressivism in the 1890s: The Policy of Containment in Orange, East Orange, and Montclair," in Schwartz and Prosser, eds., *Cities of the Garden State*, pp. 53–70; Michael H. Ebner, "Creating a Suburban Ethos for Chicago's North Shore, 1855–1900" (paper delivered at the annual meeting of the American Historical Association, December 29, 1984); and Joel A. Tarr, "From City to Suburb: The 'Moral' Influence of Transportation Technology," in Alexander B. Callow, ed., *American Urban History: An Interpretive Reader*, 2nd ed. (New York: Oxford University Press, 1973), pp. 202–12.

33. Mark S. Foster, *From Streetcar to Superhighway: American City Planners and Urban Transportation, 1900–1940* (Philadelphia: Temple University Press, 1981), pp. 18ff.

34. Jean-Pierre Bardou et al., *The Automobile Revolution: The Impact of an Industry*, trans. James M. Laux (Chapel Hill: University of North Carolina Press, 1982), pp. xiii–xv; Mark S. Foster, "The Automobile and the City," *Michigan Quarterly Review* 19–20 (Fall 1980 and Winter 1981): 461ff.; Glenn Yago, *The Decline of Urban Transportation in German and U.S. Cities, 1900–1970* (New York: Cambridge University Press, 1984), pp. 52ff.; and Holt, "Changing Perceptions of Urban Pathology," p. 333.

35. Warren J. Belasco, "Cars Versus Trains, 1980 and 1910," in George H. Daniels and Mark H. Rose, eds., *Energy and Transportation: Historical Perspectives on Policy Issues* (Beverly Hills: Sage, 1982), p. 44; Holt, "Changing Perceptions of Urban Pathology," p. 337.

36. William E. Leuchtenberg, *Perils of Prosperity, 1914–1932* (Chicago: University of Chicago Press, 1958), p. 186.

37. Charles N. Glaab, "Metropolis and Suburb: The Changing American City," in John Braeman et al., eds., *Change and Continuity in Twentieth-Century America: The 1920's* (Columbus: Ohio State University Press, 1968), pp. 402–8; Tarr, "Evolution of the Urban Infrastructure," pp. 35ff.; David Owen Wise and Marguerite Dupree, "The Choice of the Automobile for Urban Passenger Transportation: Baltimore in the 1920s," *South Atlantic Studies* 2 (1978): 153–79; and Daniel Prosser, "The New Downtowns: Commercial Architecture in Suburban New Jersey, 1920–1970," in Schwartz and Prosser, eds., *Cities of the Garden State*, p. 110.

38. Joel Schwartz, "The Evolution of the Suburbs," in Dolce, ed., *Suburbia*, pp. 21ff.; Graham Taylor, *Satellite Cities: A Study of Industrial Suburbs* (New York: D. Appleton, 1915), pp. 91–126; and Kenneth T. Jackson, "The Effects of Suburbanization

on Cities," in Dolce, *Suburbia*, p. 92. On the simultaneous location of another Allis-Chalmers plant on the periphery refer to Bayrd Still, *Milwaukee: The History of a City*, rev. ed. (Madison: State Historical Society of Wisconsin, 1965), p. 380.

39. Harlan Paul Douglass, *The Suburban Trend* (New York: Century Co., 1924), pp. 3ff.

40. Peter Marcuse, "Housing Policy and City Planning: The Puzzling Split in the United States, 1893–1931," in Gordon E. Cherry, ed., *Shaping an Urban World* (London: Mansell, 1980), pp. 23–58; Wright, *Building the American Dream*, p. 213; Glaab, "Metropolis and Suburb," pp. 418–23; Jackson, "Crabgrass Frontier," p. 210; and Schwartz, "Evolution of the Suburbs," p. 30.

41. John L. Thomas, *Alternative America: Henry George, Edward Bellamy, Henry Demarest Lloyd and the Adversary Tradition* (Cambridge, Mass.: Harvard University Press, 1983), pp. 358–61.

42. My discussion of Mumford is drawn from Park Dixon Goist, *From Main Street to State Street: Town, City, and Community in America* (Port Washington, N.Y.: Kennikat, 1977), pp.143–58, Blaine A. Brownell, "Urban Planning, the Planning Profession, and the Motor Vehicle in Early Twentieth-Century America," in Cherry, ed., *Shaping an Urban World*, p. 66, as well as Schaffer, *Garden Cities*, and Thomas, *Alternative America*.

43. Schaffer, *Garden Cities*, p. 13.

44. Mark I. Gelfand, *A Nation of Cities: The Federal Government and Urban America, 1933–1965* (New York: Oxford University Press, 1975), pp. 105–26; Blake McKelvey, *The Emergence of Metropolitan America, 1915–1966* (New Brunswick: Rutgers University Press, 1968), pp. 76–89; and Charles H. Trout, *Boston, the Great Depression, and the New Deal* (New York: Oxford University Press, 1977), p. 176.

45. Kenneth T. Jackson, "The Spatial Dimensions of Social Control: Race, Ethnicity, and Government Housing Policy in the United States, 1918–1968," in Bruce M. Stave, ed., *Modern Industrial Cities: History, Policy, and Survival* (Beverly Hills: Sage, 1981), pp. 84–109; George E. Mowry and Blaine A. Brownell, *The Urban Nation, 1920–1980*, rev. ed. (New York: Hill & Wang, 1981), pp. 79–110; and Barry D. Karl, *The Uneasy State: The United States from 1915 to 1945* (Chicago: University of Chicago Press, 1983), pp. 129ff.

46. Mark I. Gelfand, "Cities, Suburbs, and Government Policy," in Robert H. Bremner and Gary W. Reichard, eds., *Reshaping America: Society and Institutions, 1945–1960* (Columbus: Ohio State University Press, 1982), pp. 261–82; Jackson, "Crabgrass Frontier," pp. 217ff.; Mark H. Rose, *Interstate: Express Highway Politics, 1941–1956* (Lawrence: Regents Press of Kansas, 1976), passim, Robert A. Caro, *The Power Broker: Robert Moses and the Fall of New York* (New York: Alfred Knopf, 1974), pp, 947–50; Donald N. Steinnes, "Suburbanization and the 'Malling of America': A Time-Series Approach," *Urban Affairs Quarterly* 17 (June 1982): 401–18; and Prosser, "The New Downtowns," p. 119.

47. Polenberg, *One Nation Divisible*, pp. 128, 134, 180; Mohl, *New City*, pp. 195ff.; Kenneth T. Jackson, "The Capital of Capitalism: The New York Metropolitan Region, 1890–1940," in Anthony Sutcliffe, ed., *Metropolis, 1890–1940* (London: Mansell, 1984), p. 330; and Muller, *Contemporary Suburban America*, p. 133.

48. Carl Abbot, *The New Urban America: Growth and Politics in Sunbelt Cities* (Chapel Hill: University of North Carolina Press, 1982), pp. 1–14. Other additions to this literature include Gregory Jackson et al., *Regional Diversity; Growth in the United*

States, 1960–1990 (Boston: Auburn House Publishing Company, 1981); Bradford Luckingham, *The Urban Southwest: A Profile of Albuquerque, El Paso, Phoenix, and Tuscon* (El Paso: Texas Western Press, 1982); Richard M. Bernard and Bradley R. Rice, eds., *Sunbelt Cities: Politics and Growth since World War II* (Austin: University of Texas Press, 1983); and Carl Abbott, "Air Conditioned Growth Machines," *Journal of Urban History* 11 (February 1985): 235–44. For specific examples, see Howard N. Rabinowitz, "Growth Trends in the Albuquerque SMSA, 1940–1978," *Journal of the West* 18 (July 1979): 65ff.; Barry J. Kaplan, "Houston: The Golden Buckle of the Sunbelt," in Bernard and Rice, eds., *Sunbelt Cities*, p. 202; Kenneth T. Jackson, "A Nation of Suburbs," *Chicago History* 13 (Summer 1984): 10 (on Jacksonville, Florida); Michael Konig, "Phoenix in the 1950s, Urban Growth in the 'Sunbelt,' " *Arizona and the West* 24 (September 1982): 29; and Bradford Luckingham, "Phoenix: The Desert Metropolis," in Bernard and Rice, eds., *Sunbelt Cities*, p. 317.

49. Brian J. L. Berry, ed., *Urbanization and Counterurbanization*, vol. 11: Urban Affairs Annual Review (Beverly Hills: Sage, 1976), pp. 7–30; idem, "Inner-City Futures, An American Dilemma Revisited," in Stave, *Modern Industrial Cities*, pp. 187–219, and idem, *Comparative Urbanization: Divergent Paths in the Twentieth Century* (New York: St. Martin's, 1981), passim. Charles N. Glaab and A. Theodore Brown, *A History of Urban America*, 3rd ed. (New York: Macmillan, 1983), pp. 343–57, is singular in its historically minded treatment of urban-related population trends during the 1970s; also consult *New York Times*, December 12, 1981.

11 ──────── The Suburban Mosaic: Patterns of Land Use, Class, and Culture

CAROL A. O'CONNOR

In an annotated bibliography published in 1979, Joseph Zikmund II and Deborah Ellis Dennis characterize much of the scholarship on suburbia as "fugitive, faddish, and doctrinaire." In their view, too many works are not clearly labeled, and those that are too often address issues of immediate concern that bear little relation to earlier studies and that prompt scholars to bias their findings.[1] Yet if we concentrate on those studies considered lasting contributions and add several others published in the 1980s, a coherent core of suburban scholarship emerges. Despite the fragmentary nature of most research, historians, anthropologists, sociologists, economists, and geographers have attempted to analyze suburban patterns of land use and social class and the mosaic of differing class cultures that these patterns have created.

Although suburban life has a number of visible symbols, such as the detached house surrounded by lawn and the commuter car and freeway system, the assumption that a uniform suburban culture exists has never received much support among scholars except in a few works published in the 1950s. One of these, *The Organization Man* (1956) by William H. Whyte, Jr.,[2] proved especially influential, providing an air of authenticity to what Scott Donaldson has called the suburban myth.[3] The myth implies that all suburbs are middle-class, residential communities populated by harried commuters, their frustrated wives, and spoiled children. This view contributes to the humor of Erma Bombeck's *The Grass Is Always Greener over the Septic Tank*.[4] It pervades such novels as Sloan Wilson's *The Man in the Gray Flannel Suit* and Marilyn French's *The Women's Room*.[5] It serves as the basis for Malvina Reynolds' song, "Little Boxes":

> And the people in the boxes
> All went to the university
> Where they were put in boxes
> And they came out all the same,
> And there's doctors and there's lawyers
> And there's business executives,
> And they're all made out of ticky tacky
> And they all look just the same.[6]

Finally it underlies a parody, "Chicago Suburb," that appeared in *Mad* magazine in 1974:

> Hog Barbecuer for the World,
> School Segregator, Mower of Lawns,
> Player with Golf Clubs and the Nation's Wife Swapper;
> Bigoted, snobbish, flaunting
> Suburb of the White Collars.[7]

Perhaps, as Bennett M. Berger has argued, the suburban myth developed in the post–World War II era because it served the purposes both of the Right, which loved the suburbs, and of the Left, which loathed them.[8] It did not, however, reflect the complexity of suburban society either in the 1950s or the decades before or since.

Far more common among serious observers, including myself, is the notion that while a single class and its way of life might dominate one suburb and even part of a metropolitan region, other suburbs vary in the class composition and culture of their inhabitants. With the increasing urbanization of suburbia, this view has made its way even into popular magazines. Indeed, *Time* devoted a cover story to the topic, "Suburbia: A Myth Challenged," in 1971.[9] Among scholars, however, the view that suburbia consists of very different types of communities dates back to the early twentieth century. This assumption is implicit in Graham R. Taylor's *Satellite Cities*, which focuses on the conditions of workers in industrial suburbs like Gary, Indiana; Norwood, Ohio; and East St. Louis, Illinois.[10] It is central to Harlan Paul Douglass' *The Suburban Trend*, which distinguishes among "industrial," "residential," and "mixed" suburbs; "workers' suburbs and bosses' suburbs"; and "strikingly American suburbs" and "foreign and Negro suburbs." And it is a key organizing principle of George A. Lundberg, Mirra Komarovsky, and Mary Alice McInerny's *Leisure: A Suburban Study*, which divides the major communities of Westchester County, New York, into three categories: "wealthy residential suburbs," "middle class and poor residential suburbs,'' and ''satellite cities or mixed suburbs.''[11] Thus all of these early observers note the existence of relatively homogeneous local units within heterogeneous suburban regions.

The pioneering research on how this sorting out occurred belongs to a later era of the scholarship on the suburbs but examines an earlier phase of the migration to them. In *Streetcar Suburbs: The Process of Growth in Boston, 1870–1900*, Sam Bass Warner, Jr., looks at suburban development well before zoning laws and mass builders determined the character of whole communities. Nevertheless, he finds within each of the three suburbs he studies a striking degree of uniformity of class structure and land use patterns.

Warner ascribes this cohesiveness to two major causes: the economic requirements of those moving to the suburbs and the economic imperatives of those who built them. He argues, for example, that the strict transportation needs of the lower middle class restricted it to Boston's innermost suburbs. Because the work locations of many members of this group changed frequently and because a number of families depended on multiple employment for their advancement, the lower middle class required not only linear streetcar transportation but cross-town transportation as well. As a result, this class could move only to limited sites in the suburbs, later than wealthier groups but in such large numbers that they had to pay a premium for their land. In order to offset the high cost of their land, they converted single-family houses into multiple dwellings and, subdividing spare lots, erected three-decker tenements, two-family houses, and very small singles. Under these circumstances, Warner explains, the arrival of the lower middle class in a neighborhood drove out the middle and upper middle classes who could afford less crowding. As for the builders, Warner shows how the financial pressure of meeting short-term mortgages combined with aspects of their personal backgrounds to produce conformity to popular styles and adherence to neighborhood class patterns. Although more than 9,000 builders erected the 22,500 new dwellings of Roxbury, West Roxbury, and Dorchester, Warner says that ''from the extreme individualization of agency . . . came great uniformity of behavior.'' He describes the impact of this admittedly paradoxical process as a ''kind of regulation without laws.''

No synopsis of major themes can adequately convey the richness of *Streetcar Suburbs*. Based on extensive research in such sources as city directories, real estate deeds, building permits, and transit records, the book contains numerous charts, tables, and maps that support Warner's text without encumbering it. In addition, there are sixty-six photographs, many taken by the author himself, that portray shifts in architectural style and differences in the type and scale of houses for members of varying income groups. Yet while Warner is sensitive to the telling detail, he is also alert to the broadest implications of his subject. Because suburbanization broke down patterns of ethnic discrimination and brought improved living conditions to half the population of the metropolis, Warner sees it as having benefited society at least in the short run. But once most suburbs— unlike Roxbury, West Roxbury, and Dorchester—began to resist annexation to the city proper, then the existence of politically independent units segregated by class undermined the sense of there being "one great city," created barriers of mutual fear, and prevented the people of the metropolis from uniting to solve their problems.[12]

If some of Warner's conclusions sound commonplace today, it is because this book, written a generation ago, helped create the accepted wisdom. Yet while widely applauded, the book's theories were little tested. Only recently have a few historians begun to analyze whether Warner's arguments seem valid in other settings, and, as is often the case, these scholars arrive at different conclusions. For example, Robert J. Jucha finds that the evidence for the Shadyside district of late nineteenth-century Pittsburgh substantiates Warner's view that the multiplicity of participants in the building process helped produce neighborhoods segregated by class and uniform in architectural appearance.[13] Timothy J. Sehr, however, looking at three suburbs of Indianapolis, takes issue with Warner's argument. Sehr credits the decisions of the founders of Irvington, Brightwood, and Woodruff Place—rather than economic forces and shared class values—with determining the distinctive physical layout and class appeal of each of these neighborhoods. Yet although Sehr's Gilded Age focus is chronologically similar to Warner's and Jucha's, it is technologically awry. Irvington, Brightwood, and Woodruff Place were founded before the advent of streetcar service in Indianapolis. As Sehr says, this fact helps correct the misimpression that suburbanization began with the invention of the streetcar. But it also throws off the comparability of his study, for he is focusing on a period when suburbanization was not as intense. Still, with its analysis of three suburbs—one upper class, one middle class, and one working class—this is an exceptionally ambitious and interesting article. Sehr's discussion of articles of incorporation, plat maps, and real estate covenants goes far to explain how homogeneous neighborhoods developed in a varied suburban setting.[14]

Another author who has built on the insights of *Streetcar Suburbs* is Ronald Dale Karr. Looking at the Boston suburb of Brookline, Karr explains why it evolved into a more elite community than the suburbs Warner studied, located just to the south. According to Karr the upper middle class background of most developers, their willingness to adopt restrictive covenants, and a local tradition of elite rule and activist government worked to modify the influence of market forces in Brookline. With regard to the last point, Karr shows how, even before extensive regulation of building, a town exerted pressure on developers. If the town selectmen considered a subdivision to be below standard, they could create costly delays by withholding connection of the tract to the town's water, sewerage, street lighting, and gas systems. This occurred in the case of John J. McCormack's attempt to sell one hundred building lots of 5,000 to 7,000 square feet, proportions deemed too small for their location next to the country club. A more modest subdivision, promoted by two other Irish-Catholics but located near a streetcar barn, was accepted by the selectmen, however. Not even elite Brookline could insist on expensive development in substandard locations. As these comments suggest, Karr's article illumines the building patterns, political pressures, status differences, and ethnic antagonisms that prevailed in Brookline, and, we surmise, similar other communities.[15]

Of all the recent works on nineteenth-century suburbs, the most original is Henry C. Binford's *The First Suburbs: Residential Communities on the Boston Periphery, 1815–1860*. Set a half-century earlier than the other historical studies I have mentioned, *The First Suburbs* traces the evolution of Cambridge and Somerville from the time when they were part of Boston's rural-urban fringe through the 1850s when the proportion of commuters in the inner suburban work force was, according to Binford, greater than at any other point in history. The work discusses the range of economic activities in the fringe communities and the survival of many of the early industrial enterprises into the suburban era. But it also foreshadows the oncoming clash as members of the middle class increasingly felt compelled by the canons of domesticity not only to acquire a house but also to secure for it a "domestic setting"—with churches, parks, schools, and other houses but little industry.[16]

Although *The First Suburbs* does not address some of Sam Bass Warner's most intriguing hypotheses, it provides an effective supplement to Warner's study. Whereas in *Streetcar Suburbs*, growth seems to emanate from the city and to be city controlled, Binford shows how suburbanites contributed to the changes in the metropolis and adapted effectively to them. As this theme suggests, Binford pays more attention than did Warner to local issues, institutions, and leadership patterns, yet his is not a narrowly construed case study. Rather, in the best tradition of *Streetcar Suburbs*, Binford sets the experiences of Cambridge and Somerville in a broad metropolitan setting.

In addition to the analyses of nineteenth-century suburbs, the historical literature includes two books and an article that examine communities that developed in the twentieth century. One of these is Zane L. Miller's study of Forest Park, Ohio, a community whose history could not be further from that of Warner's streetcar suburbs.[17] Rather than thousands of participants in a building process that followed unconscious patterns, Forest Park had one developer, the Warner-Kantner Corporation, which proceeded according to a series of plans. Yet the growth of Forest Park was not the straightforward matter we might assume. Instead, many participants influenced the shape of the corporation's plans, and many factors affected their outcome.

As befitted an area originally intended as part of the greenbelt program of the New Deal, the plans for Forest Park aimed for a balance in industrial, commercial, and residential development. But although all of the parties interested in Forest Park's future agreed on this premise, they disagreed on the amounts of land to be allotted for various uses and particularly on the provision for multifamily, as opposed to single-family, housing construction. In other words, they differed regarding the mixture of income groups in Forest Park's population. Throughout the book, Miller effectively describes the clash of interests among planners, developers, citizens, and municipal officials. His analysis becomes especially absorbing in the chapters on the 1970s when issues of class and race combined with the impact of inflation and a downturn in the housing market to aggravate the differences among groups in the community.

Miller's book emphasizes the role of urban planning in Forest Park. Nevertheless, it contains useful insights on other issues such as the developers' early interest in creating a sense of community and the significance of the later establishment of a tax on earnings. Moreover, the work is informed by Miller's sure sense of broader developments in the Cincinnati metropolitan region of which Forest Park is part. Thus the reader is always aware that Forest Park is only one of many new suburbs vying to attract the limited number of clean industries, handsome office complexes, prestigious stores, and middle-class home buyers wanting to purchase sites on Cincinnati's circumferential interstate highway.

The intensive uses a community like Forest Park seeks to attract, an older group of more elite suburbs has been anxious to exclude. In "The Enduring Affluent Suburb," historical geographer Elizabeth K. Burns provides an introduction to the ways wealthy residential districts use such devices as local government incorporation, restrictive zoning, traffic planning, and architectural review boards.[18] Her discussion focuses on Hillsborough on the San Francisco Peninsula, with references to Lattingtown on Long Island, Scarsdale in Westchester County, Bryn Mawr on the Main Line, and Montecito near Santa Barbara.

A closer look at the reasoning behind and functioning of these devices can be found in my study, *A Sort of Utopia: Scarsdale, 1891–1981*. From early in its suburban history, Scarsdale's residents had a sense of its being "a high class residential [suburb], . . . an almost unique community." To preserve this sense of community identity, they zoned out industry in the 1920s, restricted 97 percent of the area of Scarsdale to the development of single-family houses, and regulated the quality and, indirectly, the cost of construction. Later, when mass production techniques threatened to open Scarsdale to a cheaper standard of construction, they added minimum acreage requirements and established an ordinance that prohibited excessive similarity of appearance in any neighborhood. Many of the community's other policies in areas as diverse as sanitation, education, and municipal finance reflected its domination by the upper middle class. Although my study uses local institutions, policies, and events to explicate the character of the community, it also pays attention to discordant elements: the pecking order of Scarsdale's subdivisions; the tensions among Protestants, Catholics, and Jews; and the relationship of the servant population to the rest of the community. In addition, my book consistently sets local events in the context of national developments—from progressivism, which was viewed favorably in Scarsdale; to the New Deal, which was loathed; to McCarthyism, which pointed up the liberalism of the majority of Scarsdale's residents; to the fractures of the 1960s, which ultimately defined the limits of that liberalism. Often these discussions enlarge our understanding of the mood of the era.[19]

Although the residents of Forest Park and Scarsdale differ markedly in their views of commercial and industrial development, they share an affection for the single-family detached house and an aversion to any type of residential development that deviates from it. In *Everything in Its Place: Social Order and Land Use in America*, anthropologist Constance Perin explores the cultural values underlying such attitudes. Based on extensive interviews with twenty-five people involved with land development either as public officials or as business executives and enriched by broad reading in the economics, sociology, and law of American land use, her arguments are always interesting and often persuasive.

The major contribution of Perin's book lies in its analysis of the renter-owner dichotomy. Although nearly all Americans are renters at some point in their lives, it is commonly thought that renters "live differently," "think differently," "don't care about the community," "are socially undesirable,"and are "just keeping afloat [financially]." Home owners, on the other hand, are seen as good citizens who "take better care of their property" and are "a step up the ladder of social as well as economic standing." In addition to calling attention to the fallacies behind some of these assumptions, Perin explains the reasons why people cling to them. In her view, the very fluidity of American society hardens people who were once renters against the group they came from. Moreover, the large investment most people have in their single-family houses causes them to oppose changes in the type of dwelling permitted in the community. Such opposition is not always maintained, however. Pointing out the discrepancy between the limited acreage some communities allot for apartments and the actual amount of land they devote to them, Perin suggests that developers often receive zoning variances not because they bribe municipal officials but because, given time and some concessions on the part of the developer, the already established residents adjust to the probable changes a new type of dwelling will make. Once allowed the role of gatekeeper through the ritual of a zoning appeal, the residents of a community, often as not, decide to "unlatch it."[20]

Obviously Perin would like to see additional low- and moderate-income housing in suburbia. Yet her book differs from most other studies of suburban land use and zoning written in the early to mid–1970s. While books like Anthony Downs' *Opening Up the Suburbs* and Michael Danielson's *The Politics of Exclusion* contain useful information, they excoriate current practices and present agendas for reform.[21] Perin, on the other hand, emphasizes understanding, not action. From her discussion of housing consumers as producers for the used-property market, to her comparison of the landlord-tenant relationship, to the banker–home owner relationship, Perin provides ideas, images, and insights that students of suburbia will find fascinating.

Another work that challenges us to reconsider our basic assumptions is *Shaky Palaces: Homeownership and Social Mobility in Boston's Suburbanization*. Of major concern to its authors—Matthew Edel, Elliott D. Sclar, and Daniel Luria— is the welfare of the working class. In their view, suburbanization and home ownership have brought this group of Americans inflexibility, isolation, and debt rather than stability, community, and a sound investment. The authors' most impressive piece of research is a study of changes in real estate values in met-ropolitan Boston from 1870 to 1970. In the long run these values tended to follow the rate of inflation, with the property in wealthy suburbs more likely to appreciate than the property in working-class suburbs. Far less convincing, how-ever, is the authors' treatment of the rise of suburbanization as a "compromise solution" to the labor-capitalist conflicts of the late nineteenth century. Still, with its left-wing economic analysis of the interconnections among such factors as home ownership, education, property taxes, job opportunities, and social mobility, this work offers a number of provocative insights.[22]

Given the idealization of the single-family house in American society, however ill founded that idealization might be, it is hardly surprising that the U.S. gov-ernment has attempted to spread the blessings of home ownership to a large percentage of its citizens. Although Perin, along with Edel, Sclar, and Luria, refers to the impact of some of these policies, the articles of historian Kenneth T. Jackson discuss them more thoroughly. In "A Nation of Suburbs," the best single article on the distinctiveness of suburbanization in the United States, Jackson highlights the role of the Internal Revenue Code in financing the growth of suburbia. By allowing taxpayers to deduct mortgage interest and property taxes but not rent from their income, the code provides, in Jackson's words, a "[staggering] subsidy to home ownership . . . [that] exceeds by four or five times all the direct expenditures Congress grants to housing."[23] Moreover, as Jackson shows in "Race, Ethnicity, and Real Estate Appraisal," federal programs of long-term, low-interest loans have also made it "cheaper to buy than to rent." But these loans have not been equally available for all sites and all citizens. Rather, "FHA guidelines and actual FHA assistance," at least to the mid–1960s, "favored new construction over existing dwellings, open land over developed areas, businessmen over blue-collar workers, whites over blacks, and native-born Americans over immigrants."[24]

The move to the suburbs of millions of Americans in the 1950s and 1960s, and the sociological literature it spawned, should be reconsidered in the light of these government policies. Especially interesting is the fact that writers who disagree on other matters find that their subjects moved where they did primarily for practical economic reasons. Even William H. Whyte, Jr., whose famous study of Park Forest, Illinois, helped create the suburban myth by presupposing a wide gulf between urban and suburban living says, "The people who went to Park Forest went there because it was the best housing for the money." Still, Whyte dispenses with this "eminently sensible" concern in a paragraph, devoting the rest of his study to the "significant extra"—a sense of belonging—that Park Forest provided to the transient "organization man" and his family.[25]

Other sociologists often give extended coverage to the practical economic concerns Whyte passes over so quickly. For example, S. D. Clark, who devotes an entire chapter of *The Suburban Society* to "The Choice of a Suburban Home," finds that the people who moved to the suburbs in the postwar era came from "old established residential areas" in the city, but, he says, "they wanted a house, and the only place they could find a house was in the suburbs.'' In *Class in Suburbia*, William M. Dobriner puts the situation more bluntly. For the newly married veteran, he says, ''suburbia . . . was simply survival and had very little to do with psychological selection or the pursuit of a conscious value.'' And in his monumental study, Herbert J. Gans lists the ''best house for the money'' as the major reason why buyers chose Levittown.[26] The fact that all of these authors agree that housing, not the social environment, attracted people to suburbia lends support to Kenneth Jackson's claim that federal government programs ''hastened the decay of inner-city neighborhoods by stripping them of much of the middle-class constituency.''[27]

Although the loss of middle-class residents might have had an especially damaging effect on big cities, more than the middle class moved to the suburbs in the 1950s and 1960s. Indeed, the fundamental contribution of the sociological literature of the era was to describe in detail what more serious observers had long assumed: that the culture of suburbs varied according to the class composition of their inhabitants. William Whyte's *Organization Man* is a key work not because the values of Park Forest have turned out to be, as he claims, ''harbingers of the way it's going to be,'' but because the intensive neighboring, intensive voluntarism, and intense conformity he describes are now seen as characteristic of upper middle-class communities with relatively young populations. Similarly in *Crestwood Heights*, John R. Seeley, R. Alexander Sim, and Elizabeth W. Loosley have presented not a ''study of the culture of suburban life,'' as they suggest in the book's subtitle, but a study of the values of upper middle-class suburban residents. Neither Bennett W. Berger's *Working-Class Suburb* nor William M. Dobriner's *Class in Suburbia* requires any change of title. The former, challenging Whyte's assertions about the impact of the suburban environment, shows how a group of auto workers, transferred from an urban to a suburban location, retained their political and religious identities and their working-class culture. The latter contrasts certain aspects of life in a recently built, increasingly working-class suburb—Levittown, New York—to an established community turned upper middle-class suburb—''Old Harbor'' (really Westport), Connecticut.[28]

Undoubtedly the most important work in this group is Herbert J. Gans' *The Levittowners*. Based largely on the author's experiences as a participant-observer in this New York suburb and supplemented by interviews, surveys, and broad reading, the book describes how Levittown evolved from the plans of its developers, through building and settlement, to the emergence of local institutions such as churches, schools, and political parties. As the subtitle suggests, this book analyzes the ''ways of life and politics'' in a single suburban community, not the way of life in all suburbs. Although, at the time of Gans' study, the predominant culture in Levittown was lower middle class, some residents were working class in occupation and life-style and a few upper middle class. Gans' shrewd observations allow him to compare the values and experiences of these three groups within a common community setting.[29]

Since the publication of *The Levittowners*, sociologists have turned away from suburban community studies and the subject of the quality of suburban life to examine the experiences of racial and ethnic minorities in the suburbs, the impact of suburban policies on the central city, and the question of change versus persistence in the status of suburban communities.[30] Of these topics, the position of blacks in suburbia has received the most attention from scholars. Indeed, Zikmund and Dennis devote two chapters of the 1979 bibliography and subsections of two additional chapters to this and other closely related topics.[31] Moreover, scholarly interest in the role of blacks in the suburbs has continued in recent years. The volumes of *America: History and Life* from 1980 to 1984 list twenty articles on the subject,[32] and a major study by Purdue University's John Stahura of blacks in 825 suburbs over thirty years is due out shortly.[33] Most researchers have found that nearly all moves by blacks, including those of the middle class, have been to predominantly black areas. Despite the existence of laws barring discrimination in the sale of real estate, blacks, according to Stahura, number only 2 percent or less of the population in 70 percent of the nation's suburbs.

A book that draws on both the community studies of the postwar era and the more metropolitan scholarship of the 1970s is *Contemporary Suburban America* by geographer Peter O. Muller. Although Muller's primary interest lies in the process of counterurbanization, he also addresses the human consequences of "this momentous transformation." Regarding this topic, Muller's views are mixed. On the one hand, he criticizes suburban zoning laws and discriminatory practices that limit the access of the poor and blacks to area housing and, consequently, to the growing proportion of the metropolis's jobs that are now located in suburbia. On the other hand, he applauds the suburbs for providing the "most comfortable mass-living conditions ever achieved" and doing so for an increasingly heterogeneous population.

Muller's book is at its best in discussing the patterned diversity or mosaic culture of contemporary suburbia. Dividing suburban communities into eight categories ranging from exclusive upper-income districts to satellite cities and black spillover suburbs, he argues that these types of communities can be found in metropolitan regions throughout the United States, and he implies that a resident of a cosmopolitan suburb like Princeton, New Jersey, would be likely to choose a similar suburb—say, Evanston—in the event of a move to Chicago. In addition, Muller calls attention to the recent proliferation of specialized subdivisions such as retirement compounds and singles-oriented apartment complexes. These challenge the old myth of suburbia as a place strictly for families with children.[34]

Yet in Muller's excitement over the dramatic urbanization of suburbia that has recently occurred and the intensifying heterogeneity this change has brought about, there is a danger that readers might overlook a fact that Muller acknowledges but I would stress: the differences that have always existed among suburbs. With the possible exception of black spillover suburbs, the community types Muller describes probably existed in the earliest days of suburbanization, and although retirement compounds and singles complexes might be new phenomena, "old people's suburbs and young people's suburbs" existed at least as far back as the 1920s.[35] Not only has there always been considerable diversity among suburbs, but it is possible that individual suburbs, especially at the more elite end of the scale, used to be more heterogeneous than they are today. Certainly this was true of nineteenth-century Brookline where the Irish half of the population worked as day laborers and domestic servants for the upper middle-class Yankees and upper-class Brahmins. It was also true of Scarsdale in the days before World War II when live-in servants composed 18 percent of the population and the cost of houses in some neighborhoods was within reach of members of the lower middle class.[36] As for the ethnic diversity of contemporary suburbia, it is likely that what we are witnessing now is merely the latest stir of Sam Bass Warner, Jr.'s, "selective melting pot."[37] Just as second- and third-generation Irish succeeded in moving into Roxbury, West Roxbury, and Dorchester in the late nineteenth century, so second- and third-generation Italians and Jews moved to the suburbs in the years after World War II.

To understand the degree to which contemporary suburbia builds on the patterns of the past, we need more studies that are both longitudinal and cross-sectional. Michael H. Ebner's work in progress on the evolution of Chicago's North Shore from 1831 to 1900 is a significant step in this direction.[38] Since his research design takes in not only the eight upper- and upper middle-class communities traditionally designated the North Shore suburbs but also industrial Waukegan, two federal defense installations, and the working-class communities of Highwood and North Chicago, his study promises to provide a sense of both the subtle differences among the eight contiguous suburbs and their relationship to their less affluent neighbors along the shoreline. Ebner's work, placing the North Shore in its metropolitan context, is just the beginning, however. A study of Fairfield County, Connecticut, or Westchester County, New York, especially in the years since World War II, could tell us much about the urbanization of the suburbs as well as test the selective melting pot theory. The same could be said of studies of any number of suburban counties in major metropolitan areas.

As Kenneth Jackson has shown, suburbia is one of the most distinctive aspects of American society.[39] Scholars seeking to understand the nexus between this nation's abundant land, material wealth, democratic ideals, and exclusionary practices can find no better field for study.

Notes

1. Joseph Zikmund II and Deborah Ellis Dennis, *Suburbia: A Guide to Information Sources* (Detroit: Gale Research, 1979), pp. xi–xiii. With thoughtful descriptions of over 400 books and articles, this bibliography is an essential reference work for scholars in the field. Works are divided into the following categories: general studies; metropolitan growth and development; community case studies; suburban demography; blacks in suburbia; political considerations; education in the schools; economic considerations; sociological factors; race, housing, and zoning; and new towns.

2. William H. Whyte, Jr., *The Organization Man* (New York: Simon and Schuster, 1956). See also John R. Seeley, R. Alexander Sim, and Elizabeth W. Loosley, *Crestwood Heights: A Study of the Culture of Suburban Life* (New York: Basic Books, 1956), and David Reisman, "The Suburban Sadness," in William M. Dobriner, ed., *The Suburban Community* (New York: G. P. Putnam's Sons, 1958), pp. 375–408.

3. Scott Donaldson, *The Suburban Myth* (New York: Columbia University Press, 1969). Although its defensive tone now seems dated and although it would be possible to write a new book on the subject based on materials from the 1970s and 1980s, Donaldson's study provides the one outstanding analysis of both popular and scholarly images of suburbia.

4. Erma Bombeck, *The Grass Is Always Greener over the Septic Tank* (New York: McGraw-Hill, 1976).

5. Sloan Wilson, *The Man in the Gray Flannel Suit* (New York: Simon and Schuster, 1955); Marilyn French, *The Women's Room* (New York: Summit Books, 1977). See also Kathryn Louise Riley, "The Use of Suburbia as a Setting in the Fiction of John O'Hara, John Cheever, and John Updike" (Ph.D. diss., University of Maryland, 1981).

6. From the song "Little Boxes." Words and music by Malvina Reynolds, © 1962 Schroder Music Co. (ASCAP), Berkeley, CA 94710. Used by permission. All rights reserved.

7. Reproduced by permission of MAD, copyright © 1974, E.C. Publications Inc. The entire text of Carl Sandbag's "Chicago Suburb," accompanied by an appropriately mawkish illustration, is reprinted in Peter O. Muller, *Contemporary Suburban America* (Englewood Cliffs, N.J.: Prentice-Hall, 1981), p. 2.

8. Bennett M. Berger, "Suburbia and the American Dream," *Public Interest* 1 (Winter 1966): 82–83.

9. "Suburbia: The New American Plurality," *Time*, March 15, 1971, 14–20.

10. Graham R. Taylor, *Satellite Cities: A Study of Industrial Suburbs* (New York: Appleton, 1915). For another early study of an industrial suburb, see Margaret F. Byington, *Homestead: The Households of a Mill Town* (1910; Pittsburgh: University of Pittsburgh Press, 1974). For a more recent study, see Stanley Buder, *Pullman: An Experiment in Industrial Order and Community Planning, 1880–1930* (New York: Oxford University Press, 1967).

11. Harlan Paul Douglass, *The Suburban Trend* (New York: Century, 1925), chaps. 3–4; George A. Lundberg, Mirra Komarovsky, and Mary Alice McInerny, *Leisure: A Suburban Study* (New York: Columbia University Press, 1934), chap. 2, appendixes A and B.

12. Sam Bass Warner, Jr., *Streetcar Suburbs: The Process of Growth in Boston, 1870–1900* (Cambridge, Mass.: Harvard University Press, 1962), pp. 56–58, 117, 157,163–68.

13. Robert J. Jucha, "The Anatomy of a Streetcar Suburb: A Development History of Shadyside," *Western Pennsylvania Historical Magazine* 62 (October 1979): 301–19. For a study of a Cincinnati suburb that emerged with improvements in transportation and that was later annexed by the city it served, see Henry D. Shapiro and Zane L. Miller, *Clifton: Neighborhood and Community in an Urban Setting* (Cincinnati: Laboratory in American Civilization, 1976).

14. Timothy J. Sehr, "Three Glided Age Suburbs of Indianapolis: Irvington, Brightwood, and Woodruff Place," *Indiana Magazine of History* 77 (December 1981): 305–32.

15. Ronald Dale Karr, "Brookline and the Making of an Elite Suburb," *Chicago History* 13 (Summer 1984): 36–47.

16. Henry C. Binford, *The First Suburbs: Residential Communities on the Boston Periphery, 1815–1860* (Chicago: University of Chicago Press, 1985), pp. 127, 174. For another look at early suburbs, see John Archer, "Country and City in the American Romantic Suburb," *Journal of the Society of Architectural Historians* 42 (May 1983): 139–56.

17. Zane L. Miller, *Suburb: Neighborhood and Community in Forest Park, Ohio, 1935–1976* (Knoxville: University of Tennessee Press, 1981). For a study of a planned community of the 1920s and 1930s, see Daniel Schaffer, *Garden Cities for America: The Radburn Experience* (Philadelphia: Temple University Press, 1982).

18. Elizabeth K. Burns, "The Enduring Affluent Suburb," *Landscape* 24, no. 1 (1980): 33–41.

19. Carol A. O'Connor, *A Sort of Utopia: Scarsdale, 1891–1981* (Albany: State University of New York Press, 1983), pp. 15, 30–42, 159–65.

20. Constance Perin, *Everything in Its Place: Social Order and Land Use in America* (Princeton: Princeton University Press, 1976), pp. 34, 46, 35, 129, 134, 149, 181, 183.

21. Anthony Downs, *Opening Up the Suburbs: An Urban Strategy for America* (New Haven: Yale University Press, 1973), and Michael N. Danielson, *The Politics of Exclusion* (New York: Columbia University Press, 1976).

22. Matthew Edel, Elliott D. Sclar, and Daniel Luria, *Shaky Palaces: Homeownership and Social Mobility in Boston's Suburbanization* (New York: Columbia University Press, 1984).

23. Kenneth T. Jackson, "A Nation of Suburbs," *Chicago History* 13 (Summer 1984): 6–25.

24. Kenneth T. Jackson, "Race, Ethnicity, and Real Estate Appraisal: The Home Owners Loan Corporation and the Federal Housing Administration," *Journal of Urban History* 6 (Winter 1980): 432, 437. An expanded version of this essay appears as "The Spatial Dimensions of Social Control: Race, Ethnicity, and Government Housing Policy in the United States, 1918–1968," in Bruce M. Stave, ed., *Modern Industrial Cities: History, Policy, and Survival* (Beverly Hills: Sage Publications, 1981), pp. 79–128.

25. Whyte, *Organization Man*, pp. 313–14.

26. S. D. Clark, *The Suburban Society* (Toronto: University of Toronto Press, 1966), pp. 49, 222; William M. Dobriner, *Class in Suburbia* (Englewood Cliffs, N.J.: Prentice-Hall, 1963), p. 78; Herbert J. Gans, *The Levittowners: Ways of Life and Politics in a New Suburban Community* (New York: Random House, Vintage ed., 1967), p. 32.

27. Jackson, "Race, Ethnicity, and Real Estate Appraisal," p. 433.

28. Whyte, *Organization Man*, p. 311; Seeley, Sim, and Loosley, *Crestwood Heights*; Bennett M. Berger, *Working-Class Suburb: A Study of Auto Workers in Suburbia* (Berkeley and Los Angeles: University of California Press, 1960); Dobriner, *Class in Suburbia*.

29. Gans, *The Levittowners*, esp. chaps. 2, 8–11.

30. Representative articles include Phillip L. Clay, "The Process of Black Suburbanization," *Urban Affairs Quarterly* 14 (June 1979): 405–24; Kathryn P. Nelson, "Recent Suburbanization of Blacks: How Much, Who, and Where?" *Journal of the American Planning Association* 46 (July 1980): 287–300; John R. Logan and Mark Schneider, "Racial Segregation and Racial Change in American Suburbs, 1970–1980," *American Journal of Sociology* 89 (January 1984): 874–88; Avery M. Guest, "The Suburbanization of Ethnic Groups," *Sociology and Social Research* 64 (July 1980): 497–513; John Patrick

Roche, "Suburban Ethnicity: Ethnic Attitudes and Behavior among Italian Americans in Two Suburban Communities," *Social Science Quarterly* 63 (March 1982): 145–53; Carol Agocs, "Who's in on the American Dream? Ethnic Representation in Suburban Opportunity Structures in Metropolitan Detroit, 1940–1970," *Ethnic Groups* 4 (October 1982): 239–54; Avery M. Guest, "Suburban Social Status: Persistence or Evolution?" *American Sociological Review* 43 (April 1978): 251–63; Harvey M. Choldin, Claudine Hanson, and Robert Bohrer, "Suburban Status Instability," *American Sociological Review 45 (December 1980): 972–83; John R. Logan and Mark Schneider, "The Stratification of Metropolitan Suburbs, 1960–1970," American Sociological Review* 46 (April 1981): 175–86.

31. Zikmund and Dennis *Suburbia, chaps*.5,7, 9, 10.

32. *America: History and Life: Part D, Annual Index* 17 (1980): 416; 18 (1981): 432; 19 (1982): 448; 20 (1983): 370; 21 (1984): 370.

33. John M. Stahura, "Status Transition of Blacks and Whites in American Suburbs," *Sociological Quarterly* 23 (Winter 1982): 79–93; idem, "Determinants of Change in the Distribution of Blacks across Suburbs," *Sociological Quarterly* 24 (Summer 1983): 421–33; idem, "Blacks Still Segregated in Suburbs," *USA Today*, November 30, 1984.

34. Muller, *Contemporary Suburban America*, pp. x, 81–114, 15–16, 80–81, 62–81.

35. Douglass, *Suburban Trend*, pp. 99–101.

36. Karr, "Brookline," pp. 37–38; O'Connor, *A Sort of Utopia*, pp. 100–109.

37. Warner, *Streetcar Suburbs*, chap. 4.

38. Some of Michael H. Ebner's findings are already available. See " 'In the Suburbes of Toun:' Chicago's North Shore to 1871," *Chicago History* 11 (Summer 1982): 66–77; idem, "The Result of Honest Hard Work: Creating a Suburban Ethos for Evanston," *Chicago History* 13 (Summer 1984): 48–65; and idem, "Creating a Suburban Ethos for Chicago's North Shore, 1855–1900" (paper presented at the annual meeting of the American Historical Association, Chicago, December 29, 1984).

39. Jackson, "Nation of Suburbs," pp. 10–25.

12 —————— The Neighborhood-City Relationship

PATRICIA MOONEY MELVIN

Despite its conceptual elusiveness, the neighborhood figures prominently in America's urban consciousness. During the urban crisis of the 1960s, the neighborhood became the rallying ground for numerous schemes to revitalize the nation's urban centers. Not surprisingly scholars in a range of disciplines, including sociology, geography, and political science, undertook neighborhood programs. Although these studies approached the neighborhood from a variety of perspectives, they shared a common characteristic. Whether polemical, descriptive, or analytical, these works were ahistorical. We can learn from them much about a particular neighborhood's experience or about neighborhoods in general in a particular moment in time. Historians, however, have now begun to examine the neglected historical and urban context of neighborhood dynamics. This work has shed new light on changing conceptions of neighborhoods and on the shifting views of the relationship between neighborhoods and the city.

Neighborhoods emerged as identifiable units of concern in the American cityscape at that point when urban centers underwent the transformation from the pedestrian city of the eighteenth and early nineteenth centuries to the expanded and differentiated urban structure of the early twentieth century. A few scholars, such as Carl Abbott, suggest that neighborhoods existed as early as the colonial era. Based on an analysis of land use patterns in pre-Revolutionary New York

City, Abbott argued in 1974 that the city was characterized by a series of concentric zones in which urban dwellers were sorted out on the basis of wealth and economic activity.[1] Most students of the American city, however, date the emergence of neighborhood consciousness with the demise of the walking city. Sam Bass Warner, Jr., for example, argues in *Streetcar Suburbs* that Boston, like other American cities, was small, compact, and relatively integrated before 1860.[2] Philadelphia, poised on the brink of metropolitan development in the 1850s, as Howard Gillette, Jr., suggests, was also compact and crowded. Under such conditions, Philadelphia, like Boston, was a "community experienced directly and informally."[3] Rudimentary transportation technology made walking cities of urban areas before the Civil War. In antebellum New Orleans, New York, and Cincinnati, the location of social, economic, religious, or political activities depended on the time it took to walk from one place to another. As a result, these settlements, despite the density of their populations, rarely exceeded a two-mile radius from the center of the community. The absence of rapid modes of intracity transportation made it difficult for urban dwellers to segregate themselves from one another as neatly as Abbott suggests and inhibited the development of a neighborhood consciousness based on the specialization of land uses along commercial, manufacturing, and residential lines.

Between 1840 and 1880, a series of transportation innovations broke the casement of the walking city. As Jon C. Teaford, Joel A. Tarr, Sam Bass Warner, Jr., and Clay McShane ably demonstrate, these innovations offered the elites and later, when less costly, the middling classes the opportunity to abandon the crowded conditions of the walking city. First the omnibus, then the steam community railroad, the horsecar, inclined plane, and cable cars provided small numbers of urbanites with residential options. With the electrification of the horsecar in the 1880s, these transportation innovations combined with increased immigration and internal migration to transform the American cityscape. As late nineteenth-century cities ballooned, their internal structure became characterized by distinct units, and those units that included residential structures became known as neighborhoods.[4] To put it another way, as David Goldfield has suggested in an effort to place the neighborhood in historical perspective for contemporary policymakers, "the development of neighborhoods reflected an increasingly fragmented city."[5]

With the emergence of residential neighborhoods as identifiable units, interest grew in their definition and role in the life of the metropolis. Contemporaries witnessing the development of the modern city were the first to subject the neighborhood to scrutiny. Among turn-of-the-century commentators, Robert A. Woods and Wilbur C. Phillips developed detailed analyses of the neighborhood, its relationship to the larger city of which it was a part, and its role in the nation. Woods contended in essays, "The City and the Local Community" and "The Neighborhood in Social Reconstruction," that the city was a "cluster of interlacing communities" (or neighborhoods), "each having its own vital ways of expression and action, but altogether creating the municipality which shall render the fullest service through the most spirited participation of all its residents."[6] Phillips examined the neighborhood in his autobiographical work, *Adventuring for Democracy*. Like Woods, Phillips visualized the nation as a grand union of neighborhoods that, when linked, comprised cities, counties, states, and ultimately the nation as a whole.[7] Based on their analyses of the urban environment in which they worked, Woods and Phillips identified the neighborhood as a discrete entity that operated in a complementary manner to form the larger metropolis.

Historians of the city in this period have analyzed the work of early twentieth-century students of the city, explored the ways in which these individuals put their beliefs about the city into action, and occasionally detailed their views of the relationship between neighborhoods and the city. Jean B. Quandt examined the way in which a number of intellectuals attempted to come to terms with the city in turn-of-the-century America. She argues that some progressive thinkers articulated a vision of a unified, cooperative community, and that these intellectuals consciously attempted to move society in that direction. On the city level as well as on the national level, according to Quandt, these progressives drew on their beliefs about the virtues of small town values and through their propagation hoped to create a unified civic community.[8] A study of the social unit plan, initiated by Wilbur C. Phillips in Cincinnati, suggests as well the existence of a relationship between conceptions of the city and strategies of community organization. Phillips' social unit plan represented an attempt to develop a structure through which the neighborhood could interact with the larger city so as to create a unified civic community.[9] And Mark Goldman's essay on Buffalo, New York's, Black Rock neighborhood points to the interaction between conceptions of urban structure and the direction of neighborhood activities.[10] In his larger examination of the history of Buffalo, Goldman finds, as I did in my study of Phillips' social unit plan, that changes in the way cities were viewed after 1920 created a shift in beliefs about the neighborhood and its function in the city.[11] In short, the relationship between the neighborhood and the city is not static but related to particular historical periods.

By the mid-1920s, a variety of forces seemed to be pulling cities apart and, in so doing, produced an urban form characterized by particularism rather than by the unifying interaction described by Woods, Phillips, and their contemporaries. Scholars interested in the urban environment, particularly those at the University of Chicago, found the city of the 1920s to be marked, as Gerald Suttles suggests, by a "broad pattern of segregation and sub-community formation."[12] A variety of studies by Chicago sociologists Robert E. Park, Ernest Burgess, Louis Wirth, Roderick D. McKenzie, and Harvey W. Zorbaugh, an excellent sampling of which can be found in volumes edited by Burgess and Park,[13] revealed the view that neighborhoods operated within the larger city structure as "natural areas": communities defined in terms of the "common experiences of the group," which evoked a sense of "territorial parochialism."[14]

One of the earliest manifestations of the new view of the neighborhood and the city can be found in the work of Roderick D. McKenzie. In *The Neighbor-hood: A Study of Local Life in the City of Columbus, Ohio*, McKenzie argued that neighborhoods were fragmented by "economic, racial, and cultural factors" and that these factors provided the only points of identification for neighborhood residents.[15] When neighborhood groups organized, McKenzie found, they generally sought to protect the community from outside influences or groups. Despite this orientation, McKenzie believed, as Christopher Silver has noted, that neighborhood planning focused on the demarcation of an identifiable physical unit that could allow the neighborhood to serve as the basis for the delivery of a variety of municipal services while at the same time enhancing local solidarity.[16] Despite his emphasis on neighborhood parochialism, McKenzie's suggestion of using the neighborhood as a local distributor of municipal services recognized neighborhoods as part of a larger metropolitan structure. As some historians have argued,[17] the city to McKenzie was an organism "essentially pluralistic in its composition, as much the product of competition as of cooperation."[18]

Fellow Chicago sociologist Harvey W. Zorbaugh agreed with McKenzie that neighborhoods were parochial in nature, but unlike McKenzie, whose study represents a transitional piece, Zorbaugh portrayed neighborhoods as islands apart from the larger city. Little hope exists in his work, *The Gold Coast and the Slum*, for any positive neighborhood-city interaction. Zorbaugh based his conclusions on an examination of the experiences of one of Chicago's Community Councils of National Defense, the Lower North Community Council (LNCC). Immediately after World War I, community organizers continued their efforts to stimulate democratic collaborative service and resident neighborhood organization in the area served by the LNCC. Organizers soon found, however, that the community organization theories of people like Robert Woods and Wilbur Phillips seemed inappropriate in the Chicago of the 1920s. The theories of Woods, Phillips, and their contemporaries, which looked at the urban environment in terms of "hypothetical common interests and needs," failed to confront the realities of urban life. Instead, cities appeared to be conglomerations of groups intent on protecting their own interests rather than working for the interests of the community at large. Zorbaugh concluded from his study of the LNCC that the urban community was not an integrated whole but was composed rather of "mosaics of little cultural worlds" in which most areas ignored rather than cooperated with the larger society of which they were a part.[19]

Zorbaugh's interpretation, which negated the neighborhood experience as a central element in the promotion of metropolitan identification, fit nicely with the studies undertaken by Robert E. Park and Ernest W. Burgess. Their concern with neighborhoods as natural areas led them to undertake studies that focused on the social and spatial patterns of neighborhood residents. This, in turn, led Park and Burgess essentially to depict the neighborhood as a handy container.[20] As William P. Hojnacki suggests in "What Is a Neighborhood?" Park, Burgess, and their followers conducted some of the earliest scientific examinations of neighborhood life.[21] At the same time, their studies found little relationship between the neighborhoods under scrutiny and the city of which they formed a part, and this view, which divorced the neighborhood from the city, resulted in the creation of a literature that essentially ignored the fact that neighborhoods were part of a larger structure.

The view of the neighborhood and the city that emerged during the 1920s fell out of favor during the 1930s. As Rebecca Smith suggests in her 1982 study of comparative neighborhood perspectives, the general crisis over the apparent loss of community during the 1930s and 1940s was accompanied by a shift away from viewing the neighborhood as a central element in American cities toward an increasing concern about metropolitan or regional units. Such a shift dampened research efforts that focused on the neighborhood and its role in the American urban structure.[22] Louis Wirth, for example, argued against planning on the neighborhood level. Given the "technological and cultural" trends of modern society, Wirth wrote, it was impossible to return to a "local self-contained neighborhoodly community."[23] Instead planning should focus on the city or regional level. And Jesse Steiner, who had captured the spirit of the formative years of neighborhood work with its emphasis on the local community and cooperation between all levels of society in his 1925 study of community organization, challenged the importance of the neighborhood as an integral unit of American life as the 1920s drew to a close.[24] Technological innovations, he argued, had rendered the neighborhood obsolete. "Our eyes are now turned toward the outer world of larger contacts," Steiner wrote in 1929, "instead of seeking satisfaction within a narrow circle." Community leaders, Steiner believed, should cease attempts to bring neighborhood residents together.[25]

A close examination of recent urban history textbooks suggests both that the neighborhood ceased to be regarded as an important element in the city during the 1930s and that some historians have accepted those views at face value. As a result, little attention has been directed toward analyzing the historical experience of the neighborhood between the world wars. These texts tend either merely to describe neighborhoods, as in Blake McKelvey's *The Emergence of Metropolitan America, 1915-1966* or in Charles N. Glaab and A. Theodore Brown's *A History of Urban America*, or they concentrate on the shift from the walking city to the modern metropolis and the neighborhood movement after 1960.[26] In his text, Howard P. Chudacoff stresses the emergence of the neighborhood in the late nineteenth century.[27] Manuel Castells' *The Urban Question: A Marxist Approach* essentially ignores neighborhoods as important units of the city until the resurgence of neighborhood organizing during the 1960s.[28] And Sam Bass Warner, Jr.'s, discussion of neighborhoods in *The Urban Wilderness* takes a socioreligious approach that centers on the role of the neighborhood in the process of acculturation.[29] Only in *The Urbanization of Modern America* is the neighborhood and its relationship to the city examined from its emergence in the late nineteenth century to the recent burst of neighborhood organizing.[30]

With this exception, these works examine only one aspect or another of America's neighborhood experience and, in so doing, suggest that the neighborhood as an operative unit of the city appeared either before 1930 or after 1960.

Recent research on neighborhoods paints a different picture. It indicates that neighborhoods remained important between the two world wars and that some neighborhood residents thought of the neighborhood in relation to, rather than divorced from, the city. Mark Naison explores the role of the Communist party in mobilizing community activity for social change in Harlem during the 1930s. Although the Communists failed to build a strong and enduring party in Harlem, their activities nonetheless galvanized Harlem residents to press for a variety of programs in the neighborhood, workplace, and political arena and to do so in such a way as not to isolate the various elements of home, work, and city from each other.[31] In a 1981 essay, James Borchert urged scholars to look beyond formal neighborhood organizations in order to understand the dynamics of neighborhood life for groups other than the middle class. Through an examination of black working-class migrants in Washington, D.C., Borchert suggests that the sheer magnitude of the problems faced by alley dwellers forced these urban migrants to create a series of informal institutions and primary groups that bound the residents together into a cooperative unit. Although he is careful to point out that the alley communities had life cycles during which any given area could move from cooperative interaction among residents to very loosely associated groups, Borchert believes that it is possible, using nontraditional historical sources and conceptual frameworks developed by other social scientists, to trace over time a lively neighborhood life even in poorer areas of the city.[32] And Lyle Koehler's examination of the Cincinnati neighborhood of Westwood, like my own research on Cincinnati's local improvement associations, indicates that neighborhood attachment, although its forms changed, remained an important point of identification for city residents during the interwar era.[33]

These studies underscore the fact that neighborhood activity persisted during the period when social scientists studying urban areas often discounted its importance in understanding the city. Other examinations of neighborhood life in this same period suggest that some neighborhood residents believed not only in local mobilization but also in establishing alliances among neighborhood groups. Joesph A. Spencer, in a study of tenant organization and housing reform in New York city, explores the experience of New York City's first permanent coalition of neighborhood-based tenant groups and traces the coalition's attempts to preserve living spaces, thwart evictions, stem rent increases, and end code violations in a variety of New York City neighborhoods.[34]

Despite the decline of interest among academics in the study of neighborhoods and their role in American urban life during the 1930s, members of the nascent American planning profession displayed a lively interest in the neighborhood and its place in the nation's urban structure. In general, planners' discussions of the neighborhood centered around the notion of the neighborhood unit plan formulated by Clarence A. Perry during the 1920s. Receiving its most complete description in Perry's 1929 contribution to *The Regional Survey of New York and Its Environs*, "The Neighborhood Unit, A Scheme of Arrangement for the Family Life Community," the neighborhood unit idea stressed the importance of integrating social and physical planning at the neighborhood level.[35] However, when planners began to integrate Perry's ideas into specific urban planning projects, they focused less on his interest in the neighborhood's role in social reconstruction and more on his discussion of the physical arrangement of urban space. By the late 1940s, planners concentrated on the identification of city parts, or units, in order to construct a framework for a tidy and a controlled urban landscape. Ruth Glass, for instance, in *The Social Background of a Plan*, argued that the neighborhood was a "distinctive territorial group," with the stress clearly on territory.[36] As Judith Tannenbaum noted in 1948, even Perry's most vigorous champions stressed that the major value of the neighborhood plan was "along physical lines, with social benefits as convenient afterthoughts."[37] The emphasis on territory was not new; earlier discussions of the neighborhood stressed the importance of territory in neighborhood definition. But planners elevated territory from one of many components in the definition of a neighborhood to the pre-eminent element. They were interested in constructing the neighborhood as a container. What happened inside this container was of little interest.

The changing historical context in which the shift from the neighborhood unit as a social as well as a physical unit toward the purely territorial view of the neighborhood is analyzed by Howard Gillette, Jr. In examining the evolution of neighborhood planning leading up to the 1949 Housing Act, Gillette shows how neighborhood planning became an instrument not for social reconstruction but for disruption.[38] Since this shift in beliefs about the neighborhood unit informed policymakers, Gillette has increased our understanding of the shape of legislation that had a major impact on neighborhood planning in the 1950s. His study, one of the few historical studies of the neighborhood covering the period between 1920 and 1960, reminds us that ideas about the neighborhood do not exist in a vacuum but instead are shaped by the particular historical contexts in which they operate.

Yet the planners' view of the neighborhood did not go unchallenged. Concurrent with the emphasis on territory rose a defense of local attachment based not on territory but rather on a fluid sense of identification, shifting in nature and exhibiting varying degrees of community identification. In "The Role and Concept of Neighborhood in American Cities," Zane L. Miller discusses this view of local identification through an analysis of the work of Morris Janowitz.[39] Janowitz argued that the existence of a flourishing community press suggested that the local community remained an important unit of urban life. Accordingly, Janowitz felt that social scientists needed to rethink their emphasis on the importance of metropolitan or regional units and refocus their attention on the elements that comprise the metropolis and the region. In addition, Janowitz intimated that a new view of society, gaining popularity during the late 1940s and the early 1950s, that the only "real units" of society were individuals, was equally unsatisfactory as an explanatory model for American life. Instead, Janowitz argued that urban society was characterized by "communities of limited liability."[40] In this view the city was composed of "congeries of localities," and thus neighborhood residents, all of whom maintained ties with other types of communities—occupational, religious, fraternal—"could identify and interact" in the local community as their interests and life-styles dictated.[41] As Miller points out, Janowitz's notion about the importance of the local community "failed to resurrect the spirit of the neighborhood and neighborliness" associated with beliefs about the early twentieth-century neighborhoods, but it did provide a role for the local community unacknowledged by what Janowitz described as "conventional social science wisdom."[42]

During the urban crisis of the 1960s, the notion of the community of limited liability gave way to a renewed yet modified interest in the territorial view of neighborhood. From the local level to the national grew a fascination with the utilization of the neighborhood as a staging ground for solutions to contemporary problems. This interest intensified after the passage of the Economic Opportunity Act in 1964. An important aspect of the act was the Community Action Program, which was designed to stimulate resident participation in neighborhood affairs. By the mid-1960s, numerous communities across the country began to organize in response to this federal initiative. At the same time, although residents were concerned about the neighborhood as a territorial unit, they also saw the neighborhood as an arena for social betterment. And as neighborhood residents focused on local programs, they also began to think more directly about the relationship of their area to the larger city.

Robert Fisher, in one of the first studies to look at neighborhood organizing from a historical perspective, captures the spirit of this drive to revitalize neighborhoods during the 1960s.[43] While providing details about the various federal programs and information on the neighborhood activities spawned by these programs, Fisher points out that interest in the neighborhood and its role in the city and in organizing neighborhoods did not first appear in the 1960s. Yet most social scientists date the beginning of what is called the neighborhood movement to the 1960s. Milton Kotler, writing in 1979, provides a typical example of this position. "We must remember," Kotler wrote, "where the neighborhood movement came from and what happened to create the present situation. The neighborhood movement did not fall from heaven yesterday. It began in the 1960s."[44]

At roughly the same time as programs developed under the Economic Opportunity Act began to focus the nation's attention on neighborhoods, critics of the post–World War II planning tradition raised voices of protest against what they regarded as the anti-social effects of planned change in American cities during the 1950s. In 1961, for example, Jane Jacobs' *The Death and Life of Great American Cities* provided a popular critique of the planning profession that helped direct attention to the destruction of neighborhoods and helped spark interest in the neighborhood.[45] A more recent and similar attack on the planning profession can be found in Roger S. Ahlbrandt, Jr., and James V. Cunningham's

1979 article, "The Ungreening of Neighborhood Planning."[46] Ahlbrandt and Cunningham's essay offers a convenient summation of the attacks since Jacobs' on the planning profession's approach to the city. They argue that planners have focused their efforts almost solely on the physical city and have paid little if any attention to the social context in which their efforts took place.[47] Together the federal programs of the 1960s and the anti-planning critiques of Jacobs and her contemporaries served to revitalize some neighborhoods, to create new neighborhoods, to humanize the planning process, and to focus attention on the relationship between the neighborhood and the city.

In the 1970s, a chorus of noisy neighborhood organizations advocating a variety of programs for local betterment emerged. Slogans such as"Power to the Neighborhoods" and both popular and scholarly articles focusing on resurgent neighborhoods captured the spirit of the strident localism. Advocates for neighborhood government such as Milton Kotler stressed the need to decentralize urban government and promoted the idea of the development of neighborhood economies.[48] Territory, whether precisely or ambiguously defined, remained a pre-eminent element in neighborhood definition, although it carried a fuller meaning than it did in the hands of planners during the 1950s. However, the view of neighborhoods of the 1970s, even with this broader emphasis, did not resemble the beliefs held about the neighborhood during the first quarter of the twentieth century. The vision of neighborhoods put forth in the 1970s suggested that they could be viewed as apart from rather than as part of the city.

In *Neighborhoods: Their Place in Urban Life*, Howard Hallman provides a handy synthesis of recent neighborhood studies in order to paint as comprehensive a picture as possible of the neighborhood in America during the 1980s.[49] Before examining the "many faces of neighborhoods," the process and strategies of neighborhood organization, the range of neighborhood-based activities, and strategies for the future, Hallman examines a variety of definitions of neighborhood that have emerged since the late 1960s. In general, all of these definitions stress the importance of locality. Some emphasized in addition to locality the importance of "cognition and sentiment," relating definitions neighborhood residents give to their neighborhoods to the attachment displayed and the evaluation of quality of life exhibited by the residents. Albert Hunter explored the importance of cognition and sentiment in *Symbolic Communities: The Persistence of Change in Chicago's Communities*.[50] The National Commission on Neighborhoods echoed this view in its definition of neighborhood in 1979, as did John McClaughery in 1980.[51] Hallman concludes his discussion of the meaning of neighborhood with the definition of neighborhood suggested by Anthony Downs in 1981: "neighborhoods are geographic units within which certain social relationships exist, although the intensity of these relationships and their importance in the lives of the individual may vary tremendously."[52] This view, which Hallman indicates reflects his "core definition," suggests a merger of the territorial view of neighborhoods and Janowitz's notion of communities of limited liability and captures the prevailing spirit of neighborhood today.[53] Yet as helpful as Hallman's volume is in increasing our understanding of definitions of the neighborhood, it fails to provide much insight into the evolution of these definitions or into the relationship between the neighborhood and the rest of the city.

Hallman's failure to probe beyond the basic definitions of neighborhood, in what is one of the better nonhistorical books on the neighborhood, helps point to the need for more historical research in this area. And while not issuing a call for broader, more contextual studies directly, Hallman's study echoes two earlier pleas. Albert Hunter in 1979 stressed the necessity of looking beyond mere analyses of internal neighborhood structure to its linkages with the larger society in order to understand the neighborhood more fully.[54] And Kathleen Neils Conzen suggested in her 1980 study, "Community Studies, Urban History, and American Local History," that the neighborhood, like other geographic units that touch our lives, "retains a history and an influence over the lives of its residents." What we need, she argued, are studies that analyze "the changing consequences of locality, of place itself, for those living within a place and for society at large."[55]

While few have responded to these pleas, some historians have offered a peek into the historical experience of the neighborhood and the city. Kathleen Neils Conzen's 1979 essay, "Immigrants, Immigrant Neighborhoods, and Ethnic Identity: Historical Issues," analyzes a variety of interpretations of the immigrant experience focusing on the relationship among neighborhood residence, ethnic identity, and acculturation. Although her main emphasis is on ethnic identity and acculturation rather than the neighborhood and the city, she looks at these issues in terms of process and change over time. In so doing, Conzen places the neighborhood within particular historical eras and examines as well how it operates in a variety of historical contexts.[56]

Ronald H. Bayor confronted the issue of the neighborhood and the city in *Neighborhoods in Urban America*. He recognized both the renewed interest in the neighborhood and the scattered nature of much of the literature on it. In order to remedy this situation, Bayor assembled a selection of essays "to provide a wide-ranging interdisciplinary look at the field for those interested in the research and teaching of neighborhood topics."[57] Considering this objective, Bayor has succeeded in pulling together a potpourri of essays that sample the varieties of neighborhood studies. Ultimately, however, Bayor's book is disappointing. He had an excellent opportunity to provide those interested in the neighborhood with a thoughtful introductory essay placing the articles in the book in historical perspective. Instead, his introduction does little more than indicate that a concern about neighborhoods has existed.

A more promising work that provides a look at the neighborhood over time is Robert Fisher's *Let the People Decide: Neighborhood Organizing in America*. Scholarly investigations of the history of community and neighborhood organization have been scant, and most literature in the field either has ignored the community organization tradition, suggesting that such organizational activities are a recent phenomenon, or has avoided the issue and merely examined the dynamics of the successes or failures of specific organizations. Herein rests the contribution of Fisher's study. While not ignoring the experiences of a variety of particular organizations at various times since the late nineteenth century, he addresses the larger question of how the principles and practices of community or neighborhood organization have changed over time and explores the impact of organizational activity on these developments. As with any other overview, one can quarrel with the selection of particular topics or can wish that the book contained more detail. But these concerns are of minor importance, for Fisher ably fulfills his basic goal: the discussion and analysis of important events in the history of neighborhood organizations without isolating the organizations from their historical and urban context.[58] Thus Fisher's book advances not only our understanding of the history of neighborhood organizing but also of the changing nature of the neighborhood-city relationship during the twentieth century.

Zane L. Miller has suggested in "Queensgate II: A History of a Neighborhood" that the "history of a neighborhood . . . is bound up with the history of the city, and its main theme is not continuity but flux."[59] So, too, is the case with beliefs about the neighborhood. We need more in depth studies that explore the historical experience of the neighborhood as part of the city and that examine the changing nature of this relationship over time. By doing so, historians can establish a context in which the role of the neighborhood can further illuminate our understanding of American urbanism.

Notes

1. Carl Abbott, "The Neighborhoods of New York, 1760–1775," *New York History* 55 (January 1974): 35–54.

2. Sam Bass Warner, Jr., *Streetcar Suburbs: The Process of Growth in Boston, 1870–1900* (Cambridge, Mass.: Harvard University Press, 1962), pp. 15, 46.

3. Howard Gillette, Jr., "The Emergence of the Modern Metropolis: Philadelphia in the Age of Its Consolidation," in William W. Cutler III and Howard Gillette, Jr., eds., *The Divided Metropolis: Social and Spatial Dimensions of Philadelphia, 1800–1975* (Westport, Conn.: Greenwood Press, 1980), p.11

4. Jon C. Teaford, *City and Suburb: The Political Fragmentation of Metropolitan America, 1850–1970* (Baltimore: Johns Hopkins University Press, 1979); Joel A. Tarr, *Transportation and Changing Spatial Patterns in Pittsburgh, 1970–1934* (Chicago: Public Works Historical Society, 1978); Warner, *Streetcar Suburbs*; Clay McShane, *Technology and Reform: Street Railways and the Growth of Milwaukee, 1877–1900* (Madison: State Historical Society of Wisconsin, 1974).

5. David R. Goldfield, "The Neighborhood: Islands in the Urban Mainstream," *South Atlantic Urban Studies Journal* 4 (1979): 89.

6. Robert A. Woods, "The City and Its Local Community," in Robert A. Woods, ed., *The Neighborhood in Nation Building* (1923; New York: Arno Press, 1970), p. 196. See also Robert A. Woods, "The Neighborhood in Social Reconstruction," *American Journal of Sociology* 19 (March 1914): 577–91.

7. Wilbur C. Phillips, *Adventuring for Democracy* (New York: Social Unit Press, 1940).

8. Jean B. Quandt, *From the Small Town to the Great Community: The Social Thought of Progressive Intellectuals* (New Brunswick: Rutgers University Press, 1970).

9. Patricia Mooney Melvin, "Neighborhood in the Organic City: The Social Unit Plan and the First Community Organization Movement 1900–1920" (Ph.D. diss., University of Cincinnati, 1978).

10. Mark Goldman, "Buffalo's Black Rock: A Neighborhood and the City," *Journal of Urban History* 5 (August 1979): 447–68.

11. Mark Goldman, *High Hopes:The Rise and Decline of Buffalo, New York* (Albany: State University of New York Press, 1983); Melvin, "Neighborhood in the Organic City."

12. Gerald D. Suttles, "Community Design: The Search for Participation in Metropolitan Society," in Amos Hawley and Vincent P. Rock, eds., *Metropolitan America in Contemporary Perspective* (New York: John Wiley and Sons, 1975), p. 243.

13. Ernest Burgess, ed., *The Urban Community* (Chicago: University of Chicago Press, 1925), and Robert E. Park and Ernest W. Burgess, eds., *The City* (Chicago: University of Chicago Press, 1925).

14. Robert E. Park, "The Urban Community as a Spatial Pattern and as a Moral Order," in Burgess, *Urban Community*, pp. 3–11.

15. Roderick D. McKenzie, *The Neighborhood: A Study of Local Life in the City of Columbus, Ohio* 1923; (New York: Arno Press, 1970).

16. Christopher Silver, "Neighborhood Planning in Historical Perspective," *Journal of the American Planning Association* 51 (Spring 1985): 161–74.

17. Zane L. Miller, "The Role and Concept of Neighborhood in American Cities," in Robert Fisher and Peter Romanofsky, eds., *Community Organization for Urban Social Change: A Historical Perspective* (Westport, Conn.: Greenwood Press, 1981), pp. 3–31, and Patricia Mooney Melvin, *The Organic City: Urban Definition and Neighborhood Organization, 1880–1920* (Lexington: University Press of Kentucky, 1987).

18. Miller, "Role and Concept," p. 13.

19. Harvey W. Zorbaugh, *The Gold Coast and the Slum: A Sociological Study of Chicago's Near North Side* (Chicago: University of Chicago Press, 1929), pp. 221–48.

20. See, for example, Burgess, *Urban Community*, and Park and Burgess, *The City*.

21. William P. Hojnacki, "What Is a Neighborhood?" *Social Policy* 10 (September-October 1979): 47–52.

22. Rebecca Lou Smith, "Neighborhoods Inside and Out: Comparative Perspectives on the Meaning of 'Neighborhood' " (Ph.D. diss., University of Minnesota, 1982).

23. Louis Wirth, "The Scope and Problems of the Community," in Louis Wirth, *Cities and Social Life*, ed. Albert J. Reiss, Jr. (Chicago: University of Chicago Press, 1964), p. 176, and Silver, "Neighborhood Planning," 167.

24. Jesse F. Steiner, *Community Organization* (New York: Century, 1925), pp. 117, 146.

25. Jesse F. Steiner, "Whither the Community Movement?" *Survey*, April 15, 1929, pp. 130–31. See also Howard Gillette, Jr., "The Evolution of Neighborhood Planning: From the Progressive Era to the 1949 Housing Act," *Journal of Urban History* 9 (August 1983): 429–30.

26. Blake McKelvey, *The Emergence of Metropolitan America, 1915–1966* (New

Brunswick: Rutgers University Press, 1968), and Charles N. Glaab and A. Theodore Brown, *A History of Urban America* (New York: Macmillan, 1976).

27. Howard P. Chudacoff, *The Evolution of American Urban Society*, 2nd ed. (Englewood Cliffs, N.J.: Prentice-Hall, 1981).

28. Manuel Castells, *The Urban Question: A Marxist Approach*, trans. Alan Sheridan (Cambridge, Mass.: MIT Press, 1980).

29. Sam Bass Warner, Jr., *The Urban Wilderness: A History of the American City* (New York: Harper & Row, 1972).

30. Zane L. Miller and Patricia Mooney Melvin, *The Urbanization of Modern America: A Brief History*, 2nd ed. (New York: Harcourt Brace Jovanovich, 1986).

31. Mark Naison, "Harlem Communists and the Politics of Black Protest," in Fisher and Romanofsky, *Community Organization*, pp. 89–126.

32. James Borchert, "Urban Neighborhood and Community: Informal Group Life, 1850–1970," *Journal of Interdisciplinary History* 11 (Spring 1981): 607–31.

33. Lyle Koehler, *Westwood in Ohio: Community, Continuity, and Change* (Cincinnati: The Westwood Civic Association, 1981).

34. Joseph A. Spencer, "Tenant Organization and Housing Reform in New York City: The City Wide Tenants' Council, 1936–1943," in Fisher and Romanofsky, *Community Organization*, pp. 127–56.

35. Clarence A. Perry, "The Neighborhood Unit, A Scheme of Arrangement for the Family Life Community," in *The Regional Survey of New York and Its Environs* (New York: Russell Sage Foundation, 1929), 7:22–140 See also James Dahir, comp., *The Neighborhood Unit Plan: Its Spread and Acceptance* (New York: Russell Sage Foundation, 1947).

36. Ruth Glass, ed., *The Social Background of a Plan* (London: Routledge & Kegan Paul, 1948), p. 18. See also Hojnacki, "What Is a Neighborhood?"; Suzanne Keller, *The Urban Neighborhood: A Sociological Perspective* (New York: Random House, 1968); Henry D. Shapiro, "Neighborhood and the Family: The Larger Setting. The Emergence of Ideas and Their Implication," in Thomas H. Jenkins, ed., *Home and Family in the 1980s: Insights from Past, Present, and Future* (Cincinnati: Better Housing League of Greater Cincinnati, 1981), and Silver, "Neighborhood Planning in Perspective," pp. 169–70.

37. Judith Tannenbaum, "The Neighborhood: A Socio-psychological Analysis," *Land Economics* 24 (November 1948): 358–69. See also R. J. Hacon, "Neighborhoods or Neighborhood Units?" *Sociological Review* 3 (December 1955): 235–45.

38. Gillette, "Neighborhood Planning," pp. 421–44.

39. Miller, "Role and Concept," pp. 18–24.

40. Morris Janowitz, *The Community Press in an Urban Setting: The Social Elements of Urbanism*, 2nd ed. (Chicago: University of Chicago Press, 1967).

41. Miller, "Role and Concept," p. 21.

42. Ibid.

43. Robert Fisher, *Let the People Decide: Neighborhood Organizing in America* (Boston: Twayne Publishers, 1984).

44. Milton Kotler, "The Purpose of Neighborhood Power," *South Atlantic Urban Studies* 4 (1979): 29.

45. Jane Jacobs, *The Death and Life of Great American Cities* (New York: Vintage Books, 1961).

46. Roger S. Ahlbrandt, Jr., and James V. Cunningham, "The Ungreening of Neighborhood Planning," *South Atlantic Urban Studies* 4 (1979): 9–15.

47. See also Gillette, "Neighborhood Planning," pp. 421–22, and Silver, "Neighborhood Planning in Perspective," pp. 170–71.

48. Milton Kotler, *Neighborhood Government: The Local Foundations of Political Life* (Indianapolis: Bobbs–Merrill, 1969). See also James A. Stever, "Contemporary Neighborhood Theories: Integration Versus Romance and Reaction," *Urban Affairs Quarterly* 13 (March 1978): 263–84, and Rick Cohen, "Neighborhood Planning and Political Capacity," *Urban Affairs Quarterly* 14 (March 1979): 337–62.

49. Howard W. Hallman, *Neighborhoods: Their Place in Urban Life* (Beverly Hills: Sage Publications, 1984).

50. Albert Hunter, *Symbolic Communities: The Persistence of Change in Chicago's Communities* (Chicago: University of Chicago Press, 1974).

51. National Commission on Neighborhoods, *People, Building Neighborhoods* (Washington, D.C.: Government Printing Office, 1979), and John McClaughery, "Neighborhood Revitalization," in Peter Dulgran and Alvin Ravishka, eds., *The United States in the 1980s* (Stanford: Hoover Institution Press, 1980).

52. Anthony Downs, *Neighborhoods and Urban Development* (Washington, D.C.: Brookings Institution, 1981), p. 15

53. Hallman, *Neighborhoods*, p. 17.

54. Albert Hunter, "The Urban Neighborhood: Its Analytical and Social Contexts," *Urban Affairs Quarterly* 14 (March 1979): 267–88.

55. Kathleen Neils Conzen, "Community Studies, Urban History, and American Local History," in Michael Kammen, ed., *The Past Before Us: Contemporary Historical Writing in the United States* (Ithaca: Cornell University Press, 1980), pp. 289–90.

56. Kathleen Neils Conzen, "Immigrants, Immigrant Neighborhoods, and Ethnic Identity: Historical Issues," *Journal of American History* 66 (December 1979): 603–15. This essay also provides an excellent introduction to the literature on ethnic neighborhoods.

57. Ronald H. Bayor, ed., *Neighborhoods in Urban America* (Port Washington, N.Y.: Kennikat Press, 1982).

58. Fisher, *Let the People Decide*. See also Patricia Mooney Melvin, review of *Let the People Decide: Neighborhood Organizing in America*, by Robert Fisher, in *Journal of American History* 72 (June 1985): 123–24.

59. Zane L. Miller, "Queensgate II: A History of a Neighborhood," in Zane L. Miller and Thomas H. Jenkins, eds., *The Planning Partnership: Participants' Views of Urban Renewal* (Beverly Hills: Sage Publications, 1982), pp. 51–79.

13 ——— Frontiers and Sections: Cities and Regions in American Growth

CARL ABBOTT

Cities are obvious enough. We usually know one when we see it: a vertical accent of skyscrapers, smokestacks, and grain elevators rising out of the horizontal landscape of North America.

Regions are harder to find. They are abstractions defined by common heritage and history or by intermittent flows of people, objects, and information. They can be large or small, physiographic or economic, cultural or political. Regional boundaries vary with the purpose of the discussion and the perspectives of its participants.

One of the most effective strategies for making sense of the jumble of overlapping regions that constitute the United States is to relate regional development and definition to the growth of cities and city systems. Evidence from recent work by historians and geographers shows that cities have been the senior partners in the regionalization process. City people and city-based institutions have spearheaded successive frontiers, organized production, centralized rural resources, linked local to the national or international economic system, channeled flows of information, and provided focal points for regional culture and identity.

Analysis starts with the geographer's distinction between nodal and uniform regions. Nodal regions are defined by the active connection of their parts to a center or focus. Most commonly they are urban regions created by complementary relationships between a city and the surrounding territory.[1] Movements between city and hinterland include the easily measured tangibles of raw materials, finished goods, and people; well-documented flows of economic information such as advertising and bank transfers; and elusive movements of ideas ranging from religious beliefs to styles in personal behavior.

The underlying assumption of abstract models of market systems such as central place theory is that of a hierarchy in which smaller centers are subordinated to increasingly larger cities and metropolises.[2] The nodal regions centered on smaller towns and cities are presumed to nest within those centered on the larger cities. In the actual experience of American growth, however, the varying influences of landscape and resources, swirling tides of population movement, changing transportation systems, and evolving industrial mix have given a complex layering of regional ties to every part of the United States.

Urban growth itself can add to the complexity of regional relationships by creating certain types of uniform regions—areas homogeneous with respect to defining characteristics within specified ranges. The most obvious uniform regions include climatic zones and agricultural regions. However, cities that perform similar economic functions have often clustered geographically because of the influence of a resource base or transportation system, and their common services have helped to promote regional economic specialization. The cattle trading region of the central Great Plains in the 1870s is one such example. The urban-industrial belt of the Northeast is a larger and a more permanent example.[3]

Within the framework of basic regional definitions, two descriptive models have played key roles in shaping our understanding of the role of city-based regions in American growth. Norman S. B. Gras in the 1920s and Donald Meinig since the 1960s have provided broad outlines for defining city regions, exploring their growth and internal dynamics, and examining their development and interrelations as formative influences on American social, economic, and cultural history. In the great division of the social sciences, they rank as synthesizers rather than theoreticians or technicians, suggesting inclusive strategies for framing and organizing the American experience in terms of its city regions.

An economic historian, Gras proposed a multistage model of economic evolution climaxing in the "metropolitan economy," a pattern of spatial organization in which great commercial cities function as the nuclei for large, surrounding hinterlands and control external relations among the resulting metropolitan regions. A city becomes a fully developed metropolis "when most kinds of products of the district concentrate in it for trade as well as transit; when these products are paid for by wares that radiate from it; and when the necessary financial transactions involved in this exchange are provided by it."[4] Economic initiative comes from the metropolis as it organizes markets, develops transport, manages a financial system, and administers public services.

The concept of the city-region as both engine and product of territorial expansion and economic growth has been especially applicable to North America, offering a framework to describe the development and organization of successive frontiers and to explain the relative fortunes of cities and sections. Gras applied the scheme to the development of the United States within the Atlantic economy in his *Introduction to Economic History* and in shorter essays.[5] The idea of the economic metropolis provides the basis for an interpretation of continental growth based on the interaction of resource regions and metropolitan gateways.[6] It has also furnished an intellectual context for understanding the ubiquitous American phenomenon of urban competition. In examining the development of tributary regions, Gras asserted that the "seesaw of neverending struggle" among urban rivals was "not marked by political elections, or military engagements, but by advertising, the circulation of newspapers, the activities of commercial travelers, the struggles of boards of trade, rate wars, and the migration of workers and business men."[7] His ideas supplied the rationale and often the inspiration for the studies of urban rivalry and urban imperialism that have formed a major theme in urban history since the 1930s.

Much more recently, historical geographer Donald Meinig has placed city regions at the center of cultural as well as economic change. In pioneering studies of Utah and Texas, he defined a model for cultural regions consisting of a core area, a surrounding domain, and a more distant sphere in which regional influence overlaps its neighbors. The core is defined as the "seat of political and economic power, the focus of circulation, the area of most concentrated development." Cultural influence is disseminated through patterns of migration, communication, investment, political control, and religious authority that have commonly centered in a dominant metropolis such as Montreal, Boston, Santa Fe, and Salt Lake City.[8]

Meinig has subsequently outlined the development of the American West in terms of the implantation and growth of six settlement regions centered on Los Angeles, San Francisco, Portland, Salt Lake City, Denver, and Santa Fe and has used the same conceptual model to sketch the history of the United States as an areal phenomenon. The outline traces national origins from isolated urban nuclei, follows the emergence of a hierarchy of cities and metropolitan regions, and emphasizes the dominant role of an urbanized core between New York and Chicago.[9]

By viewing city regions not only as systems of economic organization but also as part of the cultural landscape, Meinig has made Gras' model more comprehensive and more sensitive to historical nuance. From the differing viewpoints of economist and geographer, both have provided strategies for thinking about urban growth in relation to larger economic and cultural hinterlands and for understanding national growth in terms of the growth and interaction of city-centered regions.

City and City System in Small Regions

In emerging fields of historical investigation, case studies are the imperfect equivalents of experiments through which we test and refine large-scale generalizations and theory. In the past two decades, scholars interested in the textures and tensions of urban life have produced a rich fund of community studies examining social and economic processes within cities or particular city populations. The somewhat less frequent equivalent for city-region analysis is the case study of regional definition and differentiation in small regions. Although the spatial scale may range from a single township to the hundred-mile reach of a major city, "small region" is used here to mean an economic unit located within a larger economic or cultural region such as the South, New England, or Midwest. The common strategy is conceptually to isolate the small region by emphasizing the differential concentration and distribution of activities inside its boundaries and treating changes in its larger economic context as exogenous variables to which the small region reacts.

The search for isolated cases has led a number of scholars to examine American frontiers. Given a region with relatively uniform economic activity and dispersed settlement, they ask how sets of urban places evolved into ordered systems marked by functional specialization among larger and smaller centers. In theoretical terms, the question is how uniform settlement regions are organized into a nodal region or regions. In terms familiar to American historians, the question is how new frontier areas developed the internal structure that allowed them to function as parts of the national economy. For the second half of the eighteenth century, there are studies of the Carolina backcountry by Joseph Ernst and Roy Merrens and the Shenandoah Valley by Robert Mitchell. For the antebellum decades, Burton Folsom, Jr., has explored urban growth in Pennsylvania's anthracite region, Roberta Miller has looked at upstate New York, Edward Muller has examined the central Ohio Valley, and Margaret Walsh has looked more broadly at the Midwest. Barbara Bailey has followed the late nineteenth-century frontier into the isolated valleys of northeastern Oregon, and Avery Guest has examined the city system along Puget Sound.[10]

To the surprise of no one familiar with American history, urban geography, or location theory, the studies repeatedly demonstrate that changes in transportation technology or accessibility were the "disturbing cause" that determined the relative roles and importance of urban centers.[11] We can learn about the local effects of new roads across the Blue Ridge, of the Erie and Miami canals, of railroads in Massachusetts, the Midwest, and the Far West. Only in Onandaga County, where railroads appeared first as feeders to the Erie Canal rather than alternative routes, did the steam locomotive fail to alter the "relationships between cities and smaller settlements."[12]

In the tradition of older histories of interurban competition, several studies of urban system development have reemphasized the public policy context of economic change. They are concerned not only with the abstract opportunities made available by particular transportation systems but also with the ability of individual communities to take advantage of such opportunities. In Michael Conzen's terms, they are concerned with the "selective nature of growth among towns viewed as a loose system in which local aspirations can boost a settlement to the ceiling of tolerance imposed by the regional economy, relative location, technology, and other variables."[13] David Meyer has offered an integrated portrait of urban development in central Connecticut during the nineteenth century that stresses a combination of entrepreneurship, manufacturing innovation, and economies of scale in creating manufacturing and finance centers. Folsom has similarly described the emerging system of cities in the Lackawanna Valley as a result of competition for entrepreneurs, industry, capital, and transportation to outside markets. Dealing with a larger geographic region, I have examined the relative growth and differing functions of cities in the antebellum Midwest in terms of the ability of each community to define and pursue effective growth strategies.[14]

A related approach to the study of small city-regions takes the existence of a regional center as a starting point and examines its economic reach. Efforts to define twentieth-century hinterlands in terms of the market range of a variety of goods and services have produced an abundant geographic literature.[15] The constraint for comparable historical studies is the limited availability of data from which to reconstruct economic flows into and among urban centers. A common response is eclectic research like that of Francis Blouin, who has described the urban hierarchy within Boston's antebellum hinterland by combining information on transportation facilities, data on commodity movements, and records of eastern Massachusetts business.[16] Other studies organize a variety of data around the distinction between import hinterland—the area to which a city provided services, sold locally manufactured goods, and distributed merchandise—and export hinterland—the area that supplied agricultural products and minerals for processing and/or shipment to outside markets.[17] Antebellum Philadelphia, for example, had different economic interactions with the New Jersey and Pennsylvania segments of its hinterland, while Cincinnati's import hinterland covered a much larger area than its export hinterland.[18]

Several studies by geographer Michael Conzen offer an impressive contrast by showing the possibilities and problems involved in systematic analysis of limited but consistent historical data. An examination of scheduled passenger service among Midwestern cities is explicitly intended to serve as an alternative and partial surrogate for analysis based on highly fragmentary data on freight movements. Conzen has also used the national network of bank correspondence accounts to reconstruct the country's urban hierarchy between 1850 and 1910 and to explore the "extent, configuration, and internal structure of urban hinterlands at all levels of the urban system."[19]

If hinterland studies look outward from larger cities toward smaller towns and rural landscapes, a third set of historians and historical geographers have examined the effects of the urban connection on the agricultural hinterlands themselves. The topic can be termed the urban shadow effect, after Michael Conzen's book, *Frontier Farming in an Urban Shadow: The Influence of Madison's Proximity on the Agricultural Development of Blooming Grove, Wisconsin*. His focus is the process of economic change within a single township between 1850 and

1880, with particular attention to small-scale patterns of settlement and trade. The work fits within the Wisconsin tradition of detailed rural settlement studies running from Joseph Schafer to Merle Curti, with one important exception: its attention to the constant subtle pressures on land uses from the looming presence of an adjacent city.[20] Milton Newton's complementary study of Greensburg, Louisiana, emphasizes the courthouse town as the seat of civic life, legal order, and cultural sophistication. "The courthouse in its square," he argues, "spreads its power throughout the county along the roads that repeatedly ramify outward from the grid around the courthouse; reciprocally, the political, commercial, and social tribute is drawn in toward . . . the courthouse square."[21] One obvious social influence is the attraction of migrants from farm to town. John Modell, Roberta Miller, and Michael Conzen have used extraordinary state or federal census data to examine the migration sheds of Reading, Pennsylvania, in 1850, Syracuse in 1855, and Iowa cities in 1895.[22] Stuart Blumin's study of Kingston, New York, provides a less direct perspective on the cultural function of the small city in descriptions of the changing character of local politics and of civic festivals such as Fourth of July celebrations.[23]

On the whole, city growth and economic diversification seem to have meant reduced opportunities in the immediately surrounding countryside. James Lemon has found that the urban system of colonial Philadelphia was stunted within thirty miles of Philadelphia, while Diane Lindstrom has described the relative impoverishment of Philadelphia's early nineteenth-century hinterland that accompanied the city's growth as a manufacturing center. As the dominant center in the Delaware Valley, the Quaker City "gained more from specialization than did its hinterland."[24] What appears to have been a common sequence has been described by Roberta Miller and by Bayly Ellen Marks in "Rural Response to Urban Penetration: Baltimore and St. Mary's County, Maryland, 1790–1840." In southern Maryland and upstate New York alike, transportation improvements and expanded ties to a larger city initially promised new opportunities and stimulated rural enterprise. Rising expectations, however, were dashed by declining opportunities as trade, manufacturing, and talent shifted to Baltimore or Syracuse and left essentially agricultural hinterlands.[25]

The underlying theme of these small-area studies is modernization, definable variously as the replacement of traditional values by the cash nexus or the replacement of face-to-face relationships by those within large-scale social and economic institutions. In classic formulations, urbanization and urban living are therefore modernizing forces by the very nature of their scale and complexity. Urban networks that promote specialization and extend the range of the individual's regular contacts are simultaneously the product of the commercial impulse and evidence of the power of the market economy to organize settlement and production. Mitchell, for example, finds that town growth in western Virginia before and after the American Revolution was a response to the "commercialized perceptions of their new environment." Despite a small population, Camden, South Carolina, had assumed an essential commercial role by the 1760s and was a "place with ties and linkages reaching far outside the surrounding local areas for which it functioned as a center." Edward Muller provides a descriptive model for the commercial integration of frontier regions through the stages of "pioneer periphery," "specialized periphery," and finally "transitional periphery" in which access to markets for manufactured goods becomes as important as outlets for agricultural products.[26]

Work on the urban shadow effect by which cities influence and alter their immediate hinterlands approaches modernization head on, examining the changing character of rural life as well as the distribution of settlement and the concentration of higher-order economic activities. In addition, Anthony Wallace has confronted the topic in his study of an early nineteenth-century manufacturing community near Philadelphia. With the metropolis and metropolitan capitalists as the looming presence, Wallace assumes but fails to prove either a viable precapitalist society or an anticapitalist ideology.[27] The same issue of urban influence on rural values is treated with more substance in T.D.S. Bassett's dated but suggestive article on Vermont between 1840 and 1880. Tracing the increasingly intense reach of New York, Boston, and Montreal, Bassett found concentration of population, transformation of the local elite, changing cultural values, and acceptance of the business-oriented political agenda of the cities and larger towns. "By 1880," he concluded, "rural Vermont had taken to heart the message of the nineteenth century to the urban periphery: improve transportation and industrialize, find a new specialty, leave, or suffer."[28]

Work on city-region relationships in the twentieth century requires separate treatment. The message of the twentieth century increasingly is not "leave or suffer" but "stay, subdivide, sell to weekend tourists, work your five-acre ranchette, and commute to a new suburban factory."

The automobile has had significantly different effects from turnpikes, canal boats, and locomotives. As Guest has demonstrated for the Puget Sound region, hard-surfaced roads and automobiles did not introduce a new pattern of urban development in which new cities challenged the established centers. Ambitious new towns may have used canals and railroads to revolutionize the urban hierarchy of nineteenth-century Massachusetts or Ohio, but established cities in this century have been able to capture new highway links and channel automobile traffic through existing centers. When built through developed areas such as Pennsylvania, new highways at most have had incremental effects on growth.[29]

At the same time, the automobile has greatly increased the ability of major cities to control a larger retail and service hinterland and reduced the competitiveness of small towns. The result is a magnified and intensified economic shadow that has created a new sort of city-centered region that is something more than the officially recognized metropolitan area but less than the familiar commercial hinterland. The seminal effort to define this new sort of urban region was Roderick McKenzie's analysis of the metropolitan community as an "expanded pattern of local communal life based upon motor transportation." His definitions have been updated by planner John Friedmann's description of the "urban field," by geographer Brian Berry's statistical analysis of "daily urban systems," and most recently by Jane Jacobs' discussion of "city regions" as integrated and creative economic units.[30] Interest in exurban settlements and weekend amenity regions within commuting range of major metropolitan areas is a product of the same concern with new automobile-based regions that extend patterns of everyday behavior beyond the surburban ring.[31] An example that puts an amenity region in historical perspective is Richard White's fine study of Whidbey Island, Washington, a large Puget Sound island lying thirty to eighty miles from Seattle. His final narrative chapter, "The Urban Shadow: The Impact of Promoters and Tourists on the Rural Landscape," pays particular attention to the effects of improved auto access in the 1920s and 1930s.[32]

Richard Lamb has investigated the characteristic impacts of the expanding urban field through systematic statistical analysis. Evidence on population growth and explanatory factors for 224 nonmetropolitan counties between 1950 and 1970 finds a basic difference between towns located within the long-range commuting zone or daily urban system or metropolitan centers and those outside. Beyond the urban field, population and economic activity were still centralizing into the larger towns because of agglomeration economies, threshold levels for markets and labor, and other size-dependent factors. As true for more than a century, "the outlying hinterland as a whole responds to metropolitan demands for primary and first- or second-stage processed products." Within the urban fields, however, the determinants of growth are now local amenities and access to the center, since the "demands of the metropolis . . . are increasingly for land, residential sites, attractive living environments, and recreation."[33]

Cities and the American Core Region

Whether townships, counties, or metropolitan hinterlands, the development of small regions has been embraced within the process of regional differentiation on a national scale. From the mid-nineteenth into the late twentieth century, the most prominent feature of American economic geography has been a national core extending in a broad band from Boston and Baltimore to Milwaukee, Rock Island, and St. Louis. As described by Edward Ullman, the core in 1950 contained 7 percent of the nation's land area but 43 percent of its population, 50 percent of its income, and 70 percent of its manufacturing employment. It was the focus of the national rail traffic system and the major market for both consumer and producer goods. It was equally the center of political and cultural influence. The Boston-Chicago axis accounted for a disproportionate share of patents, scientists, major corporate headquarters, candidates for president, and listings in *Who's Who*.[34]

The history of the core region essentially involves a process of differential urbanization in which the fact of concentration itself became a causative factor in accentuating regional differences. Within the repeated cycles of feedback loops and size ratchet effects, it is possible to distinguish four overlapping stages in the development of the core as the location of dominant cities and city systems.[35]

The differential development of colonial cities is a well-documented process based on the interaction between economies of scale and the specific trading needs of particular hinterlands. The simultaneous processes were the urban lag in the southern colonies compared to Pennsylvania, New York, and New England and the articulation of hierarchies of smaller trading towns in the regions around Philadelphia, New York, and Boston.[36]

The rivalry among eastern ports and the emergence of New York as the control center for interregional and international trade during the first half of the nineteenth century has been described by Robert Albion, James Livingood, and Julius Rubin. Their emphasis on the external relationships of metropolitan regions has been supplemented by several recent studies that emphasize the importance of intraregional markets for the growth of cities such as Philadelphia and Boston.[37] The same decades brought the simultaneous development of sets of cities along the Ohio Valley and Lake Erie. As characterized by Allan Pred, the United States by the 1830s had three urban subsystems connected by extensive economic linkages: a northeastern subsystem of Baltimore, Philadelphia, New York, Albany, Providence, and Boston; an Ohio–Upper Mississippi Valley subsystem of Pittsburgh, Cincinnati, Louisville, and St. Louis; and a Lake Erie subsystem of Detroit, Cleveland, Buffalo, and possibly Rochester. Cities in the South, in contrast, remained isolated from each other and limited in their ability to penetrate and control extensive hinterlands.[38]

The third stage of core development involved the attachment of the Midwestern subsystems to the eastern ports to form a national core. Allan Pred has measured the strengthening of communication links between east and west during the 1820s and 1830s.[39] Canals and early railroads in the late 1840s brought increased trade and travel among the Ohio River cities, the Lake Erie cities, and an even newer Lake Michigan subsystem of Chicago and Milwaukee.[40] By the end of the railroad boom of the 1850s, the western subsystem had begun to merge into a single system oriented more and more heavily toward New York and Philadelphia and away from the river routes to the South. Recent studies have essentially provided a gloss on the findings of Wyatt Belcher in his work on the Chicago–St. Louis rivalry and of A. L. Kohlmeier in his wonderfully titled *The Old Northwest as the Keystone in the Arch of American Federal Union.*[41] One exception is Margaret Walsh's *Rise of the Midwestern Meat Packing Industry*, which adds new insight by detailing the locational shift of a major industry from Cincinnati and other river towns to Chicago.[42]

The final stage in the evolution of the national core was the regional concentration of manufacturing in the second half of the nineteenth century. David Ward's chapter, "Urbanization and Regional Economic Development," in *Cities and Immigrants* provides the best short summary of the development of a system of industrial and commercial cities organized around the multifunctional anchors of New York and Chicago. In more detail, David Meyer has offered a suggestive model for the development of the industrial belt in which the reciprocal growth of manufacturing and markets within the various metropolitan regions of the Northeast and Midwest before 1870 provided the necessary base for the subsequent emergence of manufacturing for the national market. The lack of comparable regional industrial systems in the South because of low demand accounts for its exclusion from the economic core. The interpretation builds particularly on Lindstrom's analysis of intraregional trade as the major growth force in Philadelphia in the decades after 1815 and suggests an economic mechanism that links such metropolitan regions to the establishment of a national economic system.[43]

The relatively stable division between core and periphery that has marked the national economy since the 1870s or 1880s has invited comprehensive analysis of its organizing urban system. The concern has been to describe the complete set of American cities in terms of functional differentiation, relative dominance, and territorial influence. Because such analysis requires comparable and complete data, the basis for defining urban hierarchies and hinterlands has usually been the urban economic base and flows of economic information, such as bank transfers or advertising. The first landmark in the developing social science literature was Robert Park and Charles Newcomb's 1929 study, "Newspaper Circulation and Metropolitan Regions," which parceled the country out to forty-one regional metropolises. The second landmark was *Metropolis and Region*, a 1960 publication that categorized the nation's major cities according to patterns of business borrowing, flows of bank funds, and industrial specialization. The most sophisticated historical study is Michael Conzen's 1977 article using banking data to define both an urban hierarchy and sets of banking hinterlands in 1881 and 1910.[44]

The Megalopolis of the northeastern seaboard identified by French geographer Jean Gottmann in 1961 can be viewed simultaneously as a new homogeneous region consisting of overlapping urban fields, as the focus of the national urban hierarchy and economy, and as a fifth stage in the development of the industrial core. Gottmann argued that metropolitan growth was creating an entirely new form of settlement. The string of seaboard cities from Washington, D.C., to Boston was the world's greatest concentration of industry, commercial activity, and wealth and the hinge of the American economy—its gateway to the rest of the world and the focus of its intellectual life. It was also an interlocking system of settlement and commercial facilities that functioned as a single entity stretching over 250 miles. Although its component cities retained their identities and functions, Megalopolis as an entity provided a new level of support for societal growth and change and a forecast for the world's future.[45]

Studies of the national urban system suggest two important modifications of a strict hierarchical model of dominant and subordinate regions. As Gras suggested sixty years ago and as functional classifications of cities have demonstrated, there is actually a dual system with one set of specialized cities (either manufacturing or specialized service centers) and a second set of national and regional metropolises. In addition, as Beverly Duncan and co-authors have commented, "To account for the performance of distinctively metropolitan functions by a city one must pay attention to that city's situation within the larger inter-metropolitan context." The top of the metropolitan hierarchy since the beginning of the century has been marked by extreme connectivity, with networks of economic control crisscrossing hinterlands as traditionally defined.[46]

Cities and the American Periphery

Core regions imply peripheries. In the United States, urban development in the West and South can best be understood in relation to the growth of the northeastern industrial belt. Despite obvious dissimilarities in their cultural and political histories, the two regions are linked by their common experience of subordination to the national core. Southern and western cities have been necessary links in the system of economic control extending from New York bankers to Chicago manufacturers to local resource producers. The same cities have been the carriers of national values and characteristics—the agents of refinement on the western frontier and of modernization in the South.

The most common theme in the urban history of the periphery is the role of cities as gateways between the industrializing East and market-oriented resource regions. A succession of writers from T. Lynn Smith and Rudolph Heberle in the 1950s to Leonard Curry in the 1970s, for example, have emphasized that the only significant cities in the antebellum South were river towns and seaports strung around the region's edges. Richmond, Norfolk, Charleston, Savannah, Mobile, New Orleans, St. Louis, and Louisville traded directly with Europe and the American North but carried on only limited trade among themselves. The most important impact of the South's postwar railroad building was, similarly, the rise of Atlanta and Dallas as interior gateways.[47] Farther west, gateway cities were advance bases of supply in the pioneer decades. They developed as conduits for staple exports, distribution centers for the support of miners, farmers, ranchers, and lumberman, and channels for eastern credit and investment. If the western states and territories in the nineteenth century were economic colonies of the core, as their residents often complained, then Denver, Portland, San Francisco, and the other regional metropolises were the colonial capitals.[48]

Historians have also followed the lead of nineteenth-century city dwellers by emphasizing the civilizing function of urban growth. In the context of raw frontiers, towns and cities provided the most conducive setting for reproducing the societal forms and conventions of the national core. The development of stable communities is an important theme in Duane Smith's study of western mining towns and Robert Dykstra's work on Kansas cattle towns. It is the central concern of Roger Olien and Diana Olien's recent book, *Oil Booms: Social Change in Five Texas Towns*, which directly attacks their popular image as twentieth-century remnants of the wild frontier. In a more comprehensive study, *The Urban West at the End of the Frontier*, Lawrence Larsen has compared the twenty-four western cities that had populations of 8,000 or more by 1880. He finds that the communities copied eastern patterns in their government services, religious and educational institutions, and social values. John Reps' monumental study of western town planning and promotion uses visual records, travel accounts, early gazetteers, and pioneer histories to reach the same conclusion that new cities were planned, built, and governed in imitation of the old. In an excellent case study, Roger Lotchin agrees; he says, "San Francisco was an urban colonial outpost which imported and planted the cultural forms of older, more settled areas."[49]

While the interpretation of western cities as agents of the national core culture is relatively straightforward, the parallel analysis of urban impacts on southern society is embedded in a political and ideological debate about the uniqueness of the South. For at least two generations, social scientists have been waiting for urbanization to nationalize the South and bring a "level of modernity comparable to the nation as a whole."[50] The academic mainstream has involved the definition and testing of a catch-up and convergence thesis that notes that the twentieth-century South has been urbanizing faster than the rest of the nation, closing a gap that began to appear around 1840. Economic development theory suggests that this rapid urbanization is both product and cause of economic specialization and a shift from agriculture to a modern manufacturing and service economy. The thesis is equally dependent on the sociological commonplace that urbanization creates a heterogeneous and open society. Progressive southerners have therefore applauded rapid urbanization as an end to "backwardness" and an avenue to a more open and tolerant society.[51]

Advocates of the convergence thesis have most commonly analyzed aggregate regional data on simultaneous changes in levels of urbanization, education, income, and occupational structure to demonstrate the narrowing of the gap between the South and the national core. In 1954, Rupert Vance and Nicholas Demerath reported finding "in many fields, economic and demographic, trends toward the convergence of differentials" and a reduction of southern distinctiveness. Twenty years later, John McKinney and Linda Bourque asserted that southern urbanization and economic development had brought the "national incorporation of a region."[52] The idea of convergence was also supported by a number of historians who have found that southern cities more clearly reflect national forces than unique regional experiences "in their economic origins, class structure, leadership, public policy, demographic patterns, or responses to technology."[53]

Just as it seemed confirmed beyond dispute, the convergence thesis ran into trouble in the 1970s as attention turned to cultural pecularities that persist in spite of economic and demographic change. The broad reevaluation of what John S. Reed calls *The Enduring South* has led a number of historians, sociologists, and geographers to explore the continuing identity of the South as a cultural region.[54] At the same time, a growing skepticism about the social impacts of urbanization led historian James Cobb to find that urbanization has neither erased southern traditionalism and racism nor altered southern city politics.[55]

The work of historian David Goldfield illustrates the evolving ideas. In a co-edited book, *The City in Southern History*, he emphasized the similarities in the experience of southern and northern cities. Five years later, his *Cotton Fields and Skyscrapers: Southern City and Region, 1607–1980* rejected that interpretation to proclaim that southern cities have modernized without northernizing. They have converged on the core in economic terms but not in a number of social and cultural variables. Goldfield is particularly struck by the role of race and rurality even within large cities, finding that religion, family, and regional patterns of race relations dominate large segments of everyday urban life.[56]

Since 1940, of course, something has happened to cut across regional boundaries and bring the South and West together around a set of common experiences and opportunities. To a degree as yet uncertain, parts or all of the old peripheries are facing the future as the American sunbelt.[57] The rise of the sunbelt has been viewed, although not analyzed, as the emergence of new centers of cultural change and social innovation.[58] It has also been explained as the result of a secular shift in the national economic base and in the comparative advantage of regions.[59] In either case, the most obvious manifestation has been a massive surge of urban growth dating from World War II. This era of growth has deepened the reach of southern and western metropolises into their regions and further modernized or nationalized the old periphery. Cities at both the southeastern and western ends of the sunbelt have shared significant similarities in their growth experiences and their political responses that may set them apart as a distinct group.[60]

The emergence of the sunbelt may also be rearranging the nation's basic regional structure by altering the relations among its metropolitan regions. Los Angeles is now the nation's second city. The San Francisco Bay region matches Chicago as a center of commercial and cultural influence, and Houston matches Detroit.[61] From the South Atlantic states to the Pacific, the old periphery may now enjoy the same advantages of market size, market access, and industrial innovation that led to the self-reinforcing growth of the industrial belt a century ago.

Conclusion

At the beginning of the century, Frederick Jackson Turner defined the essential subjects for American history as frontier and section. The historians and historical geographers who study American cities in their regional context operate in Turner's shadow. We may disprove his specific conclusions, but we continue to pursue his research agenda as basic to understanding the American experience. At the level of frontier, scholars of city-regions are interested in the detailed processes by which new settlement areas have been integrated into the national economy and by which regions initially specializing in primary production have evolved more complex economic bases. They are also concerned with the impacts of that growth on social structure. At the level of section, they are interested in the synthesizing process by which the economic and cultural relationships among metropolitan centers have helped to tie diverse sections into a single nation.

As we have seen, the city-region provides an arena for the study of modernization, whether the level of concern is the changing hinterland or the nationalization of the American periphery. The existence of an urban hierarchy, no matter how imperfectly articulated in reality, allows us to compare local history and community studies to each other on the basis of functional similarities and to fit them within the larger picture of national growth. When applied to regions such as the twentieth-century South or Southwest, city-region analysis based on metropolitan economics and city-centered culture regions has the capacity to suggest new interpretations of cultural differentiation and persistence. An example is Meinig's work on the Southwest, which relates ethnic interaction to the region's changing urban system.[62]

The growth and interaction of city-regions also links two central phenomena of the last century and a half: the industrial urbanization of the Northeast-Midwest core, involving massive migrations both within and into North America, and the development of successive frontiers with the exploitation of new resources and the redistribution of population and economic activity. Interaction between core and periphery has been both the source of and solution for many of the sectional issues that have marked American political history, creating regional disparities but also providing the connections of trade and communication that political theorist Karl Deutsch has defined as essential unity.[63] At the same time, the urbanized Northeast has functioned as one part of the core region for the larger North Atlantic economic and cultural system that has dominated the modern world.[64] As explored by historians as diverse as William McNeill, Immanuel Wallerstein, and Bernard Bailyn, the American core has controlled and expressed the nation's evolving role on the world scene, whether one looks westward from Europe or eastward from North America.[65] At the most inclusive scale, in other words, city-regional analysis ties case studies on the rise of western frontiers within the United States to the world-historical process that McNeill has described as the "rise of the West."

Notes

1. Preston James and Clarence Jones, eds., *American Geography: Inventory and Prospect* (Syracuse: Syracuse University Press, 1954), pp. 36–37, and Robert E. Dickinson, *City and Region: A Geographical Interpretation* (London: Routledge & Kegan Paul, 1964), pp. 227–30.

2. For summaries, see Brian Berry and Allan Pred, *Central Place Studies: A Bibliography of Theory and Application* (Philadelphia: Regional Science Research Institute, 1961), and Brian Berry, *The Geography of Market Centers and Retail Distribution* (Englewood Cliffs, N.J.: Prentice-Hall, 1967).

3. Otis D. Duncan et al., *Metropolis and Region* (Baltimore: Johns Hopkins University Press, 1960), pp. 41–42, 104.

4. Norman S. B. Gras, *An Introduction to Economic History* (New York: Harper and Brothers, 1922), p. 186.

5. Norman S. B. Gras, "The Development of Metropolitan Economies in Europe and America," *American Historical Review* 27 (July 1922): 695–708; idem, "The Rise of the Metropolitan Community," in E. W. Burgess, ed., *The Urban Community* (Chicago: University of Chicago Press, 1926), pp. 183–91; idem, *Introduction to Economic History*.

6. For Canada, see J. M. S. Careless, "Frontierism, Metropolitanism and Canadian History," *Canadian Historical Review* 35 (March 1954): 1–21; idem, "Aspects of Metropolitanism in Atlantic Canada," in Mason Wade, ed., *Regionalism in the Canadian Community, 1867–1967* (Toronto: University of Toronto Press, 1969), pp. 117–29; Donald Kerr, "Metropolitan Dominance in Canada," in John Warkentin, ed., *Canada: A Geographical Interpretation* (Toronto: Methuen, 1968), pp. 531–55. For the western United States, see Charles M. Gates, "Boom Stages in American Expansion," *Business History Review* 33 (Spring 1959): 32–42.

7. Gras, *Introduction to Economic History*, p. 298.

8. Donald W. Meinig, *Imperial Texas: An Interpretive Essay in Cultural Geography* (Austin: University of Texas Press, 1969), p. 111; idem, "The Mormon Culture Region: Strategies and Patterns in the Geography of the American West," *Annals of the Association of American Geographers* 55 (June 1965): 191–220; Raymond Gastil, *Cultural Regions of the United States* (Seattle: University of Washington Press, 1975), pp. 42–44.

9. Donald W. Meinig, "American Wests: Preface to a Geographical Introduction," *Annals of the Association of American Geographers* 62 (June 1972): 159–84; idem, "The Continuous Shaping of America: A Prospectus for Geographers and Historians," *American Historical Review* 83 (December 1978): 1186–1206.

10. Joseph A. Ernst and H. Roy Merrens, " 'Camden's Turrets Pierce the Skies!': The Urban Process in the Southern Colonies during the Eighteenth Century," *William and Mary Quarterly* 30 (October 1973): 549–74; Robert Mitchell, *Commercialism and Frontier: Perspectives on the Early Shenandoah Valley* (Charlottesville: University Press of Virginia, 1977); Burton W. Folsom, Jr., *Urban Capitalists: Entrepreneurs and City Growth in Pennsylvania's Lackawanna and Lehigh Regions, 1800–1920* (Baltimore: Johns Hopkins University Press, 1981); Roberta Miller, *City and Hinterland: A Case Study of Urban Growth and Regional Development* (Westport, Conn.: Greenwood Press, 1979); Edward Muller, "Selective Urban Growth in the Middle Ohio Valley, 1800–1860," *Geographical Review* 66 (April 1976): 178–99; Margaret Walsh, "The Spatial Evolution of the Middle Western Pork Industry, 1833–1875," *Journal of Historical Geography* 4 (January 1978): 1–22; idem, *The Rise of the Midwestern Meat Packing Industry* (Lexington: University Press of Kentucky, 1982); Barbara Ruth Bailey, *Main Street, Northeastern Oregon: The Foundation and Development of Small Towns* (Portland: Oregon Historical Society, 1982); Avery Guest, "Ecological Succession in the Puget Sound Region," *Journal of Urban History* 3 (February 1977): 181–210.

11. For example, see George R. Taylor, *The Transportation Revolution, 1815–1860* (New York: Rinehart and Co., 1951); John Borchert, "American Metropolitan Evolution," *Geographical Review* 57 (July 1967): 301–32.

12. Miller, *City and Hinterland*, p. 79.

13. Michael P. Conzen, "The Maturing Urban System in the United States, 1840–1910," *Annals of the Association of American Geographers* 67 (March 1977): 88.

14. David R. Meyer, "From Farm to Factory to Urban Pastoralism: Urban Change in Central Connecticut," in John S. Adams, ed., *Contemporary Metropolitan America*, vol. 1: *Cities of the Nation's Historic Metropolitan Core* (Cambridge, Mass.: Ballinger, 1976), pp. 291–348; Carl Abbott, *Boosters and Businessmen: Popular Economic Thought and Urban Growth in the Antebellum Middle West* (Westport, Conn.: Greenwood Press, 1981); Folsom, *Urban Capitalists*. Robert Doherty, *Society and Power: Five New England Towns, 1800–1860* (Amherst: University of Massachusetts Press, 1977), reverses the analytical relationship by treating patterns of political power and social structure as products of a community's role within the urban hierarchy.

15. For classic examples, see Mildred Hartsough, *The Twin Cities as a Metropolitan Market*, University of Minnesota Studies in Social Sciences, No. 18 (Minneapolis: University of Minnesota, 1925); Chauncy D. Harris, *Salt Lake City: A Regional Capital* (Chicago: University of Chicago Department of Geography, 1940); Edward Ullman, *Mobile: Industrial Seaport and Trade Center* (Chicago: University of Chicago Department of Geography, 1943); Howard Green, "Hinterland Boundaries of New York City and Boston in Southern New England," *Economic Geography* 31 (October 1955): 283–300.

16. Francis X. Blouin, *The Boston Region, 1810–1850: A Study of Urbanization* (Ann Arbor: UMI Research Press, 1978).

17. Harlan Gilmore, *Transportation and the Growth of Cities* (Glencoe, Ill.: Free Press, 1953), pp. 95–97; Duncan, *Metropolis and Region*, pp. 249–59.

18. Diane Lindstrom, *Economic Development in the Philadelphia Region, 1815–1840* (New York: Columbia University Press, 1978); Abbott, *Boosters and Businessmen*, pp. 77–103.

19. Michael P. Conzen, "A Transport Interpretation of the Growth of Urban Regions: An American Example," *Journal of Historical Geography* 1 (October 1975): 361–82; Conzen, "Maturing Urban System."

20. Michael Conzen, *Frontier Farming in an Urban Shadow* (Madison: State Historical Society of Wisconsin, 1971).

21. Milton B. Newton, Jr., "Settlement Patterns as Artifacts of Social Structure," in Miles Richardson, ed., *The Human Mirror: Material and Spatial Images of Man* (Baton Rouge: Louisiana State University Press, 1974), p. 352.

22. John Modell, "The Peopling of a Working-Class Ward: Reading, Pennsylvania, 1850," *Journal of Social History* 5 (February 1971): 71–95; Michael P. Conzen, "Local Migration Systems in Nineteenth-Century Iowa," *Geographical Review* 64 (July 1974): 339–61; Miller, *City and Hinterland*, pp. 107–29.

23. Stuart Blumin, *The Urban Threshold: Growth and Change in a Nineteenth-Century American Community* (Chicago: University of Chicago Press, 1976).

24. James T. Lemon, *The Best Poor Man's Country: A Geographical Study of Early Southeastern Pennsylvania* (Baltimore: Johns Hopkins Press, 1972); Lindstrom, *Economic Development in the Philadelphia Region*, p. 20.

25. Bayly Ellen Marks, "Rural Response to Urban Penetration: Baltimore and St. Mary's County, Maryland, 1790–1840," *Journal of Historical Geography* 8 (April 1982): 113–27; Miller, *City and Hinterland*. Blouin, *Boston Region*, finds a different pattern in which the growth of Boston as a manufacturing and trading center stimulated complementary manufacturing specialization in its hinterland.

26. Mitchell, *Commercialism and Frontier*, p. 230; Ernst and Merrens, "Camden's Towers Pierce the Skies," p. 316; Muller, "Selective Urban Growth."

27. Anthony F. C. Wallace, *Rockdale: The Growth of an American Village in the Early Industrial Revolution* (New York: Knopf, 1978).

28. T. D. Seymour Bassett, "A Case Study of Urban Impact on Rural Society: Vermont, 1840–80," *Agricultural History* 30 (January 1956): 34.

29. Guest, "Ecological Succession in the Puget Sound Region"; Craig R. Humphrey and Ralph R. Sell, "The Impact of Controlled Access Highways on Population Growth in Pennsylvania Nonmetropolitan Communities, 1940–1970," *Rural Sociology* 40 (Fall 1975): 332–43.

30. Roderick D. McKenzie, *The Metropolitan Community* (New York: McGraw-Hill, 1933); John Friedmann and John Miller, "The Urban Field," *Journal of the American Institute of Planners* 31 (November 1965): 312–20; Brian Berry and John Kasarda, *Contemporary Urban Ecology* (New York: Macmillan, 1977), pp. 271–304; Jane Jacobs, *Cities and the Wealth of Nations* (New York: Random House, 1984).

31. For early examples, see A. C. Spectorsky, *The Exurbanites* (Philadelphia: J. P. Lippincott Co., 1955); Jean Gottmann, *Megalopolis: The Urbanized Northeastern Seaboard of the United States* (New York: Twentieth Century Fund, 1961).

32. Richard White, *Land Use, Environment and Social Change: The Shaping of Island County, Washington* (Seattle: University of Washington Press, 1980).

33. Richard Lamb, *Metropolitan Impacts on Rural America* (Chicago: University of Chicago Department of Geography, 1975), p. 186.

34. Edward Ullman, "Regional Development and the Geography of Concentration," *Papers and Proceedings of the Regional Science Association* 4 (1958): 179–98. Also see Chauncey D. Harris, "The Market as a Factor in the Localization of Industry in the United States," *Annals of the Association of American Geographers* 44 (December 1954): 315–48.

35. For the idea of an urban size ratchet, see Wilbur Thompson, *Preface to Urban Economics* (Baltimore: Johns Hopkins University Press, 1965), pp. 21–24.

36. For superior summaries of colonial urban development, see Jacob Price, "Economic Function and the Growth of American Port Towns in the Eighteenth Century," in Donald Fleming and Bernard Bailyn, eds., *Perspectives in American History* (Cambridge, Mass.: Charles Warren Center for Studies in American History, 1974), vol 8; James E. Vance, Jr., *The Merchant's World: The Geography of Wholesaling* (Englewood Cliffs, N.J.: Prentice-Hall, 1970), pp. 68–79; Carville Earle and Ronald Hoffman, "The Urban South: The First Two Centuries," in Blaine Brownell and David Goldfield, eds., *The City in Southern History* (Port Washington, N.Y.: Kennikat Press, 1977), pp. 23–51.

37. Robert G. Albion, *The Rise of New York Port, 1815–1860* (New York: Charles Scribner's Sons, 1939); James Livingood, *The Philadelphia-Baltimore Trade Rivalry, 1790–1840* (Harrisburg: Pennsylvania Historical and Museum Commission, 1947); Julius Rubin, *Canal or Railroad? Imitation and Innovation in the Response to the Erie Canal in Philadelphia, Baltimore, and Boston,* Transactions of the American Philosophical Society, n.s., vol. 51, pt. 7 (1961); David Gilchrist, ed., *The Growth of the Seaport Cities, 1790–1825* (Charlottesville: University of Virginia Press, 1967).

38. Richard C. Wade, *The Urban Frontier: The Rise of Western Cities, 1790–1830* (Cambridge, Mass.: Harvard University Press, 1959); Allan Pred, *Urban Growth and*

the Circulation of Information: The United States System of Cities, 1790–1840 (Cambridge, Mass.: Harvard University Press, 1973), pp. 1–11.

39. Pred, *Urban Growth.*

40. Allan Pred, *Urban Growth and City Systems in the United States, 1840–1860* (Cambridge, Mass.: Harvard University Press, 1980), pp. 48–49; Harry Scheiber, *Ohio Canal Era: A Case Study of Government and the Economy, 1820–1861* (Athens: Ohio University Press, 1969).

41. A. L. Kohlmeier, *The Old Northwest as the Keystone in the Arch of American Federal Union* (Bloomington, Ind.: Principia Press, 1938); Wyatt W. Belcher, *The Economic Rivalry between St. Louis and Chicago, 1850–1880* (New York: Columbia University Press, 1947); John M. Clark, *The Grain Trade in the Old Northwest* (Urbana: University of Illinois Press, 1966); Pred, *Urban Growth and City Systems.*

42. Walsh, *Rise of the Midwestern Meat Packing Industry.*

43. David Ward, *Cities and Immigrants* (New York: Oxford University Press, 1971), pp. 11–49; David R. Meyer, "Emergence of the American Manufacturing Belt: An Interpretation," *Journal of Historical Geography* 9 (April 1983): 145–74.

44. Robert E. Park and Charles Newcomb, "Newspaper Circulation and Metropolitan Regions," in McKenzie, *Metropolitan Community*, pp. 98–110; Duncan, *Metropolis and Region*. For other sophisticated attempts to define urban hierarchy and hinterlands, see Rupert Vance and Sara Smith, "Metropolitan Dominance and Integration," in Rupert Vance and Nicholas Demerath, eds., *The Urban South* (Chapel Hill: University of North Carolina Press, 1954), pp. 114–34; Beverly Duncan and Stanley Lieberson, *Metropolis and Region in Transition* (Beverly Hills: Sage Publications, 1970); John R. Borchert, "America's Changing Metropolitan Regions," *Annals of the Association of American Geographers* 62 (June 1972): 352–73.

45. Gottmann, *Megalopolis.*

46. Conzen, "Maturing Urban System"; Duncan, *Metropolis and Region*, p. 159; Allan Pred, *City Systems in Advanced Economies* (New York: Wiley, 1977).

47. T. Lynn Smith, "The Emergence of Cities," in Vance and Demerath, *Urban South*, pp. 24–37; Leonard P. Curry, "Urbanization and Urbanism in the Old South: A Comparative View," *Journal of Southern History* 40 (February 1974): 43–66; Howard Rabinowitz, "Continuity and Change in Southern Urban Development, 1860–1900," in Brownell and Goldfield, *City in Southern History*, pp. 91–122.

48. Inclusive descriptions of the metropolitan patterns in the Far West can be found in Rodman Paul, *Mining Frontiers of the Far West, 1848–1880* (New York: Holt, Rinehart and Winston, 1963), and in Meinig, "American Wests."

49. Duane A. Smith, *Rocky Mountain Mining Camps: The Urban Frontier* (Bloomington: Indiana University Press, 1967); Robert R. Dykstra, *The Cattle Towns* (New York: Knopf, 1968); Roger Olien and Diana Davids Olien, *Oil Booms: Social Change in Five Texas Towns* (Lincoln: University of Nebraska Press, 1982); Lawrence Larsen, *The Urban West at the End of the Frontier* (Lawrence: Regents Press of Kansas, 1978); John Reps, *Cities of the American West* (Princeton: Princeton University Press, 1979); Roger Lotchin, *San Francisco, 1846–1856: From Hamlet to City* (New York: Oxford University Press, 1974), p. 346.

50. Leonard Reissman, "Social Development and the American South," *Journal of Social Issues* 22 (January 1966): 102.

51. Lorin A. Thompson, "Urbanization, Occupational Shift, and Economic Progress," in Vance and Demerath, *Urban South*, pp. 38–53; Selz C. Mayo, "Social Change, Social

Movements and the Disappearing Sectional South," *Social Forces* 43 (October 1964): 1–10; William A. Nichols, "The South as a Developing Area," in Avery Leiserson, ed., *The American South in the 1960s* (New York: Praeger, 1964), pp. 22–40; James Clotfelter and Thomas H. Naylor, *Strategies for Change in the South* (Chapel Hill: University of North Carolina Press, 1975).

52. Vance and Demerath, *Urban South*, p. viii; John C. McKinney and Linda Brookover Bourque, "The Changing South: National Incorporation of a Region," *American Sociological Review* 36 (June 1971): 399–412.

53. Blaine A. Brownell, "Urbanization in the South: A Unique Experience?" *Mississippi Quarterly* 26 (Spring 1973): 120.

54. John S. Reed, *The Enduring South* (Lexington, Mass.: D. C. Heath, 1972); John S. Reed, *One South: An Ethnic Approach to Regional Culture* (Baton Rouge: Louisiana State University Press, 1982); Charles P. Roland, "The Ever-Vanishing South," *Journal of Southern History* 48 (February 1982): 3–20; George B. Tindall, *The Ethnic Southerners* (Baton Rouge: Louisiana State University Press, 1976); Wilbur Zelinsky, *The Cultural Geography of the United States* (Englewood Cliffs, N.J.: Prentice-Hall, 1973); Gastil, *Cultural Regions*.

55. James C. Cobb, "Urbanization and the Changing South," *South Atlantic Urban Studies* 1 (1977): 253–65.

56. Brownell and Goldfield, *City in Southern History*; David Goldfield, *Cottonfields and Skyscrapers: Southern City and Region, 1607–1980* (Baton Rouge: Louisiana State University Press, 1982).

57. For a discussion of sunbelt definitions, see Kirkpatrick Sale, *Power Shift: The Rise of the Southern Rim and Its Challenge to the Eastern Establishment* (New York: Random House, 1975); Clyde E. Browning and Wil Gesler, "Sun Belt-Snow Belt: A Case of Sloppy Regionalizing," *Professional Geographer* 31 (February 1979): 66–74; Carl Abbott, *The New Urban America: Growth and Politics in Sunbelt Cities* (Chapel Hill: University of North Carolina Press, 1981): 3–33; Richard M. Bernard and Bradley R. Rice, eds., *Sunbelt Cities: Politics and Growth since World War II* (Austin: University of Texas Press, 1983), pp. 1–26.

58. James E. Vance, Jr., "California and the Search for the Ideal," *Annals of the Association of American Geographers* 62 (June 1972): 204–10; Neil Morgan, *Westward Tilt* (New York: Random House, 1963); Kevin Phillips, *The Emerging Republican Majority* (New Rochelle, N.Y.: Arlington House, 1969); John Naisbitt, *Megatrends* (New York: Warner Books, 1984).

59. Bernard L. Weinstein and Robert E. Firestine, *Regional Growth and Decline in the United States: The Rise of the Sunbelt and the Decline of the Northeast* (New York: Praeger, 1978); Alfred J. Watkins and David C. Perry, "Regional Change and the Impact of Uneven Urban Development," in Watkins and Perry, eds., *The Rise of the Sunbelt Cities* (Beverly Hills: Sage Publications, 1977), pp. 19–54.

60. Bradford Luckingham, "The American Southwest: An Urban View," *Western Historical Quarterly* 15 (July 1984): 261–80; Bradford Luckingham, *The Urban Southwest: A Profile History of Albuquerque, El Paso, Phoenix, Tucson* (El Paso: Texas Western Press, 1982); Gerald Nash, *The American West in World War II* (Bloomington: Indiana University Press, 1985); Abbott, *New Urban America*; Bernard and Rice, *Sunbelt Cities*.

61. Borchert, "America's Changing Metropolitan Regions"; Thierry J. Noyelle, "The Rise of Advanced Services: Some Implications for Economic Development in U.S. Cities," *Journal of the American Planning Association* 49 (Summer 1983): 280–89.

62. Donald W. Meinig, *Southwest: The Peoples in Geographical Change* (New York: Oxford University Press, 1971).

63. Karl Deutsch, "The Growth of Nations: Some Recurrent Patterns of Political and Social Integration," *World Politics* 5 (January 1953): 168–95; idem, *Nationalism and Social Communication* (Cambridge, Mass.: MIT Press, 1966).

64. For a demographic description of core areas, see Daniel R. Vining, Jr., "Migration between the Core and the Periphery," *Scientific American* 247 (December 1982): 44–53.

65. William H. McNeill, *The Rise of the West: A History of the Human Community* (Chicago: University of Chicago Press, 1963); Immanuel Wallerstein, *The Modern World-System II: Mercantilism and the Consolidation of the European World Economy, 1600–1750* (Orlando: Academic Press, 1980); Bernard Bailyn, "The Challenge of Modern Historiography," *American Historical Review* 87 (February 1982): 1–24. Also see Jean Gottmann, ed., *Centre and Periphery: Spatial Variation in Politics* (Beverly Hills: Sage Publications, 1980). Bailyn (p. 17) argues that one of the important frontiers of historiography is the "concept of inclusive systems with centers and margins, whose integrity as systems is essential to understanding the individual parts within them."

14 _____ Doing Local History: Monographic Approaches to the Smaller Community

ROBERT R. DYKSTRA AND WILLIAM SILAG

"If I were to anticipate history and make predictions," wrote Paul Leuilliot in 1967, "I would ask, 'What should—and what will—be the place of local history and the role of the local historian in 1985?' "[1] Unhappily, the distinguished *annaliste* refused to anticipate or predict. That very year, however, American local history (if not the French variety) lay poised on the brink of an era of inspired productivity. Eighteen years later, it is proper for the results to be critically assessed.

Two imposing essays of relatively recent vintage lighten this task by providing extensive descriptions of the monographic literature. Thomas Bender's largely theoretical *Community and Social Change in America* and Kathleen Neils Conzen's largely bibliographical "Community Studies, Urban History, and American Local History" need, to date, no replication.[2] The present inquiry instead will attempt to draw forth some larger themes having to do with what we have learned about approaches to local history rather than with substantive results. Especially (but not exclusively) in the years since 1967, what have we learned about doing local history?

This chapter will focus attention on the historiography of villages and towns in America in the nineteenth and twentieth centuries, although we will occasionally refer to studies of earlier or larger communities if these offer particularly apt examples.

The community studies of the past decades have sensitized us to an important distinction between urban history and the history of smaller communities, usually described as local history. All large cities may well merit the scholarly attention they have received, since each community of a certain large size may have played a unique role in American regional or national development. But most smaller communities do not share that claim to significance, and few of them appear to deserve scholarly treatment.

Why, then, have historians studied smaller communities? There are two reasons. First, like cities, some villages and towns have been deemed uniquely important, deserving singular scholarly treatment. Late seventeenth-century Salem Village, for example, is historically important because of its notorious witch trials; nineteenth-century Concord, Massachusetts, because of its resident Transcendentalists; early Rochester, New York, not only because of its status as the nation's first interior boomtown but also for its central role in the famous Second Great Awakening; frontier Deadwood and Tombstone and Dodge City because of their dramatic contribution to the mythology of the American West; late nineteenth-century Pullman, Illinois, because of its status as a unique experiment in utopian capitalist paternalism; twentieth-century Scarsdale, New York, because of its fame as the archetypal upper middle-class metropolitan suburb.[3]

For one reason or another, therefore, these smaller communities, and many more, have deserved separate monographic attention. The best such histories, however, not only offer a relatively comprehensive study of a community within certain chronological boundaries but also have generated results that add to our substantive, theoretical, or methodological knowledge in general. Paul Boyer and Stephen Nissenbaum's *Salem Possessed* suggests, at one point, that the witchcraft episode might have been simply another religious revival had the village minister so construed the excitement, an observation fraught with Durkheimian implications about the nature of Puritan religious energy (and of much more persuasive force than the authors' application of modernization theory). Or, to cite far less dramatic examples, Paul E. Johnson's *A Shopkeeper's Millennium* and Robert R. Dykstra's *The Cattle Towns*, in Conzen's estimate, offer insights about the "influence of hinterland values upon townsmen dependent on their [rural] trade."[4] Many scholars of the smaller community will steer toward such a goal: a good study of an intrinsically important place that also manages to say something about American culture in general.

The case study approach—"national history localized," in the words of H. P. R. Finberg—has come to dominate much, if not most, recent local history produced by professional historians.[5] Those works that reflect their authors' interest in some particular translocal phenomenon are most common. Peter R. Knights' book on Boston or Stephan Thernstrom's on Newburyport or Howard

Chudacoff's on Omaha, for example, are actually studies of social and geographic mobility. Alan Dawley's study of Lynn, Massachusetts, and Anthony F. C. Wallace's study of Rockdale, Pennsylvania, are—each in its own way—analyses of the social context of early industrialization.[6]

Far less common in recent years have been comprehensive studies of urbanization that, like their special purpose counterparts, examine communities selected more or less at random. Authors of case studies do not usually address the question of typicality with any degree of relish; most offer the reasonable hope that the chosen communities are, if not demonstrably representative, at least not uniquely atypical.[7] The main problem of picking a strictly (that is, a statistically) typical historical community, of course, is that such a community may be cursed with inferior historical resources: typicality may not match up with "do-ability."

Still, a number of highly respected local case studies can be faulted less on grounds of atypicality than by virtue of being based on source materials far less than perfect in quality. Thus Stephanie Grauman Wolf selected for study a heavily Quaker community (Germantown, Pennsylvania) that lacked Quaker records for over half her period; Robert Doherty implies that if he had it to do all over again, he would have dropped nineteenth-century Salem from his study of Bay State towns (for one thing, the 1860 census microfilm proved unreadable); and Stuart M. Blumin elected to study an urbanizing community so lacking in some early records that he ends by telling us that he cannot empirically describe the character of preurban Kingston, New York.[8] Surprisingly few case study selections have been as meticulous as Mary P. Ryan's choice of Oneida County, New York, for exploring the community context of family composition in the late eighteenth and early nineteenth centuries. The quantity and exceptionally high quality of the materials available for Ryan's study clearly help account for its apparently definitive character. Similarly, Hal S. Barron's choice of Chelsea, Vermont, is the very model of a brilliant case selection strategy. Concerned with the nature of nineteenth-century rural society within the context of agricultural decline as well as rise, his selection of an appropriate community focus involved a four-step process, his narrowing choices being: (1) New England, "the [nation's] first agricultural region to grow old"; (2) Vermont, "the least affected [of all New England states] by urbanization, industrialization, and immigration, and [which] remained predominantly rural throughout the nineteenth century"; (3) those Vermont townships that had "lost at least one-fourth of their population during the second half of the nineteenth century"; and (4) Chelsea, which possessed the "most promising records" of any of those townships.[9]

Recent historians of the smaller community unanimously agree that their research findings should be comparative. One is reminded, for example, that the most interesting datum in Boyer and Nissenbaum's study of Salem—that its witchcraft episode could instead have been a revival—comes from a specific comparison between Salem and the Northampton, Massachusetts, of Jonathan

Edwards.[10] But comparative studies are easier to applaud than to devise. Often the issue of research design boils down to a question of how many locations should be included in a single work.

The novel framework for analysis suggested by Eric E. Lampard nearly twenty-five years ago still awaits systematic testing. This social ecology approach would abstract the "changing structure and organization of communities" in terms of four quantifiable variables (indicators of population, environment, technology, and social organization), according to which any number of places might then be compared.[11] Lampard's formulation has elicited much admiration but little action; acquisition of the necessary data presents challenges that would daunt even the most energetic historian. Still, J. Rogers and Jane Hollingsworth's study of public expenditures in American cities and Edward M. Cook, Jr.'s, examination of leadership and community structure in seventy-four eighteenth-century New England towns, while not embracing Lampard's full range of variables, suggest both the attractions of the Lampardian approach—the broadest kinds of comparability—and its major drawback—such an aesthetically discouraging transcendence of traditional local history as to resemble some other genre entirely.[12]

Despite Lampard's strictures, therefore, the single-community study, or community biography, remains the most common format for local history. And whatever else one may say about it, the community biography possesses the virtue of coherence and readability. It allows for the maximum of the good historian's organizational balance, as Jacques Barzun and Henry F. Graff have described it, between topical and chronological treatments of any subject.[13] The main drawback is that the community biographer has nothing to compare with except other local studies—which leaves him or her at the mercy of others' research. The advent of statistical usage in local history—beginning with Merle Curti's famous Trempealeau County, Wisconsin, study—has enhanced comparability a good deal, but a lack of scholarly consensus about how to aggregate statistical data often frustrates measurement precision.[14] It was in response to this problem that in the 1970s five historians attempted, under the rubric of the Five Cities Project, to standardize their categories for mid-nineteenth-century occupational structures. The salutary consequences of the project's cooperative research design are exhibited in books by Blumin on Kingston, Michael B. Katz on Hamilton, Ontario, and Clyde Griffen and Sally Griffen on Poughkeepsie, New York. For example, the first chapter of the Griffens' *Natives and Newcomers* presents the urban development of nineteenth-century Poughkeepsie in a descriptive framework that includes frequent comparisons between Poughkeepsie and the project's four other cities with respect to the growth of local enterprise, the local division of labor, and the processes of geographic and occupational mobility. Likewise, the Griffens' conclusions concerning local levels of inequality are informed by the findings of their Five Cities colleagues.[15]

To be taken seriously, a community biography today must make at least some use of available quantitative data, although considerable variation exists. Katz's

The People of Hamilton, Canada West remains perhaps the most ambitiously quantitative community biography yet produced, reflecting a research devotion to statistical procedures so exclusive as to suggest that only measurable features of socioeconomic structure (that is, indicators of class) really matter. Katz assures readers, however, that his monograph is just an "initial, extended statement" about nineteenth-century Hamilton, against which more interpretive hypotheses will be evaluated in subsequent studies.[16] Similarly, Doherty's rather skeletal quantitative study of nineteenth-century Massachusetts communities is presented as only a progress report, not the final product.[17]

A promising variation on the standard community biography achieves comparability in an entirely different way. Found in Sam Bass Warner, Jr.'s, study of Philadelphia, it will ultimately characterize Robert Gross' trilogy on Concord, Massachusetts. Under its terms, different periods of the same place are compared according to such key social indicators as spatial organization, occupational structure, and political activity. Comparative attributes aside, the effect of the Philadelphia study is a rather pleasing efficiency of presentation that one could wish the writers of many a fat urban tome had discovered long before Warner.[18]

The two-community study has made its appearance in the last decades. Although providing comparability, two communities are still too few to form patterns (three being the minimal number), so that recourse must still be had to data on places external to the study. In form, the approach often seems to entail rather abrupt shifts back and forth between communities. Gunther Barth's paired examination of early San Francisco and Denver, for example, is a bit reminiscent of William Faulkner's experimental novel *The Wild Palms*, which involves following two distinct plots in alternating chapters, a task that tries the patience of some readers. The best of the two-community subgenre are probably Daniel Walkowitz's study of Troy and Cohoes, New York, and Ralph Mann's *After the Gold Rush*, which treats two California mining camps. In each instance, the duality does not damage coherence, presumably because Troy and Cohoes are geographically adjacent communities, as are Mann's frontier settlements. Locational similarities thereby reduce the significance of many ecological variables, enabling the historian to concentrate on social indicators related to political organization or economic development. This may also be observed with respect to Blumin's study of nineteenth-century Kingston, which is in fact a comparative analysis of two legally separate but geographically adjoining towns: Kingston, the overtly targeted community, and Rondout, its principal nineteenth-century suburb.[19]

It is perhaps significant that Blumin's project originally encompassed two other New York towns besides Kingston/Rondout, while Don Harrison Doyle's well-known Jacksonville study began as a comparative analysis of Jacksonville and two other Illinois towns. Blumin's research embraces forty years, and Doyle's is equally ambitious, spanning forty-five years. In each case the inclusion of additional communities—given the comprehensive approach of its author—would no doubt have required the drastic shortening of chronological coverage.[20]

Still, the advantages of a broader comparative scope are revealed in a number of local studies employing five communities. Those that come readily to mind include Carl Bridenbaugh's *Cities in the Wilderness*, the earliest important example; Richard C. Wade's *The Urban Frontier;* Dykstra's *The Cattle Towns*; Doherty's *Society and Power;* and David Grayson Allen's *In English Ways*. Each focuses on a set of relatively small communities (Doherty's Worcester, Massachusetts, with an 1860 population of 24,960, is the largest), and it is probable that for bigger cities the approach becomes much too unwieldy.[21] Take, for example, one of its more recent exemplifications, Frederic Cople Jaher's *The Urban Establishment*. Jaher's book eschews a truly comparative method and instead consists, perhaps necessarily, of five separate single-city essays connected only by concluding remarks.[22]

A number of local historians have dealt successfully with more than five communities simultaneously, prominent examples being Lewis Atherton's *Main Street on the Middle Border* and Michael Zuckerman's *Peaceable Kingdoms*. The examination of eight midwestern country towns of the late nineteenth and early twentieth centuries lies at the heart of Atherton's treatment, although their particular experiences are lost in an avalanche of materials garnered from literature, autobiography, and McGuffey's readers.[23] Similarly, at the core of Zuckerman's book are the records for eight eighteenth-century Massachusetts communities, although its author does not confine himself to this universe.[24] In both instances, while the reader obtains an extraordinarily intimate sense of the character of life in midwestern and late colonial settlements, the individuality of these communities as distinct places is necessarily lost. Such studies may therefore be considered as lying at the near end of a multicommunity continuum that ultimately stretches all the way to Lampardian transcendence, with the sacrifice of sense of place reposing rather nearer the community biography than might have been supposed.

Each sample size, if we may so describe it, has its particular rewards. The community biography possesses an essential coherence that means it can most easily be organized into a rigorous topical treatment that remains satisfyingly chronological. And it can be made broadly comparable, especially through statistical usages, with other community studies. Still, comparative references can seem distractingly intrusive when repeatedly encountered in the text of a single-community study. An attractive alternative is to be found in Mann's *After the Gold Rush*, which segregates the author's appropriate deference to the literature in a concluding chapter, an appendix, and backnotes.

The most satisfying feature of the five-community approach is that it provides a sample size large enough to generate patterns. Comparisons rise naturally within the study itself. This independence of the literature, or at least of others' research preoccupations, can be critically important if there is, in effect, not much of a literature for comparison. The incidence of town-country conflict in *The Cattle Towns* forms a case in point. There was in 1968 (and still is) virtually no historical literature on normal socioeconomic tensions between farmers and townspeople, so that the book's discussion of the topic is dependent on internal comparisons.[25] But imagine the treatment of the topic if the book were a community biography. If Caldwell alone had been its subject, the question of town-country tensions would not have arisen at all; if Abilene, it could have been dismissed as an artifact of farmer-cattleman antagonism; if Dodge City, it might have been subsumed under Spearville's political competition with the county seat. Only in Ellsworth and Wichita did the phenomenon express itself in ways that suggest its universal saliency.[26] A two-community study—of the proper two cattle-trading centers—would have brought it to light, but a five-community approach provides sufficient complexity and variation as to lend it credibility despite a lack of exogenous validation through comparison with other studies.

Any multicommunity approach should embrace only communities that are truly comparable. This means controlling for some essential variable such as economic base—so that one compares and contrasts cattle towns or mining camps or industrial villages—which will in turn tend to highlight social and political variations within each group. Conversely, one can control for some important cultural variable—ethnicity and religion, for example—so that in examining five predominantly Dutch Reform villages, one might hope to highlight economic or political variations. No doubt population size and regional location also have some bearing on ensuring that comparative local history avoids the apples-and-oranges fallacy.

Scholars of the smaller community will not find much in the way of theory to guide them, although local history has not been without its assertions of general applicability. If theory is defined sufficiently loosely, however, it becomes permissible to speak of a higher order of generalizing as theoretical, and we may observe that two theoretical preoccupations have dominated historians' encounters with the smaller place.

The first has been frontier democracy. It originated with Frederick Jackson Turner's famous hypothesis but was not explicitly the realm of local historians until publication in 1954 of the much-admired essay by Stanley M. Elkins and Eric McKitrick, "A Meaning for Turner's Frontier." The essay transposed the hypothesis into a model capable of empirical evaluation on the local level. Defining democracy as a "manipulative attitude toward government . . . a wide participation in public affairs, a diffusion of leadership, [and] a widespread sense of personal competence to make a difference," the authors hypothesized its occurrence whenever a socially and politically homogeneous pioneer settlement confronted common problems. Applying this formula to three different frontiers, they found it describing reality in early Puritan Massachusetts and the Jacksonian Midwest but not in the antebellum South, where ready-made local elites and the social consequences of cotton monoculture frustrated its emergence. They thus considered Turner validated.[27]

The Elkins-McKitrick model had not yet been critically addressed in the literature when a second conceptualization, Allan G. Bogue's prairie model, appeared in 1960. Bogue's model invited a test of four quantitative propositions:

that the frontier—in contrast to the settled East—had witnessed (1) more social conflict, (2) more interpersonal cooperation, (3) more emotional deprivation (thus more crime, religious enthusiasm, mental illness, and geographic mobility), and (4) more politicization.[28] Although the prairie model represented a quantum advance over Turner's crude environmentalism, Ray Allen Billington promptly noted its implicit support of Turner's argument for western exceptionalism.[29]

Six years later, *The Cattle Towns* offered an empirically based commentary on the Elkins-McKitrick model, suggesting that in place of the irrepressibly cooperative problem solving posited by the model, the frontier community might more typically have perceived problems as issues whose manner of resolution— cooperation or conflict—had been dictated by specific situational contexts. Dykstra also pointed out the historiographical flaw in Elkins and McKitrick's reliance on image-conscious nineteenth-century local studies for evidence, and he noted that the typical pioneer settlement may have been less devoted to the political formalism of the model than to a resolution of problems by conflict.[30] Since his largely self-contained study had suggested no major perspectives on frontier exceptionalism, however, he waived comment on Bogue's prairie model.

Meanwhile, a second preoccupation—the idea of community—increasingly monopolized the attention of local historians. The concept is Ferdinand Tonnies' gemeinschaft ("common-ship"), devised to describe an organic social relation- ship characterized by strong reciprocal bonds of sentiment and kinship within a common tradition—as, for example, in a peasant village. Apparently prompted by Perry Miller's portrait of Puritan religious declension in New England, Amer- icanists recruited geminschaft into a "decline-of-local-community" formulation that implicitly debated—in a kind of parody of Roman historiography—which century (or even decade) had witnessed the definitive decline. In time, Page Smith's "covenanted" and "cumulative" typology for pioneer towns, if not methodologically useful, implicitly resolved the issue by demonstrating that local gemeinschaft had been revitalized at will throughout American history.[31] By the mid-1970s, the decline scenario had lost its attraction, and a more sophisticated approach to community had emerged, largely stimulated by the work of Stuart Blumin and Michael H. Frisch.

Frisch's study of urbanizing Springfield, Massachusetts, argued that by 1880 geminschaft had not so much declined as been redefined in terms more appropriate to a newly emergent city: "Springfield traded an immediate sense of community for an exalted and abstract one."[32] Blumin's treatment, embracing an urbanizing town of similar population, mainly made use of the changing character of local newspaper contents—from international and national news to local news—in arguing that Kingstonians had never enjoyed a sense of community until the 1840s, when the intrusion of cosmopolitan economic and cultural influences "created a countercurrent of parochial, community-based action and identity." As to whether his or Frisch's interpretation was the more widely applicable, Blumin asserted that "perhaps on Yankee soil [these influences] simply altered a strong, preexisting sense of local community. But on Yorker soil, and no doubt in other regions outside communal New England, the effect seems to have been more creative: urban growth and regional integration strengthened communal sentiments and processes that earlier had been only weakly developed."[33]

Certainly Blumin's interpretation can be seen as the more empirical of the two. It may simply be wrong, however, if (as seems the case) Blumin assumes that the emergence of a new communal sense caused the appearance of a Kingston-oriented local journalism.[34] A less complicated explanation for this change might be the antebellum pre-emption of national and international news by the *New York Herald* and its imitators, which left small-town editors in the city's hinterland with no entrepreneurial choice but to begin—at last—reporting the local news. Contrary to Blumin's argument, not a change in local attitudes reflected in the local press but rather a scheme for economic survival initiated by the local press may well account for what Blumin found in the newspapers.[35]

The two major themes, frontier democracy and community, finally converged in Don Doyle's highly regarded 1978 monograph on early Jacksonville, Illinois, a study that for many readers definitively exhausted the historiographical potential of both themes and resolved all important theoretical questions relating to their use. In writing it, Doyle employed the major literature on frontier decision making while disclaiming any intrinsic interest in it, preferring, he said, "to proceed toward what I see as the central problem of an expanding mobile society—the problem of community."[36] In doing so, he paired the Elkins-McKitrick model and the prairie model as conceptual alternatives (which they are not), construed *The Cattle Towns* as an empirical test of the prairie model (which it was not), and—having noted the coincidence of Bogue's theoretical emphasis on social conflict and *The Cattle Towns'* methodological cautionaries—extrapolated a linkage between the two that ignored the independent judgment of each on the equal importance of both conflict and cooperation.[37]

Significantly, only the first and third propositions of the prairie model—more conflict and more emotional deprivation—merited emphasis by Doyle. The fourth—more politics—he dismissed as agreement with Elkins and McKitrick. The second proposition—more cooperation—he did not mention at all. The resulting composite was then measured against the Elkins-McKitrick model, revealing the "polarity between Elkins and McKitrick's instant community of expectant boosters and the contentious atmosphere of Bogue and Dykstra's frontier communities," a juxtaposition later phrased even more starkly as a contrast between the "harmonious band of boosters" depicted by Elkins and McKitrick and the "disordered anarchy of strangers portrayed by their critics."[38]

Having fabricated a historiographical disagreement between simple Lockean and Hobbesian models, Doyle proceeded to an unsurprising conclusion: the truth lay somewhere in between. He found Jacksonville's early experience shot through with social conflict, yet a gemeinschaft much as Blumin defined it had emerged and survived.[39] But his explication rose less from his survey of Jacksonville's early history than from sociological logic. First, said Doyle, a network of middle-class voluntary associations theoretically modulated social conflict: "by [the

1840s] local leaders and citizens came to accept certain ground rules for public discussion, even when they disagreed violently on the point at issue."[40] Second, the sheer number of conflicts theoretically ensured community stability by frustrating the development of any lasting polarization.

A few caveats come to mind. First, it will be noted that Doyle's interpretation is a description of interlocking abstractions (an essence—"community"—plus two social forces), leaving the interpretation empirically impossible to prove or disprove. Second, social conflict, which is instrumental in Doyle's multicleavage treatment, is defined so broadly as to include unexceptional differences of political opinion, diversities of religious doctrine, competing ethnocentrisms, and much else that scholars usually write off as mere cultural pluralism. Third, there was a moment in Jacksonville's history when all its social conflicts appear to have converged into a genuine community polarization. That it is likely to go unnoticed by readers of Doyle's book is because he distributed its component incidents among separate chapters, where only recurrence of the date "1862" is likely to alert the unusually perspicacious reader. Reconstituted from the book itself, the events of 1862 and their background may be briefly described and interpreted as follows.

Prohibition had become the town's most important political issue. Between 1858 and 1861 Jacksonville was officially dry although unable to suppress an underground traffic in liquor. At one point, frustrated dry extremists threatened arson against houses rented to Irish bootleggers. In 1861 the wets triumphed, returning Jacksonville to wide-open status, after which several disastrous fires were said to be "traceable to the liquor traffic." The state then established a Union army camp near town, which apparently raised "respectable" citizens' concern over liquor and social disorder to new heights.[41]

In March 1862 local Methodists organized Jacksonville's most enthusiastic religious revival ever, a fury of religious enthusiasm so intense that it impelled other churches to follow suit, even some Catholics joining in with a protracted meeting of their own. A month later, as one apparent result, anti-liquor candidates again won control of city hall, reimposing prohibition. A pitched battle between police and residents of the town's Portuguese quarter suggests the existence of a get-tough attitude toward pro-liquor citizens on the part of the new council. One immediate casualty was a community July Fourth celebration: Jacksonville's angered Germans and Irish commemorated the occasion outside city limits, where they might legally consume whatever they wished.[42]

This polarity of wets and drys had already largely reproduced—and gave dynamic expression to—cleavages between Democrats and Republicans and between religious liturgicals and evangelicals. But then an unhealthy dose of Civil War issues—this was, after all, southern Illinois—added its polarizing increment. In June, after a local college student had been refused permission to voice racist sentiments in his commencement address, a downtown rally against slave emancipation occurred. The opponents of such activities then formed a Union League for the purpose of surreptitiously gathering data on residents suspected of disloyalty. That autumn mysterious fires devastated both the Methodist women's college and the Presbyterian church, institutions closely associated, one may presume, with the campaign against strong drink and with ideological adherence to the Union cause. A year later, in fact, the office of the local Republican newspaper had twice been destroyed by arsonists.[43]

Eighteen sixty-two, then, witnessed a town beset by two angry blocs: the militantly wet, anti-war, heavily ethnic, and blue-collar Democrats opposing the dry, strongly Unionist, mainly old-stock, and white-collar Republicans. So much for the stabilizing power of minor social cleavages. So much for the moderating influence of enduring associational networks. Jacksonville's factions did not physically decimate one another, so far as we know, but the accumulated ambience must have been less that of Blumin's peaceable Kingston than it was the "contentious atmosphere" of the Kansas cattle towns. So much, indeed, for gemeinschaft at Jacksonville.

Where this leaves the relationship of local history to frontier history and community is problematical. If the most fully realized works of the genre to be produced in the last few years are any guide, the message is that the approach to the smaller community in America has given up both preoccupations, replacing them with a kind of eclectic empiricism that depends far less on functionalist sociology than on the findings of recent social history, both new (quantitative) and narrative. This may not mean that the older preoccupations have lost their relevance for organizing local studies but only that there seems no way to carry these themes forward to any definitive resolution. Pending the ability to decide between Frisch and Blumin, for example, or between the Elkins-McKitrick model and its critics, local historians may be resting content with lower-order generalizations that come with mastery of a literature increasingly sophisticated in terms of analytical method, quantitative and otherwise.

Without hesitation we can answer Paul Leuilliot's question for American scholarship in the affirmative: the place of local history and the role of local historians are unusually secure given the permanent advent of the case study approach to empirical social history. Yet some may prefer to be less sanguine, seeing in the declension of theoretical concerns a genre temporarily short on conceptual innovation and a coterie of scholars who know more about how to do local history than about why it should be done. And if that is true, it clearly tells us more about where local history finds itself today than it tells us about where it ought to go next.

Notes

1. Paul Leuilliot, "A Manifesto: The Defense and Illustration of Local History," in Robert Forster and Orest Ranum, eds., *Rural Society in France: Selections from the Annales*, trans. Elborg Forster and Patricia M. Ranum (Baltimore: Johns Hopkins University Press, 1977), p. 21.

2. Thomas Bender, *Community and Social Change in America* (New Brunswick:

Rutgers University Press, 1978); Kathleen Neils Conzen, "Community Studies, Urban History, and American Local History," in Michael Kammen, ed., *The Past Before Us: Contemporary Historical Writing in the United States* (Ithaca and London: Cornell University Press, 1980), pp. 270–91.

3. Paul Boyer and Stephen Nissenbaum, *Salem Possessed: The Social Origins of Witchcraft* (Cambridge, Mass.: Harvard University Press, 1974); Robert A. Gross, *The Minutemen and Their World* (New York: Hill and Wang, 1976); Paul E. Johnson, *A Shopkeeper's Millennium: Society and Revivals in Rochester, New York, 1815–1837* (New York: Hill and Wang, 1978); Watson Parker, *Deadwood: The Golden Years* (Lincoln: University of Nebraska, 1981); Odie B. Faulk, *Tombstone: Myth and Reality* (New York: Oxford University Press, 1972); Robert R. Dykstra, *The Cattle Towns* (New York: Knopf, 1968); Stanley Buder, *Pullman: An Experiment in Industrial Order and Community Planning, 1880–1930* (New York: Oxford University Press, 1967); Carol A. O'Connor, *A Sort of Utopia: Scarsdale, 1891–1981* (Albany: State University of New York Press, 1983).

4. Boyer and Nissenbaum, *Salem Possessed,* pp. 212–16; Conzen, "Community Studies," p. 291n.

5. Quoted in Conzen, "Community Studies," p. 274n.

6. Peter R. Knights, *The Plain People of Boston, 1830–1860: A Study in City Growth* (New York: Oxford University Press, 1971); Stephan Thernstrom, *Poverty and Progress: Social Mobility in the Nineteenth-Century City* (Cambridge, Mass.: Harvard University Press, 1964); Howard Chudacoff, *Mobile Americans: Residential and Social Mobility in Omaha, 1880–1920* (New York: Oxford University Press, 1972); Alan Dawley, *Class and Community: The Industrial Revolution in Lynn* (Cambridge, Mass.: Harvard University Press, 1976); Anthony F. C. Wallace, *Rockdale: The Growth of an American Village in the Early Industrial Revolution* (New York: Knopf, 1978).

7. This concern for representativeness at least partially explains historians' recent interest in central place theory, which provides a model for the spatial distribution of communities within geographic regions. The theory presumes that communities holding similar positions in their respective central place hierarchies are likely to perform similar economic functions and to exhibit similar social structures. Thus, to analyze one such community is to analyze a representative of a type of community. The utility of central place theory as a method for selecting case studies is noted by Robert Doherty, *Society and Power: Five New England Towns, 1800–1860* (Amherst: University of Massachusetts Press, 1977), p. vii. For a more extensive discussion, see James T. Lemon, *The Best Poor Man's Country: A Geographical Study of Early Southeastern Pennsylvania* (New York: Norton, 1972), chap. 5.

8. Stephanie Grauman Wolf, *Urban Village: Population, Community, and Family Structure in Germantown, Pennsylvania, 1683–1800* (Princeton: Princeton University Press, 1976), p. 346; Doherty, *Society and Power,* pp. vii, 48; Stuart M. Blumin, *The Urban Threshold: Growth and Change in a Nineteenth-Century American Community* (Chicago: University of Chicago Press, 1976), p. 44.

9. Mary P. Ryan, *Cradle of the Middle Class: The Family in Oneida County, New York, 1790–1865* (New York: Cambridge University Press, 1981); Hal S. Barron, *Those Who Stayed Behind: Rural Society in Nineteenth-Century New England* (New York: Cambridge University Press, 1984), pp. xi, 15, 141n.

10. Boyer and Nissenbaum, *Salem Possessed,* pp. 215–16. For a painstaking, but not entirely successful, attempt to extrapolate the social meaning of the Northampton revivals

from sparse evidence, see Patricia S. Tracy, *Jonathan Edwards, Pastor: Religion and Society in Eighteenth-Century Northampton* (New York: Hill and Wang, 1979).

11. Lampard's formulation appeared first in "American Historians and the Study of Urbanization," *American Historical Review* 67 (October 1961): 49–61. Later refinements may be found in Lampard's "Historical Aspects of Urbanization," in Philip M. Hauser and Leo F. Schnore, eds., *The Study of Urbanization* (New York: Wiley, 1965), pp. 519–54, and "The Evolving System of Cities in the United States: Urbanization and Economic Development," in Harvey S. Perloff and Lowdon W. Wingo, Jr., eds., *Issues in Urban Economics* (Baltimore: Johns Hopkins University Press, 1968), pp. 81–139. Roy Lubove, "The Urbanization Process: An Approach to Historical Research," *Journal of the American Institute of Planners* 33 (January 1967): 33–39, places Lampard's ideas in a larger theoretical context that also includes the urbanization theories of Robert Park and Lewis Mumford.

12. J. Rogers Hollingsworth and Ellen Jane Hollingsworth, *Dimensions in Urban History: Historical and Social Science Perspectives on Middle-Size American Cities* (Madison: University of Wisconsin Press, 1979); Edward M. Cook, Jr., *The Fathers of the Towns: Leadership and Community Structure in Eighteenth-Century New England* (Baltimore: Johns Hopkins University Press, 1976). Although to date Lampard's formulation has exerted more influence as a heuristic device than as a prescription for historical analysis, a few recent studies do employ aspects of the formulation with excellent results. Among these is Roberta Balstad Miller's fine study of the nineteenth-century economic region centered in Syracuse, New York: *City and Hinterland: A Case Study of Urban Growth and Regional Development* (Westport, Conn.: Greenwood Press, 1979). And although, as Dykstra has noted (*The Cattle Towns*, p. 380), such esoteric variables as Lampard's "level of social organization" evade precise quantitative expression, the comprehensive character of the social ecology formulation continues to interest urban historians. For a recent admiring discussion of Lampard's ideas, see Michael H. Ebner, "Urban History: Retrospect and Prospect," *Journal of American History* 68 (June 1981): 72–74.

13. Jacques Barzun and Henry F. Graff, *The Modern Researcher*, 3rd ed. (New York: Harcourt, 1977), pp. 209–17.

14. Merle Curti et al., *The Making of an American Community: A Case Study of Democracy in a Frontier County* (Stanford: Stanford University Press, 1959). The techniques now commonly associated with the new social history, however, had their inception with James C. Malin's invention of population turnover analysis back in the 1930s. See Malin, *History and Ecology: Studies of the Grassland* (Lincoln: University of Nebraska Press, 1984).

15. Blumin, *Urban Threshold;* Michael B. Katz, *The People of Hamilton, Canada West* (Cambridge, Mass.: Harvard University Press, 1975); Clyde Griffen and Sally Griffen, *Natives and Newcomers: The Ordering of Opportunity in Mid-Nineteenth-Century Poughkeepsie* (Cambridge, Mass.: Harvard University Press, 1978). Theodore Hershberg, "Occupation and Ethnicity in Five Nineteenth-Century American Cities: A Collaborative Inquiry," *Historical Methods Newsletter* 7 (June 1974): 174–216, summarizes the Five Cities Project's cooperative research design.

16. Katz, *People of Hamilton*, p. 11.

17. Doherty, *Society and Power*, p. viii.

18. Sam Bass Warner, Jr., *The Private City: Philadelphia in Three Periods of Its*

Growth (Philadelphia: University of Pennsylvania Press, 1968); Gross, *Minutemen and Their World*.

19. Gunther Barth, *Instant Cities: Urbanization and the Rise of San Francisco and Denver* (New York: Oxford University Press, 1975); Daniel J. Walkowitz, *Worker City, Company Town: Iron and Cotton-Worker Protest, Troy and Cohoes, New York, 1855–1884* (Urbana: University of Illinois Press, 1978); Ralph Mann, *After the Gold Rush: Society in Grass Valley and Nevada City, California, 1849–1870* (Stanford: Stanford University Press, 1982); Blumin, *Urban Threshold*.

20. Stuart M. Blumin, "Rip Van Winkle's Grandchildren: Family and Household in the Hudson Valley, 1800–1860," *Journal of Urban History* 1 (May 1975): 293–315; Don Harrison Doyle, *The Social Order of a Frontier Community: Jacksonville, Illinois, 1825–1870* (Urbana: University of Illinois Press, 1978), p. 4n.

21. Carl Bridenbaugh, *Cities in the Wilderness: The First Century of Urban Life in America, 1625–1742* (New York: Oxford University Press, 1938); Richard C. Wade, *The Urban Frontier: The Rise of the Western Cities, 1790–1830* (Cambridge, Mass.: Harvard University Press, 1959); Dykstra, *Cattle Towns*; Doherty, *Society and Power*; David Grayson Allen, *In English Ways: The Movement of Societies and the Transferal of English Local Law and Custom to Massachusetts Bay in the Seventeenth Century* (Chapel Hill: University of North Carolina Press, 1981).

22. Frederic Cople Jaher, *The Urban Establishment: Upper Strata in Boston, New York, Charleston, Chicago, and Los Angeles* (Urbana: University of Illinois Press, 1982).

23. Lewis Atherton, *Main Street on the Middle Border* (Bloomington: Indiana University Press, 1954), p. 373n.

24. Michael Zuckerman, *Peaceable Kingdoms: New England Towns in the Eighteenth Century* (New York: Knopf, 1979), p. 261. Zuckerman's monograph has been criticized with respect to its author's selection of case study communities and to the inferences drawn from them. See David Grayson Allen, "The Zuckerman Thesis and the Process of Legal Rationalization in Provincial Massachusetts," *William and Mary Quarterly* 29 (July 1972): 443–60, and Zuckerman's reply to Allen in ibid., pp. 461–68.

25. For a rare exception, see John R. Stilgoe, *Common Landscape of America, 1580–1845* (New Haven: Yale University Press, 1982), pp. 261–62, which provides an impressionistic description of the gap between mid-nineteenth-century businessmen and farmers. Hal S. Barron observes that, with the exception of Dykstra, only Stanley Parsons has elevated local town-country conflict into a major analytical theme. See Barron, *Those Who Stayed Behind*, p. 9; Stanley Parsons, *The Populist Context: Rural versus Urban Power on a Great Plains Frontier* (Westport, Conn.: Greenwood Press, 1973).

26. Dykstra, *Cattle Towns*, pp. 178–206.

27. Stanley M. Elkins and Eric McKitrick, "A Meaning for Turner's Frontier," *Political Science Quarterly* 69 (September 1954): 321–53, 565–602.

28. Allan G. Bogue, "Social Theory and the Pioneer," *Agricultural History* 34 (January 1960): 21–34.

29. Ray Allen Billington, *America's Frontier Heritage* (New York: Holt, 1966), pp. 53–54.

30. Dykstra, *Cattle Towns*, p. 378.

31. Page Smith, *As a City upon a Hill: The Town in American History* (New York: Knopf, 1966). For a critical discussion of Smith's typology, see Robert R. Dykstra, "Cities in the Sagebrush: Great Plains Urbanization, 1865–90," in James E. Wright and

Sarah Z. Rosenburg, eds., *The Great Plains Experience: Readings in the History of a Region* (Lincoln: University of Mid-America, 1978), pp. 217–19.

32. Michael H. Frisch, *Town into City: Springfield, Massachusetts, and the Meaning of Community, 1840–1880* (Cambridge, Mass.: Harvard University Press, 1972), p. 250.

33. Blumin, *Urban Threshold*, p. 222.

34. Ibid., p. 160.

35. The ultimate specific resolution of the debate over gemeinschaft may lie in Hal Barron's cautious comment that, at least "in smaller rural communities during the nineteenth century," gemeinschaft and gesellschaft (its conceptual opposite) were not mutually exclusive phenomena but could coexist within the same population unit. See Barron, *Those Who Stayed Behind*, p. 136.

36. Doyle, *Social Order*, p. 2.

37. Ibid., p. 9.

38. Ibid., pp. 10, 15.

39. Blumin's book had not yet appeared when Doyle was writing, but Doyle did manage to include at least three statements of his strong agreement with Blumin's treatment. See Doyle, *Social Order*, pp. 5n., 193n., 229n.

40. Ibid., p. 192.

41. Ibid., pp. 138–39, 211, 222.

42. Ibid., pp. 129, 134–35, 164, 222, 238.

43. Ibid., pp. 174, 196, 236–37.

Name Index

Subject Index

About the Contributors

HOWARD GILLETTE, JR., is professor of American civilization and director of the American Studies Program at George Washington University. He is co-editor, with William W. Cutler III, of *The Divided Metropolis: Social and Spatial Dimensions of Philadelphia, 1800–1975*, which was prepared while he was a research associate with the Philadelphia Social History Project. His articles on American politics and urban development have appeared in a number of journals and books. He is immediate past director of George Washington's Center for Washington Area Studies, a vice-president of the Columbia Historical Society, and president of the L'Enfant Forum, which is preparing a new edition of the papers of Pierre L'Enfant.

ZANE L. MILLER is professor of history and co-director of the Center for Neighborhood and Community Studies at the University of Cincinnati. He has taught at Northwestern University and the University of Chicago and has lectured widely on the history of urban politics, planning, and race relations. He is the author of many articles and books, including *The Urbanization of Modern America*, reissued in 1986, with Patricia M. Melvin as co-author. His current major research project, funded by the National Endowment for the Humanities, is

"Planning and the Persisting Past: Cincinnati's Over-the-Rhine since 1940," with Henry D. Shapiro and Bruce Tucker, associates in the Center for Neighborhood and Community Studies.

CARL ABBOTT is professor of urban studies and planning at Portland State University. Among his publications are *The New Urban America: Growth and Politics in Sunbelt Cities* and *Portland: Planning, Politics and Growth in a Twentieth Century City*. His research interests center on the history of city planning and patterns of regional growth and change in the twentieth-century United States.

EUGENIE LADNER BIRCH is an associate professor in the Graduate Program in Urban Planning at Hunter College/City University of New York. She has written extensively on urban planning in the *Journal of the American Planning Association*, the *Journal of Urban History*, and others.

ROBERT R. DYKSTRA is professor of history and public policy at the State University of New York, Albany, where he specializes in nineteenth-century American social and political history. He was the winner, with Jo Ann Manfra, of the 1986 Binkley-Stephenson Award from the Organization of American Historians for the best article published in the *Journal of American History*. He recently completed a term as National Endowment for the Humanities fellow and research associate at the American Antiquarian Society in Worcester, Massachusetts, while completing a book-length manuscript on pioneer Iowans and white supremacy in the period 1833–1880.

MICHAEL H. EBNER is chair of the Department of History at Lake Forest College. He is co-editor with Eugene M. Tobin of *The Age of Urban Reform: New Perspectives on the Progressive Era* and contributor to many journals, including the *Journal of Urban History, Chicago History*, and the *Journal of American History*. His book, *Creating Chicago's North Shore: A Suburban History*, is to be published by the University of Chicago Press. He is founder and co-chair of the Urban History Seminar of the Chicago Historical Society.

JOSEF W. KONVITZ is professor of history and an adjunct member of the Urban Affairs Program at Michigan State University, where he has taught since 1973. He is the author of *Cities and the Sea, The Urban Millennium*, and *Cartography in France*.

ANDREA TUTTLE KORNBLUH is a Ph.D. candidate in American history at the University of Cincinnati. She is working on a dissertation on Cincinnati race relations and cultural pluralism between 1920 and 1950. She directed research for the video documentary *Pregnant but Equal: The Fight for Maternity Benefits*, produced photo history exhibits, and is the author of *Lighting the Way: The Woman's City Club, 1915–1965.*

RICHARD LONGSTRETH is associate professor of architectural history and director of the Graduate Program in Historic Preservation at George Washington University. His most recent book is *On the Edge of the World: Four Architects in San Francisco at the Turn of the Century.* He is the author of essays that have appeared in the *Journal of the Society of Architectural Historians, Winterthur Portfolio,* and *Harvard Architecture Review,* as well as a contributor to the nineteenth editon of Sir Banister Fletcher's *History of Architecture.*

ALAN I MARCUS is associate professor in the History of Technology and Science Program in the Department of History and director of the Center for Historical Studies of Technology and Science at Iowa State University. He is author of *Agricultural Science and the Quest for Legitimacy: Farmers, Agricultural Colleges and Experiment Stations, 1870–1890* and of a number of articles on urban history. He has completed a book-length manuscript on the development of a broad range of municipal social services in mid-nineteenth-century America and is finishing a volume on the history of technology in America.

PATRICIA MOONEY MELVIN is associate professor of history and coordinator of the Public History Program at the University of Arkansas at Little Rock. She is co-author, with Zane L. Miller, of *The Urbanization of Modern America,* editor of a historical dictionary on community organizations, and author of *The Organic City: Urban Definition and Neighborhood Organization, 1880–1920.*

EDWARD K. MULLER is a historical geographer with research interests in the geography of North American urbanization. After receiving a Ph.D. in geography from the University of Wisconsin in 1972, he joined the Department of Geography at the University of Maryland at College Park. In 1977 he moved to the Department of History at the University of Pittsburgh, where he is an associate professor. At Pittsburgh he has directed the Urban Studies Program and serves as associate director of the Center for Social and Urban Research. He has co-edited *Geographical Perspectives on Maryland's Past* and *The Atlas of Pennsylvania* and authored many journal articles, invited chapters, and research reports.

CAROL A. O'CONNOR is professor of history at Utah State University. She is author of *A Sort of Utopia: Scarsdale, 1891–1981* and of several articles on suburbia. She is currently working on a book, *The Urbanization of Mormon America.*

WILLIAM SILAG is managing editor at the Iowa State University Press in Ames, Iowa. Formerly editor of the *Palimpsest,* Silag earned his doctorate in

American history at the University of Iowa in 1979. He has published articles on nineteenth-century urbanization in the *Western Historical Quarterly* and the *Great Plains Quarterly*.

JOEL A. TARR is professor of history and public policy, director of the Program in Technology and Society, and co-director of the Program in Applied History and Science at Carnegie-Mellon University. He has published widely on urban development. He has served as president of the Public Works Historical Society of the American Public Works Association and is a member of the executive council of the Public History Association.

JON C. TEAFORD is professor of history at Purdue University. He has published many books and articles on urban history, including, most recently, *The Unheralded Triumph: City Government in America 1870–1900* and *The Twentieth-Century American City: Problem, Promise, and Reality*.

LEONARD WALLOCK is assistant professor of history at Hunter College/City University of New York. He has served as David Heyman Fellow in Urban Studies at Columbia University, where he edited *Visions of the Modern City: Essays in History, Art, and Literature* with William Sharpe. He has served as Fulbright lecturer in American history at the Université de Paris III in France. He is completing a study of the work, culture, and politics of printers in nineteenth-century Philadelphia.